THE BOSSES OF THE BRONX

ALSO BY MIKE VACCARO

Emperors and Idiots
1941—The Greatest Year in Sports
The First Fall Classic

THE BOSSES OF THE BRONX

The Endless Drama of the Yankees Under the House of Steinbrenner

MIKE VACCARO

HARPER

An Imprint of HarperCollinsPublishers

Without limiting the exclusive rights of any author, contributor or the publisher of this publication, any unauthorized use of this publication to train generative artificial intelligence (AI) technologies is expressly prohibited. HarperCollins also exercise their rights under Article 4(3) of the Digital Single Market Directive 2019/790 and expressly reserve this publication from the text and data mining exception.

THE BOSSES OF THE BRONX. Copyright © 2026 by Mike Vaccaro. All rights reserved. No part of this book may be used or reproduced in any manner whatsoever without written permission except in the case of brief quotations embodied in critical articles and reviews. For information, address HarperCollins Publishers, 195 Broadway, New York, NY 10007. In Europe, HarperCollins Publishers, Macken House, 39/40 Mayor Street Upper, Dublin 1, D01 C9W8, Ireland.

HarperCollins books may be purchased for educational, business, or sales promotional use. For information, please email the Special Markets Department at SPsales@harpercollins.com.

hc.com

FIRST EDITION

Designed by Michele Cameron

Interior art: ©workingpens/Shutterstock, ©grey_and/Shutterstock

Library of Congress Cataloging-in-Publication Data has been applied for.

ISBN 978-0-06-341477-8

Printed in the United States of America

26 27 28 29 30 LBC 5 4 3 2 1

For Dominic Joseph Coppola (1929–2024): Yankees fan, Confirmation sponsor, lifetime role model. It was at his home in Farmingdale, New York, around 1976 or so, that I first started clacking on a typewriter. I still haven't stopped.

CONTENTS

Introduction 1

Chapter 1 10

Chapter 2 19

Chapter 3 27

Chapter 4 35

Chapter 5 43

Chapter 6 55

Chapter 7 66

Chapter 8 76

Chapter 9 88

Chapter 10 100

Chapter 11 115

Chapter 12 129

Chapter 13 143

Chapter 14 157

Chapter 15 170

Chapter 16 183

Chapter 17 193

Chapter 18 206

Chapter 19 218

Chapter 20 231

Chapter 21 246

Chapter 22 260

Chapter 23 271

Chapter 24 283

Chapter 25 294

Chapter 26 303

Chapter 27 313

Chapter 28 324

Chapter 29 333

Chapter 30 343

Postscript 352

Acknowledgments 357

Index 363

THE BOSSES OF THE BRONX

INTRODUCTION

I'm not a win-at-all-costs guy. Winning isn't everything. It's second to breathing.

—GEORGE M. STEINBRENNER III

The first thing I did was look at the clock: 3:27 a.m.

The second thing I did—because this is what you do when the telephone in your hotel room begins to jangle at 3:27 a.m.—was make a mental accounting of loved ones: mother, father, wife, niece, nephew, friends, dog; a ringing telephone at 3:27 a.m. rarely brings good news. I scrambled to turn on the light. I fumbled for the receiver. I reached for my glasses and instead sent them flying across the floor.

"Hello?"

"You sound like you're sleeping! Why are you sleeping?"

The voice. I knew the voice. Everyone knew the voice.

"Mr. Steinbrenner? It's three thirty in the morning."

"I heard you wanted to talk to me. And I've been hoping to talk to you. It's a beautiful morning here in Tampa—and it's already *SIX THIRTY* here. I hope it's a beautiful morning wherever you are."

I did want to talk to him, even half asleep in a San Diego Marriott hotel room at 3:27 in the morning, Pacific time, because I'd recently been hired as a sports columnist at the *New York Post* and it seemed time to finally have a legit one-on-one with him. I'd actually spoken to George Steinbrenner dozens of times already, mostly in press conferences or in informal gatherings around the batting cage at Yankee Stadium. One time, a few years before, I'd shared an elevator with him at the spring training ballpark that was, at that moment, still called Legends Field and would, some years later, bear his name. He had recently partnered with the New Jersey Nets basketball team and the New Jersey Devils hockey team for a brief corporate alliance called "YankeeNets," and it felt like a folly. The Nets were chronic losers, but Steinbrenner was excited about his new toy.

"You know, the first team I owned was a basketball team."

"The Cleveland Pipers," I said, pleased with myself.

"Lost my shirt," Steinbrenner said. "But I loved the game. You know, I was the first owner to ever get a technical foul at a basketball game?"

I nodded. I'd heard that story.

"Anyway. You watch. We'll get that ship headed in the right direction. I promise you that. The New Jersey Nets are going to be winners. And soon. Mark my words."

The elevator door opened onto the owner's level.

"I get out here," he said.

Now, two years later, at 3:27 in the morning, George Steinbrenner said, "Remember when I told you the Nets were going to be winners? Do you remember that?"

I told him I did. And I knew what had happened in the intervening two years had pleased him greatly. The Nets advanced to the NBA Finals in 2002 and were a few months away from doing the same thing in 2003. If they hadn't much eaten into the Knicks' dominant market share in New York, they'd become by far the more enjoyable basketball show in town thanks to a future Hall of Fame point guard named Jason Kidd.

"I'm a man of my word, you know. Now what can I do for you? I'm driving to the office. I have to be there by seven o'clock. That gives you ... twenty-nine minutes."

Twenty-nine minutes later, I'd been fully briefed on his expectations for the Nets; for the 2003 Yankees; for the 2004 US Olympic team, which would be competing in Athens, Greece; on the impression that a comic named Larry David—becoming increasingly famous in his own right—had memorably done of him on *Seinfeld* years before.

("I don't think it sounds like me," Steinbrenner said. "But my wife told me, 'George, that sounds more like you than you do.'")

And, lastly, we discussed the subject I'd called about: his old friend Al Davis. The reason I was in San Diego was because Davis's Oakland Raiders would that Sunday be playing the Tampa Bay Buccaneers in Super Bowl XXXVII at Qualcomm Stadium. In many ways, Davis's career owning the Raiders had mirrored Steinbrenner's with the Yankees. They were both larger-than-life figures, both demanding bosses, and both had enjoyed remarkable sustained success at a time when achieving that in professional sports was becoming rarer and rarer. This would be the Raiders' fifth Super Bowl appearance under Davis's stewardship, which dated to 1966, and they won the championship three times. Steinbrenner's Yankees had won six championships since he took over the team early in 1973, and they'd appeared in nine World Series. Both were unapologetic when it came to quarreling with the press, with their respective sport's commissioner, with local politicians, with their own players.

"Let's say what you mean," Davis had told me a few weeks earlier. "Neither of us is afraid to be called an asshole to our faces, and we know that we're called much worse behind our backs."

That interview had been quintessential Davis. I'd tried for weeks to talk to him, but it wasn't as simple as merely calling his secretary and making an appointment and then receiving a telephone call at 3:27 a.m. If Davis didn't know you, you needed to be vouched for. You needed to be vetted. Davis called some people. He had his personal lieutenant, Al LoCasale, call some more. And then, one night, when I was having dinner at a small restaurant in San Francisco with friends in advance of a Raiders–Jets playoff game, the waiter came over to our table.

"Is one of you Mike Vaccaro?" he asked.

I said I was.

"There's a phone call for you."

Again: Phone calls in restaurants three thousand miles away from home aren't generally bearing the news that you've won the Irish Sweepstakes. I made the same accounting in my head—parents, wife, friends, dog—and followed the waiter, expecting he'd lead me to a back office, or to a phone behind the bar.

We walked to a pay phone. He handed me the receiver.

"Hello?"

"Michael! Al Davis here!"

And yes: The first few sentences were a little blurry because I kept asking myself, *How in the hell did Al Davis know when I'd be eating dinner, where I'd be eating dinner, and how did he know the pay phone number, and . . . ?*

But then I just let Al Davis talk, and I simply listened.

"I look at what my friend George Steinbrenner has done with the Yankees, and I've always said, 'That's how it should be done,'" Davis said. "Don't accept second best from anyone. Don't settle for excuses. Don't wait for good things to happen to you. Go out and seize the damned day. I learned that from George. He would have been a damn good football coach if he'd stayed with it, because he's not only consumed with winning, he's willing to do the hard things that make winning possible."

I told Steinbrenner that last part, and that instantly made his day, even less than seven hours into that day.

"I don't think you can go that far," he said softly. "But I do know that Al's one of the few guys I've ever met who may actually care about winning more than I do. Seeing him back in the Super Bowl, back where he belongs, it gives me a great feeling inside."

The coming Super Bowl would be tricky for Steinbrenner. Davis was a close friend. But the Buccaneers represented Tampa Bay, his adopted home for more than thirty years. He was committed to staying neutral, and it killed him to be neutral about anything. Especially a man like Al Davis, in whom he saw so much of himself, right down to the fact that they shared a birthday: July 4 (Steinbrenner in 1930, Davis a year earlier).

"I mean, shit. He's the guy who invented 'Just win, baby!'" Steinbrenner said of Davis. "How do you *not* love a guy like that?"

Davis: "When George and I get together in a room and talk business . . . baby, we could tape some of those talks and it would be pure gold."

The Buccaneers routed the Raiders in the game, 48–21. The next spring, I saw Steinbrenner at Legends Field, and as he walked away from a media scrum I asked if he'd talked to Davis afterward.

"Two days later," he said. "He apologized when he called back, but he said he'd spent the day after buried in his office for twelve hours, watching the game film. You believe that? All these years later, everything he's done, and he still acts like a damned coaching intern."

As he told that story, the smile on Steinbrenner's face grew just a little broader.

"Can you imagine?" he said. "Who does that?"

Not long after, I told that story to Joe Torre, the Yankees' manager. He laughed.

"I know a guy," he said.

GEORGE STEINBRENNER OWNED the Yankees for more than thirty-seven and a half years, from the moment he was announced as the general partner of the group that purchased the Yankees for $10 million on January 3, 1973, until the day he died on July 13, 2010. He entered the fray young, brash, full of ideas, welcomed as a breath of fresh air from the corporate monolith of CBS, which had owned the Yankees for nine years and lost a small fortune on the club. He exited as a beloved elder statesman who'd twice seen his team rise back to prominence and who'd witnessed, just nine months earlier, his team win a seventh championship on his watch.

In between, he was, at alternate times, beloved and be-loathed, abhorred and absolved, deified and despised, treasured and trounced, vanquished and venerated, lampooned and lambasted, and likened to an old-school political Boss, capital "B." He was thrown out of baseball—twice. He once hired a low-level criminal to blackmail his best player. He once hosted *Saturday Night Live*. He did a famous beer commercial with a manager he'd just fired, and would go on to hire and fire four more times across the next twelve years. At various times in the eighties and nineties he'd been booed—and worse—at his own ballpark; yet by 1999, as the Yankees finished off a four-game World Series sweep of the Braves, 56,752 people roared, "THANK YOU, BOSS!" over and over, reducing him to tears. He was benevolent and baleful, worshipped and walloped, and fifteen years after his passing, no single name is more regularly brought up when lists of Hall of Fame omissions are discussed than that of George M. Steinbrenner III. And there seems to be growing belief that that will happen some year soon.

One time, in 2013, I was interviewing James L. Dolan, the owner of the New York Knicks and New York Rangers, who, at the time, was routinely considered to be the worst owner in team sports—by outsiders, yes; but almost unanimously by his own fans, especially Knicks supporters. During a break in our talk, he wondered aloud if any other sports-team owner had ever absorbed the kind of raw vitriol he endured on a daily basis.

"Well, all due respect," I said. "Steinbrenner."

"Steinbrenner? When he died it was like they were burying a king."

"At the end he was viewed that way."

"I go to Madison Square Garden and there's twenty thousand people screaming 'Dolan sucks!'"

"Steinbrenner had you beat. He once had the whole house at Yankee Stadium chant the same thing at him. That was the same day he was kicked out of baseball."

"Really?"

"Really."

"Well, then!" Dolan roared, laughing a laugh landscaped by plenty of cigarettes and whiskey in its day. "Maybe they'll love me when I'm dead!"

In death, Steinbrenner's name is never far away from the lips of Yankees fans. When the team goes on a losing streak and no coaches are fired or players released, the immediate reaction from loud segments of the public is always the same: "If only George were still alive. . . ."

Yankees lost a tough best-of-seven and the manager wasn't fired?

"If only George were still alive!"

Yankees have gone fifteen years without a championship and the general manager is still on the job?

"IF ONLY GEORGE WERE STILL ALIVE!!!"

Such is the burden inherited by Harold Zieg Steinbrenner, "Hal" to everyone, who runs the Yankees now and burns to win every bit as ferociously as his father did but shows it in a different way.

"My father was more about the back pages of the tabloids," Hal told me the first day I was introduced to him, in 2013. "I'm more about a back room, away from prying eyes. Anyone who thinks I don't want to win? Well, how does the saying go? 'Show me you've never met me without telling me that you've never met me.'"

Baseball is different from any other team sport in North America. There is no salary cap, and thus a big-market team—and the Yankees are the biggest of all the big-market teams in New York, Chicago, Los Angeles, Boston, Philadelphia and Phoenix, by a wide margin—can spend as much money as it pleases in the pursuit of talent. No owner in any sport embraced the era of free agency more than George Steinbrenner, who won his first two championships on the backs of big-ticket stars Reggie Jackson and Goose Gossage and the last of them thanks to the negotiation of nine-figure bonanzas handed out to CC Sabathia and Mark Teixeira. Steinbrenner also had his high-profile misses—there are no songs written about Dave Collins, to name one—and he actually spent brief periods of his ownership threatening austerity; he once almost lost David Cone to free agency because he was obsessing over a few thousand dollars.

But on the day he bought the team, one of his closest partners, theater impresario James M. Nederlander, had told him: "George, New York is a star-driven town. Always go for the star." And to the last, that was his mantra.

Hal also believes in that philosophy. But he is by nature less flamboyant than his father, more publicly reserved, less hungry for attention. He also, more relevantly, operates a baseball team at a different time than his father, one where there is more investment in analytics and cost-effectiveness. The fact is, when the elder Steinbrenner shocked the baseball world by authorizing (while serving the first of his suspensions) a five-year, $3.75 million contract that temporarily made Catfish Hunter baseball's wealthiest player on New Year's Eve 1974, it felt like all the money in the world, especially for the time. In 2024 dollars that still translates to only $24 million, which is just $3 million less than what Hal paid in 2023 alone for the services of Carlos Rodón, a starting pitcher who went 3–8 with a 6.85 ERA and who has never on his best day pitched as well as Hunter on his worst.

When George waited until two of his stars, Bernie Williams and Derek Jeter, played out their six-year entry-level contracts with the Yankees before re-signing them for big money, he was mostly hailed as a shrewd and clever negotiator, willing to let Bernie, for instance, dance with the hated Red Sox before bringing both back into the fold. When Hal did the same thing with Aaron Judge in 2022, he was lambasted as cheap and was even mocked, as Judge's price tag kept going north that same year as he slammed sixty-two home runs.

Different times, different game, different owners.

Different men.

"I learned a great deal from my father," Hal says. "But he didn't teach me to become him, because he didn't expect me to be."

Together, across more than half a century, the Steinbrenner family has taken what was already the most famous brand in sports and somehow increased it exponentially. That original $10 million investment (of which George's contribution was $168,000, or less than 2 percent), which, once CBS agreed to buy back the parking garages surrounding Yankee Stadium, was more like $8.8 million? In 2024 the Yankees were appraised in *Forbes* magazine at $8.2 billion. With no ceiling in sight. The Dallas Cowboys of the NFL appear atop a few lists citing the most valuable franchises in sports; the Yankees are on top of all the others. There have been various times when people wonder why the family doesn't just cash out, assuring prosperity for untold future generations of Steinbrenner, and it's a subject that makes Hal Steinbrenner laugh.

"The Yankees," he says, "is our family business."

This, then, is a story about one American family business and one city's fascination with the proprietors of that corner store.

CHAPTER 1

*The perfect afternoon at Yankee Stadium?
It's when the Yankees score eight runs in the
first inning and then slowly pull away.*
—COLONEL JACOB RUPPERT JR.

The great man was swollen a few extra pounds from when he'd been the most fearsome batsman in all of baseball and one of the most famous citizens of the planet, but he was still unmistakably recognized by the servants and support staff who moved quietly about the stately home at 1120 Fifth Avenue. This was one of the most stylish addresses on the island of Manhattan, tucked just north of Ninety-Second Street, an easy stone's throw from the Central Park Reservoir. George Herman Ruth hadn't swatted a baseball in almost four years, when he'd hit the last of his 714 home runs, a massive blast that famously was the first baseball ever to clear the roof at Pittsburgh's mammoth Forbes Field. Just as infamously, he'd hit that ball in the garish vestments of the Boston Braves, to whom he had been exiled by the man who owned this opulent mansion at 1120 Fifth. Many of Ruth's days since February 26, 1935, had been spent in anger and resentment, most of it aimed at the man who, almost four years later, now lay peacefully upstairs, wandering in and out of consciousness.

It was the morning of January 13, 1939.

Babe Ruth had come to say goodbye to Colonel Jacob Ruppert Jr.

For twenty-three years Ruppert had been the imperious owner of the New York Yankees, the single-most-powerful and influential man in all of American sport, the most ambitious, successful, opinionated and controversial figure who'd ever aspired to own a franchise. He was, in many ways, the spirit of Charles Foster Kane sprung to life, his fortune baseball diamonds rather than newspapers.

Ruppert was born into one of New York's most prosperous families, and he'd inherited the whole of the Ruppert Brewing Company—best known for its two hugely popular signature products, Knickerbocker Beer and Ruppert's Extra Pale Ale—which at its peak produced over a million barrels a year. He'd already been elected a four-term congressman from both New York's Fifteenth and Sixteenth Districts, running as a Tammany Hall Democrat, and earned his honorary military title serving as an aide-de-camp for Governor David B. Hill. A lifelong bachelor, with more money than he could ever spend, Ruppert was nevertheless filled with a specific ennui that would latch itself to many rich, ambitious men many decades later who dealt with the same nagging realities Ruppert did: "I've got all the money in the world. But nobody knows who I am . . ."

A century later, it became a common rite for such men to turn their attention to professional sports and shell out small fortunes for the Dallas Cowboys, for the Dallas Mavericks, for the Cleveland Cavaliers, for the New York Mets. But in 1915 there were only sixteen such opportunities. There was no professional basketball, no professional football. The National Hockey League was still a mom-and-pop operation, mostly focused on Canada. If you were a sportsman, your options were this: You could sponsor prizefighters, but even in those early years of the twentieth century that sport was overwhelmed by a strong underworld element. You could invest in thoroughbred racehorses, but even then much of the glory went to the horses themselves, to the jockeys who rode them and to the touts who could guide you toward bringing home a few more dollars than you'd brought with you to the track.

Or you could wait for one of those sixteen spots in Major League Baseball to open.

In 1915 one of them did.

And it was just about the least attractive one anyone could imagine.

Back in 1903 Ban Johnson, the founder of the American League, recognized that the only way his burgeoning baseball loop could survive was to place an anchor in New York City. The AL had gone its first two years without; it wouldn't survive many more. Johnson identified two of Tammany Hall's most faithful sons, New Yorkers to the bone who'd scored fortunes working both within and without the framework of established local statutes. One was Frank Farrell, a poolroom king who controlled a gambling syndicate valued at $3 million. The other was William "Big Bill" Devery, the last of the superintendents who'd (very) loosely overseen the New York Police Department before the advent of a commissioner's office; somehow, Devery had managed to cobble together enough nickels and quarters on his constable's salary to hold a significant chunk of the New York real estate market. Farrell and Devery had made their respective fortunes, legal and otherwise, by relying on sure things; Johnson promised them one. And with a stroke of a fountain pen and a payment of $18,000 to the league office on January 9, 1903, the Baltimore Orioles vanished and the New York Highlanders were born.

Except by 1915 the Highlanders had become a genuine baseball calamity. For one thing, they were awful—103 losses in 1908, 102 in 1912, seven losing records in all, eight finishes near the bottom of the league. For another, they were homeless: The rickety woodpile called Hilltop Park—sitting on the site that is now the home of NewYork-Presbyterian Hospital—had been inadequate on the day it was hastily opened in 1903 and within a decade became uninhabitable. The Highlanders had offered up Hilltop to the rival Giants when the National League team's Polo Grounds burned to the ground in 1911, and two years later the Giants returned the favor. It was an easy offer. The Highlanders drew fewer than 250,000 for their last full season at Hilltop. They were irrelevant in New York City, practically invisible, and it was impossible to see how that would ever change.

For it was the Giants who ruled the city, who ruled the sport, who saw their nickname not so much as a catchy moniker but as a central part of the team's mission statement. The new Polo Grounds was the grandest baseball basilica yet built. The team was an annual contender, led by the most famous manager of all, John J. McGraw, a fiery pepper pot of a man who suffered no fools and laughed at the notion that New York City would ever be anything but a Giants town. Brooklyn could have its Dodgers on the other side of the river. Those who couldn't get a ticket to Giants games were welcome to watch the Highlanders—who by 1913 had changed their nickname to the more headline-friendly "Yankees"—kick the ball around daffily. Giants fans were fierce and they were legion, and they included every class and caste and creed and color in the city's complex tapestry. Theater stars sought seats behind the dugout, the better to be seen. Wall Street titans gobbled up box seats, the better to conduct business.

Devery and Farrell wanted out of their sure thing.

As it happened, Jacob Ruppert and a civil engineer–turned-businessman with the delightfully lyrical name of Tillinghast L'Hommedieu Huston wanted in. So for the mutually agreeable price of $400,000, Devery and Farrell accepted a cool $382,000 return on their original investment. Ruppert installed himself as Yankees president. Huston became vice president. The Yankees continued to live deep in the Giants' shadow, even as things perked up on the field. Then on December 26, 1919, Ruppert wrote another check, this one to Harry Frazee, owner of the Boston Red Sox, in the amount of $100,000. In return, Frazee sent his best player, a twenty-four-year-old who'd been one of the best pitchers in the sport until deciding he preferred hitting home runs instead. He'd hit a total of forty-nine of them by December 26, 1919.

His name was Ruth.

Or, as Colonel Jacob Ruppert called him for most of the next 6,958 days the two men knew each other—as owner/player, as friends, as adversarial contract negotiators, as bitter enemies—"Root." Ruppert had been born in Yorkville and spent his whole life in Manhattan, but he spoke with a notable German accent, like he'd just stepped off the boat from Bavaria.

Now, this cold January morning, "Root" came quietly to the house at 1120 Fifth. He walked to Ruppert's bedside. The owner had taken ill more than a year earlier, felled by phlebitis, his legs swollen and increasingly useless. He'd listened to the 1938 World Series on the radio from this bed, followed every play as the Yankees swept the Cubs to earn the seventh world championship of his stewardship.

His eyes were closed when Ruth entered the room.

Ruth took Ruppert's hands in his.

"You're going to snap out of this," Ruth said. "And you and I are going to the opening game together."

Ruth squeezed the old man's hand.

His eyes opened. And widened. And then softened.

"Babe!" he called out softly, then closed his eyes for the final time.

He died a few minutes later, at 10:28 a.m. He was seventy-one years old.

"It was the only time in his life he ever called me 'Babe' to my face," Ruth said later that day. "He always called me 'Ruth.' When all's said and done, the colonel has been like a second father to me."

His anger dissolved, the great man bowed his head and wept.

THERE HAVE BEEN a total of nine men who have either owned or co-owned the New York Yankees—ten if you include Michael Burke, the man designated by CBS to serve as the team's de facto owner when the network had the team from 1964 to '73. Only two of them have been related to each other: George M. Steinbrenner III and Harold Z. Steinbrenner, father and son, the elder's reign lasting from 1973 until his death in 2010, when the younger replaced him.

In truth, though, George Steinbrenner and Jacob Ruppert were ideological twins.

Both were of German heritage. Both were the ambitious and earnest sons of hugely successful fathers. Both fathers were über-demanding; the elder Ruppert insisted young Jacob begin his time in the family business at age eighteen, washing barrels as an apprentice at $10 a week in lieu of attending

West Point or Columbia, while Henry Steinbrenner staked his son at age nine to peddle hens and their eggs door-to-door in their native Rocky River, Ohio. Both took the job of "boss" extremely seriously. Both came to the Yankees after dallying with other sports franchises—Ruppert had inquired about the Giants and nearly bought the Cubs before the Yankees opportunity presented itself; Steinbrenner owned the Cleveland Pipers, who played in the National Industrial Basketball League and the American Basketball League (competitors of the established NBA) and folded after two years, and he later came very close to purchasing his hometown Cleveland Indians (now the Guardians). Both started beholden to other partners—Ruppert to Huston, whom he would buy out in 1922 for $1.5 million; Steinbrenner to eleven other limited partners at the outset of his association with the team in 1973.

And both wound up the undisputed boss of bosses, quick to infuse their opinions and their standards everywhere: front office, ground crew, ticket office, farm system, manager's office, even the player's sacred domain of the clubhouse on occasion.

And both spoke their mind.

We will get to Steinbrenner's deep canon of such observations across much of the rest of this book. But if you look at some of Ruppert's greatest hits through the years, then close your eyes and let your imagination drift, it's not especially difficult to conjure Steinbrenner's voice—either the real one or the fanciful one birthed by Larry David—uttering much the same spirit, if not the same words:

> *"In the American League, there seems to have been an entire lack of any concerted campaign to build up a club in New York which should rival the Giants on an even basis."*

> *"Let the other teams in the league build up to the Yankees. We'll never weaken our team to make the others look good as long as I own the club."*

> *"Yankee Stadium is a mistake. Not mine. The Giants'."*

•

AFTER RUPPERT DIED, the Yankees were transferred to the partnership of Del Webb and Dan Topping (with Larry MacPhail, briefly, a third partner), who assumed far lower profiles but enjoyed just as much success as Ruppert had, winning ten World Series and fifteen American League pennants between 1947 and 1964. But it was when CBS bought the Yankees for $13.2 million after that '64 season that their fortunes turned sour. They tumbled to sixth place in 1965, and in 1966 they finished in last place for the first time since 1912. Attendance plummeted, thanks to a terrible triumvirate of lousy play, decaying ballpark and rotting neighborhood, bottoming out at 966,328 in 1972.

Burke, CBS's man in the Bronx, tried everything. He was an engaging raconteur who'd served in the Office of Strategic Services (OSS) in World War II (Gary Cooper's character in the 1946 movie *Cloak and Dagger* was based on him) and later served in the early years of the CIA before running Ringling Bros. and Barnum & Bailey Circus. In 1956 CBS president Frank Stanton recruited him to the network, and after ten years as a vice president, Stanton and CBS chairman William Paley asked Burke if he'd like to take a crack at running the Yankees.

Burke dove joyfully into the job.

He had Yankee Stadium repainted. He made an aggressive play for younger fans, who'd been fleeing the Yankees for the Mets. He didn't just invite old ballplayers to throw out the first pitch to important games: In 1968 the poet Marianne Moore did that on Opening Day; a year later, Paul Simon did it (with Art Garfunkel smiling by his side). In 1967 as an answer to "Meet the Mets," the first baseball fight song that was forever on the tip of every New York baseball fan's tongue—including Yankees fans—he commissioned a fight song of their own, "Here Come the Yankees." And in his most important decision, he'd commenced negotiations to keep the Yankees in the Bronx at a time when New Jersey had successfully poached the football Giants and trained its scope on the Yankees, too. When the city agreed to condemn the land under the stadium, buy it from the landlord

(Rice University) and toss in $24 million to give it a facelift, Burke agreed the team would stay.

> **INTERLUDE:** During his third day on the job in 1966, Burke fired Red Barber, one of the most accomplished broadcasters in team history. Barber had insisted that the WPIX television cameras span the vast empty grandstand at Yankee Stadium for a makeup game with the White Sox on September 22, a game that only 413 attended. CBS was furious and wanted Barber gone, and while it might not have been Burke's call, the way he soon described the dismissal—"I believe that for every man there is a time to come and a time to go. In my opinion it was Red's time to go."—was every bit as cold-blooded and detached as any transaction ordered by the man who would soon occupy his office.

But the team was still a mess. It was still losing. It was still hemorrhaging money. In 1970 the defending world champion Mets officially doubled the Yankees' home attendance (2.7 million to 1.13 million)—this in a year when the Yankees actually won ninety-three games, ten more than their NL neighbors—and then did it again the next two years. By late 1972 CBS was willing to part with the team, and Paley told Burke he was free to assemble a partnership that would allow him, at last, an official ownership stake.

But Burke, for all the fascinating adventures that filled his life, was not a wealthy man. He needed partners with pockets deep enough to woo Paley. He had one in mind.

George Steinbrenner was a forty-two-year-old shipping executive who'd spent some time as an assistant football coach in the Big Ten with Purdue and Northwestern and, later, briefly owned a pro basketball team. Burke had a friend in Cleveland with whom he'd shared the news about CBS and the Yankees, and that friend—initially, neither man wished to identify him—brought the two of them together. They hit it off beautifully. At their first meeting in New York, Burke took Steinbrenner to lunch at Brussels Restaurant on East Fifty-Fourth Street, where the veal was the specialty of the house and the tables far enough apart that they wouldn't draw attention to themselves. The men bonded over their shared love of football (Steinbrenner had been a halfback at Williams College; Burke played the same position at Pennsylvania). Burke, a progressive who'd attempted his whole time with the Yankees to diversify what had long been a lily-white operation, admired Steinbrenner for employing the first Black coach in any of the four major sports, John McLendon, with the Cleveland Pipers. And Steinbrenner admired Burke's easy panache, the way he seemed to glide about the city, always the coolest fellow in any room into which he ever walked. Soon, the men met with Paley, and in the odd vernacular of the day Paley had one question.

"Are you for real or did you come here with Chinese money?"

"No, sir," Steinbrenner said. "I come here with all the American cash I have and partners who are eager to do the same."

"That's what I like to hear," Paley said.

By New Year's Day, a deal—conducted almost entirely in secret, somehow away from the prying eyes and bionic ears of New York's aggressive corps of baseball writers—was all but done.

"We had a surprise for New York for the New Year," Burke said in 1981.

Yes. Yes they did.

CHAPTER 2

There is nothing quite so limited as being a limited partner of George Steinbrenner's.
—JOHN McMULLEN

They managed to spruce the old gray lady up as nicely as she could be spruced, after so many years and so many moments, so much history and so much glory, much of it now a faded whisper. Yankee Stadium was still mostly bedecked in its original look as the newspapermen began to arrive late in the morning of Wednesday, January 3, 1973, after being rousted early by Bob Fishel, the Yankees' PR chief, and his assistant, Marty Appel. The world-famous frieze that ringed the upper of three decks was still there, though the weather had treated the copper poorly, turning it a sickly shade of green in the weeks before the workmen would slather a final coat of white paint upon it. The outfield dimensions were as they'd been for decades: 296 feet down the right field line, 457 to left-center, "Death Valley," long enough and far enough that Yankees shortstop-turned-broadcaster Phil Rizzuto had once joked "anyone could clear that fence . . . as long as you played it as a par three." But it was an old stadium badly in need of renovation, something that was scheduled to happen as soon as the coming 1973 season was complete. In the newspapers in recent years, the adjectives had been far less kind: "crumbling" and "rat-infested" and "outdated," even "obsolete."

New Jersey had already come courting, pitching woo at CBS about a sparkling new baseball cathedral and wide-open concourses and enough parking to accommodate an entire fleet of automobiles. It was such sweet talk that had already wooed the New York Giants football team west, across the George Washington Bridge. And while the Yankees had agreed to stay in the Bronx pending a city-financed renovation to the stadium . . . well, no shovels had yet been dug into the earth. If the Yankees had decided to change their mind, there really wasn't much New York could do to stop them.

The Stadium Club was stuffed with writers and TV folks when Michael Burke stepped to the podium just after noon, as the media finished lunch. Burke, CBS's leading conduit to the Yankees since 1966, was the man who figured to be the first one out the door if CBS finally decided it had enough of its star-crossed nine-year ownership of the club. To many of the sportswriters who'd lost scent of this story in recent weeks, it was something of a surprise to see Burke step to the microphone looking far more dapper—three-piece blue suit, dark tie—than the casual wear he usually wore around the ballpark. (Although he did still favor a mop of gray hair, maybe a quarter inch shy of "unruly," a personal grooming preference that would soon become a bigger deal than he ever could have imagined.)

He got to the point quickly.

"CBS," Burke intoned, "has agreed to sell the New York Yankees."

Reporters scribbled furiously into their notebooks. Cameras clicked in rapid-fire. There had been rumors for weeks that CBS was going to at last cut bait with the world's most famous sports franchise, a shaky marriage from the start that grew only more dysfunctional with each passing year. Most keen baseball observers figured the sale would be announced by the end of the season, as surely CBS would want to haggle as high a price as it could. And one of the presumed favorites to close the deal was a group financed by Lehman Brothers, an investment bank with roots in Alabama that had, since 1858, been a foundational financial stronghold in Manhattan. The face of that group would be an old New York Giants catcher named Herman Franks, who was tabbed to run the team once the deal was done. And in a masterful marketing stroke that would surely have secured top billing in the city's tabloids for months to come, Franks had already called his favorite player from his time managing the San Francisco Giants from 1965 to 1968 to see if he'd be willing to manage the Yankees and become the first African American to hold a manager's job in MLB history.

"Yes, sir," Willie Mays said, "I would."

Even better: By late December, Lehman's offer of between $13.5 and $14 million was the clear leader in the clubhouse and would allow CBS to escape baseball and salvage a small profit for all its years of struggle with the Yankees. Veteran sportswriters figured they might see Franks, a familiar old face to most of them, when they walked into the Stadium Club that Wednesday morning.

Instead, they were greeted by a different familiar face—Burke—who, while an affable gentleman and always good with a quote and a story to fill their notebooks, had nevertheless overseen much of the Yankees' downfall in the past decade. But there was also a most unfamiliar face, lined up to Burke's left, the two men standing beneath an enormous blue banner, trimmed in red, with YANKEES stitched across the front in white. Burke's announcement of CBS's sale may have been anticipated, but it was still stunning.

So that was bombshell number one for that January 3, 1973.

"CBS has agreed to sell the Yankees to a group of individuals headed by George Steinbrenner," Burke said, before adding that he himself was one of those individuals. Steinbrenner, the man who'd put the group together, and Burke were the only two of the twelve on hand at the press conference. This had been his show, his and Burke's, a marriage arranged through that mutual friend whose identity was still hidden. Steinbrenner noted to himself that Burke left out the middle initial and the roman numeral at the end when he introduced him—something that would never happen again, whenever he could help it.

There was bombshell number two.

Number three followed quickly.

"The sale price," Burke said, "is for ten million dollars."

This sent shock waves throughout the room. Ten million dollars? Just three years earlier the city of Milwaukee—less than one-seventh the size of New York—had rescued the Seattle Pilots out of bankruptcy and paid $14 million for the privilege. It was believed that this had established a floor for what all sales would start at going forward. Only one baseball team since 1901 had ever sold at a loss and that had been in 1953, when Anheuser-Busch saw it as a civic obligation to buy the St. Louis Cardinals, paying slightly less than the $4 million Fred Saigh had shelled out to buy the team five years earlier, before Saigh had encountered huge financial setbacks and nearly moved the team because of it.

Since 1973 no baseball team has been sold at a loss (or even come remotely close).

Yet now Burke was explaining that because of CBS's corporate structure and the resulting tax loopholes it had enjoyed, as well as the depreciation of players as they aged, this wasn't a sunk cost at all.

"CBS substantially recouped its investment," he insisted, which was the one message CBS chairman William Paley had demanded Burke get across. CBS was no hayseed, and it hadn't agreed to the twelve-man Yankees partnership offer of $833,833.33 apiece out of any kind of charity (although it would soon be revealed the partners hadn't all paid that amount. Some paid more. One fellow paid only $168,000 of his own money. He was the one who put the group together. And he was the one standing at the podium).

Paley was adamant: Spin this to show that we made money on this deal, that we weren't taken to the cleaners by these out-of-towners from Ohio. Whatever else happened, that had to be high in every story that appeared that afternoon and the next morning.

Burke understood and agreed. He relayed that message to his new partner.

Then he introduced Steinbrenner.

And Steinbrenner immediately said: "This is the best buy in sports today. I think it's a bargain."

With those thirteen words, Steinbrenner ended the near twenty-year friendship between Michael Burke and William Paley. The two men never spoke again.

Steinbrenner—taking to the spotlight easily, and naturally—was just getting started.

"The Yankees," he said, "are an important thing to New York, but equally important as they are to New York, they're that important to baseball."

And with that, Steinbrenner allowed Burke to reveal bombshell number four: The Yankees would, indeed, be staying in New York; they would no longer be romanced by the Jersey Meadowlands (for another few years, anyway). Burke passed along a message from Mayor John V. Lindsay: "'As landlord of the New York Yankees, the city welcomes today's news.'" And soon enough, it would be revealed that while the Lehman Brothers bid had indeed outpaced the Steinbrenner/Burke group by at least three and a half million dollars, the Lehman offer had come with a caveat: They were absolutely committed to flee the Bronx for North Jersey. That, it turns out, had been the deal-breaker for CBS. For all the hassles the Yankees had beset CBS with, one thing Paley did not want to leave behind as part of his legacy was being forever known as the man who let the Yankees leave New York.

So it was Steinbrenner "and eleven partners to be named later," as the *Daily News* quipped.

The New York press was struck by Steinbrenner's presence, his self-assuredness and also by his youth.

"Finally!" crowed Phil Pepe in the *Daily News*. "A young owner instead of the usual roster of old-fogeys."

"A Yankee owner out of the Woodstock generation," enthused Vic Ziegel in the *Post*, undoubtedly the last time anyone would ever again intimate, even as a matter of satire, that George M. Steinbrenner III was a hippie.

The day's fifth and final surprise came later, after the official part of the program broke up and Steinbrenner was surrounded by a thick ring of writers—delighting in the attention more and more. As Larry Merchant would later write in the *Post*: "Nobody puts your name in the paper after you build a really good ship." But after holding court for fifteen minutes, Steinbrenner left his new friends in the press with one assurance.

"We plan absentee ownership as far as running the Yankees is concerned," he said. "Nobody is going to pretend to be something we aren't. I'll stick to building ships."

"OF COURSE I never should have said those words," George Steinbrenner would concede in January 2003, as he'd said for most of the thirty years since they were first uttered. "Because I didn't believe it. Oh, maybe in the glare of the moment it reflected what I was thinking—I really was new to baseball; I really did understand that I had some things to learn about this new world."

He laughed.

"But even from day one I knew I wasn't going to be an absentee owner. Anyone who'd ever spend five minutes around me at work knew that right away."

Some have called Steinbrenner's promise of absentee ownership the greatest lie in sports history. It was certainly—given the thirty-seven years to follow—among the most *ironic* things ever said. Steinbrenner was the principal owner of the Yankees for exactly 13,705 days; few of those days passed without someone, somewhere, for some reason, hearkening back to those four words.

"We plan absentee ownership."

In truth, Steinbrenner arrived precisely at the outset of the era of sports-owner-as-celebrity. From the beginning of Major League Baseball the exclusive club of men who owned the teams—sixteen of them from 1901 to 1960, twenty from 1962 to '69, twenty-four on the day Steinbrenner was introduced—enjoyed the primacy and the privacy of their select strata. Dick Young, who for thirty years was the most powerful sportswriter in America, once dubbed them "Lords of the Game," and later "Lords" for short, and it wasn't designed as a compliment. But none of the Lords minded all that much.

For years, they were padlocked inside a sure thing and knew it. Some teams did better than others, sure. Even in the thirties and forties baseball's economics favored big-market cities like New York and Chicago over the smaller burgs like St. Louis and Cincinnati. In the 1950s, the Kansas City Athletics became in essence an unofficial feeder system for the Yankees, and players who'd labored in obscurity in western Missouri found stardom—and championships—just north of Broadway. But even the poor teams had it fine; thanks to the "reserve clause" that bound players in perpetuity to the clubs that originally signed them, the athletes had zero leverage. They could be traded or released on a whim. The owners set the rules and thrived by them.

The game that George Steinbrenner joined in 1973 still resembled what it had looked like in 1933 but barely, holding on by fingernails. Marvin Miller had arrived to mobilize the players' union in 1967, and in 1972 they struck over pension benefits and salary arbitration—and, to the surprise of almost everybody, the players got most of what they demanded. Emboldened, the next target was the reserve clause, and the possibility of free agency that would follow. Baseball was barreling toward a much colder existence, one that would ultimately consist of billionaires on one side and millionaires on the other.

And Steinbrenner would be ready for that transition.

In the moment he was quick to say that, while his first baseball loyalties as a child were with his hometown Cleveland Indians, "I always admired the Yankees because how couldn't you admire them? They were the *Yankees*." A few weeks earlier, the Yankees had pulled off a high-profile deal, trading for Cleveland's best player, third baseman Graig Nettles, and Steinbrenner admitted: "I hated that trade then. Now, I'm a big fan."

"You know," he said as the press scrum began to thin, "there's a lot of reaching back these days for things that were meaningful. Look at the success of *No, No, Nanette* on Broadway. . . ."

INTERLUDE: Decades later, Steinbrenner would've taken great glee in gratuitously mentioning *No, No, Nanette* at any point in any conversation because the story goes that back in 1919 Red Sox owner Harry Frazee needed cash to bankroll that show, and that's the reason he sold Babe Ruth to the Yankees for $100,000. This story doesn't take into account that the play didn't actually open until 1924 . . . but, no matter. It became a foundational element to the "Curse of the Bambino" myth that grew around the Sox, and Steinbrenner delighted in deepening the mythology. But that was later. In January 1973 *No, No, Nanette* had just ended an electric 861-performance revival on Broadway, which was of great interest to Steinbrenner, himself a nascent theater impresario.

"That's part of it. And I think the Yankees are, too. That's why I'm part of it. But at the same time, I'm for new ideas in baseball."

It wouldn't take long for him to share those ideas. About as long as it took for him to return to his hotel and dial the Cleveland number of the mutual friend he'd shared with Michael Burke who started all of this in the first place.

"I think it went well today," Steinbrenner said.

"I thought so, too," Gabe Paul agreed.

CHAPTER 3

He shouted and blustered from a lack of fundamental self-assurance. From the very first, George had been bugged by my New York visibility and the amiable relationship I enjoyed with a variety of people.
—MICHAEL BURKE

January 3, 1973, had been Michael Burke's show.

But January 10 was for George Steinbrenner. This was his official coming-out party. This is when he would address, at length, his vision for the New York Yankees, after one full week at the helm, "absent" though he may have been. This is when he would reveal the identities of his other partners, the men who'd filled in the rest of the $10 million around the $168,000 sum for which he himself had written a check. He rented out the 21 Club on West Fifty-Second Street, an old speakeasy still in its prime as a meeting place for New York's beautiful people. He made sure to fill the room with as many sportswriters as he could, and many of the ones who weren't assigned to cover Super Bowl VII in Los Angeles that week would indeed be on hand, and none would ever have to worry about such nettlesome troubles as an empty glass. He fed them chicken curry and beef bordelaise.

The 21 Club had long been an object of obsession for Steinbrenner, whose business interests in the late sixties and early seventies often brought him to Manhattan, a time and a town that the writer Dick Schaap had coined "Fun City." The main room at 21 was reserved for big shots—actors, authors, politicians, judges, TV news anchors. Every time Steinbrenner visited New York, his secretary would call for a table; every time, he arrived to a table upstairs at four o'clock in the afternoon. The day after his opening press conference at Yankee Stadium, Howard Cosell invited him to lunch at 21, and when Steinbrenner arrived he discovered they'd be joined by Cosell's *Monday Night Football* partner Frank Gifford and Pete Rozelle, commissioner of the NFL. They sat at the featured table in the main room.

Now he'd rented a whole room. The rest of his life, *George Steinbrenner* would be the main room at 21.

As the writers polished off their lunch, refilled their rye and gin and bourbon, Steinbrenner walked to a dais at the front and made his elevator pitch.

"It's important to me and it's important to all of us and it's particularly important to New York and the Yankees that the group that gets behind the Yankees at this point has the wherewithal and the interest to get the kind of job done that the sportswriters, that the fans, that the city and the media in New York deserve."

Read what you will into the fact that the first and third targets of Steinbrenner's presentation were the press, although the man *would* spend more time on the back pages of the city's three warring tabloids—*Post*, *Daily News*, later *New York Newsday*—than any other sporting figure across the next thirty-seven years, not once by accident. Someone asked Steinbrenner how long he expected it to be before he and his group would deliver the Yankees back to the sport's apex, a place the Yankees hadn't reached since 1962, when they'd won their twentieth championship in the previous thirty-nine years. Steinbrenner, in the moment, didn't yet know the names of any of his players. If Bobby Murcer—the Yankees' best, a two-time All-Star who'd hit thirty-three home runs, led the league with 102 runs scored, and finished fifth in the MVP vote for 1972—had walked into 21 at that moment, Steinbrenner wouldn't have known who he was (though he would've had something to say about the length of his hair; Murcer would learn that lesson soon enough). No matter.

"Three years!" Steinbrenner declared.

"We're gonna hold you to that!" the *Post*'s Maury Allen crowed from his seat, drawing laughter.

One man who wasn't in the mood for chuckles, merriment or any manner of hilarity at all was the man standing to Steinbrenner's left on the dais. That was Michael Burke. It had taken a week, but already their roles had metaphorically shifted, symbolized by their places on the dais. But Burke could sense something else afoot.

That morning, he and Steinbrenner had shared a car from the Carlyle hotel over to 21. At breakfast at the Carlyle, Burke met many of Steinbrenner's moneymen for the first time. He expected most of them. One was a surprise.

It was Gabe Paul.

And until that morning, Paul hadn't just been the general manager of the Cleveland Indians, but he owned a 10 percent stake of the team. Paul was a baseball lifer, whose first gig in professional ball had been as a batboy at age ten for his hometown Rochester (New York) Tribe of the International League. At twenty-seven, he got his first taste of the major leagues when he became the traveling secretary for the Cincinnati Reds, and he rose to serve nine years as the club's general manager, from 1952 to 1960. He'd been the GM in Cleveland since 1961, and the next year bought into the team. He'd grown to know and like Burke from nearly a decade's worth of baseball executive meetings, and he'd been friendly with Steinbrenner, a fervent local sportsman who, a few years earlier, had nearly bought the Indians from food magnate Vernon Stouffer. When that deal collapsed, Paul promised Steinbrenner he'd keep his ears to the ground, listening for hints if any other teams might come up for sale.

Gabe Paul was the mysterious "mutual friend" who'd brought Steinbrenner and Burke together. Burke already knew that Paul was likely to jump into the Yankees fray now, something of a finder's fee for arranging the marriage. But this was the first time it dawned on him that his involvement was more than as a backroom dealmaker. That morning, Paul had resigned as Cleveland's GM and divested himself of his owner's share of the club. He cheerfully relayed those updates to Burke. And Burke suddenly sensed at once that Gabriel Howard Paul, sixty-three years old, a baseball man for fifty-three of them, wasn't going to get involved in the Yankees simply to oversee Bat Day and Cap Day and Fan Appreciation Day.

"Son of a bitch," he muttered to himself.

SO IT WAS that Michael Burke—who'd hunted Nazis as a spy in World War II, then chased Communists as a spook at the start of the Cold War—learned the first bracing lesson of the week-old Steinbrenner Era, one that would replay itself time and again as the years flew by: No matter how many bosses, there is but one Boss. No matter how many partners, there was but one voice that would matter, and it would always belong to Steinbrenner. This would take a few months to play itself out. But Burke had expected to parlay the inside scoop Paley had given him months earlier—that the Yanks were going on the block and he'd have first crack at bagging that baseball elephant—into an arrangement where he would be the point man who would restore the Yankees to glory. He would be the one calling the shots. He'd be the savior riding into town on a white steed, and he would ride him at the front of the parade when he finally returned the Yankees to the Canyon of Heroes. Burke had trusted Paul when he said Steinbrenner was too busy building ships to care about baseball—and believed Paul when he hinted that he was also ready to leave the daily grind of running a ball club, happy to consult whenever his opinion was sought.

Burke tried. He pushed the tide off as long as he could, which is to say: about as long as a ramshackle lifeguard stand could against a real tide. By the time the car reached the 21 Club that day, he'd cornered Steinbrenner into a concession: He, Burke, was the one who would call the baseball shots. Paul would be there as an adviser. Steinbrenner knew just seeing Paul at the press conference would stir the muckraking instincts of the sportswriters;

in the interest of peace he agreed. And Paul, knowing (as Burke by now surely knew, as well) that he had an open line of communication with Steinbrenner, nodded his head.

A week earlier, Steinbrenner had been unambiguous when he'd declared flatly, "Mike will be in charge."

Now, with Paul in the room, someone asked if that was still the case.

"Mike is the main guy, yes," Steinbrenner reiterated.

Burke, in what would prove to be his final gasp of and grasp for power, made sure to emphasize the point: "I don't expect to have fifteen voices telling me what to do. Gabe Paul will join the Yankees in a major post within the context of not throwing out my present organization."

Then, categorically: "We have one general manager, Lee MacPhail."

And then, just to make sure everyone understood: "This is a nice way for Gabe Paul to close out his baseball career. He's sixty-three and intends to retire to Florida in a couple of years. We'll simply use his baseball knowledge as constructively as we can."

Paul smiled a cherubic smile. It almost camouflaged how much he was seething inside. But there would be a time and a place to settle such scores. This day, he was just one of many loyal foot soldiers whom Steinbrenner had assembled to pay the bill from CBS, a total of thirteen men, including such luminaries as Nelson Bunker Hunt (son of oil baron H. L. Hunt and brother of American Football League founder Lamar Hunt); John Z. DeLorean (vice president of General Motors and head of its Chevrolet division, and later the namesake for the DMC DeLorean that was prominently featured in the *Back to the Future* trilogy); Thomas Evans, a partner in the law firm Mudge, Rose, Guthrie and Alexander who'd served as the trial lawyer for another partner, Richard M. Nixon, before Nixon had left that job four years earlier for a higher profile one in Washington, DC; and James Nederlander, a theater owner and producer whose Broadway plays would win nine Tony Awards.

INTERLUDE: Not long after the deal with CBS was consummated, the network bought back from New York City two parking garages that neighbored Yankee Stadium for $1.2 million. So the total cost was really just $8.8 million. Steinbrenner, who'd burned Burke (and ended his friendship with Paley) over declaring the Yankees a "bargain," probably undersold it; it was really a steal. Steinbrenner did keep that part of it private until long after Burke died in 1987 and Paley passed in 1990.

"I sat down and drew up a list of men I know to be doers, and these are the kind of men I wanted to bring into the New York picture," Steinbrenner said. "When you pay ten million dollars and want to operate in a first-class fashion, I don't care how wealthy you are, it's an awful strain on one man. When you want to get the job done, you need people like this."

Added Burke: "The identity with New York and the Yankees is a visibility they wouldn't get anywhere else."

Added Steinbrenner: "They're not the kind who will stick their noses in, but when they're asked, they'll help."

In time, most of Steinbrenner's partners would come to know that to jut those noses too close to the boss's purview was to wind up needing them x-rayed and reset. But for now all the men in attendance (plus Hunt and Lester Crown, who were absent) seemed perfectly happy, content to have just purchased an extra-expensive season ticket to watch a fourth-place team. And since all knew Steinbrenner a lot more intimately than Burke did, they probably all chuckled quietly to themselves as Burke kept reminding the room who was in charge. Like Steinbrenner a week before, all insisted they would keep Yankees business at arm's length other than Evans, whose law firm would now serve as the team's general counsel; Nederlander went so far as to say, "I wouldn't call Burke and tell him how to run the Yankees any more than I would expect him to call me and tell me how to run theaters."

Unlike Steinbrenner, they meant it.

PAUL, PUBLICLY TAKING a bullet on the issue of power, wound up facing an array of questions from the writers about the ethical dance he'd executed working for Cleveland while knowing he was leaving for the Yankees. After all, he and MacPhail had executed a huge deal on November 27, just forty-four days earlier, in which he'd traded Cleveland's slugging, slick-fielding third baseman Graig Nettles along with backup catcher Jerry Moses for four talented but unproven Yankees prospects: Charlie Spikes, Rusty Torres, John Ellis and Jerry Kenney—a deal that would look even more suspicious in years to come since not one of the ex-Yankees ever made an All-Star team while Nettles made five as a Yankee.

"I'm not concerned in the least about any suspicion that people may have," Paul insisted. "When you are right, there is nothing to be afraid of. And I was right. That deal was a benefit for both clubs. The Yankees strengthened themselves, but the Indians made a hell of a trade."

The reviews were, universally, favorable, because New York's sagging faction of Yankees fans was eager for a sign that reversal was even possible. It had been bad enough when the Yankees—at the end of a stretch when they'd won five straight American League pennants—had been passed in their own town in 1964 by the woeful Mets. The Yankees won forty-six more games than the 53–109 Mets but had drawn 425,000 fewer customers thanks in large part to the Mets fleeing Manhattan's Polo Grounds—a building just as dated and dilapidated as Yankee Stadium—for Shea Stadium in Queens' Flushing Meadows. But then in 1969 the Mets also surpassed the Yankees on the field, winning the World Series.

"It was hard being a Yankees fan, man," says Spike Lee, the noted filmmaker and even more notable New York sports fan who, despite growing up in the erstwhile National League stronghold of Brooklyn, had opted to go with the Yankees. "All the cool kids were all about the Mets. And for a while, before George, it was hard to argue the point."

For now, though, George Steinbrenner was done. He flew home to Cleveland to tend to his shipping business. He vanished from the newspapers; over the next two months, his name wouldn't appear even once in the *Post*, the *Times*, the *Daily News* or *Newsday*. For now, he was content to let the Knicks take much of the spotlight, as they built momentum toward another title run. He'd let mighty UCLA roam as kings of the sports page as the Bruins built an eighty-eight-game winning streak. He'd even let the Mets' owner, Joan Whitney Payson, have her share of the limelight solo as she spoke about her championship aspirations for her team. For now, George Steinbrenner was content to loom in the shadows of Northeast Ohio.

For now.

CHAPTER 4

I didn't get along with George and it was partly my own fault. He was taking over and doing stuff himself. He was getting so personally involved, making the decisions on his own and not giving anybody else any credit for anything. So I was happy to leave him.
—LEE MacPHAIL

George Steinbrenner had arrived at Yankee Stadium in a salty mood to begin with, and nothing he saw across the two hours and thirty-seven minutes of a baseball game was going to lighten his mood. As he looked around his vast new ballpark, one thing deeply troubled him: acres upon acres of empty seats. There had been a time—and there would be, again—when the Yankees' home opener would be treated almost as a secular holy day of obligation, an unofficial civic holiday. There was the usual pomp and circumstance attached to the day; it was festive; the weather was about as nice as you could ask for early April in New York City: partly sunny, on the cool side, a little wind. But as the day inched forward, and as Steinbrenner took his place in the owner's box just behind the Yankees' dugout on the first base side of the field, he had a question for his two companions: his partner Michael Burke and the team's general manager, Lee MacPhail.

"Where are all the people?"

Three days earlier, on April 6, Steinbrenner accepted an invitation from Joan Payson, owner of the Mets, to sit with her and her baseball cabinet at Shea Stadium for the Mets' opener. The Mets, too, were disappointed with the turnout: only 27,326 to watch a team that was one of the favorites to win the National League's East Division—and to watch two Cy Young Award–winning pitchers, New York's Tom Seaver and Philadelphia's Steve Carlton, duel each other. But Steinbrenner spent much of the game with his ear glued to a transistor radio, where Phil Rizzuto, Bill White and Frank Messer were taking turns describing a nine-inning calamity taking place at Boston's Fenway Park.

In future years, Steinbrenner would make a regular habit of attending such games in person, especially once he became familiar with the long and entangled (and mostly one-way) rivalry between the Yankees and Red Sox. But he decided to wait a few days, for the home opener, to see his team—which was also considered the betting favorite to win the American League East—in person. Early on, the news was terrific. One of his players, Ron Blomberg, became the first-ever designated hitter in baseball's history (two days after Steinbrenner's 21 gathering, the AL had voted in favor of the DH, which would take the place of the pitcher in the batting order; the NL wouldn't adopt the rule for another forty-nine years), and Blomberg drew a bases-loaded walk against Boston's Luis Tiant, part of a three-run top of the first for the Yankees.

That was as good as it got. The Red Sox throttled Yankees ace Mel Stottlemyre for six runs and eight hits in two and two-thirds innings, and the Red Sox demolished the Yankees in the first game of Steinbrenner's reign, 15–5—all of this as he sat through a 3–0 Mets victory at Shea. The Sox won the next two days, too, including an excruciating game Sunday afternoon in which the Yankees rallied in the top of the ninth to tie the game at 3–3 only to have Boston's DH, Orlando Cepeda, clobber the first pitch he saw from Sparky Lyle for a game-winning home run.

So to begin with, Steinbrenner wasn't in a chipper mood, with his team already 0–3 on the season. The thin crowd—only 17,028 would make it through the red-painted entrance kiosks—clouded his mood further. And a few minutes before the game began at 2:13 p.m., Steinbrenner angrily removed a pen and a piece of paper from the pocket of his sports jacket. MacPhail took notice of what he wrote: *17. 1. 15. 28.*

Steinbrenner didn't yet know their names. And as they stood at attention right in front of Steinbrenner, listening to opera singer Robert Merrill sing the national anthem, facing the American flag in center field, he couldn't see their faces, either. He just knew that he didn't at all like the length of the hair spilling out the back of Yankees caps belonging to number 17 (Gene Michael), number 1 (Bobby Murcer), number 15 (Thurman Munson) and number 28 (Sparky Lyle).

MacPhail, sitting to Steinbrenner's left, had no idea what the numbers were in reference to. Burke, sitting to Steinbrenner's right, probably would have been able to guess. A few weeks earlier, on the first day pitchers and catchers reported to Fort Lauderdale Stadium for spring training, Steinbrenner and Burke also had an assignment. They were scheduled to take a picture together for the Yankees 1973 yearbook, a page that would be titled "Yankee General Partners" at the top and would feature both men's autographs at the bottom.

But the picture itself . . .

On the left is Michael Burke, bedecked in what can best be described as straight from the 1973 Mike Brady line of fashion: a long (though well-groomed) mop of gray hair, theoretically parted on the left side of his head, with a blue denim work shirt open to two buttons north of his belt. He is wearing a bemused smile. On the right is George M. Steinbrenner III (the signature used all four segments), wearing a blue golf shirt buttoned to his neck, a blue blazer, his close-cropped hair neatly parted on the right side of his head, his expression not unlike the father who comes home early to discover a three-keg party overtaking his house.

"I don't have a problem with long hair," Steinbrenner would soon declare in a letter to MacPhail, referring directly to his players and peripherally to his partner. "But some of our guys look a little shaggy."

The shaggiest of Steinbrenner's hirsute holdouts would soon receive an extra dose of Steinbrenner's venom, as would each of his seatmates.

The opponent was the Cleveland Indians—the same club Steinbrenner had tried to buy two years earlier. This was also Steinbrenner's hometown team, and for as long as Steinbrenner would own the Yankees, every loss to Cleveland would register as two for the erstwhile Indians fan.

Steinbrenner hadn't yet spent much time around MacPhail, the future Hall of Fame executive who'd helped build the Baltimore Orioles into the most powerful franchise in baseball before joining the Yankees in 1965 and accepting the difficult task of trying to rebuild a crumbling dynasty. He'd done so with great deliberation, and by 1970 the Yankees won ninety-three games, ten more than the crosstown Mets, thanks to finding and developing fine players like catcher (and future captain) Munson, outfielder Roy White and Murcer, the franchise cornerstone. Despite the slow start, many baseball experts still believed the Yankees had an excellent chance of halting their postseason drought at eight.

But sitting in his box on April 9, Steinbrenner sure couldn't see it. For one thing, the infamous trade that Gabe Paul and MacPhail had engineered while Paul was still working for Cleveland (even as he was pushing the Yankees sale along) was looking like a one-sided steal—in the wrong direction—and Steinbrenner was furious at both men: MacPhail for getting snookered and Paul for snookering MacPhail. The jewel of the trade, Graig Nettles, went 1-for-4 and booted a double-play grounder that allowed Cleveland to take the lead; meanwhile three of the ex-Yankees—Charlie Spikes, Rusty Torres, John Ellis—combined for six hits.

So there was that.

Then there was Bobby Murcer.

Early in March MacPhail made Murcer just the third Yankee (after Joe DiMaggio and Mickey Mantle) to ever sign a $100,000 contract—a plateau that, in 1973, was the top of the mountain for baseball salaries. Steinbrenner exploded. That was a $32,000 raise from 1972, and Steinbrenner didn't find it at all funny when he read in the newspapers that MacPhail said, "I was hoping Bobby would call back and tell me 'You know, I'm too young [at twenty-six, he'd be the second-youngest player—behind Reds catcher Johnny Bench—to ever hit $100K] to make this kind of money.'" But

MacPhail was smiling as he said it, and the baseball writers saluted the GM for identifying the most popular Yankee and paying him a fair wage.

Steinbrenner seethed.

Now, at the home opener at Yankee Stadium, Steinbrenner was eager to be found wrong. Cleveland led the Yankees 2–1 in the bottom of the eighth, but with two outs Matty Alou singled and the sparse crowd rose and roared as Bobby Murcer stepped to the plate with that lefty swing custom-designed for Yankee Stadium's inviting right field porch. Murcer had walked and flied out twice in three appearances so far; he represented the game's go-ahead run with the tying run on base.

Murcer struck out looking.

Maybe other crowds in other years would've booed Murcer mercilessly, but he was the favored son, so most of the 17,028 in attendance just groaned, and then groaned some more when the Indians added an insurance run and finished off a 3–1 win.

In the owner's box, as soon as umpire Larry Barnett's arm had risen high to ring up Murcer, George Steinbrenner turned sharply to Lee MacPhail.

"SO THIS IS THE BUM WE'RE PAYING A HUNDRED THOUSAND DOLLARS?"

MacPhail said nothing. Years later, he would write, "It was in that moment I realized that things were going to be a little different around the Yankees."

In truth, they already were.

ON JULY 15, 1972, George Steinbrenner was still licking his wounds after coming so close to purchasing the Indians, and he busied himself with work at American Ship Building Co. That day at Yankee Stadium the Yankees dropped a 6–2 game to the eventual-champion Oakland A's in front of a modest Saturday-afternoon gathering. Fritz Peterson, the Yankees' flaky left-hander, had pitched well, surrendering only three runs in seven innings against a powerful Athletics lineup. That night, Peterson joined his wife, Marilyn, and a few other Yankees teammates and their spouses—Mike Kekich and his wife, Susanne; Ron Swoboda and his wife, Cecilia—at a barbecue at what seems like a most unlikely place: the home of Maury and Janet Allen in Scarsdale, a Westchester County suburb just north of the Bronx. Allen was the Yankees' beat writer for the *New York Post*, but in those simpler times it wasn't unusual for the writers and the players to have a cozy enough relationship that they would mingle for a night of hamburgers and beers. And the night was a success, the party not breaking up until two in the morning.

By three, Maury and Janet had cleaned up and were headed for bed when Maury looked out the window and noticed the Petersons and the Kekiches were still there, leaning against their cars in front of the house.

"We remarked about it and went to bed," Allen would remember years later. "These are ballplayers, remember, different from you and me."

What the Allens had witnessed, on the sly, was a burgeoning romance that was about as 1973 an event as 1973 could yield. A few months before, the Kekiches and the Petersons had discovered that while they enjoyed one another's company immensely, they'd begun to believe they were going home with the wrong spouse.

So they swapped. Literally.

"We didn't change wives," Fritz Peterson would say. "We changed lives."

It had been a whisper around the Yankees for weeks in 1972, and slowly became an open secret within the soundproof walls of the clubhouse. Peterson moved to Kekich's house in Mahwah, New Jersey, living with Susanne Kekich, her two daughters and their family pet. Seven miles south, in Franklin Lakes, Kekich moved into Peterson's house, living with Marilyn Peterson, her two sons and their family pet. Their teammates afforded the two lefties their privacy. And for a while it was blissful. Until it wasn't. Fritz and Susanne fell madly in love. Within a few months, Marilyn left Mike and moved in with her mother in Chicago. The original agreement was that if anyone felt uncomfortable with the arrangement they'd all go back. Falling in (and out of) love changed the calibration. And also sparked a little bitterness.

Which is how it came to pass that late in the afternoon of March 5, a story moved on the United Press International wire, written by UPI's ace baseball writer Milton Richman. The open secret was now an open feeding frenzy. The Yankees called a hastily arranged press conference, summoning the four traveling beat writers to hear the players' tortured testimony. Sheila Moran, whom the *Post* had sent to Florida as the first woman to cover a baseball team, wasn't invited. She was told the Yankees hoped the story would be treated "gently" by the veteran male scribes.

"This isn't as big a deal as it seems," she was told.

Moran figured she'd find that out on her own. She dialed up Susan Kekich and Marilyn Peterson, got them both to open up about this real-life, baseball-flavored take on *Bob & Carol & Ted & Alice*. And suddenly this wasn't going to be a story buried in the back with the harness-racing roundups.

"Well," Lee MacPhail said dryly. "I guess Family Day is off this year."

INTERLUDE: Years later, Ben Affleck and Matt Damon—just about the highest-profile Red Sox fans in creation—attempted to write and produce a movie, *The Trade*, based on the Peterson/Kekich swap. They wrote a treatment in 2010, and by 2014 got Jay Roach attached as a director, although by then they'd aged out of being able to play their two favorite Yankees. The movie has yet to be green-lit.

George Steinbrenner, to put it mildly, saw little about this that was terribly funny.

But he was also awaiting final approval from the other American League owners. So he kept his profile low. It had already been a flustering stretch for Steinbrenner. In January he'd attended the annual Baseball Writers' Dinner in New York and was introduced to his star relief pitcher, Sparky Lyle; Lyle was on crutches. The next day, Steinbrenner picked up a newspaper, turned to the sports page and learned that Murcer—his hundred-thousand-dollar bum—had broken his hand.

And now . . . well. *This.*

Still, after the news broke, providing Johnny Carson with a few days of easy material, Steinbrenner found himself in Fort Lauderdale Stadium, watching the Yankees. Peterson had yet to officially report to camp, since he was unsigned, although he watched the game from the stadium's rooftop. But Kekich was there. He started a game against the Orioles March 10, pitched two innings, allowed two walks and two hits and a run. He had a tender elbow, which didn't help. He also had a few admirers scattered in the stands.

"Hey, Kekich!" one yelled. "Where's your wife?"

"Which one?" the guy next to him asked helpfully.

"Hey, Kekich!" another leather-lunged commentator screeched. "Let your wife pitch!"

Steinbrenner, admittedly and proudly as conservative as trickle-down economics, quietly admonished: "Shut up, you bum." Then, a few seconds later, he saw that a few of the fan's neighbors in the stands offered the same advice.

"That shut him up immediately," Steinbrenner said. "I was happy to see that. Mike didn't deserve that kind of treatment."

Perhaps those words camouflaged what he was really feeling about the whole, um, affair. But the fact was: In his first public opportunity to show compassion for a man who was clearly going through a spell, George Steinbrenner chose kindness. That wouldn't always be his playbook.

CHAPTER 5

George told me he wanted me to stay, and he was sincere about it. He said, "I'm going to do whatever it takes to get the ballplayers that will make us great again and I want you to be the one who manages us when that happens." Funny thing, too: That's exactly what he did.
—RALPH HOUK

The Yankees tried for the better part of four months to give George Steinbrenner's maiden voyage smooth seas. From May 11 until the end of July they were the hottest team in baseball, climbing into first place on June 20 and staying there for the next forty-two days. Steinbrenner quickly learned the only thing that made him feel better than Yankees victories was when they paired with Mets losses, and that happened plenty across June and July, even as the fans kept flocking to Shea Stadium.

On August 1, the Yankees woke up in first place, 60–48, a game better than the Orioles, two up on the Tigers, three and a half ahead of the Red Sox. The night before, at Fenway Park, they rallied from two runs down in the ninth inning against Boston, the key hit a two-run single by Bobby Murcer, the hundred-thousand-dollar bum, who added to his growing credentials to win the Most Valuable Player award and kept the Yankees alone in first place. That same night, in New York, the Mets lost 4–1 to the

Pirates to fall a season-high thirteen games under .500, some ten and a half games out, dead last in the NL East.

But it was even better for Yankees fans. Earlier that year, the Mets' chairman of the board, M. Donald Grant, insisted that the job of Yogi Berra—the Mets' manager who'd been a Yankees legend in his playing days, a man George Steinbrenner would come to know quite well—was safe despite the team's struggles, "unless the fans tell me different." Never shy about stirring the pot, the *New York Post* promptly conducted a poll from the back page of its newspaper: WHO SHOULD THE METS AX? Grant was greatly displeased that the fans overwhelmingly chose either himself or Mets GM Bob Scheffing as the man to face the music, with Berra a distant third.

It surely amused Steinbrenner to no end to see a baseball team's dirty laundry washed, spun and dried on the back page of a newspaper.

But the Yankees lost an excruciating game on August 1, the Red Sox walking them off in the bottom of the ninth after Gene Michael failed to get a suicide squeeze bunt down in the top of the inning, leaving Thurman Munson out to dry, forcing Munson to try to steal home and barrel over Boston catcher Carlton Fisk. The resulting brawl marked a warning shot, of sorts, to a renewal of the dormant Yankees–Red Sox rivalry after a quarter century in repose, and also a grudge between Munson and Fisk that would fester for most of the next six years. The Yankees lost the next day, too, and the day after that in Detroit, falling out of first place. They lost all eight games on a road swing with games against Kansas City, Oakland and California. By the end of the month, they were stuck in fourth, nine and a half games back, and when they dropped a 7–3 game to Cleveland on September 11 in front of only 5,637 customers at Yankee Stadium, they dipped under .500, 72–73. And to make matters worse, the Mets—still in last place themselves on August 31—pulled off one of the greatest comebacks in baseball history in September, winning twenty of their final twenty-eight games to steal the NL East, then beating Cincinnati in the playoffs before finally losing Game 7 of the World Series to the defending-champion Oakland Athletics.

Somehow, even as the Yankees attempted to bring some dignity to the closing of their basilica of a ballpark, which would be boarded up for two years as it underwent its $24 million facelift (a price tag that would swell to $100 million by the time the final nail was hammered), they became even more of an afterthought. The final three games attracted 9,313, then 9,502 and, at last, a quasi-respectable 32,238, many of whom helped themselves to their seats at game's end.

INTERLUDE: Thirty-five years later, the renovated version of Yankee Stadium closed. The 2008 Yankees drew 4,298,543 people, many of whom left the building weeping. That entire season, fewer than 125,000 seats went unsold across eighty-one games. When the doors shut, everything—down to the blades of grass— was put up for sale or auction. By contrast, in 1973 the boxing writer and sports iconoclast Bert Randolph Sugar called the Yankees' offices the day after the season to see if he could stop by and bring home a few souvenirs. He was told he could have whatever he wanted. He rented a U-Haul, drove to the park and filled it with all manner of worthless junk that became priceless memorabilia as the years passed.

Steinbrenner received another surprise that day: His manager, Ralph Houk, tired of the constant booing by even the smallest crowds as the year progressed, resigned. Steinbrenner protested; he admired Houk's background (a Marine, he'd fought at Bastogne and the Battle of the Bulge, earned a Purple Heart and rose to the rank of major), and was generally a no-nonsense old-school type who, in many ways, Steinbrenner would try to hire again and again over the next twenty years. Houk couldn't be swayed, insisting he needed a break (although, as Steinbrenner would soon discover, he'd already been approached by the Detroit Tigers to gauge his interest in managing there). A few days later, Lee MacPhail also left to take the job as president of the American League at year's end. He'd gotten along fine with Steinbrenner (though that would change profoundly in MacPhail's ten years as Steinbrenner's de facto supervisor), and Gabe Paul had been true to his word, mostly staying out of MacPhail's way.

But MacPhail could also see what was coming.

"George *listened* to Gabe," he said in 1988. "He *tolerated* me."

That small percentage of New York still paying attention to the Yankees as the Mets flew off to Cincinnati to begin the playoffs might have been surprised by all of this, but all across that 1973 season Steinbrenner had been laying bread crumbs that led directly to this moment, laying as a new organizational foundation his preferred infrastructure, one in which the power was mostly confined to the top. One that would stay in place, more or less, for the next thirty-seven years.

THE FIRST TO go had been Michael Burke. As the weeks passed early in 1973 it finally dawned on Burke what had been evident to just about everyone observing the changeover. Burke believed this was his chance to finally run a baseball team, his way, top to bottom. And there were certain things he did very well. He had, by himself, made the Yankees a far more diverse and inclusive organization in his seven years there. He'd aggressively attempted to make the Yankee demographic younger. He'd done everything in his power to make Yankee Stadium look as attractive as possible in the days ticking down to its date with a wrecking ball, and he was ever mindful of the fact that despite present predicaments the Yankees had long been a bastion of class. And he'd done all he could to ensure that the Yankees would remain in New York City for decades to come. Those qualities had very nearly won Burke the job as baseball's commissioner in 1969.

But the Yankees had also gone 489–475 on Burke's watch, finished a collective 111 games out of first place and seen nearly 500,000 fans disappear from the last season before CBS took control. The Yankees lost an estimated $11 million under CBS—all while the Mets impossibly became world champions and a money-printing phenomenon. Burke graciously telegrammed Mets owner Joan Payson after the Mets rallied to the '69 pennant:

As a New Yorker I am ecstatic; as a baseball person I am immensely pleased and as a Yankee I consider suicide the easy option.

It was enough to make any true-believer Yankees fan ill.

"He's a good man," Gabe Paul had told George Steinbrenner after he'd put the two of them together. "He's a smart man. But he doesn't know a thing about baseball."

By late April, Burke and Steinbrenner stopped sitting next to each other at the stadium, Steinbrenner keeping his dugout seats and Burke spending more and more time on the press level, where he would regularly tell his allies in the newspapers, "You wouldn't believe what it's like," without ever having to identify who he was talking about. Increasingly, baseball matters were discussed among Steinbrenner, MacPhail and Paul that Burke would learn about in a memo a few hours later.

On April 29, he stepped away. He did so with head high and a 5 percent stake in the team in his pocket, which he happily cashed in a few years later, after he'd had a similar run of high-profile PR wins and relentless on-court and on-ice miseries as the head of Madison Square Garden, overseeing its two teams, the NBA Knicks and NHL Rangers, to almost identical eras of disappointment.

Paul, who never cared for Burke as a work colleague, raged a few years later, when Burke would take the occasional shot at Steinbrenner: "He should get on his knees and be grateful every day for George Steinbrenner. Ask him how much money he made thanks to his Yankees share." (This would come before Paul's own messy divorce with Steinbrenner.)

Through much of this, Steinbrenner followed a blueprint far different from the one he'd rely on in most of his years as owner. The New York press, whom he'd so fervently courted in January, suddenly had a hard time cornering him at the ballpark, or getting him on the phone, or getting him to talk on the record when they did. Steinbrenner stayed mostly quiet through the Burke endgame. He'd stayed mum when it was leaked that his displeasure with the hair length of numbers 17, 1, 15 and 28 had actually progressed from a fit in the owner's box on Opening Day to an official memo handed to Ralph Houk one day at Cleveland's Municipal Stadium, with the insistence that it be read aloud to the players.

"Neatness on a team is meaningful to me," Houk told his players, serving as a vessel for Steinbrenner. "A sports performer carries a certain aura to it. His uniform should be neat and so should the player."

This didn't sit well with some of the players. Ron Blomberg fumed, "If George Steinbrenner thinks he can mess with my individual rights, he can get himself a new first baseman."

Blomberg's teammates had a laugh at that one. For one, Blomberg's adventures at first base were the reason he became the first primarily designated hitter in history. For another, he wasn't one of Steinbrenner's targets; he wore number 12. He was also on a career-high tear that would have him hitting as high as .403 as late as June 28.

"If you were hitting like me," Graig Nettles needled him, "you'd have been the first number on the list."

The Yankees' corps of beat writers were irritated when they arrived in Minnesota for a series with the Twins and picked up a copy of the *Minneapolis Tribune* on May 9, turning to the second page of sports and seeing that George Steinbrenner had given a lengthy interview to longtime *Tribune* columnist Sid Hartman. He said little of consequence, other than trying to throw Burke a bone to (unsuccessfully) help repair his shattered relationship with William Paley—"CBS made a good deal selling a losing proposition"—but Steinbrenner had not selected Hartman at random. Eighteen years earlier, as an assistant football coach at Northwestern, one of Steinbrenner's duties had been to scout Big Ten rival Minnesota. Hartman befriended the unknown coach and remained a confidant. When Steinbrenner was ready to clear his throat there was no question who he'd talk to.

"His loyalty," Hartman, still working at age ninety, would write the day after Steinbrenner died in 2010, "was fierce and knew no limit."

And once Steinbrenner opened the lid . . .

Well, there was a better chance of pushing toothpaste back in the tube. And as would prove to be the case for a string of Yankees media relations directors almost as long as his list of managers and GMs, that could cause trouble. As it did on June 6 when Steinbrenner went on a television program in Tampa—the city to which he was increasingly moving both his home and business interests—and said the Yankees were about to trade Mike Kekich to Atlanta for Pat Dobson, a former twenty-game winner with the Orioles, a move that would make plenty of sense for a thousand reasons. Kekich, of course, was already miserable, abandoned by both his family and his "new" family, pitching to an unsightly 9.20 ERA.

"It's time," Kekich sighed, when told the news.

Except it was wrong.

The Yankees would actually acquire Dobson the next day (and he'd be a good pitcher for the Yankees for a couple of years) but not for Kekich. They did finally have mercy on Kekich, shipping him to Cleveland on June 12. (And just to give a crazy story a crazier epilogue, a year later Fritz Peterson would also be sent away, and also to *Cleveland* . . . although by then Kekich was pitching in Japan.)

Neither MacPhail nor Houk was terribly pleased by the boss's new chattiness, even as Steinbrenner offered early hints of his willingness to write checks for talent—Dobson, fireballer Sam McDowell, former Giants slugger Jim Ray Hart, Athletics handyman Mike Hegan. Mayor Lindsay enjoyed hearing Steinbrenner put to rest once and for all a persistent rumor that the Yankees were still open to being wooed by New Orleans, which was completing a state-of-the-art facility to be called the Superdome. MacPhail had already agreed to play a few games there in 1975, a year in which the Yankees would share Shea Stadium with the Mets and thus were happy to entertain a couple of gates of sixty thousand plus (this never ultimately happened). Steinbrenner told Phil Pepe of the *Daily News* in late August, before visiting his reeling team in Oakland: "Leave New York? Never. I give you my solemn oath on that. I wouldn't leave New York City if they shot me out of a cannon."

(Less than twenty years later, when that oath wavered a bit as New Jersey began recruiting the Yankees again, many of those fans might've likely been fine revisiting the shoot-him-out-of-a-cannon idea. . . .)

Houk and MacPhail, by this time, were already metaphorically bleeding out by a thousand paper cuts. The last straw for MacPhail came in Arlington, Texas, on August 17. The Yankees were already trailing the dreadful Rangers 5–0 in the eighth inning when Johnny Callison, a fifteen-year veteran who played infrequently, trundled out to right field. Callison misplayed a ball into a base hit and three more runs, and Steinbrenner—to Callison's great misfortune, sitting in a seat by the Yankees' dugout—was incensed.

He would make a habit of doing what followed through the years, a standard in the Steinbrenner songbook. As soon as he could, he got MacPhail on the phone and shouted: "Get that son of a bitch Callison out of here! I will not have him on my team!"

MacPhail released Callison before lunch the next day, and there was a part of him that wouldn't have minded joining him.

So both the manager *and* the general manager could barely wait for Hegan to fly out to end an 8–5 loss to the Tigers, the season, the fifty-year history of the original Yankee Stadium, and their professional relationships with the Yankees. In the twenty-five years between 1973 and 1998, Steinbrenner would change managers twenty-four times. He would change general managers fourteen times.

The only two who ever left of their own volition were Ralph Houk and Lee MacPhail.

THE REPLACEMENT FOR MacPhail was obvious: Gabe Paul was the one who'd told George Steinbrenner about the Yankees possibly being for sale in the first place. He'd put Steinbrenner and Michael Burke together. He'd quit as Cleveland's GM and divested his share of the team to move to New York and then had willingly stayed out of MacPhail's way and quickly abrogated Burke. Now the Yankees would be in his hands.

Steinbrenner was poised to make a huge splash to succeed Houk.

Dick Williams scraped together a thirteen-year career for five different teams by agreeing to play anywhere he was needed and because he had an off-the-charts IQ for baseball. As a rookie manager in 1967, he'd taken over the annually underachieving Red Sox—losers of ninety games the year before—and catapulted them from ninth place in the American League all the way to the pennant, which they clinched on the last day of the season before a riotous atmosphere at Fenway Park. The Sox pushed the Cardinals to seven games before losing the World Series and Williams was hailed a baseball savant. But his fiery demeanor wore out in a hurry and the Sox dismissed him two years later. In 1971 he took over the Athletics, a franchise that hadn't been to the postseason in forty years. The A's won 101 games that first year, won ninety-three in 1972 along with the World Series, and were attempting to repeat in October 1973, when Williams gathered his players in the Shea Stadium visitor's clubhouse on the off-day between Games 2 and 3.

His message was simple.

"Win or lose, at the end of this season, I'm done here."

The players were surprised, but not stunned, and understood why Williams would willingly choose to leave baseball's first true dynasty since the end of the Yankees' reign. Their paychecks were signed by the same man who signed Williams's: Charles Oscar Finley, "Charlie-O" to much of the baseball world, known by a slew of far more unprintable names in the Oakland clubhouse. Finley had made his fortune in insurance, bought the Kansas City Athletics in 1960, threatened to relocate them to no fewer than a half dozen cities from the minute he took over, then did move them to Oakland before the 1968 season. He was a hands-on owner, a man with opinions. His had been the loudest voice promoting the DH; other ideas—such as different-colored baseballs and outfield fences the home team could adjust according to the batter—died deaths in owners meetings featuring nineteen rolling pairs of eyeballs. He chose a mule as a mascot, then named it after himself. Finley was also tightfisted with his players, openly combative, and if it sounds like a certain young owner might've been taking notes on all this, George Steinbrenner did say of Finley in 1976, "I find that man distasteful."

Finley's latest stunt—and the final straw for Williams—was his attempt to fire A's second baseman Mike Andrews after Andrews made two errors to help the Mets win Game 2 of the series. This infuriated the entire Oakland roster and angered Williams most of all. The commissioner quickly rebuked Finley's maneuver, fined him for it, and in a fairly remarkable public referendum, the sold-out Shea Stadium crowd gave Andrews a standing ovation when he came to the plate to pinch-hit late in Game 4. By then, Williams had alerted his players and news had begun to leak that he already had his next gig lined up.

"The Yankees need to be kicked in the ass," Reggie Jackson said. "He won't take anything lying down."

Steinbrenner may have been a rookie owner but he also knew what tampering looked like, so he tried to downplay such talk. Besides, what Steinbrenner, Paul, Williams and only a few intermediaries knew was: He'd already been tampering, and for almost two months. Back in August, with Williams growing increasingly frustrated at his deteriorating relationship with Finley and Steinbrenner sickened by the losing meanderings of his own team, they'd made contact through a series of buffers. Williams knew Steinbrenner wanted him. Steinbrenner knew Williams wanted the Yankees.

Of course, nobody could admit any of that yet.

"As successful as he's been, he must be a good manager," Steinbrenner said on the eve of Game 3. "*If* he were available I'm sure he'd be in demand rather quickly."

The A's won the World Series. Williams formally resigned. And Steinbrenner waited a respectful twenty-four hours to reach out to Williams. But Finley knew baseball's dark arts as well as anyone and smelled a rat. When Steinbrenner approached at an owners meeting two days after Game 7, he wasn't subtle.

"Should I let Williams go—which I have no intention of doing at present—they will certainly have to compensate me handsomely," Finley announced.

Steinbrenner's first instinct was to pull a similar maneuver with Ralph Houk, who was about to sign on to manage the Detroit Tigers despite having a year left on his Yankees contract. It didn't take much to realize that Houk played the exact same game that Williams had. But making an issue of Houk would mean making an even bigger deal out of Williams. Steinbrenner let Houk go and simply figured he'd handle Finley the way he'd handled so many other rivals in the shipping industry: He'd out-wait him, and outwit him, and ultimately pay him off. On December 13 Williams was officially introduced as the Yankees' new manager. The next day's newspapers featured Williams wearing the Yankees' interlocking "NY" cap inside a deserted Shea Stadium. Williams would get $270,000 spread across three years, and full indemnity from the Yankees if Finley chose to sue. Paul, who knew how baseball worked from the inside, was still unsure of all this.

But Steinbrenner assured him Commissioner Bowie Kuhn urged Steinbrenner to close a deal with Williams (he had not) and that Kuhn would leave the matter in the owners' hands (he did not) and that Finley would settle for secondary prospects and a couple hundred thousand in cash as compensation (he most certainly would not). Instead, an angry Joe Cronin—in his final act before handing the office of American League president over to Lee MacPhail—summoned Steinbrenner and Finley to his office in Boston to address both Williams *and* Houk. Finley's demands were high, and he was firm: a significant cash payment *and* any two of the Yankees' three-highest prospects. Steinbrenner balked. Two days later, two teletypes arrived at the Yankees' offices.

Houk was free to take the Tigers job.

And Williams's contract with the Yankees was voided.

Steinbrenner raged at Paul, his new baseball man, and at MacPhail, the outgoing one, who by now was counting down the days until January 1, when he'd start his new job: "*YOU BLEW THIS, BOTH OF YOU!*" he bellowed. Paul's face reddened with anger. MacPhail simply tried not to smile.

"George," he said, not long after settling into his new office, "can be a little impetuous."

He also would have to settle on a different manager: the mild-mannered former Pirates skipper, Bill Virdon. Steinbrenner would have to wait a few years before identifying another fire-and-brimstone specialist with whom to entrust his team, and when he did he'd keep him around, more or less, for the next fifteen years.

By January 1 Steinbrenner, who was becoming more and more of a horseman in addition to his baseball interests, had broken his maiden as an owner. It had been quite an apprenticeship.

He, and the Yankees, and baseball, and professional sports in North America, would never quite be the same ever again.

CHAPTER 6

*Rose, he knows he's such a credit to the game
But the Yankees grab the headlines every time...*
—BILLY JOEL, "ZANZIBAR"

On the morning of Monday, May 16, 1921, the 100,000 or so New Yorkers who read the *Daily News* as part of their morning ritual were treated to the same back-page features the newspaper had used in its short, unprofitable history. The *Daily News* was the first-ever American paper printed in the "tabloid" format that had gained popularity on London's Fleet Street, and founder Joseph Medill Patterson was especially fond of the way the *Daily Mail* grabbed Londoners by the lapels every morning with big headlines and bigger photographs. Soon after it debuted in 1919 he dubbed his new invention "New York's Picture Newspaper" and installed a cartoon camera between the words "*Daily*" and "*News*" in the front-page flag. The paper lost buckets of money out of the chute and wouldn't really become a phenomenon until January 12, 1928, when a *News* reporter strapped a small camera to his leg and shot a photo of Ruth Snyder, convicted of murdering her husband, being executed in the electric chair at Sing Sing. The next day's headline—DEAD!—inspired equal parts fascination and outrage, but the paper was soon selling a million copies a day.

However, by May 16, 1921, the paper was still finding its footing. And the back page was, as usual, a breezy collection of life-in–New York snapshots, most of them centering around a fleet of naval vessels docked in New York Harbor, one of them a battleship called the USS *Arizona*. It was the next day—Tuesday, May 17—that readers witnessed a silent revolution that the *News* never even heralded. Instead of those breezy photos were action shots and results from the previous day's thoroughbred activity at Jamaica Race Course. The same thing happened Wednesday, and then Thursday. Soon, the back page became a daily array of photographs and headlines focusing on Jack Dempsey and Georges Carpentier, two heavyweight prizefighters scheduled to box in the "Fight of the Century" on July 2 at Boyle's Thirty Acres in Jersey City, New Jersey, and after that and for the remainder of summer it became a haven for headlines and pictures about the Yankees and the Giants, on a collision course to face each other in the World Series.

And thus was the Back Page born.

William Randolph Hearst would introduce a rival tabloid, the *New York Mirror*, in 1924. The *New York Post*, founded by Alexander Hamilton in 1801 and the longest continually published paper in the United States, would convert from a broadsheet format to a tabloid briefly in 1934 and then permanently once Dorothy Schiff purchased the paper in 1939. From then until 1963—when the *Mirror* ceased publication—those three tabloids warred on the back page as well as the front; later, in the 1970s, the Long Island–based tabloid *Newsday* would make a run at New York City, too, which is when the back page became stuffed with humorous hot takes and venomous rebuttals and all manner of jazzed-up alternate nicknames for the city's teams: Bombers, Amazin's, Gang Green, Big Blue.

And nobody worked the back page the way George Steinbrenner worked the back page. Nobody knew how to play one newspaper against the others, one writer or one columnist against the others, like Steinbrenner, who played them like a Stradivarius. In the years before cell phones and pagers, traveling beat writers would be terrified to stray from their hotel rooms to grab a quick breakfast because if you had a call out to Steinbrenner and he returned it when you were away, you'd pay severe consequences when his latest commentaries were featured in every other newspaper except your own.

Joel Sherman, now perhaps the most well-known newspaper baseball columnist in America but in the early nineties a rookie beat writer for the *Post*, still shivers as he recalls the nightmare that awaited a newbie on the beat when a big story was brewing. At the ballpark, the press box announcer would, every few minutes, announce: "Michael Kay, phone call . . . Moss Klein, phone call . . . Jon Heyman, phone call . . . Michael Martinez, phone call . . ."

There was no mystery who was making those calls, and little chance that Sherman, barely out of NYU, would be receiving one of those calls.

"And your soul died a little bit with every announcement," he says.

That was the power Steinbrenner wielded. He could make sportswriting careers. He could break them. Some columnists had enough clout to take him head-on, but the reporters on the beat were beholden to him. Another young writer, Jack Curry of *The New York Times*, had tried for six months to get a call back from Steinbrenner. One day the phone rang in his parents' home in Jersey City, and for the first time in weeks he could exhale. It was Steinbrenner. Curry began to ask his questions, grateful in the knowledge his job was safe for another day, when soon a third voice cut in on the telephone line.

"Doesn't anyone know there's a dinner hour around here?" the third voice said. It was Curry's mother.

Curry was stunned. He tried to regroup, ask his questions, but Steinbrenner interrupted him: "Who was that? What did they say?"

Curry explained it was his mother calling him to the supper table. He started to stammer a question but again Steinbrenner stopped him. "She's right! Family time is important! Why are you talking to me, we've talked enough, we'll talk baseball another time!"

And hung up.

In the moment, Curry wondered how he'd explain that to his editor. But at the start of the call Steinbrenner briefed him on the cardinal rule in dealing with him: "If you never lie to me, if you tell me the truth, I'll always return your call."

Later, after Curry went to the kitchen ashen-faced and ate with his folks, Steinbrenner did call him back, and the men enjoyed a good working relationship for years thereafter. He got his story. When it came to George Steinbrenner, what always mattered was getting the story.

IT WAS LATE in that 1973 season when Steinbrenner not only became proficient at playing the tabloid game—Phil Pepe would have an exclusive in the *Daily News* on Tuesday, Murray Chass in the *Times* on Wednesday, Maury Allen of the *Post* on Thursday, Steve Jacobson of *Newsday* on Friday, with a new mix the next week, and the next—but he also began to learn about the flip side, too. On September 28, the ongoing Watergate investigation yielded a story listing all the citizens who had contributed $50,000 or more to the reelection campaign of President Nixon before new laws mandating full disclosure of the identities of even the more modest donors had gone into effect. There were hundreds of names on the list who'd given a total of just under $20 million, all of which had been done secretly—but, as the story stressed, in large part legally.

Among the notables were Joan Payson, owner of the Mets; J. Willard Marriott, head of the hotel corporation; four Rockefeller siblings, including Nelson, who happened to be governor of New York at the time; and George M. Steinbrenner III, who was listed simply: "Cleveland, Ohio, $75,000."

Steinbrenner had long contributed to political campaigns on both sides of the aisle, and he was eager to contribute to Nixon's reelection because his administration had guided waterfront legislation friendly to Steinbrenner's shipping business. Nixon's personal attorney, Herbert Kalmbach, suggested it would be more efficient if Steinbrenner made thirty-three different contributions of $3,000 in order to both comply with the new law and keep him as an anonymous donor as well as to earmark the payments for a number of the reelection committee's subdivisions. Steinbrenner could have simply paid the entire amount before April 7, 1973, and still remained unnamed. And had he simply written thirty-three checks for $3,000 he would also have gone undetected. But he was sloppy. Two of the checks he wrote were for a sum a bit larger than $3,000. That's what got his name noticed by the Watergate Committee, and then they began investigating Steinbrenner, who, it turned out, had violated the limit for contributions to both Republican and Democratic candidates, and had also coaxed some of his employees to cover for him if they were called before the grand jury.

Steinbrenner knew he was in a fix. He hired Edward Bennett Williams, about as high-powered a Washington attorney as has ever hung a shingle inside the Beltway and a man who, in 1979, would join Steinbrenner's own exclusive baseball club when he purchased the Baltimore Orioles. Steinbrenner publicly insisted his innocence, even as he was indicted on fifteen counts by Watergate prosecutor Leon Jaworski in April. Privately he hoped Williams could get his case dismissed or, at the least, plead it down so there would be no felony conviction. Steinbrenner knew Bowie Kuhn—up for reelection himself in 1975 for a second six-year term as baseball commissioner—would be following the case closely. He tried to keep a low profile. It was hard. At the press conference introducing Bill Virdon as the new Yankees manager on January 3, 1974—the one-year anniversary of Steinbrenner's tenure with the team—Steinbrenner was the star of the day, spinning that Virdon wasn't simply a consolation prize when it became clear the Yankees couldn't hire Dick Williams.

Virdon was a quiet man, serious but mild-mannered, a manager who'd won a pennant in 1972 with the Pirates but had been fired the next year—with Pittsburgh in first place, in September—because his bosses deemed him not fiery enough. He believed in treating his players like men, preferred simple spring training practices, and was, in every way possible, exactly the emotional opposite of the kind of manager Steinbrenner was attracted to.

Quickly, it was obvious Virdon had been hired because he was willing to work cheap and on a one-year contract, the better to keep the Yankees' options open in case their number one choice became available; Virdon's only alternative in 1974 would've been the Triple-A Denver Bears.

"No," Steinbrenner insisted, "we haven't given up on signing Dick Williams. If he gets free, we'd have to cross that bridge."

Virdon was standing right next to him inside at the Shea Stadium Diamond Club.

"All I know," Virdon said, "is that I'm the manager of the New York Yankees."

A curious, most unexpected thing happened across the next few months. The Yankees won their first four games, including a 6–1 Opening Day victory over Steinbrenner's hometown Indians, which drew only 20,744 fans to Shea Stadium in the first game of their two-year crash pad in Queens. They struggled some after that. Steinbrenner was getting restless. His instinct was to fly to Arlington, Texas, to meet the team in the midst of a thirteen-game road swing, maybe offer an old-school locker room pep talk. He decided not to. Instead, the Yankees began to play much better. They began to win. Virdon wasn't an especially popular figure in the clubhouse; he was tougher than advertised and had little problem telling Bobby Murcer that he was no longer the team's center fielder—career singles hitter Elliott Maddox was.

Incensed when Virdon made the move, Murcer decided to appeal his case higher up the Yankees ladder, to a man with whom he had developed a most unlikely friendship.

"You'll play where the manager tells you to play," George Steinbrenner told his erstwhile hundred-thousand-dollar bum. "You know you're better than you've been playing."

Murcer did start to hit more. So did everyone. Graig Nettles, who'd been such a disappointment in 1973 after arriving from Cleveland, tied the American League record for most home runs in April with eleven, and he kept hitting the ball hard. Doc Medich and Pat Dobson became co-aces of the staff, after longtime staff centerpiece Mel Stottlemyre hurt his shoulder, ending the career of the final active Yankee who'd participated in their last playoff run in 1964. Gabe Paul once again fleeced his old friends in Cleveland, this time acquiring Chris Chambliss and Dick Tidrow, two men who would be stalwarts on some terrific teams to come. The Yankees won two of three in Arlington, swept the Royals in Kansas City, and when they walked into the Royals' stadium visitor's clubhouse, traveling secretary Bill Kane greeted each player by peeling from a roll of ten-dollar bills.

"Car fare for when we get home tonight," Kane announced. "Mr. Steinbrenner is very pleased. He doesn't want you guys to have to take the bus."

But Steinbrenner had one more surprise up his sleeve: When the Yankees plane landed at LaGuardia Airport, just after three o'clock in the morning, he was there to greet the team, and shook everyone's hand as they deplaned.

"Hell of a job!" he barked, over and over.

"Sure, we were surprised to see him," Virdon said. "But I guess nothing he does really surprises us."

The Yankees kept winning. If Virdon was worried that he was merely keeping his dugout seat warm for Dick Williams, that ceased being an issue on June 28, when the California Angels hired Williams. Charlie Finley did not object.

"Finley doesn't hate the Yankees," Gabe Paul said with a laugh. "He hates one guy."

Steinbrenner, meanwhile, retreated more and more to his home office in Lorain, Ohio, and consulted regularly with his lawyer, who'd seen enough of the Watergate investigation to know Steinbrenner would undoubtedly have to pay a certain price. That bill came due on August 23, when Steinbrenner pled guilty to one count of conspiracy and one count of obstruction of justice, a felony, as he'd instructed some of his workers to lie before the grand jury. American Ship Building Co. was also found guilty of two counts of conspiracy and making illegal campaign contributions. A week later, Steinbrenner avoided what could have been a six-month jail term when he was instead fined $15,000 personally, while his business was docked an additional $20,000.

Steinbrenner had already promised when he'd been indicted that he'd step away from his day-to-day involvement in the Yankees until justice ran its course, although he'd been about as successful at doing that as a smoker cold-turkeying Pall Malls. Now he announced an immediate public withdrawing from all baseball business for the foreseeable future, a preemptive act he hoped would convince Kuhn to show mercy while he pondered how to punish the Yankees' owner. Kuhn had the authority to force Steinbrenner to sell the team thanks to the felony admission. The only other baseball owner ever so convicted had been Fred Saigh, guilty of tax evasion in 1953, and it was because baseball reacted by banning him from the sport that Saigh had been forced to sell the St. Louis Cardinals for slightly less than he'd paid for it—the only other instance in which a baseball team sold for a loss, other than George Steinbrenner's purchase of the Yankees in 1973.

Kuhn sniffed at Steinbrenner's self-imposed ban, later saying, "George tried to beat me to the punch." He was also unmoved. Kuhn met with Steinbrenner and his attorney a few days after Labor Day, then retreated to his Park Avenue office to mull over what he had to do. Steinbrenner disappeared from public view as his baseball team, for the first time in ten years, made a furious run for first place. They got there at last on September 4, the latest they'd held that spot since the last day of the '64 season. They clung to first for eighteen of the next nineteen days, at one point stretching their lead to two and a half games. The Orioles caught fire, winning their last nine games and passing the Yankees on September 24. One day in September, with the Yankees about to play the Orioles in a critical game at Shea Stadium, Steinbrenner sent a cassette tape to Virdon—packed with full-blown football coach clichés (absent the 18.5-minute gap of another famous tape from that Watergate summer)—and asked him to play it for the team.

The Yankees lost that night. Steinbrenner was undeterred. He ignored his own quasi suspension and was on hand for the season's final five games: three in Cleveland, two in Milwaukee.

"You just wait until next year!" Steinbrenner crowed after the final out of the season. He'd decided he could no longer simply keep to himself in his stadium seat, but he also didn't want to taunt the commissioner by explicitly violating his self-suspension, so he held court outside the visitor's clubhouse at County Stadium and filled the reporters' notebooks gleefully. "Next year this club will really be something!"

Kuhn had other ideas about the next year for Steinbrenner.

•

IT WAS THANKSGIVING EVE when Bowie Kuhn finally rendered a verdict, and it flabbergasted the sport. Kuhn had spent much of his time in office trying to duck almost every important decision that passed across his desk. He'd shamefully stayed away from Atlanta on the night of April 8, 1974, when Henry Aaron had blasted his 715th career home run, passing Babe Ruth for the sport's most revered record. He'd been taken to the cleaners by Marvin Miller and the players' union in the brief 1972 strike, and seemed determined to grasp foolishly to the status quo as baseball's economic revolution inched closer and closer to his doorstep. He was up for reelection, and so most in the baseball community expected him to go easy on Steinbrenner, not wishing to make any new enemies among the owners with him needing 75 percent of them to ensure six more years.

"He will hit him with a feather duster," one anonymous owner surmised.

Instead, Kuhn opted for a sledgehammer.

"An essential element of a professional team sport is the public's confidence in its integrity," Kuhn wrote in his judgment, which lasted twelve pages. "If the public does not believe that a sport is honest it would be impossible for the sport to succeed. Attempting to influence employees to behave dishonestly is the kind of misconduct which, if ignored by baseball, would undermine the public's confidence in the game."

Steinbrenner was suspended for two years, "ineligible and incompetent to have any association whatsoever with any major league club or its personnel."

Steinbrenner reacted as you might expect.

"Naturally we are shocked beyond belief by Mr. Kuhn's decision," he said. "It is certainly a wonderful Thanksgiving present. I will be meeting with my attorney, Edward Bennett Williams, in the next few days and will announce our plans early next week."

INTERLUDE: As would be a regular part of Steinbrenner's game plan over the years, he was less angered by the punishment as by one word. "How *dare* he call me incompetent!" he raged at his public relations VP, Marty Appel. Kuhn, a by-the-book lawyer, understood that in strictly legal terms "incompetent" merely emphasized Steinbrenner was incapable of being involved with the Yankees because he'd just forbidden him. If Kuhn was going for an extra elbow to Steinbrenner's ribs . . . well, if so, he took it to the grave.

Steinbrenner's first instinct was to fight. His lawyer calmed him. Williams believed just keeping his client out of jail when just about everyone else with a whisper of "Watergate" attached to his name had wound up incarcerated was enough of a win. On the courtside steps back in August, asked if he planned to appeal, Williams had looked incredulously at the gathered reporters and asked, "Appeal *what*?" Now his only appeal was to Steinbrenner's common sense. *Lay low. Deputize people you trust. Prove to Kuhn you have learned the error of your ways.*

"Nobody is going to expect that when it's time for money to be spent that they're not going to call you," Williams told him. "Of course they will."

There was also this: The very office of commissioner had been invented in the interest of keeping discipline—oftentimes Draconian—in the game. Judge Kenesaw Mountain Landis had been appointed in 1920 and given free rein at a time when eight members of the Chicago White Sox stood accused of throwing the 1919 World Series. Those eight players—notably Shoeless Joe Jackson, one of the game's most feared hitters—were acquitted in a Chicago court. But a day later, they were thrown out of baseball for life by Landis, no questions asked. Happy Chandler later suspended Leo Durocher from managing the 1947 Brooklyn Dodgers because of his association with "unsavory elements," and Durocher, like the White Sox players, had little recourse. The commissioner had sweeping "best interests of the game" powers, and Kuhn was using them aggressively.

Steinbrenner relented. He appointed Patrick J. Cunningham, the Bronx Democratic leader, to replace him as general partner for the duration of his suspension. And he fully deputized Gabe Paul, who that day was about to enter the most blissful period of his baseball existence. Already, Paul had grown weary of Steinbrenner's interference, but it especially galled him when he tried to lend his limited expertise when Paul honestly believed he wouldn't be able to explain the infield-fly rule if asked.

Beginning now, this would be Gabe Paul's show, and Steinbrenner would, for the time being, be reduced to a shadow figure. And the *Daily News*, the *Post* and friends were ready for all of it, the *News* proclaiming on its back page Thanksgiving morning:

BENCHED FOR TWO YEARS!

CHAPTER 7

George is a great guy unless you have to work for him.
—LOU PINIELLA

Some wondered if he would sell, rather than endure the humiliation of suspension. They clearly did not know George M. Steinbrenner III very well. Quitting was anathema to Steinbrenner. His father, years earlier, had hammered home a credo that stayed with him forever: "You show me a quitter, I'll show you a loser." And the only thing Steinbrenner detested more than quitting was losing. He thought about suing Kuhn. He filed the papers. He was eager to fight. In February he withdrew.

"It's humiliating to take the punishment," he said. "But people who should be concentrating on winning a pennant will be called away to testify, and that could detract from the job they have to do. I could win the battle and lose the war. I'll take it if I have to, but it's a small price to pay to win a pennant. I'll be better for it."

So, in truth, would the Yankees.

Gabe Paul had waited his entire baseball life for an opportunity like this. He'd waded through some difficult seasons in Cincinnati, and just as he was assembling the final pieces for what would be a pennant winner in 1961—including signing a young Black slugger from Oakland named Frank Robinson—he left the team to help the start-up baseball operation in Houston. He regretted that move almost as quickly as he made it, and by

1962 was back in the game, in Cleveland, a team that hadn't been a champion in fourteen years and was beginning to crater. Dwindling fan interest, a series of shallow-pocketed owners and a crumbling ballpark conspired to tie Paul's hands, and his teams finished .500 just once in twelve years, never closer than fifteen games out of first.

Steinbrenner had been the white knight he'd been looking for his whole career. Michael Burke had been an impediment, but Paul knew from the jump he could steer Steinbrenner away from Burke, and did. Lee MacPhail was the GM, and Paul respected MacPhail, but he could sense MacPhail was restless, unhappy that Burke hadn't included him in his scheme to buy the Yankees from CBS. It was also clear MacPhail had his eyes on the American League presidency. So by January 1, 1974, Paul was the top baseball man in the organization. And it was around that time that he developed a new nickname for his boss, one he'd share with anyone so long as he was out of earshot.

"*This Steinbrenner* . . ." became a regular beginning to a lot of Paul's sentences.

Even as Steinbrenner's legal woes mounted, and even as he agreed to step away in the months before the commissioner decided his fate, Steinbrenner never forgot Paul's phone number. He called every day, sometimes twice a day. And he wasn't shy about including his opinion about Virdon, about the Yankees players, about stars on other teams who may be available that perhaps Paul should consider. Paul could name all twenty-five players on all twenty-four major league rosters; he was pretty sure Steinbrenner only knew half the players on his *own* roster.

"I had to take his calls," Paul said years later. "I mean, he was the *boss*."

But now those calls came less frequently. For the first time in his career Paul's baseball acumen was backed up by resources that would allow him to take big swings. He still felt compelled to back-channel his opinions to Steinbrenner in exile, but now it seemed that Steinbrenner, faced with little other choice, had learned to trust his GM. He backed Paul at almost every turn. Late in the year, he approved a raise for Sparky Lyle to $92,500 for the 1975 season, the highest amount ever paid a relief pitcher and one that pleased most of Steinbrenner's fellow Lords because Lyle had been talking about playing out his option and mounting an official challenge to the century-old reserve clause, binding players forever to their teams; this proved a temporary ebb against an oncoming tide. He approved a two-year contract extension for Bill Virdon, after Virdon led the Yankees to eighty-nine wins and second place in the AL East and was named the AL Manager of the Year.

Most important to Paul, Steinbrenner stood firm when he called him during the 1974 World Series and informed him that the San Francisco Giants would be willing to part with Bobby Bonds, the gifted but enigmatic outfielder who'd become only the fifth player in baseball history to hit thirty home runs and steal thirty bases in the same year, 1969, and then repeated that trick in 1973. But the cost would be stiff: Bobby Murcer. Murcer had tailed off in 1974, but he'd still been an All-Star. He failed to hit a home run at Shea Stadium until late September, and he disliked playing for Virdon, but he was still the Yankees' most popular player since Mickey Mantle. Paul believed Murcer, at age twenty-eight, was showing early signs of decline. Bonds was the same age and had an off year in '74 that yielded twenty-one homers and forty-one steals and was still an elite athlete in center. Paul's professional motto drilled into him by his mentor in Cincinnati, Warren Giles, was "there is no substitute for talent." And Bonds was one of the game's most talented players.

But before Paul could close the deal, he needed to give Steinbrenner a heads-up, and he knew Steinbrenner had grown fond of Murcer. No longer a bum in Steinbrenner's eyes, the man who wore number 1 had become his favorite player, and a friendship followed, and so did this promise in the summer of 1974:

"As long as I'm the owner here, you'll be a Yankee."

This was the first time Steinbrenner had made such a vow. It would not be the last. And it would certainly not be the last time he would have to walk words back. But as much as he liked to toss around his opinions like a longtime-listener, first-time talk radio caller, George-from-Cleveland also realized Paul had forgotten more baseball than George might ever know.

"If you think it's for the best, do it," Steinbrenner said.

Paul did.

INTERLUDE: A few months later Paul would have to make a similar decision about another Steinbrenner favorite when the two of them couldn't stop haggling over a few thousand dollars for his 1975 contract. When Paul told shortstop Gene "Stick" Michael that he was being released on January 21, Michael laughed, "You're not serious?!" and then called Steinbrenner, by now fully relocated to Tampa, and asked the same question.

"I'm afraid we are," Steinbrenner said, before assuring Michael—who would play one more year for Ralph Houk in Detroit—that there'd be a job waiting for him with the Yankees when he retired.

Michael wound up with several (scout, coach, eye-in-the-sky, manager) before assuming the general manager's job in 1991—at precisely the moment when, with Steinbrenner temporarily tossed out of baseball again, the Yankees would again need steady veteran instincts and guile with an eye to the future and an unflinching devotion to improving the team's depth in trying to build the team back up from the dust. Someone who had the same skills as Gabe Paul.

By the end of the year, with Steinbrenner now officially gone and by the letter of Kuhn's agreement technically unable to discuss any baseball matters at all, Paul would have to quietly ask Kuhn's approval to consult with Steinbrenner, because Paul wanted to enter the wildest baseball sweepstakes ever, and he wanted the full muscle of the New York Yankees and their coffers behind him. A few weeks earlier, arbitrator Peter Seitz—you may wish to bookmark that name—had ruled that Steinbrenner's old nemesis, Charlie Finley, failed to make insurance payments due his star pitcher, Jim "Catfish" Hunter, and so he found Finley in breach and declared Hunter a free agent, able to sign with any other team besides Oakland, presumably to the highest bidder.

Hunter was exactly the kind of superstar Steinbrenner craved, and even an old-school man like Gabe Paul was blown away that the winner of the 1974 AL Cy Young Award—25–12 in '74 and 106–49 with a 2.89 ERA the past five years as the undisputed ace on the best team in the sport—was suddenly available.

Kuhn relented. It was Steinbrenner's money that Paul would be flashing, after all. So the race began, and twenty-two teams sent representatives to Ahoskie, North Carolina, to visit the law offices of Hunter's attorney, J. Carlton Cherry. Only the A's, who were forbidden to do so, and their Bay Area neighbors, the financially imperiled Giants, abstained. Paul flew to Steinbrenner's new offices in Tampa to brief the owner on what he believed the parameters would be to hook this extraordinary fish. Early estimates had the total costs at $2 million but Paul had come armed with some helpful information courtesy of Clyde Kluttz, a Yankees scout and fellow Carolinian who'd signed Hunter for Finley when he was working for the A's back in 1964. Kluttz was privy to the bids. He knew $3 million was the likely ante and that some teams might be willing to go even higher. Paul told Steinbrenner all of this.

"We have to get this guy," Steinbrenner said.

It wasn't easy. Kluttz's intel had been spot-on. One team, the San Diego Padres, had just been bought by McDonald's founder Ray Kroc, and they were willing to essentially hand Hunter a blank check and a lifetime supply of Quarter Pounders. When Paul was granted an audience he did what he'd been doing in baseball negotiations for a quarter century and led with a bid so low that Kluttz immediately shook his head quietly at Paul, subtly gesturing an upraised thumb. Paul's clever games weren't going to carry the day. Steinbrenner's money would, or else Kroc would add a new star to his stable alongside Grimace, Hamburglar and Mayor McCheese.

After a few days, it was clear the two choices were San Diego or the Yankees. Both were offering fairly complicated structured contracts that between salary, deferred payments, insurance, no-interest loans and annuities would clear $3 million, a number that had been unheard of in baseball at the start of the month. Hunter and his team knew that Kroc, trying to make a huge splash in a city where baseball had fizzled since arriving in 1969, would take whatever the Yankees' final offer was and nudge it as high as was necessary. So now it became a simple choice.

Cherry, the lawyer, told Hunter: "Can you be happy in New York?"

Kluttz countered. "Tom Seaver seems happy in New York." (Which he was, though whatever Hunter signed for was bound to alter that cheerfulness.)

Cherry: "There's sun in San Diego."

Kluttz: "How many Hall of Famers played in San Diego? Would you like me to list all the Hall of Famers who played with the Yankees?"

That one got Hunter's attention.

"What about Steinbrenner?" he asked. "I hear things about him."

"You've just played for Charlie Finley for ten years," Kluttz said. "How much worse could Steinbrenner possibly be?"

That was that. Hunter agreed to sign with the Yankees and flew to New York for a press conference on December 31 so the contract—final total: five years, $3.25 million, much of it deferred—could be a part of the Yankees' 1974 books. Hunter smiled easily and won the press conference (despite being confronted with a room full of cranky sportswriters who were especially salty at having their New Year's Eve plans torched).

"What are you going to do with all that money?" Hunter was asked.

"I don't know," Hunter replied. "But maybe when I get through playing I can sit down and count it."

DESPITE THE PRESENCE of Catfish Hunter—who had an elite season in 1975 (23–14, 2.58 ERA, an astonishing thirty complete games and 328 innings pitched)—and a solid bounce-back year from Bobby Bonds (thirty-two homers, thirty steals), George Steinbrenner's exile was not a happy one. The Yankees started 1–6 and 11–18 before Virdon once again settled the waters, and on June 24 they actually snuck into first place when Hunter threw a four-hitter at the Orioles in Baltimore.

Steinbrenner visited spring training in Fort Lauderdale briefly. He occasionally skulked into Shea Stadium, usually sitting on the press level but waving off any press that approached. On Opening Day he'd revived his old standby, getting a tape recorder in Virdon's hands before the game and instructing his field manager to play it for the troops. The players had a hard time stifling laughter after Virdon pressed Play.

"It was a cross between Knute Rockne and George Patton," Graig Nettles remembered years later. "It was . . . something else."

Still, as aggravating as he could be to Gabe Paul, Steinbrenner was still looked upon as a kindly uncle by most of the Yankees. At the All-Star Game at Milwaukee's County Stadium, catcher Thurman Munson saw Bowie Kuhn settling into his seat next to the American League dugout. The men shook hands.

"Commissioner," Munson said, "when are you going to let us have George Steinbrenner back? We really miss him. We need him. He's done a lot of good things for us, and we think he's good for the Yankees and good for baseball."

A few years later, if someone could've handed Munson a tape of that conversation he'd have looked for the nearest incinerator to throw it in. But for now, this represented the majority opinion in the Yankees' clubhouse. When Steinbrenner went to Dallas to watch the Yankees play the Rangers a few weeks later, there was a line of players waiting to shake Steinbrenner's hand as he ate breakfast in the team hotel. By this point, the Red Sox had zoomed past in the AL East standings, and the Yankees were at the start of a dreadful skid that would carry them to the end of the month.

"He's dying to have a clubhouse meeting and chew out a few behinds," a Steinbrenner ally told Phil Pepe of the *Daily News* and Maury Allen of the *Post*. "You can see how it's eating him up inside, how he'd like to have a talk with the players. Of course he won't. He can't."

Steinbrenner's frustrations bubbled over on the afternoon of Sunday, July 27. The Yankees and Red Sox had split the first two games of an important four-game series at Shea Stadium, leaving the Yankees eight games behind. There was still a lot of baseball to be played in 1975, but if the Yankees couldn't salvage at least a sweep of that day's doubleheader they'd be ten back, and Boston was playing so well and the Yankees so poorly that it would feel like twice as much. There were 53,631 at Shea, which would prove to be the single-highest attendance the Yankees would draw in their two years in Queens. One of those fans, eschewing his usual spot on the press level, settled into his box seat just to the left of the Yankees' dugout behind first base, shortly before the first pitch, which Catfish Hunter threw to Boston DH Bernie Carbo at 1:06 p.m.

And from the start, George Steinbrenner was in a foul mood. For the first four innings the Yankees couldn't scratch a hit off Boston pitcher Bill Lee. And if Steinbrenner wasn't exactly encyclopedic in his knowledge of the American League, one thing he did know is he didn't care for Lee—nicknamed "Spaceman"—who was an odd flake, notably outspoken, quite conversant on all matters counterculture, a proud radical in a mostly conservative sport. In later years, Lee would return the favor plenty, once referring to the Yankees as "George Steinbrenner's Nazis, his brown shirts."

For now, he was simply making Steinbrenner's batters look foolish.

But they broke through in the bottom of the fifth. Graig Nettles and Chris Chambliss led off with clean singles. Sandy Alomar attempted to sacrifice, and bunted so perfectly nobody could make a play on him. The bases were loaded, nobody out. Due up for the Yankees was Fred "Chicken" Stanley, whose .224 batting average and beanpole physique helped explain his nickname. As well as Lee was throwing, this was the Yankees' chance to seize the game. A large portion of the crowd waited to see if Bill Virdon would send in a pinch hitter for his good-glove/bad-bat shortstop and many of them stirred uneasily when Stanley took his place in the batter's box.

One of them was especially aggrieved.

"What are you doing?!" Steinbrenner yelled, standing and craning his neck from his field-level seat, aiming his displeasure into the home dugout, where his fury was easily audible to Bill Virdon. "Where's the pinch hitter?!"

Stanley drizzled a ground ball to third, and Nettles was forced at home. Boos cascaded from the grandstand, and rage filled the owner's box, none of it assuaged when Bobby Bonds followed with a strikeout and Rick Dempsey with a pop-out to end the threat. Steinbrenner's verbal assault continued unabated. Two innings later Alomar led off by flying out to left;

now, Virdon called Stanley back and sent up Alex Johnson—a former AL batting champion—to hit for him.

"*Now* he uses the pinch hitter!" Steinbrenner thundered, raising his arms in disgust.

When Johnson grounded out—to the soundtrack of more Steinbrenner screaming—Virdon was caught smirking in the dugout. The problem was, Stanley's defensive replacement, Jim Mason, booted a one-out grounder by Fred Lynn in the top of the ninth, who then came around to score after a steal and an RBI single by Rick Miller. Lee retired the Yankees one, two, three in the bottom half, and the Red Sox won, 1–0, then blanked the Yankees again, 6–0, in the second game.

"He was a roaring maniac as he left the ballpark" was how a helpful usher described the way Steinbrenner departed that day to inquiring newsmen.

Being a detached observer was getting old.

THERE WERE A few knives under the table on July 17, when baseball's owners gathered in Milwaukee to vote on a new six-year term for commissioner Bowie Kuhn. Things did not look good. His old sparring partner Charlie Finley had formed a strong alliance with Baltimore owner Jerold Hoffberger, and in the days leading up to the vote the pair believed they also had Brad Corbett of the Texas Rangers lined up on their side. They needed one more vote. They went to bed on the sixteenth believing they had it: Patrick J. Cunningham, serving as George Steinbrenner's proxy at the Pfister Hotel. Steinbrenner promised he wouldn't use his vote as a cudgel seeking revenge for Kuhn's suspension, but it sure seemed like he was about to do just that. So sure were the renegade owners that they informed Kuhn of the straw poll the night before the vote.

A funny thing happened, though.

When the owners gathered in the morning and began casting their ballots, Cunningham changed his vote. That clinched Kuhn's reelection. Corbett decided to switch his now-meaningless vote to yay, and Finley and Hoffberger stormed out of the room.

Finley, especially, smelled a rat.

"What a joke," he railed bitterly.

Finley wasn't alone in assuming the Yankees' change of heart might have had something to do with Kuhn promising to reduce Steinbrenner's suspension in exchange for his—er, *Cunningham's*—vote.

"I realize people will think George was instrumental in my vote," Cunningham said. "But so help me God, he wasn't."

God was unavailable for comment, and neither was Steinbrenner, though he did offer a terse—and somewhat ironic—statement: "I think the Yankees did what was in the best interests of baseball," a line Kuhn had used, and would use, an incalculable number of times in rendering decisions in his mostly forgettable time as commissioner.

If the fix was in, nobody—certainly not Kuhn—was going to say so, or ever did. Still, it was Kuhn's decision on March 1, 1976, to reinstate Steinbrenner and slice his suspension by six months that finally made him feel whole again. Much of baseball might have rolled its eyes, but that didn't bother Steinbrenner a bit.

"I'm going to be more active than ever," he said, words that undoubtedly sent a chill down the spine of Gabe Paul—and made others who easily recalled his "absentee owner" vow laugh. "Very active. I'm going to be right in the middle of things."

By then Steinbrenner had already approved the hiring of the man with whom he would be singularly and uniquely associated for most of the next fifteen years, a man who would, more than any other, not only relish looking Steinbrenner in the eye but also, on occasion, spit in it.

CHAPTER 8

GEORGE STEINBRENNER: You know, a lot of people think Billy and I argue all the time. Actually, we agree on just about everything, right, Bill?
BILLY MARTIN: You betcha, George.
GEORGE: We even drink the same beer!
BILLY: Lite Beer from Miller! Lite's got a third less calories than their regular beer, and it's less filling.
GEORGE: And the best thing is, it tastes so great!
BILLY: No, George, the best thing is it's less filling.
GEORGE: No, Bill, it tastes great.
BILLY: Less filling, George.
GEORGE: Billy, it tastes great!
BILLY: Less filling, George!
GEORGE: Billy?
BILLY: Yeah, George?
GEORGE: You're fired.
BILLY: Not again!

It was Michael Burke who first envisioned Billy Martin in pinstripes. Whenever Martin would come to New York—with the Minnesota Twins in 1969, later with the Detroit Tigers beginning in 1971—Burke invited him to lunch. Burke admired the way Martin led the Twins to ninety-seven wins and the AL West pennant in his year there, an eighteen-win improvement over 1968. Burke noted how the 1971 Tigers won ninety-one games, a twelve-game upgrade over 1970. When the Tigers visited New York in late May 1972, the Yankees were already scuffling. The Tigers were at the top of the division, in a year when they would win the AL East by half a game over the Red Sox, but Martin was already beginning to feel his chronic restlessness and was generally unhappy with his relationship with the Tigers' front office. Burke sensed that, took note of it, and on the ride back to Yankee Stadium began to wonder if maybe it was time for the Yankees to ask if the Tigers would be open to a deal for Martin. Burke walked into Lee MacPhail's office.

"What do you think about Billy Martin?" Burke asked him.

MacPhail was midway through a career that would land him in the Hall of Fame. There, he would join his father, Larry, a colorful character who in World War I had taken part in an unsanctioned (and unsuccessful) mission to arrest Kaiser Wilhelm II and bring him to the Paris Peace Conference; for his troubles MacPhail helped himself to one of the Kaiser's ashtrays. He later helped build pennant winners in both Cincinnati and Brooklyn and, after World War II, briefly partnered with Del Webb and Dan Topping in the Yankees ownership group. The MacPhails remain the only father/son duo in Cooperstown. The elder MacPhail was also a raging alcoholic whose booze-fueled rants ultimately landed him out of baseball far too soon, and when he was fired as president of Bowie Race Track in 1953 after only thirteen months on the job for "drunk and disorderly conduct," he never worked in sports again.

That, understandably, left a deep impression on Lee, and it wasn't exactly a secret to anyone in baseball that Martin long held a similar affinity for boozy late nights.

"I don't think it would be a good idea," MacPhail quietly told Burke.

Inevitably, Martin wore out his welcome in Detroit and he was fired early in September 1973. His name immediately surfaced in the New York newspapers as a potential replacement for Ralph Houk (though Steinbrenner vowed Houk would stay on for 1974, unaware that Houk had different ideas), or even Yogi Berra, though the Mets soon rescued Berra's job with their run to the pennant. Besides, it was presumed Martin was reluctant to replace Berra, as the two were still friends from their time as teammates in the 1950s (as we'll see, that small detail wouldn't get in Martin's way twelve years later).

Instead, with twenty-three games left in the season, Martin headed to Arlington, Texas, to manage the hapless Texas Rangers, who would finish 57–105 and draw less than 700,000 to their ballpark. Just as inevitably, Martin sparked an immediate turnaround. In '74 the Rangers won eighty-four games—a remarkable plus-twenty-seven—and kept the Rangers in the AL West hunt most of the year before settling for second, five games behind Oakland. Even more notably attendance nearly doubled, to just under 1.2 million. This time felt different, too. He immediately took to the Texas lifestyle, and the Berkeley, California, native fashioned himself a baseball cowboy, replete with boots, hat, bolo tie, mustache and a deep affinity for country music. His longtime friend and perennial drinking buddy Mickey Mantle lived nearby, in Dallas. The Rangers were a young team on the rise with the 1974 MVP (Jeff Burroughs), Rookie of the Year (Mike Hargrove) and Cy Young runner-up (Fergie Jenkins) anchoring the roster, which seemed custom-built for Martin, who figured on spending years in North Texas.

He lasted ninety-five more games.

The same patterns of behavior that shadowed him in Minnesota and Detroit crushed him in Texas. He openly warred with the front office (a problem expedited in Arlington by the fact that the man who hired him, Bob Short, promptly sold the club to Brad Corbett, a thirty-six-year-old multimillionaire who'd made his fortune in plastic piping).

"I don't tell him how to make pipes," Martin decreed late in his time in Texas. "He shouldn't tell me about baseball."

He picked unnecessary feuds. At each of his stops there were some Black players who played for him who thought if Martin wasn't quite a full-blown racist he didn't always hold all players to the same standards. In Texas, toward the end, he was known to bring companions who weren't his wife on road trips, which led to some hard-to-forgive accusations that Martin's attention span was prone to drifting.

Then there were saloons, where too often Martin would wind up confronting his own equally well-watered players. When he managed the Twins, he had an alleyway confrontation outside a Detroit bar called Lindell AC with a Twins pitcher named Dave Boswell. Martin punched him against a wall; later he was asked what occurred next.

"Well, when he came off the wall, I hit him again."

Three years later, in another Detroit tavern, this time the Leland Hotel, Martin had another angry encounter with one of his players, a young outfielder named Ike Blessitt, after Blessitt refused to give a ride home to a woman—actually, a sixteen-year-old girl—with whom Martin was talking. (Blessitt, who was Black, decided it would not be a good idea in 1972 suburban Detroit to be giving a white teenage girl a lift at night; he called her a cab instead.) Martin accused him of insubordination. Police were called. Both men were arrested and fined $32 each for disturbing the peace.

In Texas, the inevitable encounter happened not in a bar but at thirty thousand feet, after the Rangers were eliminated from the 1974 pennant race and flying to Kansas City for the season's final week. Martin already helped himself to a handful of small bottles of whiskey and spotted the Rangers' longtime traveling secretary, Burt Hawkins (who, in a past life as a newspaperman, was nominated for a Pulitzer Prize for his work with *The Washington Star*). Hawkins's wife had created a "wives club" for the Rangers' spouses, a stone in Martin's shoe; he thought team planes and road hotels should be off-limits to all but players.

"You need to shut your wife up," Martin sneered.

Hawkins, fifteen years Martin's senior, threw a punch. Martin blocked it. The men were quickly separated, and Martin actually apologized the next morning. But another notch had been added to Martin's belt.

Thus, Lee MacPhail to Michael Burke: "I don't think it would be a good idea."

A little over three years later Gabe Paul was filled with similar dread the morning of July 23, 1975, when he saw in the morning papers that Martin had finally been axed in Texas. Paul was as plugged-in as any man in baseball; he quickly learned that Martin's last stand was a doozy: As the Rangers cruised to a 6–0 win over the Red Sox, Martin called the press box directly before the seventh-inning stretch and ordered them to play John Denver's "Thank God I'm a Country Boy." Martin and Texas owner Brad Corbett argued about this all season; Corbett preferred the traditional "Take Me Out to the Ball Game." As Corbett stood and waited to sing about buying some peanuts and Cracker Jack, trying to enjoy a rare night of pleasure in a tough season, he heard "Well, life on the farm is kinda laid back, ain't much an old country boy like me can't hack . . ."

Corbett fired Martin at game's end.

Paul laughed at the absurdity of it all.

Then his phone rang. It was George Steinbrenner.

He wasn't calling with a stock tip.

WHAT MAY BE hard to understand is when George Steinbrenner, who was born into wealth and comfort in upper-middle-class Ohio to a demanding father, saw Billy Martin—born into poverty in the poor section of Berkeley, California, abandoned by his father as an infant—he saw much of himself. The two men were fueled by ambition. Steinbrenner was forever trying to prove his mettle as Henry Steinbrenner's son, as a student, as a sportsman, as a businessman; Martin was forever trying to prove he belonged in the big leagues despite looking like a bantamweight.

"Some people have a chip on their shoulder," *Los Angeles Times* columnist Jim Murray once wrote. "Billy has a whole lumberyard."

Both were quick to anger and uncontrollable rages, especially when they believed they were in the right and, often, thanks to a shared stubborn streak, when they were wrong. Both men had galactic egos, which sometimes proved ruinous but just as often allowed them to fulfill the preposterous dreams they'd crafted for themselves.

Both enjoyed the reputations they developed as fighters willing to occasionally cross boundaries to stand up for what was right, and both were reluctant to allow those images to be compromised when their softer sides would emerge. Some fifteen years after George Steinbrenner's death, stories would still regularly surface about Steinbrenner's bountiful kindnesses, financial and otherwise, many of which he refused to publicize. And Martin was fiercely loyal, almost to a fault, and would regularly find himself seeking penance both within and without a confessional booth for his missteps. When Martin was young and often hungry, in the teeth of the Depression, he became expert at pilfering fruit from the pushcarts on Berkeley's San Pablo Avenue. Years later, after he'd made a little money, he figured how much he'd stolen and one offseason handed each merchant the equivalent in cash of what he'd taken as a child. That story only became public when one of the men he'd reimbursed called around in the aftermath of one of Martin's public blowups, demanding equal time.

Mostly, the men bonded over one thing.

"All we cared about was winning," Steinbrenner said in 1994, five years after Martin died in a Christmas Day car crash.

"Winning was breakfast, lunch and dinner for Billy. And for me."

On the day Michael Burke formally cut ties with the Yankees partnership agreement, when the rancor between him and Steinbrenner finally dissipated and Steinbrenner felt comfortable enough to talk to him once again as a baseball neophyte seeking counsel from an established elder, he'd asked, "When the time comes to find Houk's replacement, who would you suggest?"

Burke immediately answered, "Billy Martin."

"Get him at the first chance," Burke urged. "Billy's driving ambition is to become the Yankees' skipper and baseball's first hundred-thousand-dollar manager. He'll be difficult to work with. But as soon as he's free, I'd get Billy."

Billy was free.

And Gabe Paul realized that he was going to have an impossible time fending off Steinbrenner once Steinbrenner fixed his attention on Martin. If Bill Virdon—quiet, unemotional, an umpire-baiter only in the most extreme, egregious examples—was counter to everything Steinbrenner the ex–football coach coveted in a manager, then Martin was the ideal blueprint. He liked to outthink and outwit opposing managers, and was never shy about explaining every angle of his wisdom on the record when those plans worked out on the field as they had in his head.

"Good managers think two or three hitters ahead of the game," longtime Yankees outfielder Roy White once said. "Billy thinks two or three *innings* ahead."

Martin also wasn't afraid to rip his own players if they deserved it, and never anonymously; once, with the Tigers, he'd actually replaced his All-Star left fielder, Willie Horton, in the middle of an inning when the manager believed the player loafed after a fly ball.

(Dramatic foreshadowing: There's a chance you'll hear about a similar type of incident in the pages to follow.)

And as for umpires . . .

"They're out to get me," he told *Sports Illustrated* in a cover story that ran three months before he was fired in Texas. "Two National League umpires asked me in spring training why the umpires in my league were all out to get me. And if they're out to get me, it will be very difficult for my ball club to win this year. I've got to protect my team."

Martin argued with umpires. He heckled them. He challenged them, especially young, green umpires, to see who would fight back and who would quaver with anger and quiver with intimidation. He feuded with some. He openly disdained an American League umpire named Ron Luciano, once declaring: "I don't want him fined, I want him *fired*." He would get kicked out of both ends of a doubleheader before a pitch was thrown just to prove a point. He once ordered his Tigers pitchers to throw nothing but spitballs after umps refused to eject admitted spitballer Gaylord Perry as he was shutting down Detroit.

All of that was catnip for George Steinbrenner.

And when the 1975 Yankees continued to slide as July melted into August, the calls to Gabe Paul became more frequent, until Paul agreed at last to talk to Martin. Martin was hard to find at first; after his firing he'd taken his family to a quiet outpost in western Colorado to fish and decompress and stay away from a phone that was ringing off the hook inside the Martin home back in Arlington. But when Paul kept frantically calling Martin's lawyer, Eddie Sapir, Sapir realized this was a meeting his client had to take, no matter how disillusioned Martin might be. Because Martin always fashioned himself as a Yankee. He'd become an unlikely star on four Yankees championship clubs and been at his best in October, including hitting 12-for-24 with an astonishing OPS of 1.478 in the 1953 World Series against the Dodgers. That followed a year after he'd come dashing in from out of nowhere to grab a Jackie Robinson pop-up at his shoe tops with the bases loaded in Game 7, a play that saved *that* series for the Yankees.

> **INTERLUDE:** There is no way the great *New York Post* columnist Jimmy Cannon could have possibly understood the enormous irony when he quietly dubbed Martin "Mister October" deep inside a column during the '53 series. But we will soon surely laugh together at that one with the benefit of 20/20 hindsight.

Martin's time with the Yankees ended traumatically for him, and served as a harbinger for so much of what would follow. On May 15, 1957, a day before his twenty-ninth birthday, Martin (who was single) was feted by teammates Yogi Berra, Hank Bauer, Mickey Mantle, Whitey Ford, Johnny Kucks and their wives with a night on the town. That culminated after midnight at the Copacabana, the best-known nightclub in New York in those years, where they caught the last show there by Sammy Davis Jr. At some point, someone at a neighboring table—a team of bowlers from Washington Heights and *their* wives—drunkenly yelled a racist remark at Davis. Bauer, an ex-Marine, took exception, and things grew increasingly heated as the bowlers started heckling the Bombers. Finally, it was Martin who suggested if the two parties had an issue they should take it outside. The bowlers agreed, to their immediate regret: They were pummeled. When one of them came to, he called the cops. It was Bauer, not Martin, who was charged (though later cleared). Sixty-three years later, a man named Joey Silvestri admitted to *The New York Times* that he'd been the one who knocked out Edwin Jones, a forty-two-year-old delicatessen owner and lifelong Yankees fan, with two quick punches. To best describe "Joey at the Copa's" job, think of the man who Henry Hill dukes $50 in the movie *Goodfellas* to bypass the velvet rope and get choice seats for the Jerry Vale show. That was Silvestri in real life.

"There were no Yankees involved in the fight," said Silvestri, coming clean in 2020. "Nobody threw a punch but me."

But Silvestri was unavailable to offer witness testimony to Yankees GM George Weiss in 1957, when Weiss was gravely concerned Martin was being a negative influence on Mantle and Ford, his two closest friends. The fact Martin wasn't charged was just an annoying detail to Weiss. It was all the ammunition he needed. He traded Martin to the Kansas City Athletics a month later, which in itself was devastating to Billy. Worse, he believed Casey Stengel hadn't put up a strong defense on his behalf. Casey and Billy first teamed up in Oakland in the Pacific Coast League; when Casey got the manager's gig with New York in 1949, he'd encouraged Weiss to sign Billy. They were so close that Martin was called "Casey's Boy" in the press, and when Martin was traded, they didn't speak for years.

But by 1975 they'd reconciled, and Martin fully reembraced his connection with the Yankees. On an offseason fishing trip with Bob Short, soon to be the ex-owner of the Rangers, he'd declared, "I'll always have the 'NY' logo tattooed on my chest." When he became a manager his contract stipulated he was permitted to leave his team two days a year: the day before and the day of Yankees Old-Timers' Day. On his final trip into New York as Rangers manager in July, he gathered some of his friends in the New York press to air a grievance. He'd been notified that Gabe Paul enacted a new policy: No player working for another team could be invited to Old-Timers' Day. Paul didn't think that terribly outlandish; Yogi Berra hadn't attended since he'd become a Mets coach in 1965, after all.

Martin didn't care. Martin was pissed.

"I oughta call up Mickey and tell him not to come," Martin huffed. Then, privately, he told a handful of writers, "Fuck Gabe Paul. What has he ever won?"

Now Gabe Paul was standing in the Denver airport, waiting for Billy Martin's shuttle flight from the Colorado boondocks to land so they could alight to a nearby hotel. Martin arrived with his then-wife, Gretchen, and Sapir. At the hotel, Paul cut to the chase quickly: He was offering Martin the job to manage the Yankees for the rest of 1975 and all of 1976.

Casey's Boy could have Casey's old job. But on a one-year trial.

"Gabe," Martin said. "I'm flattered. But I don't think I can take another firing. And if I take this job, at some point, I'm gonna get fired."

Something else concerned Martin and Sapir: The Yankees wanted a clause put into the contract stipulating Martin "would personally conduct [himself] at all times so as to represent the best interest of the New York Yankees and to adhere to all club policies." Sapir knew his client better than anyone. And he knew that was a trapdoor Martin would likely fall (or stumble) through sooner or later, giving the Yankees an easy out.

He told Paul that Martin wasn't bluffing.

Paul was stunned. At once he was also delighted, because this meant he could either retain Bill Virdon (his preference) or pick a replacement more to his liking. But before he let Martin, Gretchen and Sapir leave the hotel, he called Steinbrenner.

"Put Billy on the phone," Steinbrenner ordered.

Technically, Paul knew, this was in direct violation of Steinbrenner's suspension, and he was in essence aiding and abetting. But Steinbrenner insisted. So Paul called Martin over, handed him the phone.

"Billy," Steinbrenner said, "this is the only job you've ever wanted in this world. And I'm giving it to you."

Martin hung up. He shook Paul's hand.

"OK," he said. "I'm in."

SO BILLY MARTIN got his invitation to Old-Timers' Day 1975 after all—and as the featured guest of honor, too. He was introduced last to the buzzing crowd of 43,968 on Saturday, August 2, which regaled Martin with a welcome-home cheer and so outraged Joe DiMaggio—for years the unquestioned final name announced on this day—that he vowed to never attend another until George Steinbrenner himself called and apologized for the unintended insult. What Steinbrenner was decidedly unapologetic about was his decision to big-foot Gabe Paul into hiring Martin; the reception at Shea only confirmed that. Better still, Martin gleefully took the lineup card out to home plate before the game, and would do so every day, something that fired up Yankees crowds every single time he did it. Virdon, by contrast, sent coach Dick Howser to perform that task, and had taken to sending Whitey Ford out to make pitching changes.

To Steinbrenner, whose desk was dominated by a sign that read LEAD, FOLLOW, OR GET THE HELL OUT OF THE WAY, that was Virdon all but begging to get pink-slipped. One thing he wouldn't have to worry about was Martin hiding in the dugout, away from the tumult of his loyal, faithful throng of admirers.

The first few days were a nonstop parade of kudos and congratulations. It was an irresistible story, the exiled Yankee prince restored to the castle, charged with the task of reclaiming the kingdom, Steinbrenner serving as the wise, benevolent despot. There were a few dissenting voices. One Yankees player, shrewd enough to keep his identity private, said, "I'll tell you something. The first time Martin second-guesses me on a pitch or any play, I'm taking off my uniform, handing it to George, and going home."

A few days later, in a remarkably prescient column in *Newsday*, long-time baseball writer Steve Jacobson typed out the following lead as if he were staring into an actual functioning crystal ball:

"The marriage of Billy Martin and George Steinbrenner is the stuff of great novelists and playwrights—like *Who's Afraid of Virginia Woolf?* There will be brilliant flashes of lightning and great claps of thunder. They are madly impetuous, each in their own way."

And he ended the column thusly: "Steinbrenner will love the fire and its illusions, for a while. But what happens when he and Martin conflict, as they surely must? It will be a wondrous thing to watch—all sparks and rockets and lightning. How long will it last? Martin has a contract through next season. So did Bill Virdon."

Martin's fifty-six games as manager in 1975 were mostly a period of quiet and calm. At season's end he said, "There are a lot of players here who believe we will finish first next year," and what he left unsaid was obvious: Everyone else can hit the bricks.

By the time Steinbrenner was officially reinstated, baseball would experience one last seismic shift that would not only change the game's look forever but also allow Steinbrenner to assemble what in his worldview was manifest destiny for the Yankees. He had the manager he wanted. He had the system he wanted. He had the bully pulpit he wanted, beginning with the back pages of the tabloids and extending to an army of TV reporters eager to air his thoughts on every subject under the sun.

On March 1, 1976, with a stroke of Bowie Kuhn's pen, George Steinbrenner returned, fully reinstated.

He was rested, and restless, and eager to get back to work. Napoleon had returned from Elba.

CHAPTER 9

I may not have been the greatest Yankee to put on the uniform, but I was the proudest.

—BILLY MARTIN

To understand just how vexing George Steinbrenner's exile had been, let's begin with a story he told on March 3, two days after his suspension ended. There was a day he'd sat on the press level at Shea Stadium in the summer of 1975 and saw Rod Carew, the brilliant batting champion of the Minnesota Twins, foul off a pitch that scooted down the left field line. As had been protocol forever, all across baseball, the ball boy stood up from his folding chair near the stands, scooped the ball with his glove, and tossed it back to the dugout so it could be reused in the days ahead for batting practice. Dozens of kids in the lower box seats reached out, pleading for the souvenir.

"That pissed me off," Steinbrenner said. "That foul ball business. What's it going to cost us to give the balls to the fans? Twenty, twenty-five bucks a day? If we can't afford that, we better get out of business."

Grumpy ballplayers also irritated him. By 1975 it wasn't uncommon for a lot of players to ignore autograph seekers—sometimes without even a trace of self-awareness. One day, hiding in the plain sight of a crowd of fans in Cleveland, Steinbrenner witnessed a young fan ask a Yankee, "My dad thinks you're the greatest. Can I get your autograph?" And it was all

Steinbrenner could do to keep from jumping the fence when he heard that Yankee say, "Kid, tell your old man that he can go fuck himself."

No more.

"Any Yankee ballplayer seen shoving aside a kid asking for an autograph will be wearing another uniform before he knows it. If you're working or pressed for time, say so. Don't be rude."

He was bursting with ideas and thoughts, observations and opinions, and they spilled forth like an open faucet in those first weeks of March 1976.

"I know it sounds corny," he said. "But we're going to restore the Yankees to what they used to be, the greatest name in sports. I don't mean we're going to win five World Series in a row. Nobody will ever dominate that way again. The talent is spread out too evenly. I'll promise you one thing for this season: We won't finish in third. We'll be knocking the Red Sox right out of there."

Steinbrenner was emboldened by the knowledge that two months earlier, on December 23, 1975, baseball was turned upside-down. The sport's three-man arbitration panel issued a ruling that abolished the century-old reserve clause—which bound a player in perpetuity to the team that originally signed him. It had been the linchpin of a system that bolstered the owners, controlling player salaries and knowing the athletes had little choice but to be beholden to them.

The committee *was* technically composed of three men but one was Marvin Miller, chief of the players' union, whose opinions were every bit as predictable and partisan as the second man, John Gaherin, the owners' counsel. That left Peter Seitz, a seventy-year-old professional arbitrator, a self-styled "lapsed Brooklyn Dodgers fanatic" and a veteran of forty years' worth of labor disputes involving steelworkers and steamfitters and electricians. A year earlier, it was Seitz's decision that set Catfish Hunter free; the owners were annoyed at that, but enough of them took delight in watching Charlie Finley suffer and sweat that they shrugged their shoulders and then sprinted after Hunter with their checkbooks wide open.

This time, the owners weren't nearly as sanguine. The reserve clause was dead, and while Bowie Kuhn vowed to fight all the way to the Supreme

Court, baseball's lawyers assured him it would be hard to mount an appeal without also putting into peril baseball's other sacred cow, the Anti-Trust Exemption granted in 1922, which the court upheld thirty-one years later.

"This [is] a disaster for the great majority of the players, for the clubs, and most of all for the fans," Kuhn raged, though he didn't elaborate how life would turn instantly miserable for the jubilant players and for fans who now knew their favorite team wouldn't be imprisoned for decades with awful players who kept returning year after year. "It is just inconceivable that after nearly one hundred years of developing this system for the overall good of the game, it should be obliterated in this way."

The owners reacted as you might expect: First, they fired Seitz, accusing the one impartial panelist of gross prejudice, though Seitz was the one who'd agonized about the decision for over a month. The *Daily News*' Dick Young, for decades an unapologetic shill for management, raged: "Peter Seitz reminds me of a terrorist, a little man to whom nothing important has happened in his lifetime, who suddenly decides to create some excitement by tossing a bomb into things. That should make people pay attention to him, get him in the headlines, maybe even into history books."

Second, they ordered a lockout that began the same day Kuhn unlocked Steinbrenner from his baseball cell: March 1. They took their case to federal appeals court and were quickly dismissed. Later, in July, the owners and players would agree on a four-year collective bargaining agreement that put into place the framework for free agency we still know today: A player becomes free after six years of major-league service time. For now, there were two test cases: pitchers Dave McNally—retired, merely offering his name as help for the cause—and Andy Messersmith—very much in his prime at age thirty, coming off two years in which he'd gone 39–20 with a 2.43 ERA, thrown thirty-two complete games and twice finished top five in the Cy Young Award voting for the Dodgers.

It was killing Steinbrenner to toe the company line. He saw right away free agency would become his most useful and devastating weapon. He wanted to open the camps, and his coffers, and quietly threatened to do so on his own if Kuhn and his fellow owners refused to accept the inevitable.

When the camps finally did open on March 17, Steinbrenner gathered with Gabe Paul and together they hatched a plan. Paul had already enjoyed a bountiful offseason, trading Bobby Bonds to the Angels for speedster Mickey Rivers and rugged starter Ed Figueroa, swapping Doc Medich to the Pirates for Dock Ellis—still a useful starting pitcher—and twenty-one-year-old Willie Randolph, a Brooklyn native who would collect 2,210 hits in his career, 1,731 of them as a Yankee. They still had perennial All-Stars in Hunter, Munson and Nettles, and a borderline one in first baseman Chris Chambliss. Now there were two targets who would strengthen the roster (and likely vault them past the Red Sox).

One was Messersmith, engaged in the same kind of recruiting tour Hunter had enjoyed a year earlier.

The other was All-Star Reggie Jackson, once Steinbrenner caught wind that Charlie Finley was planning to sell for parts a team that had finished in first place in the AL West five straight seasons, with three world championships in the middle. The boss coveted this key piece of the A's dynasty.

Jackson always enjoyed playing in New York: the passion, the energy and especially the dimensions of the old stadium. In August 1973, after planting one in the third deck, he'd admitted, "I'd like to hit in this park all the time. There's still a lot of unexplored territory for a hitter."

And a few years later Jackson would add this gem while the A's were visiting Shea Stadium: "If I played in New York, they'd name a candy bar after me."

Jackson wouldn't come without compensation, and he planned on doing what dozens of players decided to do in the wake of the Seitz ruling: play out his option year—the "reserve" in the reserve clause—and then seek the highest bidder. He was eager to get away from Finley, as most of the A's were by 1976, and Finley was just as zealous to slash payroll. Steinbrenner figured the cantankerous A's owner might be willing to go for a deal for a scattering of second-tier Yankee prospects or, better, a fat six-figure check.

But Charlie Finley still detested George Steinbrenner.

And he wasn't in the business of helping him build a champion, no matter how high Steinbrenner was willing to push the price. On April 2 he traded Jackson and Ken Holtzman in a six-player swap with Baltimore, no doubt rejoicing that he'd not only dealt the Yankees a blow but also helped fortify the Orioles, still an AL East force to be reckoned with. Jackson was shattered. He wanted no part of Baltimore and threatened to retire, but as Baltimore manager Earl Weaver said, echoing baseball's company line in the dying hours of the old ways: "In what other line of work is he going to make $200,000 this year?" Jackson reported and had a solid year, twenty-seven homers and ninety-one RBIs in 134 games, what would come to be known in future decades as a "good walk year."

Messersmith was a different matter, already free to sign with anyone, and the sides were so close to a deal that, on the last day of March, reports surfaced he'd be joining Hunter, Ellis and Figueroa at the top of the Yankees' rotation. But on the first of April, the deal fell apart amid wild accusations from both sides. Messersmith's agent, Herb Osmond, suggested the Yankees had tried to change the deal, requiring them to get 40 percent of Messersmith's off-field earnings (illegal by baseball law), and further hinted Steinbrenner and Paul had plied him with booze to influence him.

"Completely untrue!" Steinbrenner raged, then helpfully pointed out he had witnesses who would attest that Osmond drank exactly one and a half bottles of beer during a seven-hour meeting.

"I value my integrity too much to ever play for the Yankees," Messersmith said after Kuhn voided the deal, allowing him to sign a million-dollar pact with Ted Turner's Atlanta Braves instead.

"Anyone who doesn't want to play for the Yankees," Billy Martin sneered, "we don't want 'em on the club."

> **INTERLUDE:** Messersmith had a fine season in 1976, going 11–11 for a terrible Braves team that lost ninety-two games. But he hurt his elbow in 1977, and at that December's winter meetings in Honolulu Turner was trying to sell him to the Texas Rangers when Steinbrenner immediately offered $100,000. Turner said yes.
>
> "This might be the best deal we've ever done!" Steinbrenner

predicted, delighted he'd finally bagged Messersmith, himself suddenly happy to adjust his parameters of integrity.

Messersmith's arm never healed. He pitched six games in 1978, eleven more for the Dodgers in '79, then called it a career.

With his first two swings at free agency Steinbrenner had two whiffs and was starting to understand an old truth of the game: Even the best hitters fail 70 percent of the time.

IN 1976 THE YANKEES were restored to glory. Steinbrenner set the mood early when he convinced Billy Martin to name Thurman Munson the first Yankees captain since Lou Gehrig's forced retirement in 1939. Munson was reluctant until Martin assured him that he, Martin, would keep taking the lineup card to home plate; in his first official game as captain, Munson launched a home run to fuel a 10–0 win over the Twins, the first Yankee to hit one out of the renovated park. Steinbrenner approved Martin's wish to add Yogi Berra to his coaching staff. Berra had been estranged from the team since 1964, fired two days after leading the Yankees to Game 7 of the World Series in his only season as skipper. Berra joined the Mets in 1965, became manager in '72 and was fired just before the Yanks hired Martin. Berra was a quick sell, but his wife, Carmen, was instinctively suspicious of Steinbrenner.

On April 15 Yankee Stadium was reopened, and 52,613 stuffed the rejiggered palace to watch the Yankees spot the Twins a 4–0 lead before roaring back to win 11–4. Steinbrenner showed up in a pinstriped suit with the Yankees logo stitched on his dress shirt and declared, "It's been a two-year road trip." By then, the Yankees were already 4–1 and in first place in the AL East, and they would remain there for the season's final 174 days. Martin was masterful, guiding the club to ninety-seven wins, ten clear of the second-place Orioles, fifteen and a half up on the Red Sox. The Yankees took on the pugnacity of their manager—much to the delight of their owner—on the night that officially ushered in a new chapter of Red Sox–Yankees contempt.

On May 20, the first time the teams played, there were 28,418 inside Yankee Stadium on a Thursday night. Bill Lee, the Yankees' old antagonist, held them to one run over five and two-thirds innings, but the Yankees made the lead stand up. Rookie Otto Velez singled to right, and Lou Piniella tried to score against the rifle arm of right fielder Dwight "Dewey" Evans. The ball beat him by about six feet. With no other recourse, Piniella flattened Carlton Fisk with his shoulder and rolled over him, trying to jostle the ball free (all perfectly legal). Fisk punched back. The benches cleared. Out of the melee Lee emerged with his pitching arm dangling, his shoulder separated, his season interrupted for fifty-seven days.

Afterward he was philosophical. "How can I hold anything against the Yankees?" he asked. "They're just tools of that madman Billy Martin."

A few years later he'd say: "I had a terrible dream last night, a vision, the ghost of Christmas past. It came into my room and had Steinbrenner's face on Billy Martin's body."

The Yankees drew 2,012,434 to Yankee Stadium, their highest figure since 1950. As delicious to Steinbrenner: That was 500,000 more than the Mets drew to Shea Stadium that summer, the first time since 1963 the Yankees drew more. The normally benign rivalry even saw a salty exchange early on. When the lockout ended, the first exhibition game was supposed to be Mets–Yankees on Wednesday, March 24, but the Mets agreed to that day only because they were supposed to play a few games in San Juan and figured Fort Lauderdale would be a natural stopover. When the lockout wiped out their trip to Puerto Rico, they wanted no part of a five-hour bus ride from St. Petersburg or a charter flight for an exhibition game. But the game was already a sellout, more than seven thousand tickets, and televised back to New York on WPIX/Channel 11, the Yankees' station, which had set viewership records for a Mets–Yankees exhibition in 1975.

"We have a contract," Steinbrenner insisted.

The Mets chartered a plane, got hammered 7–1 and Steinbrenner reveled in every pitch, imagining columns of Mets fans tearing up their tickets and trading in their Mets caps for Yankees hats.

It especially delighted Steinbrenner to watch Billy Martin work, though as the summer progressed, Steinbrenner, wittingly or not, developed a template he would follow often across the rest of his days, picking fights and quarreling publicly with managers and his best players. In this case it was Catfish Hunter, who had a difficult year two of his mega deal, allowing the most homers in the league and a run more per nine innings than he had in '75. Still, he was a gamer: On May 9 he pitched into the twelfth inning against his old teammates in Oakland before losing on a walk, a sacrifice bunt and a sacrifice fly. Five days later he was scheduled to make his next start at home against another old friend, Reggie Jackson, in town with the Orioles. First, he came to the stadium early in the morning to film a commercial for Red Man tobacco, which was paying him $7,500 for two hours of work.

Jackson, as Jackson often would, didn't just step into the moment but seized it, scalding Hunter's first pitch to him deep into the right field seats, a home run in his first swing at the renovated stadium with even more unexplored territory than the prior incarnation. Baltimore battered Hunter. The next day, when Hunter picked up the newspaper, he read this:

"It was a disgrace," a temporarily anonymous "high Yankees official" screamed, stripped across the top of the back page of the *Post*. "And it showed a complete lack of regard for his teammates and some very bad judgment. Maybe if he didn't pitch and pose for pictures all morning he wouldn't have given up those two homers at night. He's being paid enough money not to have to do that."

Hunter certainly knew the identity of the "high Yankees official" even before the *Daily News* gleefully outed Steinbrenner.

Hunter was already annoyed at Steinbrenner's insistence that he and his teammates maintain their hair short enough so "the skin on your neck is visible." On the first day of spring training Steinbrenner posted a list of commandments for the team that would still be the law of the Bronx almost fifty years later: "No beards. No muttonchops. No long hair. No high stirrups." It was signed "By George Steinbrenner and Billy Martin," and the players noted the higher credit line. Hunter, who wore his hair modestly but did sport a mustache, always believed Steinbrenner kept a closer eye on him, and Steinbrenner admitted that was so: "I pay him the most money."

"Maybe George is trying Charlie Finley's old trick of getting us to hate him enough to win," he mused.

To which Steinbrenner retorted: "If being angry with me makes Catfish pitch the way he can and should that's fine with me."

Later, in August, with the Yankees in a brief tailspin, Steinbrenner visited the Yankees' clubhouse and gathered the starting rotation, saying he was tired of "paying good money to guys who aren't trying one hundred and ten percent."

He wasn't necessarily talking about Hunter. But Hunter was pissed anyway.

"He's a fan who thinks you should win every time you pitch," said Hunter, bound for the Hall of Fame despite losing 166 games in his career.

So there was that.

There was also this: Dick Williams was fired on July 22 after parts of three unhappy and unsuccessful seasons with the Angels. Two weeks later, on the evenings of August 2 and 3, Williams was George Steinbrenner's guest in the owner's box as the Yankees, who'd seen their lead slip to nine and a half games, swept the Tigers. Steinbrenner insisted he was merely hosting a friend, seeing if he'd have interest in joining the Yankees in a consulting role down the road.

"It's obvious we feel he's a great baseball man, and we wanted to talk about the future, if there's a fit for him here," he said. "But we already have a manager."

Martin understood better than anyone the inherent Sicilian message: *Don't blow the big lead. Nobody is irreplaceable. Even you.* Especially *you.*

It wouldn't be for another six weeks, with the Yankees' magic number getting smaller by the day, that Steinbrenner finally offered Martin a three-year extension through 1979, which Martin happily signed before anyone could remind Steinbrenner that Martin had never come remotely close to staying in one place for four years. He'd be paid $90,000 per year. Now he had his dream job and was inching closer to his dream salary.

But Martin, being Martin, was still simmering even before the ink dried.

"I told George I thought he was a bigger man than that," he said. "I told him: 'You piss me off.' His taste was poor. He said he was just talking about a job in the organization. Well, I think there could've been another way to handle it that wouldn't embarrass me. He's the boss, but I'm not sure what he was trying to prove."

Perhaps that sounds paranoid. But it was exactly eleven days later that even the most skeptical sports reporter would be forced to admit Martin's working conditions weren't exactly ideal. The Yankees went into a four-game series with the second-place Orioles up eleven and a half games. Just one win in those four games would cinch the division, with eleven games to play. The mathematics were secondary; the Yankees were going to finish first. Except they lost the first game, 11–8, squandering a 7–0 lead. They were shut out by Jim Palmer the next day, shut down by ex-Yankee Rudy May the next. And by the time the Orioles were done with the sweep with a 2–1 win, the lead was cut to seven and a half and the Orioles were still breathing, if barely.

When the door opened to Martin's office, the manager was gone; he'd escaped to the trainer's room for forty-five minutes because he knew what was coming. He knew his team would be fine, but he also knew there was someone who didn't share that opinion. Before the first question could be fired off, the phone on his desk rang. And rang. And rang.

Martin didn't answer it.

Martin barely looked at it.

It rang ten times. Twenty times. Thirty times. Reporters shouted over the ringing. Martin answered over the ringing. It kept ringing.

Finally he said, "Do you believe this fucking guy?"

None of the reporters had to be told who that fucking guy was. As they departed, the phone rang again and they heard Martin's side of the conversation: "George, if I'm seven and a half games back you can yell at me all you want. But when I'm seven and a half games ahead, get the hell off my ass. . . ."

●

ON THE EVENING of September 25, most of the Yankees along with George Steinbrenner and Gabe Paul gathered in a private dining room in downtown Detroit for a celebration twelve years in the making. The Yankees pounded the Tigers that afternoon to secure a tie for the AL East; now, if the Red Sox could beat the Orioles in Baltimore that night, the Yankees would clinch a postseason spot for the first time since 1964. Back at Steinbrenner's coming-out party at 21 in January 1973 he'd vowed it would take three years to return the Yankees to glory. Now, exactly three years later, a group of men anxiously circled a telephone, where Yankees PR man Mickey Morabito was connected with an Orioles PR man at Memorial Stadium, providing long-distance play-by-play. When the players arrived around nine o'clock Dewey Evans had just given Boston a 1–0 lead. Now it was the bottom of the ninth. There were two outs and nobody on. Morabito reported that Bobby Grich was at the plate, and worked the count to 3-and-2 against Luis Tiant.

"Hey, somebody get George away from the phone," crowed Lou Piniella, owner of a license to needle the boss because he'd replaced Murcer as Steinbrenner's favorite Yankee. "With your luck, this guy will hit a two-run homer with nobody on."

"Ground ball to short," Morabito relayed. "We win!"

Champagne popped, and Steinbrenner was targeted before the players remembered they weren't in a clubhouse. They guzzled it instead. Steinbrenner hugged everyone.

So this is what it feels like, he marveled to himself.

The Yankees enjoyed another wild celebration when they knocked off the Kansas City Royals in the best-of-five AL Championship Series (ALCS), Chris Chambliss hitting a pennant-winning home run in the bottom of the ninth of Game 5. Steinbrenner enjoyed that game with New York mayor Abe Beame on one side of him and Hollywood icon Cary Grant on the other; in the clubhouse, Grant rejoiced as player after player dumped bubbly on him. Martin was quieter than you'd expect; he was delighted that he'd finally get a chance to manage in a World Series game, but he was sad Casey Stengel—who'd died the previous September—didn't live to see it. Martin alone had chosen to wear a black armband on his left uniform sleeve to honor his mentor all year. Now he choked up as he talked to Yankees television announcer Bill White in the joyous clubhouse.

"I think he'd have been awfully proud of me," he said.

But Cincinnati's Big Red Machine of Johnny Bench and Pete Rose, Tony Pérez and Joe Morgan, was on a mission to win back-to-back championships. The Reds quickly ended the party, sweeping the Yankees in four. Steinbrenner arrived back at his room at Essex House around 1 a.m. after the series clincher. By seven he was up and by nine he was at his desk at Yankee Stadium, summoning his lieutenants. The night before, walking into the devastated home clubhouse, Steinbrenner had growled at Gabe Paul, "Look at them! They should hang their heads after that!" but then he'd also spent an hour circling the clubhouse shaking hands, offering thanks for a hell of a run and Martin for a hell of a job. That was then.

Now, his eyes narrowed as the meeting began.

"That," he said, "can't ever happen again. That is inexcusable."

Gabe Paul knew what that meant.

More important, he knew *who* that meant.

CHAPTER 10

It's a fickle town [New York], a tough town. They get you here, boy. They don't let you escape with minor scratches and bruises. They put scars on you here.
—REGGIE JACKSON

The player had never exactly been subtle about his intentions or his ambitions. From the time he first visited Yankee Stadium as a twenty-one-year-old Oakland Athletic, Reggie Jackson salivated at the inviting right field porch at Yankee Stadium and conquered it. His very first game there, April 15, 1968, he hit a home run, off Mel Stottlemyre, a mammoth blast that cleared the 407-foot sign in right-center field and landed halfway up the bleachers. Then, afterward, he found himself swarmed by newsmen who wanted to hear all about the 450-foot blast.

"I felt Yankee Stadium, all of it," he told them, although with 58,421 of the park's 67,000 seats unoccupied that day, he didn't hear much of it. "Mickey Mantle, Babe Ruth. All those guys. All of it."

Ever a suitor to the moment, Jackson greeted the renovated version of the stadium the same way eight years later, hitting a homer his first game there in 1976, this time as an Oriole, this time in his first at bat of the game, this time against his old friend Catfish Hunter on the day Hunter filmed his Red Man commercial. Later, when the Yankees visited

Baltimore's Memorial Stadium in July, Jackson held court with the New York writers and made little effort to disguise his intentions.

"What's Graig Nettles doing wearing my number?" he said with a laugh. Nettles wore number 9 for the Yankees. Jackson had worn 9 since his first day in Oakland.

He was just warming up.

"The next time I sign a contract I'll be in some deep water. I'll need a Brink's trunk with mag wheels and tinted windows all the way around and a candy-apple paint job. When you shop at Tiffany's there's no deals. They don't discount anybody. All cash. They don't even take credit cards."

Picking up steam now. Someone mentioned New York City.

"New York, man," he said. "I already got deals with Revlon and Puma and Colgate. I had a feeling this was coming one of these days. It was 'Just wait and be patient.' The people in New York love me. They love people who put on a show."

And in case anyone was still confused . . .

"Steinbrenner?" He was smiling his best Colgate smile now. "Some guys can sell ships. Some guys can sell insurance and some guys can sing songs. I can play baseball."

He could also sell Reggie Jackson.

George Steinbrenner was an eager customer.

In October, in Kansas City, the two men crossed paths behind the batting cage on a workout day before Game 1 of the ALCS. Jackson was moonlighting as a broadcaster for ABC TV. They spoke briefly. Bob Fishel, a former Yankees PR man who'd followed Lee MacPhail to the American League office, said playfully, "You know I can report this, right?"

"We're just discussing philosophy," Steinbrenner said.

"Actually," Jackson said, "he's permitted to tell me New York has great restaurants and lots of fine clothing stores. And I'm permitted to say that ABC is where I work, and Puma. They're both in New York."

A week later, at Yankee Stadium for the World Series, Jackson was left off the guest list to a pregame party upstairs in the Yankee Club. A few panicked Yankees officials rectified the situation before he could reach the elevator, but Jackson just smiled at them.

"Forget it," he said. "Next year I'll own that fuckin' room."

THIS WAS GEORGE STEINBRENNER'S moment. This was his play. That meeting at Yankee Stadium, the morning after they'd been swept out of the World Series, he listened to his lieutenants' thoughts. There would be twenty-two players taking part in the first class of free agency, a bonanza that would kick off in November. Steinbrenner knew this was the time to flex the Yankees' big-market muscle and didn't plan on being bashful. His partners had already begun to bitch about how often they were asked for cash calls, were already getting frustrated at their modest dividends. A lot had already thrown up their hands, sold their shares back to Steinbrenner. If they were replaced, it was by investors of smaller measure, and quieter voice. It allowed Steinbrenner to consolidate his considerable powers. The Yankees were already making money, thanks to much-improved attendance and a favorable stadium lease that allowed a generous share of parking and concessions. Their improved play yielded fatter deals with both WINS AM radio and WPIX TV, and his advisers promised there would be more, much more, when cable TV, then in its infancy, was properly mined.

He had money to spend. He intended to spend it.

Now it was about identifying the players to whom he would write those checks.

Gabe Paul piped up first. In a few weeks he would be named baseball's Executive of the Year for 1976 by UPI, the crowning achievement of his professional life.

"Bobby Grich is the best player," Paul said of the Orioles' second baseman, who'd played out his option. "We're good at second, but he's got the range to play shortstop, and we desperately need a shortstop."

Steinbrenner wrote down the name.

"I agree on Grich," rasped Billy Martin, puffing a pipe, his voice a scratchy mess since he'd been ejected from Game 4 the night before, one more last-stand fight for a lost cause. "And I also think Joe Rudi would be a perfect fit for us. He gives us a right-handed bat, which we badly need, and he's a top-notch defensive outfielder."

Steinbrenner nodded.

A few more names were tossed out: Don Gullett, the Reds' pitching ace. Rollie Fingers, Oakland's shutdown reliever. Wayne Garland, who'd come out of nowhere to win twenty games for the Orioles. Don Baylor, who . . .

"What about Reggie?" Steinbrenner asked impatiently.

He wasn't really asking. Paul knew he could explain why any of the other players would be better fits and the boss would respond as if he were talking in Japanese. Martin desperately wanted to recite the list of red flags he'd assembled on Jackson through the years, from his ego to the fact that he wasn't near the fielder Rudi was. But Martin knew anything he said now he'd probably see on the back page of the *Post* in June or the *Daily News* in August. Maybe sooner.

"Those guys are good," Steinbrenner said. "But they aren't *stars*."

The men nodded.

"They don't put fannies in the seats. Reggie Jackson will put fannies in the seats."

The meeting adjourned.

The courtship commenced.

IT HAD TO be 21, of course. The place gave George Steinbrenner chills because this was where he first became a participant in New York, a *player*. This was where New York's players did their moving and their shaking. Not long before, Steinbrenner took Thurman Munson here, too, to congratulate him for winning the AL's Most Valuable Player award for his 1976 season (.302, seventeen homers, 105 RBIs) and to take Munson's temperature. When Munson received the MVP, he'd joked about Steinbrenner promising him a raise. Steinbrenner stood stone-faced and now asked Munson about his comment.

"Well, you always said I'd be the highest-paid player on the team besides Catfish," Munson said. "And I know you're a man of your word."

Steinbrenner smiled; he knew he'd probably made that promise at some point, though he couldn't quite remember it. He told Munson he'd always take care of him.

"Now, about Reggie . . ." he said.

"Go get the big guy," Munson said. "He's the only guy in baseball who can carry a team for a month, and don't believe all the other stuff. He plays hard."

With the captain's endorsement, Steinbrenner flew Jackson to New York the Monday before Thanksgiving. Jackson had heard of 21, knew its reputation, knew enough that he should wear a jacket and tie to this first meeting with Steinbrenner, who brought along a friend, William Fugazy, a limousine magnate and one-man rolodex to the who-est of the who's whos in New York. Jackson walked inside 21 and thought he'd stumbled into a TGI Fridays: red-checked tablecloths, beat-up chairs, tin jets dangling from the ceiling, uncarpeted floors. *This* was where New York's elite came to meet?

Jackson ordered a steak. It was overcooked.

At lunch's end, Steinbrenner bypassed the taxi line.

"Let's take a walk, Reggie," he said.

Here is where Steinbrenner allowed New York to do the recruiting. They walked past the Plaza Hotel; as if on cue, the drivers of the horse carriages started calling his name, exhorting him: "See ya in the Bronx, Reggie!"

As they walked along Central Park South, cabbies honked their horns. "Sign him, George!" they crowed.

Pedestrians pleaded with him to make New York his new home, and a gaggle of schoolkids handed him scraps of paper from their spiral notebooks to sign.

"We were falling in love," Jackson would say. "New York with me, me with New York."

This lovely stroll out of a movie culminated at George Steinbrenner's apartment on the tony Upper East Side, and that's where reality splashed both men cold in the face.

"Reggie," Steinbrenner said, "we'd like to offer you two million dollars over five years."

Jackson's thousand-watt smile dimmed. He'd kept this information in his pocket, and he'd nearly forgotten about it as half of Manhattan tried to romance him that day, but his prior meeting had been with Charles Bronfman, one of the world's wealthiest men, whose two biggest assets were Seagram's whiskey and the Montreal Expos; his profits from the former had allowed the latter to offer Jackson $5 million if he'd be willing to take his talents north of the border. He wasn't sure about playing in Canada, and he was less sure about switching leagues, and he *really* wasn't crazy about the weather there.

Still, five mil was five mil.

"George," Jackson said, "what I want is three million dollars. And a Rolls-Royce."

Steinbrenner had to play poker now. The money would be split between yearly salary, deferred payments and annuities. He figured with $200,000 a year as a base, he'd be able to hold off the prone-to-pouting Munson, who wasn't making *that* much less than that. He could nudge it closer. He still didn't want to take it all the way to three. He told Jackson about all the benefits of living so close to Madison Avenue; Jackson said he understood, but he already was making six figures in endorsements living in California. The men agreed to meet at the O'Hare Hyatt in Chicago two days later.

Steinbrenner managed to keep much of this out of the papers, to the extent that the tabloids all called it "unlikely" Jackson would sign with the Yankees, because they *had* heard about Bronfman's offer. Steinbrenner wanted it that way. By Wednesday, some were lamenting that Steinbrenner, after whiffing on Messersmith a year earlier, might be on the verge of getting shut out since both Grich and Rudi signed with Gene Autry's California Angels. All the Yankees had to show for this unprecedented baseball auction so far was Gullett, a nice pickup who would've helped the club but literally wouldn't draw one extra fanny to spend a night in a stadium seat.

Steinbrenner felt confident as he walked into the Hyatt . . . until he saw a few of his fellow owners milling about the lobby and realized they weren't in town to visit the observation deck of the Sears Tower. He'd come hoping Jackson would agree to meet in the middle at $2.5 million and now realized he'd better lead with his best offer. He did: $2.9 million.

"What about the Rolls, George?"

Steinbrenner grabbed a cocktail napkin, wrote down the details. And the final official figure: $2.96 million, with the sixty grand added on to cover the car. Jackson took the napkin, scrawled, *I will not let you down. Reginald M. Jackson.*

Steinbrenner kept that paper linen under glass in his office the rest of his days. He'd bagged his star—or, as Jackson himself preferred to be called, his "superduperstar."

"He hustled me, man," Jackson would say a week later inside the Versailles Terrace Room of the Americana hotel. He wore a Yankees cap and a brass-buttoned three-piece suit of gray flannel as he was officially welcomed to the Yankees. He had black alligator shoes, sported a bracelet with his name spelled in gold and made sure to wear one of the championship rings he'd earned in Oakland. "George Steinbrenner outhustled everyone else. He dealt with me as a man and as a person. I feel like I'm a friend of his. He's like me. He's a little crazy, and he's a hustler."

On the grandest day of his nearly four years owning the Yankees, with his entire plan falling into place just as he'd planned it, Steinbrenner opted for humility: "Anyone can sell New York. That's really all I sold him."

Munson, the captain, was there, as was Roy White, the longest-tenured Yankee. Together they put the cap on Jackson's head and helped him into a pinstriped Yankees jersey, interlocking "NY" on the left breast and a temporary number, 42, on the back.

> **INTERLUDE:** Jackson knew he was never really going to pry number 9 away from Graig Nettles, a mostly easygoing man who'd grown to appreciate his kinship with another Yankee 9, Roger Maris. Jackson initially requested number 42 to honor Jackie Robinson before concluding, twenty years ahead of the rest of baseball, "There should only be one forty-two." He'd always admired how regal the

number 44 looked on the backs of Henry Aaron and Willie McCovey; it was available—no prominent Yankee had ever worn it before. And it now hangs in Monument Park and will never be worn by another Yankee.

It was all smiles and hugs, and in his prepared remarks everyone heard a Jackson who was humble, grateful, eager to fit in.

Later, as Jackson chatted up a smaller group of writers, Munson and White overheard—and then read—something else entirely: call it the first riff of Jackson's Yankees career.

"I didn't come to New York to become a star. I brought my star with me."

He delivered all sixteen words with what one of the men around him, columnist Dave Anderson of *The New York Times*, would call "perfect notebook speed."

White looked at Munson. Munson looked at White.

They rolled their eyes.

BILLY MARTIN WASN'T at the Americana. He wasn't invited and didn't much want to be there anyway. He was still angry at Steinbrenner, and watching him escort Jackson around the city didn't help his mood much. Living in the Sheraton Hotel across the river in Hasbrouck Heights, New Jersey, Martin seethed as a player he didn't want began a platonic love affair with an owner he was beginning to mistrust.

"George was taking Reggie to 21 for lunch, going out to dinner, and I was sitting in my room and he never once called and asked me to come to lunch with him," Martin fumed.

The storm was gathering, and it was headed for Fort Lauderdale, which promised to be the most interesting spring training in baseball history, and it would be George Steinbrenner who would play the part of Jim Cantore, right in the middle of every hurricane, every tornado, every monsoon, every blizzard. Before the Yankees could even make it to Florida Steinbrenner had to deal with a disillusioned Munson, who took to the offseason banquet circuit to lob grenades. Steinbrenner was treated to the first with his morning coffee one morning in February: "I wouldn't mind being traded to Cleveland [near Munson's home of Canton, Ohio], or buying out my contract so I can go to Cleveland."

Steinbrenner summoned Munson to New York. Munson accused Steinbrenner of misleading him with the Jackson contract. Steinbrenner let Munson rant, then met with him later that day. They reached an agreement: Steinbrenner would add two years to his deal and would allow Munson to live in the offseason in Ohio. As a way to compromise his own feelings about spending so much time apart from his family, Munson began to ponder his options. One day, walking out of Fort Lauderdale Stadium with Lou Piniella, he took a long look at a Beechcraft Duke aircraft parked at the executive airport next door, and his imagination began to whirl.

"I think I'm going to start taking flying lessons," Munson said. "I can get home on off-days that way."

Piniella figured he was kidding.

GRAIG NETTLES WAS up next. In the middle of the 1976 season, with Nettles struggling, Steinbrenner nevertheless signed him to a three-year deal to head off free agency. But then Nettles unhappily saw the new level of riches the Seitz decision yielded. Nettles also failed to seek proper advice on how to deal with his new income, didn't shelter it properly and got killed by his tax bill. He tried to renegotiate, but Steinbrenner refused and took to the back pages to hammer his point home. Nettles jumped the team for two days in spring training. Steinbrenner fined him, threatened to trade him. Nettles returned and, at Steinbrenner's insistence, read a public apology for ditching the team.

"This was pretty goddamned important," Steinbrenner said, "because a lot of players might have gotten into their heads that these contracts are unilateral."

Nettles, chastened, was asked to respond. He simply waved the apology that was still in his hand.

"All I want to say," he said, "is what's on this fuckin' paper."

It was only March, and the tempests were everywhere, but Steinbrenner figured maybe the worst was over. He had no idea he was only watching minor squalls.

NOT EVERYONE LAUDED the Yankees' merry band of baseball mercenaries. A few weeks before the Yankees were due in spring training came a most public rebuke of George Steinbrenner's methods by a man named Joseph Iglehart, a holdover from the CBS days who'd signed on for a 5 percent share when Steinbrenner bought the club. Previously he'd been the chairman of the Baltimore Orioles and hired Lee MacPhail there; for three years he'd been the most active and visible of all of the minority partners. But he was gravely concerned about Steinbrenner's spending habits, particularly with Jackson.

"I told George I was mad at the whole damned thing," Iglehart said. "If we can't sign players for reasonable salaries I don't want to be a part of it anymore."

The men parted on good terms, and Steinbrenner happily bought out Iglehart's share, which further increased his grip on the team. As he departed, Iglehart issued a warning shot that could've doubled as a horoscope reading.

"One of the really big problems with the Yankees," he said, "will be how the three biggest egoists in baseball—George Steinbrenner, Billy Martin, Reggie Jackson—get along."

HE WALKED INTO the home clubhouse at Fort Lauderdale Stadium carrying an equipment bag that bore the logo of the Oakland Athletics, and from the moment he unpacked it Reggie Jackson began filling reporters' notebooks.

"I'm not just a ballplayer," he said. "I'm a multifaceted person, a myriad of personalities. I'm a businessman who happens to be an athlete. I've got my case here, my files, my tools."

The Yankees who'd played with him in Oakland greeted him warmly. Catfish Hunter embraced him, then joked about getting mustard on his hands after hugging such a hot dog. Ken Holtzman pitched his first round of batting practice and "accidentally" hit Jackson in the side with his first offering.

"I hope George has paid up the insurance!" Jackson laughed.

The rest of the team was distant. It was subtle, mostly. Thurman Munson walked in and barely acknowledged him. The rest of the Yankees took their cue from the captain. They weren't freezing him out. But they'd also seen the comments Jackson made a few weeks earlier on the ABC program *The Superteams*, where he'd volunteered there'd probably be jealousies and other petty human frailties to deal with and mentioned Munson by name. The Yankees were one of the participants in the show, but Jackson spent most of his time with the TV folks. He'd quickly tried to walk all that back, but a clubhouse has a long memory; the Yankees were hoping Jackson would make the first move. That first day—a lot of days that followed—Jackson instead chose to keep collecting neat sound bites.

"Part of the reason they pay me is this," he said. "I like living in this environment. They're looking for me here. I'm the hunted. I'm the hunted on the team of the hunted."

As those first weeks passed, the early chill became a full frost. One night, after another day when he was removed from all the banter and ballbreaking that constitute a clubhouse, Jackson walked into a Fort Lauderdale restaurant. He had a meeting with a reporter for *Sport* magazine named Robert Ward. Ward had some questions for Jackson. And Jackson, he had some answers for Ward.

STILL, MOST OF the spring, whatever unease was percolating below the surface with Jackson remained muted. It was Billy Martin's growing uneasiness with George Steinbrenner that became the issue. One day, sitting in the Yankees' dugout, Steinbrenner was chatting about his colt, Steve's Friend, which had just won the Florida Derby and was likely to enter the Kentucky Derby in May. Martin wheeled and faced Steinbrenner.

"In this dugout," he snapped, "we only talk baseball."

Steinbrenner opted not to tell Martin who actually *owned* the dugout.

Steinbrenner planted himself at spring training and was around the club every day and didn't like what he was seeing. The Yankees were losing, for one thing, often looking like they were treating the games with half interest.

"It's spring training, George," Martin reminded him after one panicked postgame visit to the manager's office. "You don't want to leave your best baseball in Florida."

Steinbrenner, the ex–football coach, couldn't understand why Martin wasn't punishing the Yankees by making them run stadium steps after a tough loss to the Tigers in Lakeland, why he wouldn't threaten to make them walk home after dropping one to the Red Sox in Winter Haven. It infuriated him that Martin and his coaches drove to road games rather than sit on the team bus. Martin argued it offered time to better assess players and the team privately; Steinbrenner believed his manager should sit in the front row of the bus like Woody Hayes.

Steinbrenner stewed and simmered. The Yankees kept losing. He boiled, and broiled, and . . . finally, on March 26, he blew.

The Yankees lost to the Mets in St. Petersburg, 6–0. The game was telecast back to New York on the Mets' station, WWOR/Channel 9, and with every passing inning Steinbrenner envisioned a vast traffic jam eastward over the Triboro Bridge, Bronx to Queens. The Yankees actually surpassed the Mets in season ticket sales for the coming season for the first time since 1963—even in '76, while the Yankees drew more fans, the Mets had a larger base—but that didn't matter to Steinbrenner. The Mets humiliated the Yankees, and Channel 9 reported it was its largest baseball audience ever.

After the game, Steinbrenner stormed into the visiting clubhouse. Martin was sitting in a corner, drinking a beer with Mickey Mantle.

"I want to talk to you!" Steinbrenner roared. *"Now!"*

In that moment, to Martin, Steinbrenner was every other punk who'd ever approached him in a bar looking to get his name in the papers, scaring up a fight.

"Get the fuck out of here, George! How dare you yell at me in front of my players!"

"I'll yell at you wherever the hell I want!"

"No, you won't. Not here."

"Oh, really? Do you want to be fired right here?"

"If that's what you want to do, George, then fire me."

The two men retreated to the trainer's room. There was a bucket of ice water on a desk; at one point Gabe Paul feared Martin might take a swing at Steinbrenner, but instead he punched the water, and it splashed all over Paul, who must have wondered how he'd found himself in the middle of this odd baseball sitcom. Steinbrenner stormed out. Later, he called Yogi Berra and told him he was going to replace Martin as manager.

"Not a chance, George," Berra answered.

Within a few days, Steinbrenner calmed down and Martin did, too. Martin, knowing he'd have amped his players' routine up anyway, agreed to take the rest of the spring games more seriously.

Steinbrenner said, "I think we'll have some arguments along the way that will wind up being a lot worse than that."

WHAT KILLED MARTIN was, Steinbrenner was right. The Yankees *did* play all spring like a team enjoying its press clippings. And much to the manager's dismay, that carried into the season. The Yankees stumbled out of the gate 2–8, including back-to-back losses to the expansion Toronto Blue Jays (run by Pat Gillick, Gabe Paul's former lieutenant, a fact not lost on Steinbrenner). Martin went with an old standby, having Reggie Jackson pick names out of a cap to build a batting order and break the slump, and it worked. The Yankees immediately won six straight, lost one (at which point he reverted to his original lineup) and won five more in a row.

There was always a fissure waiting just below the surface. In late April, on the Yankees' first West Coast swing, Martin grew frustrated at the lack of left-handed bats on his bench. Steinbrenner demanded the Yankees carry only two catchers, so veteran Elrod Hendricks was sent to Syracuse against Martin's wishes.

"George and Gabe must think I'm kidding," he said. "Why are we going with twenty-four players? Are we that friggin' great?"

Steinbrenner immediately announced that he was fining Martin $2,500, and for an ever-so-brief moment, that actually seemed to unify the Yankees: Jackson offered to pay the fine.

Catfish Hunter said, "This reminds me of the Oakland clubhouse. There are going to be fights soon."

He was right. He just had the wrong combatants.

By May 23, the Yankees were 21–17 and welcomed the Red Sox to the Bronx for the first time. In the bottom of the seventh, trailing Bill Lee 2–1, Jackson provided his first genuine Yankee Moment by drilling a Lee fastball over the right field wall to tie the game. Jackson admired it, toured the bases, drank in the adulation from the 31,261 fans, touched home plate and headed for the dugout.

But instead of going in the side nearest to home plate—where his teammates and manager gathered to greet him—Jackson went to the extreme opposite side, where all that awaited was an empty bench. He did this in full view of television cameras and at least half the stadium crowd.

Afterward, Jackson explained, "My hand was hurting."

Thurman Munson replied: "His hand? He's a fucking liar. How's that for a quote?"

It wasn't the hand. That morning, the latest issue of *Sport* magazine had been published. The conversation Jackson had with Robert Ward early in spring training, when he most felt like a disgraced West Point cadet enduring The Silence from the rest of the corps, was the centerpiece of the issue.

"This team, it all flows from me. I'm the straw that stirs the drink. Maybe I should say me and Munson, but he can only stir it bad."

With those twenty-eight words, a line had been drawn. And Jackson was now the only person standing on the other side of it. There was a Yankees backup catcher named Fran Healy who'd befriended Jackson and was serving as something of a conduit to Munson. Healy, trying to foster a truce, told Munson, "Maybe what Reggie said was taken out of context."

"For six fuckin' pages?" Munson raged.

This was clear: If Jackson had previously just been paranoid that his teammates didn't like him, he was a full-blown pariah now.

The next day, Steinbrenner went to Martin's office and closed the door. There'd been some stories in the papers that Steinbrenner insisted to Gabe Paul that Martin had to go.

Steinbrenner assured Martin, "I'm on your side here."

Martin appreciated that.

"But, Billy," Steinbrenner said. "You have to fix this shit. And soon."

CHAPTER 11

Some kids dream of joining the circus, others of becoming a major league baseball player. I have been doubly blessed. As a member of the New York Yankees, I have gotten to do both.
—GRAIG NETTLES

For the first time in two years, the Yankees couldn't even sniff the back pages of the New York papers those first few weeks of June 1977. That was the exclusive purview of the Mets and their chairman, M. Donald Grant, engaged in a stare-down with Tom Seaver, the greatest player in team history. Seaver was among baseball's disgruntled class of players who'd signed multiyear contracts before the Seitz decision, and was markedly underpaid. He wasn't looking to renegotiate so much as sign an extension that would reflect his status at the top of the pitching market. The Mets balked, finally used Dick Young's bully pulpit to plant a nasty story in the *Daily News* hinting that Seaver's wife was jealous of Nolan Ryan's wife, and that was that. Seaver was shipped to the Reds at the trading deadline of June 15, and, for good measure, they'd also exiled their best offensive player, Dave Kingman, to San Diego. METS' MIDNIGHT MASSACRE! the tabs gleefully dubbed it.

(George Steinbrenner, unaccustomed to being overshadowed, nevertheless offered his two cents on the Seaver matter, to a reporter from the *Post* gossip column Page Six: "I would never have traded him. He's a star. New York is a star town.")

Ever so quietly, the Yankees slithered into Boston on June 17, and they arrived in first place, too, by a half game over the Red Sox, two over the Orioles. Though there'd been a notable thaw between him and his teammates, and Thurman Munson had started talking to him again, Reggie Jackson was still unhappy, primarily because Billy Martin refused to hit him fourth in the order.

"I was born a cleanup hitter," he groused.

"Chambliss was our cleanup hitter last year, and we won the pennant," Martin reasoned. "Why would I break up a successful hand?"

The Yankees lost the first game to fall back into second place, but even that was muffled by stories previewing Seaver's first start as a Red Saturday in Montreal. It was the last time the Mets would bump the Yankees off the back pages for about six years.

In the bottom of the sixth inning Saturday afternoon at Fenway, with the Sox leading the Yankees 7–4 on the way to a 10–4 win, Boston's Jim Rice hit a lazy fly ball to right that dunked in no-man's-land between Jackson and second baseman Willie Randolph. Jackson retrieved the ball, threw it back in, but not before Rice eased into second with a stand-up double. Jackson retreated to his position, turned to get ready for the next hitter and was greeted by a puzzling sight.

Reserve outfielder Paul Blair was jogging out to right field.

"Billy says to come get you," he said.

Jackson trundled back to the dugout, and when he got there he asked, "What did I do?" What he also did, as the TV cameras saw, was remove his eyeglasses immediately and put them on the bench, as if in anticipation of . . . something.

"You don't hustle, you don't play for me!" Martin growled.

By now bench coach Elston Howard had gotten in between the two men. Another coach, Dick Howser, took a towel and covered the NBC TV camera in the Yankees' dugout, which was a nice idea, except the image filling screens across the country was from the camera in the *Red Sox's dugout* on the other side of the field.

"Billy, nothing I do will ever please you. You don't like me. You don't think I can play ball. You never have from the first day."

By now the Yankees' DH Jimmy Wynn grabbed Jackson and tried easing him toward the clubhouse. Martin spewed more venom.

Jackson snapped back, "You son of a bitch. Take your best shot, old man," and Martin lunged at him again, and this time Yogi Berra joined Howard in holding him back. Finally Jackson disappeared into the Yankees' clubhouse. His one ally on the team, Fran Healy, urged Jackson to get changed and go back to his hotel room before anything else could happen. He did.

"If a player shows up the team," Martin said later, "I'll show up the player."

George Steinbrenner watched all of this unfold on WKYC, the NBC affiliate in Cleveland, where he was spending the weekend, and he was horrified.

"Twenty-five million people are watching this!" he said. "This is a disgrace!"

He blamed one man. And it wasn't his $2.96 million outfielder.

"It was kind of humiliating," Steinbrenner said. "I would have waited to talk to him in the locker room later. It was a scene that good sense would have avoided."

Steinbrenner was particularly incensed at the impromptu boxing match.

"No manager should do that," he said. "He tried to get at him three times."

Soon, Steinbrenner was on a plane to Detroit, where he would meet the Yankees on Monday, and the entirety of the flight was spent pondering who he'd hire to replace Martin, who clearly had to go. Yogi Berra? He'd already rebuked Steinbrenner out of loyalty to Martin. Howser? He'd been up for several jobs in recent years, and the players respected him.

Howard? He had coveted the job for years, and Steinbrenner liked the idea that he might hire the Yankees' first African American skipper, and why not Elston Howard, a faithful Yankees soldier for twenty years and a fan favorite?

One thing he knew for sure as he touched down in Michigan.

Billy Martin was as good as gone.

EXCEPT BILLY MARTIN found salvation in a most improbable place: Gabe Paul, who never wanted him hired in the first place, who didn't care for how Martin managed a ball club on the field or himself off it. Yet it was Paul who ordered Martin and Reggie Jackson into the tiny manager's office at Fenway Park the morning after the dugout incident. He knew better than to expect either man to apologize.

"We cleared the air," Paul said.

"It was a good talk," Martin said.

"No comment," Jackson said.

It was something else Jackson said, in addition to Paul's conviction it wasn't yet time, that convinced Steinbrenner he couldn't fire him. Following his quick exit from Fenway Saturday, Jackson walked back to the team hotel; a few reporters found him there after they'd finished writing their first-edition stories.

"I'm a good ballplayer and a good Christian and I've got an IQ of 160," Jackson said. "But I'm a n—— and I won't be subservient. The Yankees pinstripes are Ruth and Gehrig and DiMaggio and Mantle. They've never had a n—— like me here before and treat me like shit."

Steinbrenner read this, and he was incensed. He'd been unyielding in his support of Jackson from the second he'd signed the cocktail napkin in the O'Hare airport hotel. He'd publicly sided with Jackson while trying to cool down Thurman Munson's various Jackson-themed tantrums. He'd continually sided with Jackson against Martin. Now Jackson was essentially calling Steinbrenner a racist. It cut deep.

"George isn't a racist, at all," John McLendon, the African American coaching pioneer who'd coached for Steinbrenner's Cleveland Pipers in the

ABL, would say about him. "He isn't anti-Black. He may be anti-human, but he isn't anti-Black."

There was something else. Steinbrenner knew fans in Minneapolis still hadn't forgiven Clark Griffith for firing Martin eight years earlier, and that night, in Tiger Stadium, 47,236 Tigers fans would welcome Martin the way they had every time he'd returned to Detroit since being axed in 1973: with a standing ovation. Steinbrenner knew his approval rating was still high among Yankees fans, but he also knew if he ever fired Martin, there would be a steep tax to pay for that in public opinion. New Yorkers might've liked Steinbrenner's deep pockets; they respected Martin's brass balls to regularly (and publicly) tell his boss to go to hell, as so many of them fantasized telling their own bosses.

So Steinbrenner announced Martin was staying on. Then he had separate, private talks with Jackson and Martin.

"Cut out the racist shit," Steinbrenner chided Jackson. "Never has a man's color or where he goes to church been a part of my life. It's an insult to me when you say that, and I'm pissed off about it. I don't expect you and your manager to have breakfast together, but you've got to pull together."

To Martin he said, "You haven't been working at your job. On the field you're great, but you don't do your homework in the office. You're coasting on last year's pennant. I want to keep you here, but don't let me down this time. You push me to the wall again, I promise you I'll throw you over."

Then he assembled the rest of the team in the clubhouse.

"You guys have given me more headaches than any of my businesses. I'm not used to losers. I won't tolerate losers."

But the Yankees kept playing middling baseball. Steinbrenner was in Kansas City for the last game before the All-Star break, an 8–4 loss to the Royals that completed a series sweep and dropped them into third place, and he left the team with a decidedly mixed message postgame. In his hands were thirty checks for $300 apiece that he handed to the players, the coaches and trainer Gene Monahan.

"Have yourself a good time on me," he said. And then he added this kicker.

"If you don't turn this around, you'll be known as the greatest chokers in baseball history. Remember that."

BILLY MARTIN REALIZED one dream on the evening of Tuesday, July 19, when he managed the AL All-Star team, a perk that goes to the skipper of the defending pennant winner. The game was at Yankee Stadium, making it extra meaningful to him even though the AL fell for the fourteenth time in the previous fifteen games, 7–5.

"I enjoyed every second of this," he said.

That's a good thing. Because by the next weekend he was back on the griddle, and by now he'd lost Gabe Paul as a defender. It didn't help the Yankees lost twice to the Brewers, including one where Sparky Lyle blew a 4–0 lead in the ninth. But the break allowed Steinbrenner and Paul to further discuss Martin's qualities as a manager. And the more they talked, the more they realized they had an underachieving team on their hands. A manager takes a fall for that.

Steinbrenner called a few trusted Yankees writers—"on background only!" he advised them—and alerted them Martin was on thin ice. He further advised he was going to ask Dick Howser to take over. The next day at Yankee Stadium, Martin was confronted with the rumors and said, "Our attendance is up, we're in a pennant race, and they're going to fire the manager?"

He was angry now.

"Where do these rumors start? Probably the people who are trying to fire me," he correctly surmised. "Where are they? I don't know."

There were 41,060 people at the stadium that day, and they gave Martin a forty-second ovation when he took out the lineup card. That certainly didn't hurt Martin's case. But the larger issue was that Howser turned down the job. He believed he had a bright future as a manager somewhere but had seen enough of Steinbrenner to know he should try to chase that dream elsewhere (for now, anyway).

One more time, Martin received a stay. Steinbrenner was angry that Martin seemed to play on the empathies of the writers and the sympathies of the fans.

"He's saying, 'They're making a martyr out of me,'" Steinbrenner railed when he confirmed Martin was still on the job. "The same thing was said in Minnesota and Detroit and Texas. Comes to a point you ask, how many times are we going to go through this? Maybe the guy is in the wrong business. I do get a little tired of the self-serving statements that are made and are less than accurate."

Not content to simply censure his manager, now he added an extra dollop of humiliation. Martin, Steinbrenner said, would keep his job as long as he followed to the letter a list of demands intended to keep him focused and prepared. Martin wasn't amused.

"You mean I can sleep until tomorrow?" he said. "It's like being on death row. You never get used to it. You never know when they're coming to get you."

MARTIN WAS CONVINCED they would get him in August. The Yankees lost four out of six to the Angels in Anaheim and the expansion Mariners in Seattle. They fell five games out of first. Worse: Martin's own captain was trying to sabotage the whole season. For eleven days, Munson kept showing up at the ballpark having let his beard grow. It was stubble at first. Then a five-o'clock shadow. And then something akin to a genuine beard, which was a direct violation of George Steinbrenner's sacrosanct appearance code. Writers started to ask about it. Martin said it's a free country, even in the employ of George M. Steinbrenner III.

"I like beards," Munson said coyly. "Billy doesn't mind. George . . . is the other way."

He laughed. But by the last day of the trip, everyone was tired and cranky. It was obvious Steinbrenner was going to say something at some point, and his ire probably wouldn't be directed at the hirsute captain but at the hair-trigger manager.

Munson told Martin: "I'm keeping the beard. I hope it doesn't get you into trouble."

Martin had to laugh: After all the other crap, he was going to get fired over personal hygiene?

And then, in an instant, all was well.

First, Munson shaved. Then Reggie Jackson became the cleanup hitter.

Steinbrenner pleaded with Martin for months to make that move. Martin resisted. At first it was out of loyalty to Chris Chambliss. Then it was to refute speculation that Steinbrenner was ordering Martin who to play and where to hit them. Lastly, it was out of either stubbornness or spite, probably a little bit of both. But the Yankees were five out with fifty-three games left to play. If the team had a finishing kick in it, this was the time.

Martin alerted a grateful Steinbrenner by using a horse term: "George, it's time to go to the whip."

By now, the Yankees saw how Jackson had continued to produce even amid the daily storms that gathered around him, and his teammates had actually grown to quietly admire him. They knew how much it killed him not to hit cleanup, yet no matter where Martin batted him—usually fifth or sixth—he kept hitting. At one point a few weeks earlier, at the Pfister Hotel in Milwaukee, Lou Piniella convinced Thurman Munson to take an elevator to the presidential suite, where Steinbrenner was quartered. Piniella had a father-son relationship with Steinbrenner; Munson's was more detached, but he was the captain, and Piniella convinced him to join him. Steinbrenner answered the door, puzzled.

"George," Piniella said, "you need to give Billy some room. You need to let him breathe. If he's under pressure every day, so are we, and we can't perform that way."

"Also," Munson said, "it's time for Reggie to start hitting cleanup."

Before the discussion could get much further it was interrupted by a loud knock on the door. Martin had been passing by, heard familiar voices coming out of the room, and suspected treason. It took a few minutes for Steinbrenner to convince Martin of his players' pure intentions, and it took a few weeks before Martin finally would write "Jackson" fourth on his lineup card.

The Yankees won that night. Jackson had two hits and an RBI. Across the season's final fifty-three, he was the most dangerous hitter in the sport: a .288 batting average, thirteen homers, forty-nine RBIs. The Yankees went

38–13 in the fifty-one games he played. They jumped into first place on August 23 and stayed there for the final forty games of the season, finishing at 100–62, two and a half games clear of the Orioles and Red Sox. The keystone moment came on the night of September 14, bottom of the ninth of a tied game with Boston. Munson led off with a single. Now Jackson stepped up against Reggie Cleveland, a tough righty. Maybe that's why Martin signaled for a bunt. In June Jackson likely would've fumed; now he squared and took ball one.

Martin took the bunt sign off the next pitch, and Jackson fouled it off.

Then Martin put the bunt back on.

"I don't even know the bunt sign," Jackson said later. "I had to read [third base coach] Dick Howser's lips to make sure."

Another ball. Martin took off the bunt for good, giving his piping-hot slugger license to swing away. Jackson worked the count to 3-and-2.

Cleveland threw. Jackson swung. Four hundred and thirty feet away, the ball landed in a mass of joyful arms, the 54,365 fans inside the stadium chanting his name. This time, there was no need to wonder which side of the dugout Jackson would return to because he was swallowed by his gleeful teammates and his giddy manager as soon as he crossed home plate, sealing a 2–0 win for the Yankees.

"Tonight, they got something back from me," he said. "I'm supposed to hit. With all the money I'm making and George Steinbrenner sticking his neck out, it's great to do well."

He was hitting cleanup, slugging every day, he had New York eating out of his hand; hell, even Billy Martin hugged him as they walked off the field together. Surely, the worst was behind him.

WINNING THE AL EAST again, it turned out, hadn't added an ounce of normalcy to what was lately being referred to as "the Bronx Zoo." Martin saw to that. Two days before Game 1 of the ALCS Martin decided it would be the perfect time to renegotiate his contract, using the newspapers as a courier to Steinbrenner.

"If we win everything," he said, "I think it's a must for George to come up with another contract. If he didn't, I'd have to seriously think about asking permission to talk with other clubs."

Steinbrenner blew a gasket.

"I would just tell him he's not indispensable," Steinbrenner said. "That this is just another example of his immaturity. Do you think if we hadn't finished in first place he would take the blame? Then he's crazy if he tries to take all the credit."

Before Game 5 Martin informed a bewildered Steinbrenner he was benching Reggie Jackson against Kansas City lefty Paul Splittorff.

Jesus.

And: damned if it didn't work out perfectly, too.

The Yankees trailed 3–1 heading into the eighth, and Royals Stadium was fixing to detonate, five outs away from Kansas City's first-ever World Series appearance. Willie Randolph singled. So did Lou Piniella. Splittorff was removed after pitching brilliantly for seven full innings. Doug Bird, a righty, came in. Cliff Johnson was due up.

Martin pointed to Jackson. He already had his helmet on.

Jackson took the high road before the game, when reporters asked about the benching. He credited Steinbrenner for reminding him that sometimes what's best for the star isn't best for the team and said, "It's Billy's team, and he knows what's best."

But he'd been dying inside for seven and a third innings.

Now he dug in, and he took a mighty whack from the heels, and as it soared into the sky Royals center fielder Amos Otis instinctively took a few steps back, assuming the trajectory would match the swing. It didn't. The ball dropped right in front of him, and Randolph, reading the ball perfectly, scooted home from second to cut the deficit to 3–2. In the ninth, the Yankees buried the Royals with three more runs. They won the game, 5–3, and the Yankees retreated to the clubhouse, where they emptied case after case of champagne in a raucous celebration. Steinbrenner, hit by stray bubbly, sought out a mirror on one side of the room, trying to comb his hair and restore a little dignity.

At once a bottle was poured directly above his head. The comb disappeared.

"That's for trying to fire me!" Billy Martin squealed.

Steinbrenner squinted through stinging eyes.

"What do you mean, *try*?" he asked.

Both men laughed. Both men hugged. And then Cliff Johnson and Mike Torrez approached with bottles in both hands and finished them off with a waterfall of Moët.

Jackson? He was giddy. Also a little salty.

"All season I had to hold it in here," he said, clutching his T-shirt. "I had to eat it in here. I can't explain it because I don't understand the magnitude of Reggie Jackson and the magnitude of the event. I *am* the situation."

Steinbrenner walked over, the two men embraced. The boss said, "I think this was a crucial thing for Reggie. When he came in tonight, he delivered a hit instead of sulking. That shows everyone else in New York he's a team man."

ONE OF THE most famous nicknames in baseball history began its life as an insult. The Yankees finished a workout at Dodger Stadium on October 13, the day before Game 3 of the World Series. The Yankees and Dodgers had split the first two games in New York, and on the field in LA Reggie Jackson and Billy Martin were clowning for the cameras, arms around each other as they shagged batting practice balls together. Jackson was smiling, but he was struggling: In the first two games he'd managed only a hit, a walk and a hit-by-pitch. His swing wasn't right. The Dodgers were throwing a lefty, Tommy John, in Game 3 and so speculation already began that Martin might revisit his strategy from Kansas City and sit Jackson.

Munson, grouchy among writers even in his brightest moods, snorted.

"It's just an overheated argument," Munson said. "Reggie's been struggling, and he would like to be doing better. Billy probably doesn't realize Reggie's Mr. October."

And thus was a forever moniker born out of a mud pit of sarcasm.

But Jackson really did heat up in the warmth of Los Angeles. He had three hits, including a double and a homer, as the Yankees won Games 3 and 4 to take a commanding 3–1 lead in the series; in Game 5, won by the Dodgers 10–4, he homered off Don Sutton with his final swing of the day, in the eighth inning.

Two days later New York City was amped with possibility. The Yankees needed one win in two games to deliver their twenty-first championship, their first in fifteen years. To celebrate, before the game, they engaged in—Gabe Paul's words—"one more round of bullshit for the road." In the pregame, George Steinbrenner forced Paul to speak to two hundred reporters to announce Billy Martin would manage the Yankees again in 1978 and in 1979. This might actually have been newsworthy if not for the fact that Martin was *already under contract* for 1978 and 1979.

It was one more headline for the early edition of the papers.

Reggie Jackson would deliver for the later editions.

He walked his first time up against Burt Hooton, on four pitches in the bottom of the second. In the fourth, after Munson led off with a single, Jackson clobbered the first pitch he saw—over the wall in right—giving the Yankees a 4–3 lead. Two innings later, facing Elias Sosa, he redirected another first pitch over that fence that had been so inviting to him as a kid back in 1968. It gave the Yankees a 7–3 lead, and the stadium began to rock on its foundation as 56,407 smelled a championship.

By the eighth, police officers on horses were already beginning to stage in the bullpens, hopeful to keep the on-field celebrating to a minimum. Knuckleballer Charlie Hough was on for the Dodgers, and Jackson led off, receiving a thunderous greeting as he stepped into the box. Hough's first pitch fluttered toward the plate. Jackson swung.

"Oh, what a blow!" Howard Cosell yelled on ABC TV, trying to be heard over the gathering din as the ball rocketed over the night, finally landing in the blacked-out "batter's eye" area in dead center. After making his triumphant tour of the bases the crowd pleaded for a curtain call, the first one since Roger Maris was summoned after hitting his sixty-first home run in 1961. Jackson took off his helmet, stretched both arms and mouthed, "Thank you!"

Afterward, Jackson found himself in Billy Martin's office with a couple dozen reporters and TV cameras.

"Anybody fights you, Skip," Jackson said, "he's got to fight both of us."

"And anybody who fights you," Martin said, "has got to fight the both of us."

> **INTERLUDE:** One of the reporters in that room, Dave Anderson of the *Times*, had taken Jackson out after a game in July, the two of them sitting at a quiet table at P.J. Clarke's on Third Avenue. Jackson was grossly unhappy and said so, begging to keep his thoughts off the record. Anderson agreed.
>
> "I'm still the straw that stirs the drink, not Munson, not anyone else," he'd said. "I should've signed with the Padres. Or the Dodgers. I'd be happy there. You know what Bobby Vinton sings, 'Color me gone'? Color me gone, man. I want to hit .300, hit thirty homers, fifty doubles, drive in ninety, be most valuable player in the World Series. And then go." When Anderson got home to New Jersey, he scribbled those quotes into a notebook and put it away. Three hours after Jackson's last home run, his fourth in four consecutive swings over two games, Anderson asked Jackson's permission to put those quotes on the record, so he could contrast what he was feeling in July with this moment. Jackson agreed.

George Steinbrenner had been a year off. It took him four years instead of three to restore the Yankees to full glory, and he was beaming as he rode at the head of the parade that New York threw the Yankees up the Canyon of Heroes the day after Game 6.

"This," he said, "is the happiest I've been since I got out of school."

In the clubhouse, after hugging Jackson, Steinbrenner reminded him of a bet they'd made back in the spring. Jackson guaranteed the Yankees would draw 2.2 million fans and if they did, Steinbrenner would have to sign over a foal from his thoroughbred stable. If they fell short, Jackson would owe Steinbrenner a Porsche. Though the Yankees became the first baseball team to ever draw two-million-plus both at home and on the road, and while they drew almost 100,000 more than in 1976—a lot of fannies in a lot of seats—they'd only reached 2,103,092. And a bet was a bet. But Steinbrenner couldn't disguise his delight.

"Forget it," he said. "This makes us even."

Jackson decided to show his gratitude another way. A few weeks later he received his World Series MVP trophy. Jackson got it inscribed: *To George, No. 1, from Reggie, No. 44.*

He presented it to Steinbrenner, who was moved to tears.

The boss's generosity also extended to his manager; he rewarded Martin with a $50,000 bonus. And said he'd be immediately getting back to work on 1978.

"Maybe there was a little too much turbulence this year," he said. "If there was, you have to blame me. We'll review it. Maybe we can do with a little less."

CHAPTER 12

Being a boss is the loneliest place in the world. When things go wrong, when there's criticism, who takes the heat? I do. You have to be thick-skinned in my position.
—GEORGE STEINBRENNER

Billy Martin finally had things exactly as he'd always wanted. Reggie Jackson was out of his hair, suspended five games for insubordination. In his absence, the 1978 Yankees were playing championship-level ball, and when they beat the White Sox 3–1 that afternoon at Comiskey Park it was their fifth straight win. The Red Sox, who'd spent most of the season's first three months playing at a 113-win pace, had cooled off, and the Yankees chopped four games off a fourteen-game lead.

"If they don't sense us coming," Martin said, "they're crazy."

Jackson returned from what Martin snidely called "his vacation" that day but hadn't gotten off the bench. Before, there was a crowd five-deep at his locker in the cramped visitor's clubhouse. Sportscaster Dick Schaap had patiently waited out the crowd.

"Reggie," Schaap began, "what was uppermost on your mind during your suspension?"

Jackson paused a beat, looking for the precise words.

"The magnitude," he said, "of me."

Jackson was uppermost on Martin's mind. After eighteen months of bickering and bitterness Jackson finally leaped across the line to insubordinate, to such an extent that even George Steinbrenner refused to defend him. When Martin said he'd wanted Jackson suspended, Steinbrenner agreed, then supported his manager. Now Jackson was back. Martin would need to arrange a working truce with Jackson even if he wished he could simply trade him, or release him, or ignore him.

Still: He was in a good mood. He had a few beers to take the edge off in the manager's office, and when he arrived at O'Hare and saw the team flight to Kansas City was delayed, he ducked into a bar. A few of the Yankees' beat writers spotted him there. They were about to sour his day.

"Reggie wouldn't apologize," he was told. "He said he didn't do anything wrong."

Martin's face darkened.

"Shut up, Reggie Jackson," he said. "We don't need more of your crap. We're winning without you."

The writers scribbled furiously.

One asked, "Are you sure you want this on the record?"

"Print it," Martin said, ordering another round.

The reporters scrambled to find pay phones so the smoking-hot quotes could be included in their first-edition stories. Not long after, the Yankees were summoned to the gate to board. Martin saw two of the writers, Murray Chass of the *Times* and Henry Hecht of the *Post*, and asked if they'd printed what he said. Chass nodded; Hecht, whose paper had afternoon deadlines, said he would as soon as the plane landed in Kansas City. Martin was pleased. He also seemed, all things considered, reasonably sober despite having quaffed five or six drinks.

"I've seen him drunk enough times to know the difference," Hecht would later say.

But Martin was still angry. And standing with the two reporters, he got angrier still.

And out it came.

"The two of them deserve each other," Martin said, and Hecht and

Chass heard enough of these rants to know whom he was referring to. And then came the kicker:

"One's a born liar, the other's convicted."

THINGS HAD ACTUALLY been relatively peaceful, certainly compared to the carnival act of 1977. There were few incidents to speak of in spring training. Reggie Jackson showed up a day late but with permission: He'd attended a press gathering at the Plaza Hotel introducing Standard Brands Confectionery's brand-new contribution to sweet-toothed bliss.

It was a dark patty made of chocolate, caramel and nuts—some wise guy cracked it looked like "kind of a Baby Ruth bar if Thurman Munson sat on it."

The man had said if he ever played in New York they'd name a candy bar after him and damned if he wasn't biting into a "Reggie!" bar right now.

"Good and gooey!" said the man whose swing-from-the-heels image was featured on the bright orange wrapper.

When Jackson drove into camp in his Rolls he was immediately greeted by razzing teammates, the first sign of clubhouse acceptance.

"When you unwrap a Reggie! bar," Catfish Hunter said, "it tells you how good it is."

There were some moments, sure, but the six weeks in Florida were practically sedate. The Yankees even beat the Mets both times they played, although the first time it took a six-run ninth-inning rally to do it, a few innings after Steinbrenner showed up in the dugout, in the middle of the game, the Yankees trailing 6–3, to offer a little Knute Rockne pep talk to the players, remind them they were champions of the world even if they damn sure didn't look like the champions of New York right now.

"George," Martin said, "get the fuck out of my dugout."

Opening Day at Yankee Stadium was glorious. After twelve years Roger Maris ended his exile from the Bronx as a favor to Steinbrenner, and together with Mickey Mantle they helped raise the first world championship pennant to grace the premises since 1962, when the M&M Boys were the heart of the lineup. The Yankees beat the White Sox, and Jackson hit a home run, and the crowd showered the field with the free Reggie! bars they'd been handed upon entering the yard.

"I guess they're better for throwin' than for tastin', eh, Reg?" Hunter asked.

Jackson laughed.

The Red Sox soared out of the starting gate in 1978. They won sixty-two of their first ninety, and on July 19 that meant a fourteen-game lead over the Yankees, languishing in fourth. The Yanks weren't playing all that differently than they had to a similar point in 1977, but they weren't chasing Secretariat then. Or, as Jackson said in a quiet Fenway Park clubhouse after a 9–2 loss in June, referring to the recent Triple Crown winner: "Not even Affirmed could catch the Red Sox right now."

George Steinbrenner was in a fix. He'd vowed to take a few steps back and let his baseball people handle his baseball team. Gabe Paul had fled to Cleveland when his friend Steve O'Neill bought the Indians and promised Paul tranquility and full control of baseball operations, neither of which Paul would ever truly get with the Yankees. He was sixty-seven and tired of the daily wars with Steinbrenner. His departure was amicable, although that would change when he sold his interest in the Yankees. Steinbrenner offered $60,000. Paul, as was his right, found a buyer for almost twice that, but he came with partners. Steinbrenner was trying to reduce the number of cooks in his kitchen. It got heated.

Steinbrenner: "Gabe was in business for forty years, twenty-five as a general manager, and did he ever win a pennant before? You think he made all those moves with this team by himself? You think all of a sudden he got brilliant?"

Paul: "The guy is a mental case, a liar, an egomaniac, and a crook, and that's a pretty good parlay." Paul sued Steinbrenner, then withdrew when Steinbrenner finally agreed to his price and bought back the share himself.

To replace Paul, Steinbrenner turned to an old friend from Cleveland, Al Rosen, a terrific player for Cleveland in the 1950s, winning the MVP in 1953. Rosen befriended Steinbrenner when both were pursuing Northeast

Ohio business interests in the 1960s. Steinbrenner vowed to stay in the background, empowering both Rosen *and* Billy Martin.

"We've built a strong organization here," Steinbrenner pledged. "And it will now be in their hands, not mine."

The Yankees kept dropping. A bunch of players were banged up—Thurman Munson, Willie Randolph, Bucky Dent. Goose Gossage got off to a dreadful start.

And the Sox just wouldn't lose.

By the time June melted into July, George Steinbrenner turned back into George Steinbrenner. One day, Rosen called Steinbrenner at his horse farm in Ocala, Florida, to brief him on the status of the team.

Steinbrenner told him, "It's your problem. I'm staying out of it. It's peaceful down here, and the horses don't talk back."

A day later he was at Fenway Park, sitting next to Rosen, frowning as he watched the Red Sox pummel his team. "They keep spitting the bit," he said, a horse racing term he would convert to baseball the rest of his days.

Then he did a drive-by on almost everyone else: "Only two guys, Nettles and Chambliss, are playing up to what's expected of them," he said.

One of the boss's targets heard that one loud and clear.

"Screw my boss," Jackson said. "I don't ridicule him if he fucks up a business deal, why would he ridicule me? If he doesn't think I'm doing the job, let him get someone else. John Doe didn't pay me three million dollars, George did."

It was starting again, the same vicious cycle. Rosen announced flatly: "Billy's situation is tenuous," but, as always, Steinbrenner feared a mass reprisal from Yankees fans. He told Martin his job was safe at least until the All-Star Game, which he would manage for the second straight year. The Sox kept pulling away. In mid-July, Steinbrenner made Martin a deal: Retire, and we'll honor your contract. You can stay with the organization, be an ambassador. You'll never have to worry about money; you'll have a job for life. Steinbrenner really was beginning to worry that

Martin—skinnier than usual, his face pale and gaunt—was at risk of a serious health issue.

"No way, George," he said. "My mother didn't raise no quitter."

Steinbrenner accepted Martin's rebuke. He also had three demands:

- Make Reggie Jackson (hitting .222 since mid-May) a full-time DH until he got his swing right.

- Make Thurman Munson the new right fielder, until Munson's chronically sore knees were right.

- Replace Munson with rookie catcher Mike Heath, who would go on to a fine fourteen-year career with five different clubs but who, to that moment, had played exactly five games and taken thirteen at bats as a big leaguer.

Martin, by now, knew the difference between a request and an order. He made the switch. Nobody was happy, and at the top of the list was Jackson, who only 269 days earlier had been the undisputed king of New York.

"Did that really happen?" he asked one day, wearily. "Did I dream that?"

For the first time, Jackson felt it wasn't just his manager who was trying to make him look bad. Now it was the owner, too, eager to criticize him but less willing to confront him, ducking his phone calls every day.

All of these things were pinballing inside him when he stepped to the plate in the bottom of the tenth on July 17, the Yankees knotted in a 5–5 tie with the Royals, desperate to avoid a series sweep and a ninth loss in eleven games. Thurman Munson led off with a single against Al Hrabosky. The crowd stirred; these were the moments Jackson was born to seize.

Out of habit, Jackson looked down at third base coach Dick Howser, and he thought he might be hallucinating: Howser flashed the bunt signal.

Immediately, Jackson recalled the previous September, when Martin twice gave him the sign, then taken it off, which allowed Jackson to clobber a game-winning homer off Boston's Reggie Cleveland. He figured that purged the notion of Jackson as a small-ball specialist for good. He was wrong.

Hrabosky threw a pitch high and tight. Ball one.

Like the previous year, Martin now wanted to take the bunt off. But Jackson never looked at Howser. Howser called time and walked toward him.

"The guy wants you to swing the bat," Howser said.

"I'm going to bunt," Jackson replied.

"Reggie, Billy wants you to swing away."

Jackson retreated to the plate. On the first pitch he offered, missed and ignored Howser again. Next pitch he fouled off. Again: no look toward Howser. In the dugout, you could have fried an egg on Martin's forehead. He frantically signaled to Howser. Howser relayed the signal to the side of Jackson's head. Jackson bunted again. This time he popped the ball up, and the catcher, Darrell Porter, caught it. Jackson stepped briskly off the field, other side of the dugout, and laid his glasses on the bench; he figured Martin might really take a swing at him this time. Martin sent coach Gene Michael to inform Jackson he was being removed from the game. The Yankees lost, 9–7; Cliff Johnson, hitting in Jackson's spot in the bottom of the eleventh, flied out to the warning track representing the tying run.

The aftermath was swift. Martin told Rosen and Steinbrenner he wanted to suspend Jackson.

"For how long?" Rosen asked.

"Forever," Martin replied.

They settled on five days.

"I can't win," Jackson said as he hustled off to a plane bound for California, where he'd spend his exile. "No matter what I do, I come off like a big, greedy moneymaker against a poor little streetfighter."

Steinbrenner's worst nightmares were all being realized. His team was in shambles. His franchise player was in what appeared to be a permanent stalemate with a hugely popular manager. Five years earlier he'd enjoyed himself mightily when the *Post* ran a mail-in poll asking who was to blame for the '73 Mets' troubles; now the *Post* did the same thing with the Yankees, only this time as a phone poll, asking readers who should go, Martin or Jackson—a landslide for Martin, who carried 60 percent of the vote.

He figured it couldn't get any worse.

And then, right around eight o'clock on the evening of July 23, his phone rang. He picked up. It was Henry Hecht.

"George," he said, "you're not going to believe what Billy said."

THE BOSS WAS so angry, he shook as he spoke and his voice quivered.

"It's hard to believe he said those things," George Steinbrenner said, before adding to Hecht: "My only question is, 'Was he drinking?'"

Hecht told him Martin had five or six over the course of a few hours but was fully coherent when he'd called him convicted, called Jackson a liar.

Now, there was no debate. Billy Martin had dredged up the one thing Steinbrenner tried mightily to keep locked in his attic, and it was there, in black and white, for close to two million readers to see, with a few million to follow once the other papers and the wire services picked it up. Martin had to go. Even people who loathed their bosses would have to understand: *You can't push it* this *far*.

Steinbrenner knew something else, too.

The Yankees had played six home games since Rosen had declared Martin's situation tenuous. There'd been 157,601 people at those games. And every one—every one—had stood on their feet when Martin brought the lineup card to the umpires. Every time, Billy Martin, man of the people, doffed his hat, waved, milked the moment. Steinbrenner could already see the *Post* running another of its infernal polls, this time him versus Martin.

> **INTERLUDE:** And, sure enough, the *Post* did just that, and to no one's surprise Martin received a 99-percent approval rating from the paper's readers. The sports editor, Jerry Lisker, demanded a recount. And he was right; that number was off. "It's more like 99.3," he was told.

Rosen was sent to Kansas City to encourage Martin to resign instead of being fired for a fourth time in nine years.

"In view of the past twenty-four hours, it was inevitable," Rosen said. "As president of the Yankees, I could not allow a man to make the statements that were made."

Not long after, Martin appeared on the balcony of the Crown Center Hotel—a few steps away from where he'd alerted Steinbrenner that he was benching Reggie Jackson from Game 5 of the ALCS the previous year. Reporters cornered him.

"I don't want to hurt this team's chances for the pennant with this undue publicity," Martin said. "The team has a shot at the pennant, and I hope they win it. I owe it to my health and my mental well-being to resign. At the same time I'm sorry about these things that were written about George Steinbrenner. He does not deserve them nor"—he paused here, staring daggers at Chass and Hecht, to whom he was brazenly lying—"did I say them."

Martin's voice began to break, his tears hidden only by a dark pair of eyeglasses.

"I would like to thank the Yankee management, the press, the news media, my coaches, my players, and most of all . . ."

Now he was weeping.

"The fans . . ."

He was led away from the scrum by a Kansas City friend, Bob Brown, and by his old Yankees teammate Phil Rizzuto, now a Yankees broadcaster, who wrapped an arm around his broken friend.

"I thought the bottom of the world had dropped out watching him make that statement and break down," Rizzuto said later. "I was really afraid he was going to have a heart attack. The Yankees were his whole life."

It was a sad—borderline pathetic—scene.

And yet, twelve hundred miles away, watching all of this unfold in his Tampa office, George Steinbrenner somehow didn't see a shattered man but instead one seeking some manner of peace. Maybe he was just seeing what he wanted to see. Nevertheless, once Martin was out, once Bob Lemon (a

Hall of Fame pitcher and former Rosen teammate in Cleveland) was chosen to replace him, Steinbrenner softened, his anger dissolved.

"We have never worked better together than we have the last three weeks," Steinbrenner said. "The Chicago thing, I was shocked. You could have knocked me over.

"His apologies over the recent incident are accepted with no further comment necessary. I think Billy knows of our concern for the well-being of his family and himself."

Steinbrenner had another idea gurgling in his imagination, one that was so absurd that nobody could possibly see it coming.

AND ONCE IT happened, it was still hard to believe.

But there Billy Martin was, trotting onto the field, a smile as wide as the Grand Concourse, 46,711 fans aiming with great intent to crack Yankee Stadium's fifty-five-year-old foundation with their voices and their stomping feet. Bob Sheppard, in his twenty-eighth year as the Yankees' voice-of-God public address announcer, had just made a staggering pronouncement near the end of the Yankees' Old-Timers' Day ceremonies.

"The Yankees agreed to a contract today that Bob Lemon continue managing the Yankees through the 1978 and 1979 seasons . . ."

The booing was boisterous, same as it had been when Lemon was introduced a few minutes earlier as part of the roster of Old-Timer invitees; when Rosen was introduced it was even louder and more vicious because he was essentially serving as George Steinbrenner's surrogate, so he received all of the reflected venom.

"Your attention to the rest of the announcement," Sheppard insisted. "In 1980, Bob Lemon will become the general manager of the Yankees. . . ."

The booing intensified.

"And the Yankees would like to announce . . . that the manager for the 1980 Yankees and hopefully for many years after that will be number one, Billy Martin. . . ."

Suddenly it was a Led Zeppelin show at Yankee Stadium.

Back in the Yankees' clubhouse, the mood was a bit different. That's where Reggie Jackson was sitting when he heard thunder bleed through the walls, as he watched it all unfold on a small black-and-white TV. In that moment, Jackson later said, he had the distinct feeling that the entirety of New York City was flipping him the finger.

"I'm bewildered by this," he said, and figured it was now "fifty-fifty I'll finish the season somewhere else." He did manage a thin smile.

"I'll have to ask my parents if I was born a liar," he said.

Martin and Steinbrenner appeared at a joint press conference, and Martin looked ten years younger than he'd seemed just five days earlier.

"When I quit the other day, I called George and told him how I apologized for what I said. I did say it. I don't know why I said it. I was angered at the time. I had no reason to say it, and I feel very bad about it, and I am not afraid to admit as much. The challenge is there for me. I'm going to do whatever I can for George. He deserves it."

Said Steinbrenner: "I am undoubtedly going to get ripped a little for being soft, maybe, or being stupid. But there are times in life when you should be tough and times when you have to be rigid and times you have to understand and have compassion."

(Lemon and Rosen agreed if Steinbrenner had *really* wanted to be compassionate he could've maybe made the announcement *before* they'd both almost been publicly executed by 46,711 people.)

Steinbrenner beamed through the entire briefing. He had his man back. He'd thrown one of the largest olive branches ever at his fans. He'd have to repair his relationship with Jackson, because there wasn't a chance in the world he was trading his meal ticket, but he believed he could do that.

And hell: If his team could get a few breaks they might scare the Red Sox yet. . . .

GEORGE STEINBRENNER HATED the idea. He wanted Billy Martin Bubble Wrapped until 1980, wanted him to go off to the sticks of Colorado, fish to his heart's content, heal his liver, gain some weight, disappear for a while. But Martin had been coming to games, sitting in Steinbrenner's box. The writers were bugging Mickey Morabito, Steinbrenner's PR chief, about getting some time with him before he went into witness protection. Morabito kept pitching Steinbrenner directly, knowing Rosen would sooner keep Martin locked in a basement than allow him to chat with the scribes. Steinbrenner relented.

With a caveat.

"If anything goes wrong," he told Morabito, "it's your ass."

It was a handful of reporters that arrived at a small Italian restaurant not far from the stadium on the afternoon of August 9. They found Martin cheerful and bronzed and spry, already polishing off his first Miller Lite. Lunch was served: spaghetti, sausages, ravioli, steak pizzaiola. But those were mere appetizers once Martin started talking.

"I probably made the comment about George," he said. "I don't know why, I say a lot of things just to be cute. But I was mad at the other guy. He set me off. He won't admit he made a mistake, denies he deliberately disobeyed an order."

That was batting practice.

"When Reggie got his money I read the comments, 'I got no problem, George and I are eye-to-eye on everything.' But he forgot one man. Billy Martin."

The writers looked at Morabito, whose face was ashen.

"If Reggie is here in 1980, he can expect to be treated like one of twenty-five players. If he abuses the privilege, he'll have his hand spanked again. I never looked at him like he was a superstar because he never showed he was a superstar. I never put him above Chris Chambliss, Thurman Munson, Willie Randolph, Mickey Rivers, Roy White or Lou Piniella. At times I put Fred Stanley [a lifetime .216 hitter with ten home runs in a fourteen-year career] higher than him. . . ."

Morabito, on the verge of passing out, quickly ended lunch, hustled Martin back to his Lincoln Continental Diamond Jubilee Mark V with the New York license plate YANKEES on the front, then headed back to the office. He knocked on Steinbrenner's door.

"How'd it go?" he asked.

"Not good," Morabito said. He debriefed him. And wondered if he should duck.

"If this Reggie shit hits the papers tomorrow," Steinbrenner said, "you're fired."

Morabito knew he was a goner. Except just past midnight, after the Yankees had rallied for five runs in the bottom of the ninth to stun the Brewers, 8–7, one of the writers called Morabito in his office.

"See you when I see you," the writer said. "We just went on strike."

There would be no *Times*, no *Post*, no *Daily News* the next morning to deliver Morabito's head to Steinbrenner. The Jersey papers, the other suburban papers (even *Newsday*, which didn't belong to the city guild) would have every word, but this was 1978: Martin could've called Steinbrenner a serial killer and he wouldn't have cared as long as those words were limited to the boondocks. The *city* papers were what mattered. And, miracle of miracles, now there *were* no city papers.

Mickey Morabito was spared.

So were the Yankees, remarkably enough.

FROM AUGUST 10 on, the Yankees went 37–13. They chased the Red Sox, caught them one memorable weekend in early September in Fenway Park, and watched the Sox win their final eight games, setting up a one-shot playoff on Monday, October 2, at Fenway. The Yankees won that, 5–4, thanks in large measure to one of the most famous home runs in Yankees history, a seventh-inning blast by Bucky Dent that turned a 2–0 deficit into a 3–2 lead.

The whole thing happened in blissful quiet: no newspapers, no backpage bloodlettings. Oh, Reggie piped up once, after Martin's remarks got back to him. He still hadn't gotten much satisfaction from Steinbrenner. The fans at Yankee Stadium routinely booed him. In Game 2 of the World Series in Los Angeles, the Yankees trailing by a run with two outs and men on first and second, Jackson battled Dodgers rookie Bob Welch for nine pitches. On 3-and-2, with the runners in motion (as runners automatically do when there's a full count and two outs), Jackson swung through a Welch heater and raged angrily in the box, approaching third base coach Howser with what looked like malicious intent before Bob Lemon interceded. Jackson wheeled and shoved the fifty-eight-year-old Lemon, screamed at him for starting the runners, which he called "distracting"; Lemon shoved him back, screamed, "Base runners have been running on full counts since the time of Abner Fuckin' Doubleday!"

Of course, with a certain other manager, this would have been like shooting Archduke Franz Ferdinand, a prelude to war. Lemon just shrugged it off. "That ain't no fight," he said. "I've had worse fights with my wife."

The Yankees rallied back to win the World Series after spotting the Dodgers the first two games. Jackson hit .391 and had two more homers, but it was Dent, enjoying the month of his life, who won the series MVP, hitting .417.

Lemon was the center of another intramural tangle when word escaped that a bloc of Yankees players wanted to vote him only half a playoff share. Cooler heads prevailed in that one, and Lemon was voted his full share of more than $31,000 once the Yankees finished off the Dodgers. Back home, it was Reggie Jackson (who'd further solidified his status as "Mr. October") who got the last word—literally—when he took to the microphone at city hall after the Yankees' second straight tour up the Canyon of Heroes. Steinbrenner, who believed *he* should be the prime spokesman, stalked redfaced to the back of the stage, where Al Rosen was sitting.

"Sometimes," he said, "it's easy to see why Billy was pissed all the time."

CHAPTER 13

Mr. Steinbrenner and Thurman were very close. George was grooming Thurman to be a manager someday. The question I always had was how many times George would have fired Thurman and rehired Billy.
—DIANA MUNSON

Through all the craziness, they'd never actually come to blows, any of them. Billy Martin and Reggie Jackson had come close. Thurman Munson, heart of hearts, would've loved nothing more than to take a swing at Jackson, and there were times when Jackson wouldn't have minded rearranging the faces of fifteen or twenty of his teammates. There was an endless parade of verbal jousting, mostly on the back pages, some of it in the back of planes or buses. There was some awkward sniping. But nobody had ever thrown a punch before.

Then, on April 19, 1979, the Yankees lost a game to the Orioles, 6–3. Jim Palmer went the distance for Baltimore; Luis Tiant, one of George Steinbrenner's prized free agent acquisitions the previous winter, got hammered. Afterward, the Yankees were picking at dinner plates, engaging in quintessential clubhouse bullshitting before the reporters came in. Reggie Jackson, seated between Goose Gossage and Cliff Johnson (neither had played in the game), was something of the master of ceremonies.

"Hey, Cliff," he asked the hulking six-foot-four backup catcher, "how'd you hit Goose when the two of you played in the National League?"

Gossage, himself built like a linebacker, answered instead: "He couldn't hit what he couldn't see."

The room broke up laughing, even Johnson, who threw a rolled-up piece of tape at Gossage. But a few minutes later, as Gossage emerged from the shower room, Johnson approached again.

"Did you mean what you said before?" he asked.

Gossage laughed him off. But Johnson wasn't playing around. There were pushes. There were shoves. There were soft punches. Then harder ones. Then Gossage felt a shooting pain in his right thumb, which was attached to his three-million-dollar right arm.

Jackson—amazed and more than a little relieved that something like this had happened and didn't involve him—said, "The Big Guy with the boats ain't gonna like this."

The Big Guy with the boats was, in fact, enraged when he heard about it. Steinbrenner called Bob Lemon, asked him, "How could you let this happen?" and Lemon reminded Steinbrenner that he managed a baseball team, not a kindergarten.

"I had a few fights in my day," Lemon said.

"Were you smart enough not to hit anyone with your right hand?" he was asked.

"If you're smart," he said, taking a long drag on a cigarette, "you wouldn't be fighting in the first place."

Steinbrenner wanted to fine both his players, withhold their paychecks for as long as Gossage was out. That meant close to $100,000 for Gossage, and Steinbrenner knew that would never fly with the union, but it reflected just how incensed he was. Winning had become an addiction, and now the Yankees would have to play two months without their top relief pitcher.

"Terrible judgment," Steinbrenner said. "Like two juvenile delinquents."

The Yankees actually won the next day to move into first place in the East, the only day they would spend there all year. For the first time,

Steinbrenner was learning that reaching the summit in baseball was a whole different assignment than staying there.

THERE WAS ACTUALLY a name for it now. Bowie Kuhn used it privately, whenever he began to fret about escalating player salaries and the shift in the balance of power in his sport. Newspaper columnists used it constantly. Fans of teams other than the Yankees used it as a certain path toward prosperity for their franchises of choice.

The word was "Steinbrennerfication."

It was especially felt in New York City, where after Steinbrenner's rapid run to the pinnacle no team executive in any sport would ever again be able to sell five-year rebuilding plans. Executives would grumble that the people who wanted them to behave as Steinbrenner had conveniently forgot the chaff that went along with all the wheat in a true Steinbrennerfication—the egos, the headaches, the indulgences—but those laments, more and more, were being aired either at farewell press conferences or in angry phone calls with one another.

"People ask me all the time, 'Why can't you be more like George Steinbrenner?'" Wellington Mara said in 2000. "And I tell them, 'I'm exactly like George Steinbrenner.' We both act like fools when we lose, and the people who work for me don't want to answer the phone the day after. I just keep my feeling private. George likes to play newspaper folks one off the other. Different strokes."

Mara, whose family bought into the NFL in 1925 and who co-owned the Giants for forty-six years beginning in 1959, had a close look at how his fans—many of whom were also Yankees fans—steadily lost patience with the old ways of team building. By 1978 the Giants had gone fifteen years without making the playoffs. In early December, a group of fans organized a protest. In the parking lot they burned their tickets for that day's Giants–Rams game; in the sky they rented a small plane that carried a message for Mara: 15 YEARS OF LOUSY FOOTBALL—WE'VE HAD ENOUGH.

One of the ringleaders, a fan named Ron Freiman, summed up their feelings:

"They need a different philosophy here," Freiman said. "They need to spend money. Call up George Steinbrenner and ask him how he does it."

In a compelling irony, it was Michael Burke who most closely and publicly tried to emulate—even outdo—Steinbrenner. Burke, now running Madison Square Garden, engaged in a yearslong struggle to put the financial muscle of the Garden and New York City into reloading the Knicks, chasing an endless list of big-ticket players to restore the basketball team to prominence. Kareem Abdul-Jabbar. George McGinnis. Wilt Chamberlain. Julius Erving. Bill Walton. He whiffed on all of them. And the big-ticket players he did get—Bob McAdoo, Spencer Haywood—were so unpopular they virtually emptied the Garden by themselves.

"A lot of swings," was how Burke described it in 1981, "and a lot of misses."

INTERLUDE: A few weeks later Burke would leave the Garden and retire to Ireland. Before he did he divested himself of his Yankees stock. At his final partners meeting he and Steinbrenner parted warmly.

Burke stood and said, "George's performance as general partner has been unique, an unmatched formula for success."

And Steinbrenner rose and reminded his partners, "Never forget that Mike laid the foundation here—the rebuilt team, the new stadium. If it weren't for Mike, none of us would be here."

Nobody suffered by comparison more than the Mets, though. By 1979 they drew 788,905 fans to Shea, just nine years after they'd set a New York City record with more than 2.7 million. M. Donald Grant, the team's chairman and chief decision-maker, had proudly and defiantly declared he would take the extreme opposite path Steinbrenner did at the dawn of free agency, opting for in-house development and patience (when in truth neither he nor Joan Payson's heirs wanted to spend any money to actually acquire good baseball players). To the end, to the day he was removed from power, he believed he was right. A year later the family sold the Mets to a group headed by publishing scion Nelson Doubleday, and for the first time,

Steinbrenner would finally have a rival within his own city willing to match him dollar-for-dollar.

But it would take them a while—seven years, in fact—to finally catch up. By then, Steinbrennerfication was rampant in sports. For better and for worse.

IN THEORY IT sounded wonderful. Steinbrenner looked at his roster, saw not only the surplus of six-figure contracts but also realized that, necessarily, most of those players had already passed thirty. In 2025 the prevailing school of thought is to maximize players in their twenties, when they have, in most cases, failed to cash in on their talent. Steinbrenner was actually well ahead of the curve on that. He would still use the checkbook when needed—Luis Tiant and Tommy John came for a cool $5 million between them, and he dabbled with free agent Pete Rose, toyed with trading for the Twins' Rod Carew—but he was determined to find alternate ways to build sustainable rosters.

"I think he meant it, too, he said it enough," Gene Michael laughed one day in 2014. "But, you know, it wasn't ever going to be his way to sit idly by and comfortably watch an eighteen-year-old kid blossom over the course of six years."

Michael spent that 1979 season leading the Yankees Triple-A team in Columbus to the International League title. Steinbrenner had big plans for him. For now, he didn't much care for what he was seeing at all at Yankee Stadium. The Yankees dipped into fourth place in late April and there they sat in the middle of June. Reggie Jackson hurt his leg. Ron Guidry lost his bulletproof vest and volunteered to go to the bullpen when Gossage was hurt, and Lemon complied.

"My teammates picked me up last year," he said. "I wouldn't have won twenty-five without them."

Steinbrenner praised Guidry's selflessness. Others had differing opinions.

"You're a fuckin' idiot," Thurman Munson, the captain, told him. "They'll screw you over this. You watch."

As the weeks trudged along, one thing was certain: The team lacked energy. They played without fire. And it wasn't just Steinbrenner who noticed it, and sadly it was clear what the issue was. Just one month after riding shotgun with Steinbrenner at the Yankees' victory parade, Bob Lemon's world came shattering down around him: His youngest son, Jerry, was killed in a car crash.

"When he died," Lemon admitted that spring, "a part of me died with him."

Lemon's stern-but-quiet personality had been the perfect remedy for the Yankees in 1978. Now it was seen as a hindrance. He was drinking more. He was laughing less. It didn't take a lot of clairvoyance to see Steinbrenner's brain was stirring.

Billy Martin, the sequel, awaited.

But Martin hadn't exactly spent his time away in a monastery. He'd opened a western-wear store in Manhattan, and when someone asked what he'd recommend Reggie Jackson to buy if he ever stepped into the store, Martin couldn't help himself.

"Something in shark would fit," he said. "Don't you think?"

A few days later, asked again about Jackson, Martin said, "I don't like pitchers coming into my office every day and saying, 'I'm not going to pitch if he plays right field.'" When the Yankees pitchers were contacted none of them backed that one up.

But Martin's biggest problem was his oldest problem.

In November Martin flew to Reno, Nevada, to help out an old friend, Bill Musselman. If there was a basketball-coach soulmate to Martin, it was Musselman: a brilliant strategist whose anger and inner demons always sabotaged him. They'd met in Minneapolis when Musselman was the head coach at the University of Minnesota (one of his players was a forward named Dave Winfield). By 1979, after American Basketball Association stops in San Diego and Norfolk, Musselman was coaching the Reno Bighorns of the Western Basketball Association. He invited Martin to a game to sit courtside. After, Martin retreated to a bar near the entrance of the Bighorns' arena, Centennial Coliseum.

A twenty-five-year-old reporter for the *Reno Evening Gazette* named Ray Hagar approached Martin there, asked if he could talk a few minutes. Martin was annoyed at first, and also a few drinks in, but after Hagar said his boss was on his ass to get a story from him, Martin—not exactly unfamiliar with a demanding boss—relented.

"OK, kid," he said. "I'll give you the interview."

Hagar nervously asked about Sparky Lyle being traded that day. Martin hadn't heard anything about that, so his mood immediately turned foul, knowing Steinbrenner had dealt away one of his favorites without even a heads-up.

Then Hagar asked, "Will you be able to get along with Reggie Jackson . . . ?"

"Reggie Jackson," Martin said, his voice rising, "will have to play on my terms, not his. I've got one set of rules for guys. There are no superstars in my eyes."

Hagar read from a recent Associated Press story that quoted Martin saying Jackson "lacked true Yankee spirit and would never be a true Yankee."

"Did you hear me say that?" Martin said, his face reddening.

"No," Hagar said. "It's in this AP story . . ."

And that was that. Martin demanded Hagar's notebook, lunged for it, said, "You writers are always looking to stir me up" and started spitting out the names of Murray Chass and Henry Hecht and Phil Pepe. Hagar refused to give up the notes.

Martin punched him in the face. Hagar's glasses flew off his face. His body sagged.

Some people jumped in, tried to calm Martin, thought they had.

Then Martin hit him with another.

Hagar went to the hospital, and when he was patched up he pressed charges for battery. He later filed civil charges, too. He had a cut lip, three chipped teeth and a blackened right eye. That image of his battered face was in every newspaper in America by morning, including the *Tampa Tribune*. George Steinbrenner spit out his coffee.

Then he called Al Rosen.

"Billy has to be found innocent of the criminal charges," he said. "And if he pays any settlement money in the civil suit, that's the same thing as losing."

Rosen called Eddie Sapir. Sapir called Martin.

"Judge," Martin said, "I slugged the guy. I didn't mean to, and I wish I didn't. But how are we going to get away with saying it never happened?"

Sapir, a municipal court judge and New Orleans city councilman for many years, knew his way around the judicial system every bit as well as his friend knew when to call for a suicide squeeze. He convinced the Bighorns to cover Hagar's medical costs, so Hagar abandoned the civil suit. He then persuaded Hagar to drop criminal charges in exchange for an apology—which Martin never made, settling instead for an all-smiles-and-handshakes photo on May 24 that also made all the papers.

Steinbrenner saw that one, too. He was satisfied.

Three weeks later Steinbrenner flew to Dallas. On Friday, June 15, he had a two-hour breakfast with Lemon and at the end delivered his verdict: "I think it's time for a change."

Lemon, ever the good soldier, said, "OK." And he agreed to manage through the weekend, even as the lamest of ducks. Rosen, Lemon's close friend of thirty years, wasn't nearly as understanding. Within a few weeks he tendered his resignation, saying: "When an employee can't get along with the boss, then the employee has to leave."

That night, word began to ricochet through the Yankees' clubhouse, and the news kneecapped Reggie Jackson. He'd begged Steinbrenner to, at the least, give him fair warning when he planned on bringing Martin back. He'd heard nothing. Still on the disabled list with a bad leg, he spotted Steinbrenner sitting beside the Yankees' dugout at Arlington Stadium.

"How can you do this?" he asked. "You know how I feel about that man."

"You'll play for who I tell you to play for," Steinbrenner said, and then he saw the hurt in Jackson's eyes, and he leaned closer.

"You'd better get your head screwed on straight, boy."

In the moment, Jackson was focused on just how miserable his life was about to become. Steinbrenner had revised Martin's contract, given him two years at $120,000 per, finally making him a six-figure manager. And as the season dragged, something else about that last sentence, *the last word of that last sentence*, ate at him, too. Reggie Jackson wasn't going to forget that.

SOMETIMES, A FOURTH-PLACE club is just a fourth-place club. The 1979 Yankees were a fourth-place club for Bob Lemon, they remained a fourth-place club under Billy Martin, they would've been a fourth-place club under Miller Huggins or Joe McCarthy or Casey Stengel. By August the Yankees were fourteen games out again, but the '79 Orioles weren't the '78 Red Sox. Even a three-game sweep of the White Sox in early August didn't move the needle in the AL East, although it did bring a moment of hilarity and a few more moments of hysteria when a woman visited the Yankees team bus and dropped her shorts. Invited on to the team bus, she repeated the trick a few more times, and volunteered to flash her top, Mardi Gras–style, too. A Chicago reporter dutifully reported this but erroneously added that a few Yankees volunteered to autograph her, er, assets. Steinbrenner flipped until photographic evidence emerged that the woman had left the bus uninked.

By the time that story made the rounds in late August, everyone could use the laugh.

Because the phone call that arrived in George Steinbrenner's office late in the afternoon of August 2 shattered everyone.

"I must talk to Mr. Steinbrenner!" the frantic voice on the other end of the line said. "It's a matter of life and death!"

Steinbrenner took the call. That's how he learned that Thurman Munson had died in a plane crash at the Akron-Canton Airport, practicing takeoffs and landings in his new Cessna Citation jet.

"Oh my God," Steinbrenner gasped, his eyes watering. "Oh no."

For three years, Munson had all but begged Steinbrenner to trade him to Cleveland, an hour north of Canton, which is where his wife and three young children lived full-time. Not long after the bitter back-and-forth with Steinbrenner after the Jackson signing, Munson began to think about buying his own plane to commute home on off-days. He'd bought his first one, a Beechcraft Duke, in the summer of 1978 and mastered it quickly;

he'd recently upgraded to the Cessna, a heavier, more difficult aircraft for inexperienced pilots to conquer.

"Every opportunity I had, I tried to talk him out of the jet," Steinbrenner said later. "Time and time again, in the presence of many people, I said: 'Sell it, you don't need a jet. Being a jet pilot is a full-time business. You couldn't do it [and also be a baseball player]. It's just too demanding and too exacting an operation.'"

But Munson was unmoved. Before the '78 season he threatened he'd retire if he didn't get traded; when Steinbrenner called his bluff he insisted on an amendment to his contract allowing him to fly on off-days. Steinbrenner reluctantly agreed. Ironically, in the days before the crash, Steinbrenner called his old friend Gabe Paul in Cleveland to gauge his interest in acquiring Munson.

"Of course," Paul said. "Let's see what we can put together."

Instead, they gathered for a funeral on the afternoon of Monday, August 6, a celebration of Munson's life that filled a civic center. The Friday before, the Yankees held an emotional ceremony honoring Munson before a game with the Orioles, leaving home plate unoccupied during the national anthem while Reggie Jackson openly and unabashedly wept in right field. Now, at the funeral, his best friend, Bobby Murcer—whom Steinbrenner had reacquired from the Cubs a few weeks earlier—delivered a eulogy so powerful that George Steinbrenner, publicly stoic till then, began to cry: "He should be remembered as a man who followed the basic principles in life," Murcer said. "He lived. He led. He loved."

Hours later, insisting on playing that night to honor his friend, Murcer drove in all five runs—including a two-run walk-off double—to help the Yankees to a 5–4 win over the Orioles on national TV. In the dugout, he fell into the arms of Lou Piniella, who'd also eulogized Munson that day. Later, on the verge of exhaustion, he told a throng of newsmen: "That's for Thurman."

Murcer, though, returned to a team that looked and felt much like the ones he'd played on from 1969 to 1974, hopelessly out of a playoff race and playing out the string. Of course, those earlier teams didn't have a centrifugal force like Reggie Jackson at their core. Not only was Jackson having his finest season as a Yankee to date—.297 average, twenty-nine homers, eighty-nine RBIs despite missing thirty-one games—he also found a certain tranquility playing under Billy Martin, who actually said late in the year that Jackson was a pleasure to manage.

But there was another scab to be picked.

This one by the owner.

Jackson was still fuming about the lecture Steinbrenner gave him back in June, and he was still angry at being called "boy." This began a weeklong game of back-page Ping-Pong.

"George slurred me racially that day," Jackson said in early September. "He emphasized 'boy.'"

Steinbrenner had been stung when Jackson hinted at racism two years earlier, and he was even angrier now. "I'm no racist," he said. "I've never uttered a racial slur in my life. One word doesn't make a man racist. Reggie knows that, and what's more he knows *me*. Look at what a man does in his life."

He vowed to trade Jackson once and for all, and to a losing team, any losing team.

Jackson retorted that he had an amendment in his contact forbidding him from being traded to a team not of his choice.

Steinbrenner spitefully refused to allow Jackson to talk at a ceremony honoring the retiring Catfish Hunter, Jackson's teammate for ten seasons, with whom he'd won five World Series. Steinbrenner also hinted Jackson was in financial peril.

Jackson laughed at that one.

"What does he want me to do, shine his shoes and wash his boats?"

Steinbrenner answered back: Billy Martin, he said, had started to demand Jackson be traded because he was disruptive in the clubhouse and abusive of fans near the dugout who heckled him.

"I never said that," Martin insisted. "I *never* said that."

Steinbrenner visited Martin in his office. When it was over, Martin said, "If you pay me $500,000 a year, I'll kiss your butt in Times Square. It's an honor to be a Yankee."

A day later Steinbrenner said, "I pity Reggie. I do."

To which Jackson said, "I'll never trust a word that man says ever again."

And yet, after all of this, in the season's final week, Jackson said he wanted to stay with the Yankees, stay in New York, stay and play for Martin and Steinbrenner and all the emotional taxes and surcharges that went along with it.

"George has to win this battle, he has to have the last word, and when he gets his back up he does something like this," he said. "But this is where I want to be. I hope it just ends right here."

For Jackson, for now, it did.

For Martin?

Well, Steinbrenner for one believed Martin was officially transformed. In early October he said, "Billy's more relaxed now. He's cooperative. He's interested in a lot of things about the welfare of the team he wasn't before and that makes me feel good. I don't care what he says, he's a different Billy Martin."

It would take less than a month for Steinbrenner to find out just how wrong he was.

THIS TIME, YOU could make a reasonable case Martin did what almost any man in a saloon would have done—if only these kinds of incidents hadn't seemed to follow him around from saloons to taverns to bars and grills from coast to coast in four different decades.

This time, it was a man named Joseph W. Cooper, a fifty-two-year-old resident of Lincolnshire, Illinois, who happened to take the seat next to Billy Martin at the Chez Colette, the restaurant on the ground floor of L'Hotel de France in Bloomington, Minnesota. Martin was there with his friend Howard Wong, a local restaurateur who had also been with Martin in Reno eleven months earlier. Martin was a couple of drinks into a nightcap. So was Cooper. Martin was not an aloof barfly; he regularly chatted up his fellow patrons enjoying the gargle.

So it was that Cooper and Martin started talking baseball.

"I think Dick Williams did a hell of a job this year with Montreal," Cooper said. "And Earl Weaver, he did a great job with the Orioles, too."

It's possible Cooper could have picked a more flammable subject than this, but not likely. Martin intensely disliked Weaver, who he thought was able to get away with intimidating umpires freely and being called "colorful" while he, Martin, was regularly roasted for being out of control, often called "maniac" or "lunatic." And Williams? Jesus, how many times had Steinbrenner held Dick Williams over his head? And Williams had never—not once—resisted Steinbrenner's offers when he was between jobs to come and take in a few ball games Martin was managing.

"Well, Weaver's an asshole and Williams is an asshole," Martin told Cooper. "And you're an asshole for bringing them up."

Cooper shrugged.

"What do you know about baseball anyway?" Martin asked. "What do you do for a living?"

"I'm a salesman," Cooper said.

"What do you sell?"

"Marshmallows."

Martin burst out laughing.

"Everyone laughs when I tell them," Cooper said later.

Now Martin peeled off five hundred-dollar bills and slapped them on the bar.

"Here's five hundred dollars to your penny that I can knock you on your ass," Martin said, and by this point Cooper admitted he was a bit in the cups himself.

"The time comes when pride comes into focus," Cooper explained. "I put a penny on his five hundred dollars and said, 'Let's go.'"

They made it as far as an archway separating the bar and the lobby when, Cooper's version, Martin wheeled and slugged him in the mouth.

"I assume all of his fights have been sucker punches," Cooper said.

Cooper, like Martin, wanted to forget it. He never went to the hospital. He never went to the police. He didn't go to the press because he knew that would mean trouble for Martin. The bad news for Martin was that a security guard who didn't witness the fight felt compelled to alert the Bloomington Police. Someone in the police department tipped off a local newspaper. And suddenly Billy Martin was back in the news again. His first instinct was to deny; he actually said Cooper slipped and fell on his own. When he did that's when Cooper cleared his throat in an effort to clear his own name. But even before that, Steinbrenner knew better than to believe Martin's absurd side of the story. Not again. Never again. He called Eddie Sapir.

"Eddie, who the hell is Howard Wong," Steinbrenner asked him, "and why is he always around for these fights?"

Sapir laughed, but Steinbrenner wasn't in the mood.

"Eddie, that guy in Minnesota fell and hit a marble floor. *The manager of the New York Yankees probably put him there!* The guy could've hit his head and been killed! What would we do then? I can't keep going through this."

Steinbrenner told Sapir he was firing Martin, even before he began investigating the incident. "If I don't do it, Bowie [Kuhn] might beat me to it. He's sick of his shit, too."

Sapir would raise an appropriate fuss when Steinbrenner announced the firing, although thirty-five years later he would admit to Martin biographer Bill Pennington: "The fact was, Billy was in trouble. And, you know, we couldn't turn that around."

Billy Martin's second—and presumably final—tenure with the Yankees lasted ninety-five games, and he'd won fifty-five of them. Steinbrenner quickly called Dick Howser, the former third base coach who'd spent 1979 coaching at his alma mater, Florida State, and hired him to replace Martin. He elevated Gene Michael to general manager. He'd spent October watching the Orioles, Angels, Pirates and Reds, and he didn't like it one bit, so he busied himself to make sure there would be another trip up the Canyon of Heroes, and if someone had told George Steinbrenner that it would be seventeen years before that would happen he'd have screamed you out of his office.

CHAPTER 14

I'm not a guy who ever wanted to see my name in lights. I've seen people like that. When things go bad, those kinds of guys are the first to get hurt.
—DICK HOWSER

Most of what people saw, and heard, was anecdotal and, hell, it was kind of funny, too. From the moment George Steinbrenner assumed control of the Yankees he referred to himself as The Boss, capital "T," capital "B." Sparky Lyle won the Cy Young Award? There'd be a bouquet of roses for his wife signed *The Boss*. Catfish Hunter pitched a shutout? There'd be a magnum of champagne awaiting him on his locker stool, with a card that said *Congrats! The Boss*. It used to infuriate Billy Martin when he'd receive a memorandum on just about anything—player decorum, second-guessing a hit-and-run, the incompetence of various umpires across the American League—signed simply *The Boss*.

But it was on August 17, 1979, when Mike Lupica, writing in the *Daily News*, first referred to him as "Boss Steinbrenner," and almost immediately that became the appellation of choice for just about every newspaper save for the *Times*. Lupica borrowed the term from Mike Royko, whose bestselling book on Chicago mayor Richard J. Daley had been titled *Boss* and who often referred to him in his *Chicago Daily News* columns as "Boss Daley." Headline writers for the next thirty-one years borrowed from Lupica, "Boss" being a lot more headline-friendly than "Steinbrenner."

BOSS RAPS BILLY

JAX BLASTS BOSS

BOSS FIRES STICK

The occasional story from a former secretary, or an ex-PR man—by 1980 he was on his fourth one; he went through them like pitching coaches—would surface about how hard a boss he was, how irrational he could be based upon the whims of his day. But it wasn't until the night of October 9, 1980, when the rest of the world got an uncomfortably up-close look at it. The Yankees won 103 games under rookie manager Dick Howser, then dropped Game 1 of the American League Championship Series to the Royals in Kansas City and were trailing in the eighth of Game 2, 3–2, with two outs and Willie Randolph on first. As Bob Watson stepped to the plate, the ABC TV cameras pointed to an intense observer sitting among Yankees executives and the wives of players and coaches.

"There's a man," play-by-play man Al Michaels said, "who won't be happy until he has a team that goes 162–0."

"He just wants to win," said one of Michaels's analysts, a guy moonlighting from his day job in Oakland, California, by the name of Billy Martin.

"Don't we all?" asked Jim Palmer, third man in the booth.

Royals pitcher Dennis Leonard got a couple of quick strikes on Watson, but then Watson yanked an inside pitch down the left field line. Willie Wilson retrieved the ball as Randolph—who'd tripped running from first—roared around the base path as the tying run. When Wilson overthrew shortstop U. L. Washington, the cutoff man, it looked like Randolph would score easily.

That's sure what Mike Ferraro, coaching third base, thought.

Ferraro waved Randolph home, though Randolph had already made up his own mind to do that. What neither man anticipated was that the Royals had third baseman George Brett purposefully backing up Washington. That's not a common play, but for the Royals it was part of their defensive plan. Brett wheeled and threw to Darrell Porter behind the plate. Randolph was beaten by two steps, tried a hard slide to jostle the ball free. It didn't work. The Yankees lost 3–2, and the next night, back in New York, the Royals finished up a sweep when Brett hit an upper-deck three-run shot, late, off Goose Gossage.

A few seconds after home plate umpire Joe Brinkman punched out Randolph, ABC went with a full-screen replay of Steinbrenner reacting to the play, the Boss wearing approximately the same expression as if he'd been T-boned on the Cross Bronx Expressway. He flailed his arms. He pulled his blue blazer on and stormed toward the aisle.

What the camera didn't catch was Steinbrenner staring down Ferraro's wife as he walked past her, sneering, "Your husband just cost us the damn season!"

Although if there was any doubt how Steinbrenner was feeling, he was plenty helpful filling in the blanks after the game was over.

"My guys didn't lose this one," he steamed. "We got taken out of this one."

It probably didn't help Steinbrenner's mood that Martin, settling into his new job as a baseball Walter Cronkite, said on ABC: "Mike was right sending him home. Every time a guy makes a great play people blame the third base coach. It's the hardest job in baseball."

Steinbrenner was unmoved.

"He's been doing this all year," he said. "I never wanted him at third, I thought he belonged somewhere else. I told that to Dick Howser over and over again."

In some ways, this was simply the capstone to a slow but steady sea change for Steinbrenner. He no longer had Martin as a daily foil in 1980. Jackson, playing like he'd been released from a prison camp, enjoyed the best season of his career, hitting .300 for the first time, forty-one homers, finishing second in the MVP vote. On August 11 he blasted his four hundredth career home run, only the twentieth player to reach that mark at that point; there wasn't much for Steinbrenner to find fault with there, either.

He'd found other targets. When Graig Nettles got off to a slow start (and before he was shelved the final two months with a frightening case of hepatitis), Steinbrenner began to poke that bear regularly, harping on Nettles's weight, insistent the third baseman had ballooned past where a proud professional athlete should (which was odd; Nettles was never going to be confused with Chicken Stanley but he hardly looked like Don Zimmer, either). Steinbrenner made a mistake picking a verbal fight with Nettles, though, who was one of the most quick-witted players in baseball. After his hepatitis diagnosis, for instance, when he was told his Yankees teammates would need to be inoculated, he said, "I feel bad for Louie [Tiant, who by this late stage of his career was tipping the scales around 240-plus]; they're gonna need a harpoon for him."

With Steinbrenner, Nettles waited, sharpening his needle. One day, as he was emerging from the clubhouse shower, he saw a crowd gathered around his locker; Steinbrenner had set up shop there, just under Nettles's nameplate, and was busy filling notebooks and tape recorders. And, well, overfilling his own trousers, truth be told.

"Goddamn, Steinbrenner's right," Graig said. "Nettles really *is* a fat piece of shit."

But it was Nettles's backup, a pleasant professional hitter named Eric Soderholm, who presented evidence that not all the Boss's barbs so easily and innocently rolled off the backs of his high-priced employees. Soderholm missed a season to a blown-out knee, won Comeback Player of the Year after that, and when he arrived to the 1980 Yankees he started mashing left-handed pitching as the Yankees built a big lead; he was hitting .351 in mid-July. But as the Yankees came back to the pack, Soderholm fell to earth. And one day, he picked up a newspaper and saw this:

"I'm not saying Soderholm is a bad ballplayer. He just hasn't been doing the job for us. If we are going to win it, we have to get production out of Eric Soderholm, who is hitting just terribly. He's left more men on base than I care to count."

At the time of Steinbrenner's impromptu public job evaluation, Soderholm was at a respectable .285. He did not handle the scolding well, tumbling into a three-week tailspin. He actually sought out the help of a therapist to deal with the matter and talked about that freely, a remarkable admission for a 1980 baseball clubhouse.

"I've been worrying myself into the nuthouse," he admitted a few weeks later, after his two-RBI single gave the Yankees a critical walk-off win against Cleveland. "I would've been a lot better off if [Steinbrenner] just called me into his office and privately asked me what the matter was."

That wasn't the Steinbrenner way. In later years, as veteran players watched the impact Steinbrenner's harangues would cause newcomers, they'd invent a word for it: The player had been "George-ed." But they also had an alternate term for this plague: "Soderholm's disease." In 1981, Larry Milbourne was playing his first season for the Yankees after seven quiet, happy years in Houston and Seattle. In a game against the Indians, Milbourne made two errors, leading to a loss. Afterward, knowing he was about to become a Steinbrenner dartboard, Milbourne started muttering to no one in particular.

"What's it going to be like? Does he do it to your face? Do I have to wait until the papers to read what he's going to say? Is there a chance he wasn't watching the game?"

Nettles and Bucky Dent happened upon this mid-stream, listened carefully, like Beatles fans searching for Paul-is-dead clues by slowly spinning a record backward. Then, at the end, they turned to each other, reached the same diagnosis.

"Soderholm's disease," they agreed.

THE 1980 SEASON had, for the most part, been a dream ride. Dick Howser was an instant success. The Yankees assumed first place for good on May 2, stayed there for the season's final 157 days, their lead peaking at nine and a half on July 17. Jackson was over the moon with the new manager.

"Honestly," he said on July 31, after hitting his twenty-ninth homer of the year, "it feels like someone opened a door and a few windows and let the air in here for a change."

Billy Martin wasn't looming over his shoulder anymore. On February 21, he signed on to become manager for his hometown Oakland Athletics, trading in one opinionated owner for another when he agreed to work for Charlie Finley. The only holdup had been Finley's insistence that Steinbrenner cover about a third of Martin's salary and Steinbrenner balked. A friend of Steinbrenner's explained, "He may dislike Billy. But he hates Finley a *lot* more." Adding to the intrigue, when Martin's Tigers and Finley's A's met in the 1972 AL playoffs they'd engaged in a war of words in which Martin had said this of Finley: "He's a liar. I hate liars with a passion. *He's a born liar.*"

You really can't make any of this up.

Martin, for his part, did what he usually did when inheriting an expired franchise. In 1979 the hollowed-out A's had gone 54–108 just five years after winning their third straight championship. They'd drawn only 306,763 people to cavernous Oakland-Alameda Coliseum and Finley nearly moved the team to Denver. His fellow owners blocked that move, one final fuck-you-for-the-road to Finley, who promptly announced he'd sell the team once and for all. Then he hired Martin. And soon "Billy Ball" became a fever in Northern California. The 1980 A's won eighty-three games. They more than doubled their attendance, to 842,259. And Martin signed on for $300,000 to write a tell-all book called *Number 1*.

He even buried the hatchet with Steinbrenner—temporarily. In early June, with the Yankees winning three out of four in Oakland, Steinbrenner sent a telegram to Martin congratulating him for turning things around with the A's and noting that Oakland would be in New York on June 21— Old-Timers' Day, which was now becoming regularly integrated into the Martin/Yankees narrative. Steinbrenner invited Martin not only to take part in the ceremony but also to wear his Yankees uniform. Martin had sworn after his last firing, "I'll never wear the pinstripes the rest of my life," and as a final kick of dirt said, "George is sick, I really believe that." But Steinbrenner knew his quarry too well to believe he'd show up for the ceremony in the garish green-and-yellow vestments of the A's.

Martin wore the pinstripes, and he jogged out to an extended ovation.

Before that Martin and Steinbrenner would reprise their Miller Lite glory days by filming a Pepto-Bismol commercial Friday morning, Martin chiding that he got his part down in just three takes while "George needed fifty-seven of them."

(This time the punch line had Martin holding a bottle of the pink stomach-relief goop and saying, "I'll take a swig of this!" Steinbrenner emerges from a crowd and says, "Billy, can you use a spoon?" and Martin exclaims, "Oh noooo!")

A few weeks later, excerpts of Martin's book would end the era of good feeling. Though Martin mostly spared Jackson his wrath, he infuriated Steinbrenner with several accusations, notably that Steinbrenner had bugged Martin's telephones at Yankee Stadium to monitor his conversations. Steinbrenner flatly denied it and threatened to sue; Martin agreed to omit that and several other shaky allegations from future printings, but that seemed, for all the world, to be the denouement of this odd and tempestuous relationship.

Silly world.

HOWSER QUICKLY SHOWED how different he was from Martin. Jackson strolled into camp two days late, and in past years that would've been kindling for a five-alarm fire; Howser simply smiled when asked about it, said dryly, "That's for Gene Michael and George Steinbrenner to worry about." When Jackson finally arrived they met privately; Howser fined Jackson same as he would anyone else and left it at that.

His players tested Howser periodically. Luis Tiant, angry at being removed from a game, threw the ball down before Howser could take it from him, then heaved his glove into the stands. Howser stalked Tiant into the clubhouse, gave him a private earful and fined him $500. Tiant apologized. More wounding to Howser was the behavior of Bobby Murcer and Lou Piniella, two of his closest friends, who publicly sniped at Howser for lack of playing time. Murcer's betrayal especially stung; Howser had a large picture of their families hanging prominently in his office. One angry night in Anaheim Murcer cut him deep: "You're talking to the wrong guy about Howser. Better ask someone who likes him."

Howser shook that off publicly, but privately the men never repaired their relationship (Piniella, for his part, did apologize a few years later and asked Howser's forgiveness, which he granted). Howser knew if Murcer was willing to share that much with the sportswriters, the reports he was delivering his pal in the owner's box must be even more devastating. He was right.

In years past, when Steinbrenner entangled himself in back-page black ops, he did so mostly to prevent his regular sparring partners, Martin and Jackson, from getting the last word in against him and partly—he would admit later—for "the spectacle of it. It kept people talking about the Yankees every day of the year." And while the sentiments might have been harsh, in the end they were mostly harmless. Mostly.

In 1980 Steinbrenner first revealed a less-agreeable public trait that would tail him the rest of his days. The Orioles began to peck away at the Yankees' lead, reducing it to five as the teams began a critical eight-games-in-eleven-days stretch on August 8. Steinbrenner was already uncomfortable with Howser's quiet strength, his unwillingness to humiliate struggling players or engage his frustrated boss. In advance of the Orioles series Howser said, "I never believed the standings when we were nine ahead of the Orioles. I knew they were a damn good team."

That did not play well with Steinbrenner, whose mood was doubly foul because of Earl Weaver, the Orioles' fiery manager, whose tactics Steinbrenner publicly deplored but whose managerial acumen (and gleeful willingness to slug it out with umpires) he privately cheered. Envied, even. Then the Orioles went out and swept the Yankees at Yankee Stadium, took three out of five in Baltimore. The Orioles were within two and a half games as both teams headed west for identical trips through Seattle, Anaheim and Oakland.

"I expect to go home from this road trip in first place," Sammy Stewart, an Orioles relief pitcher, said. "The Yankees have George Steinbrenner getting on them now, and I think maybe they're looking over their shoulder."

He was right on both counts. The Yankees were now girding for a legit pennant race.

The owner was officially spooked. By the time the Yankees reached Seattle Howser was greeted by this observation from on high: "As a fan, I have a right to question Howser's strategy. He knows his job rests on the bottom line and the bottom line is winning. You've got to give Earl Weaver all the credit. He's a wizard, and our guy's a rookie manager. I wouldn't invite Weaver to Christmas dinner, but you've got to give the devil his due."

Howser's players read that. They also saw how Howser responded. He gathered the writers around him. He pointed to Maury Wills, another first-year manager, who was leading the Mariners, and he complimented Wills. Then, smiling thinly, he added this:

"You know, now that I'm competing against a rookie manager I know it's very important for me to win."

The smile widened just a hair.

The Yankees won twenty-eight of their final thirty-seven games even though Weaver tried to trash-talk his way into Steinbrenner's head in September.

"The 1964 Phillies," he said one day, referring to a team that famously blew a six-and-a-half-game lead with twelve games to go, "those poor bastards have been remembered forever. Hell, it's time somebody fucked up to get them off the hook. I hear George Steinbrenner is building a boat and calling it 'the *Titanic*.'"

Weaver would have to settle for one hundred wins and second place. Steinbrenner's team would play in the ALCS for the fourth time in five years.

IN MANY WAYS, 1980 was the pinnacle of George Steinbrenner's ascendance. The Yankees would set an American League attendance record with 2,627,417 paying customers. Early on, those fans would be treated to the start of a tradition that would last, uninterrupted, well into the next century.

One day in June Steinbrenner walked from his press-level office at Yankee Stadium into the main stadium. Steinbrenner had become quite the aficionado of the city's finest nightspots—not just 21 for him anymore—and this included "Le Club," a trendy discotheque located on East Fifty-Fifth Street, steps from the FDR Drive. Steinbrenner wanted to expand the stadium's musical selections from the standard between-innings organ stylings of Eddie Layton to some more contemporary-sounding numbers. A disc jockey at Le Club made a few suggestions, none of which moved the needle in Steinbrenner's imagination.

Then the DJ sent a tape of a song he'd been playing regularly from one of Steinbrenner's all-time favorites, Frank Sinatra. Steinbrenner heard "New York, New York" plenty, because it was impossible to own a radio that spring and not hear it.

But he was about to hear it a whole different way.

"CBS didn't leave a lot of memorable legacies," says author Marty Appel, Steinbrenner's one-time PR chief. "But they did install a state-of-the-art public-address system in 1967, using their very best technicians to enhance the sound. That was still in use in 1980 and still gave you chills."

Now an electrician hooked "New York, New York" into that system and hit Play.

It was thrilling.

Then, for the first time, Steinbrenner paid attention to the lyrics—and for a kid from Cleveland who dreamed his whole life of making it in New York, you can only imagine the impact of hearing Sinatra sing, "These little-town blues . . . are melting away . . ."

But that wasn't what sold him.

This sold him:

"A number one . . . top of the list . . ."

"That's us!" Steinbrenner exclaimed in the empty ballpark. *"That's the YANKEES!"*

Immediately—as in the very next game, a date lost to the fog of history but somewhere awfully close to June 16 or so, the start of a thirteen-game home stand—the final out of every game was greeted with the cymbals, with *bob-bop-BOP-ba-bop*, with "Start spreadin' the news . . ."

Forty-five years (and counting) later, an essential part of the rhythm of a Yankees game is walking out of the ballpark to the Chairman crooning about his vagabond shoes, longing to stray (although, early in 2025, it was announced that the Yankees would play the song only after wins; after losses they'd use an array, with an early candidate another Sinatra standard: "That's Life").

There was much joy on 161st Street and River Avenue.

But then, come October, Steinbrenner found himself congratulating Royals owner Ewing Kauffman and pretending he was happy about it. At the dawn of free agency Kauffman told the *Sporting News*: "When I talk about ego and pleasure in owning a major-league club, I'd say the Yankees situation is a little one-sided. George takes all the ego trips."

Steinbrenner went home to Tampa to sulk and think. He remembered the little shots Howser took at him. He decided he wanted Don Zimmer to coach third base and send Ferraro off to baseball Siberia. He began compiling a list of requirements Dick Howser—winner of 103 games his first time out of the chute—would have to agree to in order to come back for the second year of a three-year, $300,000 deal. Howser figured maybe he'd earned a little more trust, maybe even a bit of respect.

"As a manager," he said, "I should be able to say who's going to coach and who's not going to coach."

That was as good as writing a resignation note.

"Howser, I can't figure out," the Boss fumed. "I am upset. My staff and I are in agreement: We are not quite ready for Dick Howser to start running the New York Yankees totally yet. Please quote me on that, too."

Actually, Steinbrenner's most trusted staffer and the man who, theoretically, *was* running the Yankees, Gene Michael, was immediately trying to do damage control. If Steinbrenner hadn't noticed how completely the Yankees and their fans had fallen for Howser, Michael certainly did. He'd seen Howser grow into the job. Michael and Howser were teammates on the Yankees in 1968, and they'd both been targeted early as future manager/GM candidates, Howser by Ralph Houk (who'd made him his third base coach at age thirty-three, in 1969) and Michael by Steinbrenner.

INTERLUDE: Although it started as something of an odd partnership. One day early in the 1973 season, the Yankees were playing the Rangers in Arlington. During infield practice Michael—skinny as an exclamation point his whole life, thus nicknamed "Stick"—suddenly tossed his glove and let out a piercing shriek. Michael was deathly afraid of bugs and critters and thought he felt something in his glove. He had. It was a hot dog.

As Houk reported to an angry Steinbrenner later: "Someone put a weenie in there."

Steinbrenner didn't find anything about this funny and tried in vain to identify the weenie wielder. "You've heard of omerta, the code of silence gagsters use?"

Michael said years later, laughing, "That was Yankees omerta."

Michael understood if he wasn't able to calm Steinbrenner, his own days as GM—his dream job—would be numbered because Steinbrenner would expect him, Michael, to succeed Howser. Michael believed he was far better suited to the GM gig than the skipper's office (as would be proven correct). He wasn't able to calm Steinbrenner; if anything when he saw how much support Howser was accumulating it hardened him further. On November 21, Steinbrenner invited a handpicked crew of fourteen newsmen to his office at Yankee Stadium. Gene Michael was there. So was Dick Howser.

"Dick has decided," Steinbrenner said, "that he will not be returning to the Yankees next year. I should say: not returning to the Yankees as manager."

Michael was quiet. So was Howser. Steinbrenner insisted Howser could have returned if he'd wanted, without restrictions. He was selling that version hard.

Someone asked Howser why he didn't want to stay. Howser waited a few seconds to answer, then said: "I have to be cautious here, but the other thing 'popped up.'"

Howser stared straight ahead. He was asked if he was satisfied that he could've returned without conditions.

"I'd rather not comment on that," he said quietly.

"Were you fired, Dick?" he was asked directly.

"I'm not going to comment on that," he said.

"I didn't fire the man!" Steinbrenner insisted.

That didn't play, not to the cynical newsmen in the room, not to Yankees fans at large. Howser was still due $200,000. He wasn't going to jeopardize that. He took the Fifth, then took a flight to Tallahassee, where he knew there would be other suitors calling soon. Midway through the 1981 season he was hired by Kansas City. In 1985, he led the Royals to their first-ever world championship. It would take a while, but Steinbrenner would ultimately agree with the way everyone else took the news of November 21, 1980.

"I've made two awful mistakes in my time," Steinbrenner said. "One was letting Dick Howser go."

The other was just around the corner.

CHAPTER 15

Hell, when you're a shipbuilder nobody pays any attention to you. But when you own the New York Yankees . . . I'm a ham.
—GEORGE STEINBRENNER

The ham was on his way, and he was pissed. Nobody inside the Yankees' clubhouse this Saturday evening, October 10, 1981, was especially pleased. They'd had a half dozen opportunities to beat the Milwaukee Brewers, send them home from this first-ever AL East Division Series (ALDS) (necessitated by a two-month strike in the middle of the summer), send the Yankees to the ALCS against their old pal, Billy Martin, whose remarkable Oakland A's had already secured a place there.

But the Yankees couldn't get a clutch hit when they needed one.

Sure enough, word was, the Man was on his way.

"Shut the door!" screamed Reggie Jackson, who knew better than anyone what pearls of wisdom George Steinbrenner was capable of sharing if he wasn't happy with his baseball team. "And don't say a word."

Minutes later, in walked Steinbrenner, red-faced and spitting mad. As he blew through reporters in the corridor he carpet-bombed his team, specifically catcher Rick Cerone, who'd taken too far a turn off first base after what should have been a clutch single in the seventh, a misstep that forced Larry Milbourne at third to try to scamper home. He didn't make it. Then, with two on and two outs in the ninth, Rollie Fingers struck out Cerone. The Yankees lost, 2–1.

"There are guys here who are on trial, and Rick Cerone is one of them," Steinbrenner fumed. "Stupid baserunning. Now we'll see who some of these guys are and who deserves to be in the playoffs and if some of the guys here deserve to be Yankees."

Once in front of his team, Steinbrenner revved his engine into overdrive.

"Tomorrow we will find out what kind of men you are," Steinbrenner said. "Now you've got to show *me*."

Most of the players simply sat with heads bowed, trying like hell not to laugh at Steinbrenner's latest locker room screed. Manager Bob Lemon (we'll get to *that* shortly) was so mad he worked his way through a cigarette in about three drags.

But Cerone didn't find any of this even remotely funny. He'd been tasked with the unenviable job of replacing the sainted Thurman Munson, and after the Yankees brought him in from Toronto he'd responded with a terrific year in 1980, hitting .277 with career highs of fourteen homers and eighty-five RBIs. He was durable with movie-star good looks, and he instantly became a fan favorite. Just as quickly, he fell into disfavor with Steinbrenner because he'd taken the Boss to arbitration and won a $450,000 contract, about two hundred grand more than Munson had ever made in a year. He also broke his thumb in spring training '81, costing himself a month, but Cerone, a tough kid from Newark, came back two weeks early as much to spite Steinbrenner as anything else.

Still, Steinbrenner remained livid Cerone fought him over his salary, and took a measure of odd delight that Cerone scuffled through a difficult 1981 season. A few weeks before the playoffs began Steinbrenner said, "Cerone's gotten a big head. Suddenly he's Mr. New York, the Italian Stallion. He's going to disco joints. I have a way of bringing guys down to size, and I'll bring him down."

Now, in the Yankees' clubhouse, Steinbrenner said, "You haven't lost anything yet."

And that was about all Cerone could take.

"Fuck you, George, you fat son of a bitch," he snapped. "You never played the game. You don't know what the fuck you're talking about."

The room went instantly silent.

"Most of us wanted to give Rick a standing ovation," one of the players in that room would recall years later.

Steinbrenner shot back.

"And you won't be playing this game as a Yankee next year, either!" he snapped. And then stalked away.

By now, there were no barriers in place to keep Steinbrenner from his most basic instincts. Gabe Paul was in Cleveland. Al Rosen was in Houston, running the Astros (taking great delight when he signed free agent pitcher Don Sutton when Steinbrenner thought he had Sutton locked up). He was even about to part ways with Lou Saban, a well-traveled football coach whom Steinbrenner installed as team president mostly as a thank-you for hiring Steinbrenner on his coaching staff at Northwestern back in 1955.

"By '81 or so," Gene Michael would say, "George was pretty much unfiltered."

His players were tired of it. Yankees fans were becoming less and less enamored with it. But there was a problem:

In *his* mind, it worked.

Take the day after his friendly exchange with Cerone. The Yankees trailed the Brewers 2–0 in the fourth when Moose Haas tried to sneak a fastball by Reggie Jackson, and instead Jackson launched one that hit a few hands in the upper deck and then fell into the lower stands in right.

More tellingly, later that inning Cerone drove in a run with a groundout, and three innings later crushed a game-clinching home run off Jim Slaton. Cerone was feted with a curtain call by fans who saw him as something of a new version of Billy Martin, standing up to the Man. And later, the Boss interrupted a crowded interview session around his locker to shake Cerone's hand.

"When people put fear in you," Cerone said, "sometimes you play beyond yourself."

Jackson, a veteran of so many Steinbrenner battles, watched that exchange and couldn't help but smile.

"Jaws roams the city," he said. "You must adjust or be consumed."

THE METS HAD occupied precious little of Steinbrenner's thoughts. Yes, he'd blow up if the Yankees lost in spring training games beamed back to New York, but once the regular season began the Mets would dutifully take their position in or near last place in the National League East. By the end of the seventies, they'd traded away most of their good players and refused to pursue replacements in free agency. The ghost town formerly known as Shea Stadium was redubbed "Grant's Tomb" after chairman M. Donald Grant.

But on January 24, 1980, a group led by publishing scion Nelson Doubleday bought the Mets for $21 million. Doubleday and his chief partner, an old high school teammate of Sandy Koufax's named Fred Wilpon, declared they would bring the Mets back to relevance by building the team up from the dust, pursuing star players and selling them on all the possibilities of New York City—essentially borrowing Steinbrenner's blueprint for rehabilitating the Yankees. Steinbrenner knew Doubleday socially, and he welcomed him sportingly to the exclusive club of twenty-six major-league baseball owners.

But he also realized the stakes were different now.

The clues were subtle at first. When the schedule for the 1980 season was released, there was a notable absence. The Mayor's Trophy Game had started as a round-robin charity exhibition between the Yankees, Dodgers and Giants in 1944 and later became the one time the Yankees and Mets appeared on the field together during the season. That was the toughest ticket in town most summers. As recently as 1972 it drew 52,308 people to Yankee Stadium, more than all but one of the Yankees' regular-season games that year. By 1979 the crowds were smaller and the players even more disinterested. In his book on the 1978 season, *The Bronx Zoo*, Sparky Lyle alleged that Graig Nettles purposely threw a ball ten feet over Chris Chambliss's head in the eleventh inning in an attempt to expedite the end of a game that would drag into the thirteenth and drew fewer than ten thousand fans to Yankee Stadium (Nettles vehemently denies that to this day).

The game was designed to raise money for amateur baseball in New York, and the Mets were still eager to play. But Mets' GM Frank Cashen said, "I have been told that the Mets were notified by George Steinbrenner prior to the start of the current season that the Yankees no longer wished to play the Mayor's Trophy Game." Or any other. In 1981, the Mets proposed a home-and-home series after the two-month strike ended; the Yankees said no, again, choosing instead to fly the rookie-league team from Bradenton, Florida, to serve as the Yankees' warm-up for relaunching the season.

Things turned nasty in spring training 1980. The Mets hired Madison Avenue legend Jerry Della Femina to put together an advertising campaign for their new-look team and Della Femina delivered beautifully with a new slogan: "The Magic Is Back." As he was promoting it Della Femina—an admitted lifelong Yankees fanatic—took it a step further by taking shots at the Yankees.

"This is a town where we had to settle for Reggie Jackson," Della Femina said. "Let's face it, if the Mets were where they were in 1969, Reggie Jackson would have trouble getting arrested in this town. We're looking to Mets with star quality, like Lee Mazzilli. We believe he's the big glamorous player in this town, a handsome Bucky Dent who can hit and doesn't do fur commercials."

Bowie Kuhn was just as mad about that as Steinbrenner and fined the Mets $5,000—which Della Femina offered to pay, so the Mets took it out of his fee. But Steinbrenner stepped into the cage to take his swings, too.

"If talk produced pennants and World Series, these guys would be champions before the season even starts," Steinbrenner said. "For reasons unknown to me the Mets management has gone out of its way to snipe at the Yankees. Perhaps in desperation."

It was pointed out that neither Doubleday, Wilpon nor Cashen had done any of the sniping, and had in fact denounced Della Femina, but Steinbrenner put his hand up and said, "When you hire an ad agency, it speaks for management."

The Mets weren't good enough to challenge the Yankees on the field yet, so Steinbrenner settled for victories where he could. He set his sights on the biggest fish of the free agency class of 1980, Dave Winfield, an outfielder for the San Diego Padres. Steinbrenner had been enamored with Winfield for years, and as early as 1978 Winfield welcomed the idea of playing in New York, asking, "Do you think I'm an unknown star? I think so. We're never on TV. The Yankees are on TV all the time."

Two years later, with Winfield about to play out his option in San Diego, Steinbrenner pondered trading Ron Guidry—who himself would soon be due for a steep raise—to the Padres for Winfield, straight up; that never worked out. Later that summer, with the Padres visiting Shea Stadium, Winfield insisted he would love to play in Gotham: "I can live anywhere. I'm not a country boy."

He took great care to not single out a team because by now it was clear the Mets were eager to shed their frugal ways, and if Winfield picked the Mets he would immediately become their biggest star. So Yankees versus Mets it was. And the Mets, as promised, were aggressive.

"I believe what I hear, and what I hear is that the Mets offered eight years and $1.2 million per," Steinbrenner said early in December, lounging on the patio of Tampa Downs, the racetrack he owned, waiting to make his bid. "That's formidable. But we also will offer something the Mets can't right now: We can offer a winner."

In the end, what Steinbrenner also offered was to extend the Mets' deal by two years, and to add a cost-of-living escalator clause that would ultimately land the two men in court a few years later. But in the moment, facing his first real piggy-bank-versus-piggy-bank battle with the Mets, Steinbrenner got his man.

And that got Reggie Jackson thinking.

Jackson spent the offseason talking about wanting to end his career as a Yankee. Steinbrenner agreed that should happen. But he also never formally made Jackson an offer. Not in the offseason. Not in spring training, to which Jackson (as usual) showed up late, angering (as usual) the man with the boats. Not in the early portion of the season, when Jackson started slowly, hampered by a leg injury. Jackson took note of the Mets' willingness to go eyeball-to-eyeball with Steinbrenner.

One day he asked, "How many people did the Mets draw the other day?"

"Two thousand, something like that," he was told.

"I could have batting practice on a Monday afternoon in the parking lot, wearing my street clothes, and I'd draw two thousand people."

The season began. No contract. Jackson couldn't get on track. On June 11, he pinch-hit late in a 3–2 loss to the White Sox. He walked. His batting average was .199. It would stay there—a buck-ninety-nine—for fifty-nine days as baseball players walked out after those games of June 11. Jackson still didn't have a contract.

"I'm going to the beach," he announced. "I'm not thinking about baseball for a while."

JACKSON AND THE rest of the Players Association sunned themselves, played golf, took odd jobs to occupy their time. Most baseball owners vowed a hard line this time—they were demanding strict player compensation for lost free agents (which meant those agents wouldn't have been free at all)— but George Steinbrenner was not among them, and with good reason. He'd utilized free agency as often (and as well) as it could be used, but he'd have been less inclined to sign, say, Dave Winfield if it would've meant surrendering, say, prized pitching prospect Dave Righetti. There was also the small matter of commerce: The Yankees drew so well Steinbrenner dreamed of becoming the first American League team to bring in three million fans (the Dodgers had done it in 1978 and again in 1980 in the National League, in a city that didn't fear rainouts).

One person who didn't mind the fifty-nine-day layoff?

Gene Michael. For fifty-nine straight days the rookie manager didn't lose a baseball game, and so for fifty-nine days he could relax at his home in Closter, New Jersey, and not have to worry about getting a phone call— often multiple phone calls—wondering why the Yankees didn't bunt more, why they didn't steal more bases, why this player was sitting and that player was playing and why, oh why, can't the Yankees win every baseball game they play?

Isn't that what the good managers do?

"I was friends, good friends, with George for a lot of years," Michael recalled in 2014. "I did a lot of jobs for him, and he was great to work for. I was even a manager for another club [the Chicago Cubs] and we still got along great. The only time I ever had a problem with him was when I was his manager. Because anyone who was his manager, it was *impossible* to get along with him. Impossible."

Michael had actually been a hair away from getting fired already. The Yankees got off to a slow start, always a terrible thing for a manager who worked in the Bronx. Worse, the Yankees went to Baltimore for the first time in late May and got swept by the Orioles and their infernal tyrant, Earl Weaver. They were already four and a half games behind the Birds. Steinbrenner began to boil and there was nobody to turn the burner down.

"He doesn't listen to anyone anymore," Saban told a friend.

Bad news for Michael.

"There's going to be some things happening very shortly," Steinbrenner pledged. "I'm going to sit with my people tomorrow. Don't be surprised if some things happen."

Such as . . . firing the manager? After *forty-two* games?

"That could be the decision that's made," Steinbrenner replied.

Michael was flown to Tampa for a sit-down with Steinbrenner on an off-day while the team traveled from Baltimore to Cleveland. He didn't beg to keep his job. Mostly, he listened. When he'd been the GM, Michael learned that listening quietly was the best way to endure a meeting with an angered Steinbrenner.

"I don't agree with everything George does," Michael said afterward. "But I know George pays the bills and can do what he wants. He has that right."

What he'd lost, much to Michael's good fortune, was the ability to hire Gene Mauch, longtime manager for the Phillies and Twins now working with the Angels as an adviser to Gene Autry. Steinbrenner called Mauch to gauge his availability before summoning Michael to Tampa, and Mauch said he was, indeed, interested. But by the time Michael's plane landed, Autry fired manager Jim Fregosi and replaced him with Mauch.

Michael was safe. For now.

Then a funny thing happened. The Yankees won nine in a row—including a payback sweep of the Orioles in New York—and barreled into first place by three games. This became a significant thing when the strike was finally settled—the owners had their clocks cleaned again by Marvin Miller—and the owners agreed to a split-season format. All the first-place teams from before the strike would play the winners from after the strike in a one-time intra-division best-of-five series, prior to the League Championship Series.

Good news for the Yankees. Great news for their fans, and for their owner: guaranteed playoff games two months before the end of the season.

The bad news for Michael? The Yankees were about to play baseball games again.

EVEN FOR STEINBRENNER, this seemed, and felt, ridiculous. The Yankees came out flat in August, perfectly understandable given they quite literally had nothing to play for: Even if they went 0–51, they were still guaranteed a spot in the playoffs. Even if they went 51–0 it wouldn't matter because the owners, absurdly, decided that if a team won both halves they'd still face the team with the second-best record in a division series. It was actually something of a tribute to Gene Michael that he got the Yankees to Labor Day weekend in Kansas City with a 14–12 record.

But when the Yankees walked into the clubhouse that day, and peered into the manager's office, the familiar face that greeted them from behind the desk wasn't Gene Michael's. It was Bob Lemon's.

"Condolences, mate," Graig Nettles said with a laugh, shaking Lemon's hand.

Michael had never been more popular with the team than in his final hours. When he'd been hired, there was grumbling Steinbrenner had embedded a double agent in their midst. Michael was close with the Boss, and unlike with Billy Martin, Dick Howser, Lemon and Ralph Houk, they weren't sure Michael would take their side in high-level battles of wills. Michael proved them wrong, especially when he stared Steinbrenner down in May. At the time, the one move Steinbrenner did enact was firing pitching coach Stan Williams—a close Michael confederate—and installing Clyde King, a deep part of Steinbrenner's inner circle.

So Michael really *was* on their side.

And now he was gone.

> **INTERLUDE:** Interestingly, one who managed to survive the purging of both Michael and Dick Howser was Mike Ferraro, the third base coach who'd sent Steinbrenner into such a bitter rage in the 1980 playoffs. He was affable and likable, and Steinbrenner allowed him to stay, switching him to first base coach.
>
> "I've received invaluable advice from some of the great first base coaches of our time," Ferraro quipped early in '81. "Both Yogi Berra and Whitey Ford have told me my most important duty will be to keep my back pocket buttoned. Plus, I get to pat the players on the butt. If I do all those things, Yogi and Whitey tell me I have every chance to be remembered as the complete first base coach."
>
> It also seemed every time he went to Pompano Park to watch the trotters with Ferraro and Michael, Steinbrenner came out ahead thanks to Ferraro's handicapping.
>
> "Your job," he always kidded Ferraro, "is safe for another day." After the '82 season Ferraro was hired to manage the Indians, then after reuniting with Howser in Kansas City he had a second stint as a coach with the Yankees from 1986 to 1991. He died in July 2024.

Michael was gone because he couldn't tolerate the lack of respect Steinbrenner showed him, or the job of manager. He'd seen it with Martin. He'd seen it with Lemon. He'd seen it up close with Howser, which is why Michael went so far as to beg Howser to return within days of Steinbrenner's announcement that Howser would leave the job to pursue exciting real estate opportunities. Michael knew what was coming, and more than anyone who would ever occupy the post, he was ready for it . . . *and still got run over.*

Steinbrenner was adding new items to his playbook, too. On August 19, after a 6–5 loss at home to the White Sox, Michael was characteristically frank about his team's performance: "I told them they were horseshit, and they knew they were horseshit." Steinbrenner piled on: "I don't pay this kind of money to see mediocrity. They'll practice till they get it right."

He meant that literally. The Yankees had an off-day August 20—or did, until Michael announced a mandatory workout. Days off in August are essential to keeping baseball players from burning out, and Michael knew that better than anyone, which is why there wasn't a single Yankee who believed this was Michael's idea. It was all Steinbrenner.

A week later, Michael finally blew.

"It bothers me," Michael said of the constant barrage of phone calls to his home, to his office, to the dugout. "I can't manage this way. He's always saying it's my fault. It happened again today and he indicated he might have to make a managing change. I told him, 'George, do it now. Don't wait.' I don't like the threats."

From there, it was just a matter of when, not if.

"You can't say those things about your boss and expect to get away with it," Steinbrenner reasoned.

Steinbrenner's timing was lousy, though. Just as he was considering whom to replace Michael with, the Royals fired their manager, Jim Frey, and replaced him with Dick Howser, who was first on Steinbrenner's wish list. Then, just two days after he pulled the trigger, the Montreal Expos axed Dick Williams, Steinbrenner's perennial dance partner.

So it would be Lemon, and even as he said hello to his players Lemon was absolutely certain of one thing: He'd be saying goodbye to them soon enough, too.

"Don't get too comfortable, Meat," Lemon said, chuckling, when he met with Michael to discuss the transition, using the nickname he used for everybody. "I'm just keeping your seat warm."

Steinbrenner had owned the Yankees for just over eight years. Including two-timers, Lemon would be his ninth manager.

THE WRITERS WERE groggy as they assembled in the owner's suite at the Wilshire Hyatt. It was 11:30 p.m. local time—2:30 in the morning back home—and they were eager to get a few hours of sleep before flying back to New York between Games 5 and 6 of the World Series. They'd been summoned for an "emergency briefing."

They were greeted by a most remarkable sight: Steinbrenner's left hand, bandaged. There was a cut on his right hand. His lip was puffy. There was a bump on his head. Steinbrenner wore a plaid lumberjack shirt, which might have been the oddest twist of all.

Well, until Steinbrenner began telling his story.

It seems he'd gotten on the elevator at the Wilshire to head down to dinner following the Dodgers' tense 2–1 win in Game 5, which gave LA a 3–2 edge in the series. At one point the elevator stopped and two men walked on—Dodgers fans, Steinbrenner could tell, because one was wearing a Dodgers cap and the other recognized him and sneered, "Steinbrenner, right?"

"That's right," said the Boss, according to the Boss.

"Why don't you go back to those fucking animals in New York and take your choke-ass players with you?"

In his suite at the Wilshire a few hours later Steinbrenner said, "I'm sick of people in other cities knocking Yankees fans, and I especially couldn't take it when he said my players were chokes. It's OK for me to criticize them because I pay their checks. I'm not going to listen to some drunk fan say that about my players."

The writers in the room looked at each other, wondering if they'd somehow made a wrong turn and landed thirty miles away in Disney's Fantasyland.

Steinbrenner: "I cursed at the guy, and he hit me in the side of the head with a bottle. I clocked him with my left hand, and the other guy hit me in the mouth. I slugged him, too. The elevator door opened, and I got off.

I left them there, one guy on the floor and the other kneeling over him. I went to the washroom, washed blood off my face and went to dinner."

Did this really happen?

Steinbrenner insisted it did, and said so right to the end. A few LA radio stations tried to find the mystery elevator men for a couple of days, got inundated with crank callers, and gave up. Forty-four years later, nobody has stepped forward to confirm the story. But nobody has stepped forward to debunk it, either.

One man who chose to believe it was one Alfred Manuel "Billy" Martin.

"Just heard the news. You're fired," Martin crowed in a telegram he sent Steinbrenner the next day. "I understand exactly how you must have felt in that elevator. I only hope you don't have a good-behavior clause in your contract."

If the effect was to rally the troops behind John Wayne, the mission failed. The Dodgers wrapped up the series in Game 6 at Yankee Stadium with help from Bob Lemon, who made the curious decision—in a World Series played without a DH—to pinch-hit for Tommy John, pitching well, in the fourth inning of a 1–1 game. The Dodgers blasted his replacements for seven runs the next two innings. The Yankees lost 9–2.

"I want to sincerely apologize to the people of New York and fans everywhere for the performance of the Yankees team in the World Series," Steinbrenner said in a statement issued minutes after the final out. "I also want to assure you that we will be at work immediately to prepare for 1982."

The ball club did not take Steinbrenner's apology well.

"I have nothing to apologize for," said Reggie Jackson, who hit .333 and slugged .667 with a homer in the series.

"Hell," Lou Piniella fumed. "We could've played better. We just didn't."

It would be 5,471 days before the Yankees would again play a World Series game.

Before the Revolution: The Yankees' brain trust in the years before George Steinbrenner, pictured boarding a "fan caravan" in the winter of 1969. *From left to right:* President Michael Burke, third base coach (and future manager) Dick Howser, broadcaster Frank Messer, general manager Lee MacPhail, player Bill Robinson and manager Ralph Houk.

Courtesy of New York Post

Pledge Absentee Ownership: Michael Burke (*front left*) introduces George Steinbrenner (*back left*) as the head of a syndicate purchasing the Yankees at Yankee Stadium on January 3, 1973. Deputy Mayor Edward Hamilton is to Steinbrenner's left.
Courtesy of New York Post

The First Architect: Gabe Paul, who ran the Yankees with only minimal interference during Steinbrenner's first suspension from baseball, celebrates the Yankees' 1977 World Series championship.
Courtesy of New York Post

The Odd Couple: Steinbrenner (*left*) and Billy Martin (*right*) couldn't have come from more divergent backgrounds, but both shared two common traits: boundless ambition and an unrelenting fear of failure. Steinbrenner hired Martin to manage the Yankees five times and had promised him a sixth opportunity not long before Martin died on Christmas Day 1989.

Courtesy of New York Post

The Game Changer: Steinbrenner's pursuit of Reggie Jackson defined his early years as owner and changed the course of Yankees history forever. Here, Reggie takes a curtain call before the watchful eyes of ex-Yankees boss Michael Burke (white hair), who by then was running Madison Square Garden.

Courtesy of New York Post

Challenging the Boss: Steinbrenner thought he'd found his dream manager in no-nonsense disciplinarian Dallas Green, but when Green tired of the Boss's interference and merrily returned fire, he was canned just 121 games into his tenure.
Courtesy of New York Post

The Third Steinbrenner Son: Steinbrenner's closest personal relationship with one of his players was with Tampa native Lou Piniella. Steinbrenner hired him twice to be his manager. But it wasn't until Piniella left the Yankees that he found managerial success with the Reds, Mariners and Cubs.
Courtesy of New York Post

The Architect, Part II: Gene "Stick" Michael became close to Steinbrenner as a player and later served a number of roles in the front office. While the Boss was suspended from baseball for the second time, Michael laid the foundation for a team that would win four championships from 1996 to 2000.
Photo by Charles Wenzelberg

The Boy Wonder: Gene Michael told Buck Showalter he wouldn't be considered for the Yankees manager's job after the 1991 season—a decision that Michael admits nearly sank his rebuild before it could get off the ground. Together they restored the Yankees to prominence.
Photo by Charles Wenzelberg

Gentleman Joe: Joe Torre helped add four Commissioner's Trophies to the Boss's collection, in large part due to his skill in serving as a buffer between Steinbrenner and his more destructive impulses.
Photo by Charles Wenzelberg

The Lightning Rod: Brian Cashman (*right*) was the last man the Boss ever hired to be general manager, and he was instrumental in acquiring Alex Rodriguez (*left*), who helped the Yankees to the 2009 title and invited scores of headaches thereafter.
Photo by Charles Wenzelberg

The Boss's Backyard: George Steinbrenner, surrounded by the plaques and memorials that populated Monument Park in the old Yankee Stadium, at the peak of the Yankees' most recent dynasty of 1996–2000.
Photo by Charles Wenzelberg

Game Knows Game: The two centerpieces of the two iconic eras of George Steinbrenner's stewardship: Reggie Jackson (*left*), who powered the Yankees to back-to-back titles in 1977 and '78, and Derek Jeter, a star on five Yankees champions (1996, 1998–2000 and 2009).
Photo by Charles Wenzelberg

Hank's Yanks: For a brief but very colorful time, the Boss's eldest son, Hank, was the face and voice of the team before he tired of the spotlight and eagerly agreed to let his younger brother, Hal, lead the franchise following their father's semiretirement.
Photo by Charles Wenzelberg

Meet the New Boss: Hal Steinbrenner has never shied away from the legacy he inherited, or from the responsibility he and his family feel as proprietors of the greatest dynasty in the history of North American sports. "It's a privilege," he says.
Photo by Charles Wenzelberg

The Steinbrenner children flank their mother in front of the Boss's imposing memorial in new Yankee Stadium's Monument Park. *From left to right:* daughters Jennifer and Jessica; wife Joan; sons Hal and Hank.
Photo by Charles Wenzelberg

CHAPTER 16

It's a nice feeling to go to the ballpark and just work and not worry about who's going to be on your ass today.
—REGGIE JACKSON

Reggie Jackson was back. He was home. It was April 27, 1982, and he was mired in a miserable slump, hitting .173 without a single home run in his new California Angels uniform.

Didn't matter.

Never mattered as far as Jackson was concerned. There were 34,458 of them sitting in the rain, a hell of a crowd for a cold April night in the Bronx. There was a reason there were so many fannies in the stands, and they cheered every move of the man wearing number 44 in road grays. They gave him a loud roar his first two times up that night, and he'd scratched out a single in the fifth. Then, leading off the seventh, with the Angels up 2–1, there was another ovation, and now Ron Guidry tried to muscle a fastball by him and Jackson swung and hit one of his specialty home runs designed expressly for Yankee Stadium and for the moment.

"I knew nobody was going to make a play on it," Guidry said later, a sporting tip-of-the-cap gesture for which George Steinbrenner would soon rip him a new one. "But at least when Reggie hits 'em, you enjoy watching 'em. He earns his."

And so the saturated masses rose to their feet as soon as they heard ball hit bat, as they watched it fly high on a beautiful parabola toward the facing of the upper deck. They summoned Jackson out of the dugout for a curtain call, unheard of for a visitor at Yankee Stadium. And then, the chant started. And got louder. And louder.

"*STEIN-BREN-NER SUCKS!*" they thundered, clapping five times.

"*STEIN-BREN-NER SUCKS!*" they roared.

"*STEIN-BREN-NER SUCKS!*" they bellowed.

"It was very hard to believe," Jackson said later on. "I was deeply touched. I feel like that was a total acceptance from them, and it made me feel extra good, knowing I was forced out of here by George."

Steinbrenner? He saw it a little differently.

"Disappointed," he said a few minutes after the chant finally died down. "Embarrassed for my family to have to hear such things."

He wasn't surprised, though.

"I just thought it was a cheap shot after all the cheers we've given them."

He paused.

"I'm happy for Reggie," Steinbrenner said. "He might not believe that. But I am."

He was right about that. Jackson didn't believe that, especially later on, in the stadium lobby, where he was chatting with friends waiting for a limo to take him to Seventy-Seventh and Third Avenue, where a postgame rib eye awaited him at the Jim McMullen steak house. He was standing maybe two feet from the elevator when the door opened. George Steinbrenner. They locked eyes. Steinbrenner pressed a button, and the door closed. A few seconds later the door opened again. Steinbrenner again. Now the Boss furiously pushed buttons and muttered, "Someone fix this damn thing!"

"Can he really hate me that much," Jackson said, "that he couldn't even get off and walk past me?"

"Hate" was probably a bit strong, but it hadn't been the best of times for the Boss. Jackson spent most of 1981 trying to get Steinbrenner to commit to a five-year deal that would allow him to close his career as a Yankee. Then Jackson went through the most difficult season of his career; even the Reggie! bar was doomed, discontinued for lack of sales.

"My baseball people all agreed," Steinbrenner said in 2002, a few days before the twentieth anniversary of Jackson's triumphant return. "They all thought—me, too—Reggie had one good year left in him. And the more time went on the more we agreed it wouldn't be smart to pay Reggie for five years and have prime Reggie for one."

Of course, by 1982, Steinbrenner's "baseball people" consisted of a party of one: himself. Everyone knew that. Jackson knew that. He loved New York. But the interest was not mutual. By January 22, he realized it never would be and signed with the Angels for five years, $900,000 per. He lobbed no verbal missiles at his former boss, refused to even talk about Steinbrenner.

"I'm a happy man," he said. "Take my word."

Later in the year, still fried about the way it ended with the Yankees, he'd admit: "I was discarded like some old baggage."

Still, he was happier now, Yankees fans less so. Much of that ovation was to remind Jackson how much they'd enjoyed watching him for five years. Part of it was their way of flipping a double bird at the Boss—and only partially because he'd let Jackson go. And to be fair . . . he was proven right over time. Jackson played the next five years with the Angels. He was productive for four of them. But he was vintage Jackson in only one: 1982, when he led the Angels to the AL West title, hit thirty-nine homers and drove in 101 runs, finishing sixth in the MVP vote. He would become the thirteenth member of the 500 Home Run Club on September 17, 1984, as an Angel (after which he was presented with a commemorative silver tray from Cartier by George Steinbrenner). He finished his career where it started, in Oakland, compiling 563 homers—which even thirty-eight years after his retirement put him fourteenth on the all-time list. He hit 144 of them as a Yankee.

Steinbrenner developed an alternate plan. He decided speed and defense was the right path to follow. He signed Dave Collins from the Reds, who'd stolen seventy-nine bases in 1980. He traded for Ken Griffey, father of a future Hall of Famer and a speedy perennial All-Star. In January he "urged" his team to report to spring training a couple of weeks earlier than the March 1 due date, and most did that, some begrudgingly. When they arrived they spent much of the time running sprints, jumping into sliding pits and learning the secrets of running from Harrison Dillard, a four-time Olympic gold-medalist hurdler.

Broadcaster Phil Rizzuto was commissioned to teach bunting. When a young shortstop named Andre Robertson muffed one in an exhibition game, Steinbrenner ordered him to bunt one hundred balls after the game, until Robertson's arms were numb. The Yankees, famous for decades for their power, were specializing in small ball. And the nicknames that came flying out of the clubhouse were catnip for headline writers.

FROM BRONX BOMBERS TO BRONX BURNERS!

FROM MURDERER'S ROW TO MURMURER'S ROW!

STEINBRENNER'S STRIDERS!

"This is by far the best team we've ever assembled," Steinbrenner said in March, and the Yankees spent the next six months making that seem like the funniest thing anyone had ever heard of since the words "absentee ownership."

STEINBRENNER ALWAYS COVETED bold-faced names to manage his team, but the ones who qualified—Earl Weaver, Tommy Lasorda, Sparky Anderson—were never available when he had an opening. Dick Williams was in San Diego now. Bob Lemon was sixty-one, and he'd hardly distinguished himself in his brief return, but during a January meeting Lemon told Steinbrenner he'd lost twenty-four pounds and was trying his best to stay away from the cigarettes and the Canadian Club. Steinbrenner was duly impressed and announced Lemon would manage the Yankees in 1982 in something of a victory lap for a long and meritorious baseball life. In 1983 he'd restore Gene Michael to the job.

"Bob Lemon is going to be our manager all year," he declared. "You can bet on it. I don't care if we come in last place. I swear on my heart he'll be the manager all season."

Lemon got fourteen games.

The Yankees were 6–8, and Steinbrenner couldn't take what he was watching. He fired Lemon and guaranteed him a job in the organization for life. He summoned Gene Michael a year early. Lemon spent some time with Michael before flying home to California.

"What did I tell you, Meat?" he said with a smile.

The Yankees spent the season mired in fourth or fifth place, because what Steinbrenner assembled amounted to a fourth- or fifth-place club. The team was supposed to be built around speed but wound up eleventh in stolen bases with sixty-nine, or sixty-one fewer than Rickey Henderson of Billy Martin's Oakland A's stole *by himself* that year.

To make matters worse the Mets got off to a 27–21 start and saw a surge in attendance while the Yankees' numbers flattened. Steinbrenner agreed to reinstate the Mayor's Trophy Game in late May, and 41,614 fans—the highest total at the stadium all year to that point, many wearing Mets caps—showed up to see the Mets win, 4–1.

"I'm disgusted with this ball club," Steinbrenner railed in late June, and none of his pet tricks had any impact.

After a 6–5 loss to the Mariners in July that lasted twelve innings and tickled the midnight hour, Steinbrenner ordered seven players, by name, to report an hour and a half early the next day to work on the various things they'd done wrong in that loss.

"I'm depressed; it's no fun here anymore," said Gossage (just warming up, trust us). "It's getting worse. If you don't perform here you don't need Steinbrenner on your ass every day. The people will let you know."

The Yankees were dull. They were losing. And they were old.

INTERLUDE: By 1982 it became harder for Steinbrenner to make trades because the minor-league system was bereft from his emptying it of scores of prospects. In a few months Willie McGee would be a World Series star with the Cardinals and would win an MVP and a batting title in his career; the year before McGee had been stuck in Double-A Nashville, where he'd hit over .300 but found, as many other Yankee farmhands did, that it was impossible to move up in the system because of Steinbrenner's fascination with big-ticket veterans. McGee was swapped for Bob Sykes, who never pitched another inning in the majors.

"Your initial response when you're drafted by the Yankees is that it's great. After about three years of playing in the minors you find it's about the worst thing that could have happened to you. I don't think the Yankees farmhands are fooled anymore." Those words came from the Nashville first baseman, a career .294 hitter who never played an inning in the bigs. His name was Buck Showalter.

Gene Michael never allowed the season to spin completely sideways; he simply didn't have the talent to compete with the Orioles and Brewers. Every winning streak seemed to be halted by a brutal loss. On August 15, with a chance to crawl back to .500 and inch within ten games of first-place Milwaukee, Gossage inherited a 4–2 lead in Chicago and got boxed around by the White Sox for four eighth-inning runs. The next day, back home, he woke up to this subtle headline in the *Post*: WILD GOOSE RIPPED.

In the short term, Gossage reacted as you would expect the premier rubber-armed, flame-throwing stopper of his generation to react: He saved both ends of a doubleheader sweep of Dick Howser's Royals, retiring all ten batters he faced across the two games. Afterward, reporters gathered around him; Goose had his moments and his moods but mostly he was a good guy and a good quote.

Someone asked if he'd seen the newspaper. He had *absolutely* seen the newspaper.

"Everybody . . ." he said. And then he was off.

The way they boo fucking Griffey and everybody else . . . and you motherfuckers, all you motherfuckers with a fucking pen and a fucking tape recorder, you can fucking turn it on and take it upstairs . . .

. . . to the FAT MAN!

OK?

Because I'm fucking sick and tired of this fucking shit, the negative fucking bullshit. Everything you guys read and write these motherfuckers read it—these dumb motherfuckers in the seats . . .

He caught his breath. Spotted a writer dutifully turning on his tape recorder so he wouldn't miss even one syllable of the monologue. Continued.

Yeah, turn it on. Turn it on, you greasy cocksucker! They read everything you write and we hear the same fucking lines, you know what I mean? Fuckin' negative motherfuckers. No wonder you carry a pad and a fucking paper around, you ain't worth a fucking shit to do anything else. Motherfuckers!

It should be noted that none of the writers ever felt physically threatened by Gossage's tirade; there was in fact audible laughter when Gossage got to the "greasy" part. And the next day, he made sure to apologize to the fans, and to the female reporters who'd been at his locker stall. And he even apologized to the Fat Man, who himself actually took the invective in stride, saying, "I consider Rich Gossage more of a son than anyone else on the team."

He was unhappy being called, you know, "fat."

"Tell him I've lost eleven pounds the last couple of weeks," Steinbrenner said, "and that when I was thirty-one [Gossage's age] I would have beaten him in the hundred-yard dash."

Gossage laughed when that was relayed. And while he was sorry about the R-rated part of his diatribe, this most accountable of all Yankees stood by its crux.

"I mean everything I said. I can't take it back. I'm sincere."

●

GENE MICHAEL WASN'T around to hear Goose's rant. Back on August 3, around the seventh inning of a 14–2 pasting by the White Sox (after Chicago had already won the opening game of the doubleheader 1–0), he heard Bob Sheppard announce over the PA system that any of the 34,172 fans who'd retained their ticket stub could turn it in for a free ticket for a future game.

Michael turned to Yogi Berra on the bench.

"You know what that means," he said. "I'm gone."

Michael kept a stoic profile in public. Steinbrenner called him the next day, said there was a job waiting for him in the front office if he wanted it. Michael wasn't so sure.

"George, this one stings," he said. "I'm hurt by this."

"Why do you want this job anyway?" the Boss asked. "You don't need a guy like me on your ass every day."

"Because I know I'm a good manager," Michael said.

In 1986 the Cubs hired him to manage, but Stick struggled there for two years, and by 1988 he was back in the employ of Steinbrenner. Soon enough, he would save Steinbrenner's baseball empire from sliding into the abyss.

Soon enough.

For now, the Yankees would be in the hands of Clyde King—a former pitcher who players had long suspected was more of a spy for Steinbrenner than an employee—and in what was probably the biggest surprise of the year King won the clubhouse. King took over with the Yankees still only eight games out at 50–50, with sixty-two games to go. As the Boss insisted to Michael, "We did it before. We did it in '78."

"George," Michael said, "Thurman is dead. Reggie is in California. Guidry isn't Superman anymore. This is crazy."

It was crazy. The Yankees finished 79–83, their first losing season under Steinbrenner since '73, sixteen games out of first place and only a game out of last. Still, Clyde King, loyal lieutenant, hoped that would be enough for his general to give him a legitimate crack at the job. He never realized it, but he had no shot.

In late September Roy Eisenhardt, the president of the Oakland Athletics and the son-in-law of owner Walter Haas Jr., called George Steinbrenner, unsolicited.

"If you are interested," Eisenhardt said, knowing full well he would be talking to an interested party, "we give you permission to speak to Billy Martin."

IT HAPPENED AGAIN, amazingly (inevitably, predictably). Martin had revived baseball in Oakland. In 1981 the A's built off Martin's stunning first year by starting the season 11–0, winning twenty of their first twenty-five games; they cruised to a share of the AL West in the split season and then hammered the Royals, three games to none, in the playoffs. After the third game, he returned to his office, soaked in champagne, and opened a telegram from an interested observer back in New York: "You're a horseshit cowboy but a great manager. I hope we play you in the playoffs. G. Steinbrenner."

They did play, and the A's were slaughtered in three straight, but it sure felt like a baton had been passed between powers in the American League.

Until Martin broke the baton in two and lobbed if off the Bay Bridge.

The A's had the most electrifying young player in baseball in twenty-three-year-old Rickey Henderson, who stole a record 130 bases that season. They had baseball's most complete pitching staff. The '82 A's drew more than 1.7 million to charmless Oakland-Alameda Coliseum, at least 700,000 more than they'd attracted in any of their three championship seasons of 1972, 1973 and 1974. Martin had a five-year contract at $250,000 per, and the A's bought him a luxury house as a thank-you for all his fine work.

"I'm an Oakland A for life," he'd declared in spring, in Arizona.

One by one the pitchers all got hurt, and many blamed Martin's overuse of them in 1981 for that. He started showing up for games late, and actually left a few early. He began warring with his players. He openly questioned the manhood of his catcher, ex-Yankee Mike Heath, in one barroom and challenged one of his injured starters, Brian Kingman, to a fight one other boozy night.

By late August Martin wanted to add a year to the back end of his contract. The A's refused. Eisenhardt called Steinbrenner.

And thus was Billy III born.

"The Kid's back," Steinbrenner gleefully announced. "This is a new era . . . for the third time around."

Martin, straight-faced: "I had a long talk with George, I know people will wonder if we'll get along. We've straightened a lot of things out. For instance, I'll be handling all the trades . . ."

From behind him, Steinbrenner, also stone-faced: "What do you mean?"

"There'll be no phone calls in the dugout. . . ."

"What do you mean?"

Then George stepped to the bank of microphones. "That's not right!" he said. "I'm handling the trades—"

"That isn't the way we said, George—"

"I want you in the dugout—"

"That's not the way it's gonna be, George!"

"You're damn right it is, and if you don't like it, you're fired!"

"You haven't hired me yet!"

At that, Abbott and Costello began to laugh and so did the rest of the room, out of uncomfortable politeness as much as anything else. It was quite a show. Soon to be quite a shit show.

CHAPTER 17

*The problem with George is that he doesn't
know what it's really like to play baseball.*
—MICKEY MANTLE

He'd had enough. Ten years serving, in essence, as George Steinbrenner's dean of discipline? Please. Lee MacPhail never lost his quiet dignity, even after so many run-ins with Steinbrenner and his angry little sidekick, Billy Martin. He'd never lost his sense of fair play. MacPhail announced his retirement as American League president as of January 1, 1984, and he was eager to be done with Steinbrenner's endless, epic litany of grievances, mostly about how umpires were always out to get the Yankees.

"Anyone who knows me knows I hate to have my name in the newspaper," MacPhail said a few weeks before his retirement.

He'd loved his job as Yankees GM but saw immediately what life working with Steinbrenner would be, then happily shifted his professional life to the AL offices on Sixth Avenue. It was a blissful decade, but he was ready for something else. His son, Andy, was hired by the Twins as the sport's youngest GM, where he would assemble championship teams in 1987 and 1991. Lee would spend many happy days in Minneapolis.

He just had to make it to the end of 1983 first.

Martin and the Boss seemed determined to make that trip as miserable as possible.

"I've tried to reason with both of them," MacPhail said. "I've told them a certain level of behavior just will not do. And that will work for a time. But then . . . circumstances seem to come into play, and off we go again."

The bitching began almost from the start. Sometimes it was silly: Martin played a game under protest once because he insisted a pitcher's undershirt wasn't regulation. Sometimes it was almost hilarious: When Yankee Stadium reopened in 1976, it featured the first-ever video board, and Steinbrenner insisted every umpire call that went against the Yankees be replayed over and over, inflaming the fans. MacPhail ordered him to stop. Steinbrenner argued that was unfair.

"Life is unfair sometimes," MacPhail replied.

Once, as they were closing the gap on Boston in the summer of 1978, the Yankees mounted a comeback on a rainy Sunday afternoon in Baltimore, taking the lead in the top of the seventh inning. As they did, with threatening skies looming, Earl Weaver stalled as much as he could. Then those skies opened up, for hours. Under the rules at the time, the final score reverted to the previous full inning. Orioles win.

Steinbrenner went berserk.

"Weaver can't do that!" Steinbrenner screamed at MacPhail.

"George," MacPhail said, "he just did."

It was the umpires for whom Steinbrenner reserved his fiercest furies, and it was Lee MacPhail who received the business end of those bombasts.

"It's strange," MacPhail said. "We have seven games a day in the American League and the only noise we get is from New York."

In 1983 both Steinbrenner and Martin seemed intent on boiling MacPhail's blood every day as a parting gift. In the spring Steinbrenner accused National League umpires working spring training games of "being in cahoots" against the Yankees, a charge so irrational MacPhail didn't know whether to laugh or spank Steinbrenner with a paddle; he levied a $50,000 fine instead.

A few months later, when the Yankees got into a brawl with the A's at Yankee Stadium, Steinbrenner, watching at home, was incensed when Dave

Winfield was ejected and A's catcher Mike Heath—with whom Winfield had tangled—was not. He called MacPhail at home, where he was watching the game on TV. Then Steinbrenner demanded that his PR man, Ken Nigro, release a statement blasting the umpires, giving the impression that MacPhail agreed with him.

MacPhail released his own statement:

"Mr. Steinbrenner's intemperate blast at the integrity of the umpires is completely unacceptable and will result in disciplinary action."

Steinbrenner, true to form, doubled down.

"We are all free to express our opinions," the Boss said, "unless Lee MacPhail has authored a new Constitution or Bill of Rights of the United States."

That one earned Steinbrenner a one-week suspension. Shortly thereafter Billy Martin kicked dirt on an umpire, and that earned him a three-game ban. Martin, like his boss, never knew when to simply shut up, walk away, and he accused MacPhail of being unfair.

"He's right, it was unfair," MacPhail responded. "For behaving like a three-year-old in front of thirty thousand people on prime-time TV, a fair penalty would've been thirty games."

So . . . let all of this serve as a preamble for the hot, sticky Sunday afternoon of July 24, 1983. The Yankees, for all their quirky daily turmoil, were playing their best baseball in three years. They'd won eight of nine, were only two games behind first-place Toronto. Dave Winfield was having his best year as a Yankee. Ron Guidry was on the way to winning twenty-one. Lefty pitcher Dave Righetti, the Rookie of the Year in 1981 whom Steinbrenner had personally sent to the minor leagues during a rough patch in 1982, threw a no-hitter on the Fourth of July—Steinbrenner's fifty-third birthday. And a sweet-swinging rookie named Don Mattingly came up for good in May and started hitting line drives every day.

Good times in the Bronx. This day, with 33,944 on hand, the Yankees overcame a 3–1 Kansas City lead to take a 4–3 advantage into the ninth. Dale Murray got the first two outs. Down to his last strike, U. L.

Washington scratched out a single. Martin walked to the mound, took the ball from Murray, handed it to Goose Gossage. One more out and the Yankees would creep within a game of first place.

George Brett stepped to the plate.

Gossage threw a 97 mph fastball. Brett got a good swing on it, laced it down the left field line, but it sliced just foul. Rick Cerone put down one finger again. Gossage went into his stretch, quickly delivered. This time it was ninety-eight, and it seemed to be heading for Brett's chin. "If I was smart enough, I would've ducked out of the way of the son of a bitch before it killed me," Brett would remember years later. "But I wasn't so smart in those days."

Brett didn't duck.

Brett swung his bat.

ON TELEVISION, FRANK MESSER, the Yankees' longtime play-by-play man on WPIX, lent perfect voice to what everyone was thinking the moment Gossage's heater hit Brett's bat.

"Uh-oh!" Messer said.

Brett circled the bases slowly, triumphantly, one of the great Yankee killers of all time admiring his work as the stadium quieted and Gossage kicked dirt on the mound. As he was approaching home plate, the Kansas City batboy dutifully retrieved Brett's bat and started toward the third base dugout. Before he could get there, he was called back by home plate umpire Tim McClelland, who was engaged in quiet conversation with Billy Martin, with Graig Nettles listening in. Brett saw this happening out of the corner of his eye but thought nothing of it. What he didn't see, or hear, was Martin pointing to the Louisville Slugger now in McClelland's hands.

"Look at how far the pine tar is," Martin said. "That's an illegal bat."

For all of Martin's eccentricities and idiosyncrasies, the son of a gun knew the rule book backward and forward. A few weeks earlier, playing in Kansas City, Nettles noticed the pine tar on Brett's bat clearly extended beyond the trademark, more than the eighteen inches allowed by rule. He'd notified Martin.

INTERLUDE: Steinbrenner stunned a lot of folks—including himself—when he named Graig Nettles captain before the 1983 season, having respectfully left the position vacant for four years after Thurman Munson's death. Nettles, too, was dumbfounded, given how many skirmishes the two had through the years. But he was also humbled.

"I have mixed emotions about being named captain," he said. "I wish that as long as I played the game Thurman would be here and he'd be the captain."

"Keep it quiet for now," Martin told Nettles. "Let's save it for when we really need it, the next time that son of a bitch kills us in a game."

McClelland knew home plate was eighteen inches wide. He lay the bat across the top. In the Royals' dugout, Dick Howser muttered, "No fuckin' way . . ." to Brett. He knew what was happening.

Brett was incredulous.

"If they call me out," he said, "you're going to see four dead umpires."

A few seconds later, McClelland approached the Royals' dugout. As if to offer a happy preview to the 33,944 witnesses, Nettles merrily pounded the pocket of his mitt with his right fist—just as McClelland was raising his right arm. Brett was out, game over, Yankees win, 4–3.

Brett immediately went about his stated mission.

He stormed out of the dugout, red-faced, twice nearly choking on the chaw of tobacco in his left cheek as he screamed *"BULLSHIT!"* a dozen times, as he lunged at McClelland in blind fury before being physically restrained by crew chief Joe Brinkman. The crowd, which had already begun to filter out, roared in delight. Howser was livid, his rumpled cap in his hand, his own anger unleashed. It was lunacy, of course, and even Brinkman, who'd rendered official final judgment, admitted as much afterward.

"It wouldn't be a bit surprising if they changed that rule or threw it out altogether," Brinkman said, conceding that pine tar in no way helped the flight of a baseball.

The Royals filed a protest. Brett vowed to quit if he was suspended for charging the umpires. The Yankees rejoiced; Gossage told Martin, "I honestly have no idea how he hit that pitch." To which Martin winked, smiled and said, "What pitch?"

The matter went to MacPhail's office. Nobody expected that to mean much.

Except. *Except.* MacPhail studied rule 1.10b four hundred times. He read all sixty-three words four hundred times. Suddenly, he saw it. Or, more precisely, its absence.

Nowhere in the rule does it say the batter shall be declared out.

It simply says *the bat itself may no longer be used.*

MacPhail knew how he had to rule. And also knew that nothing in 3,496 days of his tenure as president—including about 3,125 of them in which he'd had to field a complaint from Steinbrenner—was anything close to this. He had fewer than six months left on the job. The path of least resistance beckoned: uphold the ruling, promise to throw out the rule, grant Brett amnesty for his explosion, everyone moves on.

"My conscience," Lee MacPhail would say much later, "wouldn't allow for the path of least resistance."

His conscience, instead, declared the home run should count, the game should be suspended from where it was the instant Brett's ball soared over the wall, and it should be resumed on Thursday, August 18, the next mutual off-day for the clubs. Neither Brett nor Howser would be suspended for their antics, but both would be ejected from the game when it was picked up with two outs in the top of the ninth, Royals now up 5–4.

"Although the umpires are being overruled, it is not the fault of the umpires," MacPhail said. "Rather, it's the fault of the official Playing Rules, which in some areas are unclear and unprecise."

The umps weren't pleased—"All we were doing was our job when we called Brett out. We followed the letter of the law," McClelland said—but that small brushfire was soon covered in lava thanks to Mount St. Steinbrenner.

"I like Lee," Steinbrenner said, "but I feel sorry for him. He made a very dumb decision, a putrid decision. He's opened up a Pandora's box and left his umpires out to dry."

Steinbrenner threatened to forfeit the game, then announced a festive day for camp kids instead, welcoming bands and attractions to Yankee Stadium for a two o'clock start; MacPhail doused those plans by pointing out the Royals would be flying from a game the night before and thus the resumption couldn't start before six.

Now Steinbrenner went full Vesuvius.

"It sure tests our faith in leadership," Steinbrenner said. "If the Yankees lose the American League pennant by one game, I wouldn't want to be Lee MacPhail living in New York City. Maybe he should go house-hunting in Kansas City."

A few folks noticed that the owner of the New York Yankees had, in essence, hinted that the president of the American League might now be in harm's way for rendering an unpopular decision. (Later, Bowie Kuhn would levy a $300,000 fine for Steinbrenner's remarks, the steepest in the history of professional sports to that time.) Some called to ask Lee MacPhail's thoughts on the matter. MacPhail stayed quiet.

He had only 155 days left on the job.

MONTHS EARLIER STEINBRENNER at last retired the folly that anyone other than he called the Yankees' shots. His advisers had fled. Now he was left with a kitchen cabinet of men welcome to share dissenting opinions with George just as long as they were content with those suggestions being ignored.

"I'll listen to two or three trusted guys, then I'm going to make the damned decisions," he said, shortly before ignoring those trusted guys and dusting off Billy Martin for a third ride through the pumpkin patch. "I'm going to take the full blame anyway. But damn it, if that's the way it's going to be, then it's going to be *my* damned decisions."

Steinbrenner didn't seem to quite appreciate the irony that while his own team had fallen from dominance in the AL East while he was making all the damned decisions, the rest of the division was catching them, and speeding by them, largely thanks to an unofficial Steinbrenner Alumni Association. There was Gabe Paul, who'd managed to make the Indians respectable again. There was Pat Gillick, formerly Paul's assistant, hired by Toronto when the Blue Jays were born in 1977; within six years he'd built a formidable roster. There was old friend Ralph Houk, now managing the archrival Red Sox after doing a fine job with the Tigers. And there was Joe Altobelli, formerly a coach with the Yankees, now managing the Orioles, bound for the 1983 World Series title.

Steinbrenner vowed a few years earlier that he'd used his free agency muscle simply to speed up the Yankees' timeline toward excellence, that his true desire was to build an organization that would yield younger, cheaper stars much like the Yankees machine of the forties, fifties and early sixties. But he never could help himself. He kept signing big-ticket players, his latest score slugging DH Don Baylor. Worse, he emptied his farm system in the name of adding vets, far too many of whom were well past their shelf lives.

One prospect Steinbrenner kept was an Indianan named Donald Arthur Mattingly, a nineteenth-round pick by the Yankees in 1979 who immediately started raking. Yankees scouts all but covered him in laminate so the Boss wouldn't be tempted to send him off to Seattle for a thirty-seven-year-old middle reliever or to Cleveland for a sore-kneed former speedster.

"He is our crown jewel," those scouts insisted.

On this, Steinbrenner listened.

Billy Martin . . . that was another issue. Steinbrenner was determined to give Martin more space this time around. He kept quiet when the Yankees endured another slow start. In June came reports that Martin was again showing up late for games, one time not arriving in the dugout until after the first pitch; there were other days Martin was spotted sleeping off a hangover in his office during batting practice. When the Yankees arrived in Milwaukee on June 9, they did so after receiving another Steinbrenner mandate to hold an off-day workout after losing five out of seven. When spies reported back to Steinbrenner that only eleven or twelve Yankees bothered to attend he was angry; when it was noted that one of the AWOL Yankees was the manager himself he exploded.

But there was *more*, and this was where the crazy started to metastasize. On June 11, as the Yankees dawdled through a 6–2 loss to the Brewers, the writers in the press box noticed something. On the TV monitors showing the local feed, the cameras trained their attention on an odd sight: Martin wasn't standing on the top step of the dugout, which was almost always where he watched a game. He was sitting on a stool alongside the dugout, in front of the visiting club box. It took about a minute for the reporters to notice a woman in a bright yellow sundress sitting behind Martin, and they recognized her as Jill Guiver, Martin's traveling companion, not to be confused with Heather Ervolino, to whom he was still married. Amazingly, a few minutes after *that*, the WVTV/Channel 18 cameras caught Guiver passing notes through the fence with her toes to a beaming Martin. As if the writers didn't already realize what a bizarre twist this all was, the producer of the Yankees' WPIX telecasts, Don Carney, came into the room asking if the writers intended to report this since he'd decided not to televise it.

Steinbrenner, red-faced, flew to New York. There was the usual barrage of will-he-or-won't-he. He didn't. He did tell Martin his team—still mired under .500—needed to start winning, and soon, or else he wouldn't hesitate. They started winning. They chipped away. They were playing their best ball of the season when Billy Martin placed the baseball in Goose Gossage's glove on July 24, when Gossage reared back, fired and sent a heater in the general direction of George Brett's jaw.

HERE'S HOW CRAZY the 1983 season was: You could argue the nuttiest thing wasn't the Pine Tar Game. You can actually argue that the Pine Tar Game's reign as zaniest moment of the year lasted only eleven days. The Yankees were playing the Blue Jays at decrepit old Exhibition Stadium by the edge of Lake Ontario, a place that large white seagulls saw as a fine hunting ground for discarded bits of hot dogs, popcorn and pizza crusts. When the Jays were bad, the gulls often outnumbered the paying customers. On this Thursday night, they'd descended. On the field, before the bottom of the fifth of a game the Yankees would win 3–1, Winfield, playing center field, was warming up with a catch with Don Baylor in left. As the inning started,

Winfield turned and whipped the ball to a ball boy. A seagull happened to be standing between them, maybe a hundred feet away.

Bad luck for the seagull.

"*Pffft*," was how Yankees bullpen coach Jeff Torborg described what happened when Winfield's one-hopper bounced up and beaned the bird. "Right in the head. *Pow!*"

Another ball boy sprinted to the gull, carefully wrapped it in a towel. Winfield placed his cap over his heart; maybe he was genuinely sorry. The Toronto crowd of 36,684 thought otherwise. They started chanting obscenities at Winfield. After the game, Winfield was greeted in the dugout by local authorities and charged with cruelty to animals; in Canada, it seems, the seagull was a protected species. The Yankees had to post $500 bail, and the flight home was delayed forty minutes.

Martin, for one, found the whole thing hilarious.

"They obviously haven't been watching him throw all year," he said. "That's the first time he's hit the cutoff man."

This time the Yankees gladly accepted Lee MacPhail's offer to smooth things over with the Canadian authorities, and the matter was quickly dropped. But that was a temporary truce. As August 18 crept closer, things slowly went haywire in the Bronx. First, the team collapsed. From the moment Brett's ball left the yard until the moment the Yankees and Royals stepped on the field to finish off the game, the Yankees went 12–13, and were staring down a fourteenth loss once play resumed. They were still only three and a half games back but were now buried in fifth place.

Then the morning of the eighteenth, Steinbrenner found a sympathetic voice in Justice Orest V. Maresca of the State Supreme Court in the Bronx, located two blocks from Yankee Stadium; Maresca granted an injunction forbidding the game from being played. Anticipating that, the American League immediately appealed, raced to Centre Street in Manhattan to the New York State Supreme Court and encountered none other than Roy Cohn, the flamboyant attorney best known as an eager Communist witch-hunter for Senator Joseph R. McCarthy thirty years earlier. Cohn argued that allowing the game could cause near-riot conditions because Yankee

Stadium security was only one-quarter staffed. Justice Joseph Sullivan found that to be amusing.

At three thirty he said, "My ruling can best be summed up in two words: 'Play ball!'"

Sullivan urged the Yankees to make sure there were no genuine security breaches; there were none. Despite selling tickets for $2.50 apiece, exactly 1,245 people showed up (although Mattingly put the number closer to five hundred and Ron Guidry said, authoritatively, "Two fifty. Tops"). Some of that could be blamed on a railroad strike called that day by a suburban commuter service, but that didn't prevent some seventy thousand people from cramming Shea Stadium on the other side of the Triboro Bridge to see a triple bill of R.E.M., Joan Jett & the Blackhearts and the Police, which kicked off at almost exactly the same time.

Those who did show up witnessed a bit of baseball burlesque.

First, as the Yankees took the field to play the top of the ninth, they saw Guidry, a starting pitcher, trot out to center field and Mattingly, a lefty, go out to play second base. That was a small protest by Martin. Then, before George Frazier could throw a pitch against Hal McRae, Martin ordered Frazier to throw the ball to Ken Griffey, at first, and then to Roy Smalley, standing on second, officially protesting that either U. L. Washington or George Brett had failed to touch those bases twenty-five days before. Both times, crew chief Dave Phillips waved safe.

Now Martin was ready to pounce.

"How do you know they touched them?" he demanded. Martin had been cooking this scheme for weeks, because he knew the four umpires on the field now were different from the four who'd worked the game on July 24. There was no way they could possibly know with certainty that the two Royals in question had, in fact, stepped on all the bases.

Now Lee MacPhail threw the final counterpunch of a Hall of Fame career. Martin was never one to keep his genius to himself, and he'd told a few people what he planned to do. One of them had alerted MacPhail. So when Martin reached Phillips, the umpire removed from his back pocket a sworn document signed by Tim McClelland, Drew Coble, Joe Brinkman and Nick Bremigan that they'd witnessed both Washington and Brett touch every base on their tour home.

"Billy," Phillips said, "I have an affidavit."

"An affi-what?"

Dan Quisenberry retired the Yankees one, two, three in the bottom of the inning. There were still forty-four games left in the season, but the season was done.

And so, soon thereafter, was Billy Martin. For a third time.

CARMEN BERRA HAD seen for years the way the public responded to her husband, in New York and beyond. If he wasn't the most beloved sports figure in America, he was in the team photo. She'd seen how devastated he'd been when the Yankees fired him in 1964, two days after guiding them to Game 7 of the World Series. She'd seen how disappointed he'd been in 1975, when he'd been let go by the Mets less than two years after leading *them* to Game 7 as well. Both times, she supported Berra crossing team lines to stay in the game, first serving as Mets coach from 1965 to 1971, then returning to the Yankees in 1976.

"Carm said, 'Why don't you just make a living being Yogi?'" Berra said in 2009, sitting inside the museum that bears his name in his adopted hometown of Montclair, New Jersey. "We were lucky, we'd saved a lot of money. I could golf five times a week and sign autographs twice a month and we'd be happy. 'Just be Yogi,' she told me. It made a lot of sense."

But Berra was fifty-eight in December 1983, knew he had time for one more shot at winning a World Series as a manager, and the Yankees were loading up. He'd seen Don Mattingly blossom into a star in 1983, knew Dave Winfield already was. He also knew George Steinbrenner was going to replace Billy Martin. Despite winning ninety-one games, the lingering issues were still lingering, and now there was a story about Martin having a drunken screaming match with a flight attendant. It was too much. Martin would be asked to stay in the organization as an adviser, a simple way to collect his $250,000 salary.

Steinbrenner needed a manager.

Berra said yes.

Steinbrenner swore he'd let Berra be Berra all year in 1984 and, in truth, even if he'd wanted to change his mind there was little use. The Tigers jumped out to a 35–5 start, by which point the Yankees were already seventeen and a half games behind. The Yankees closed the season red-hot, 51–29. Mattingly and Winfield went down to the season's final day battling for the batting championship, with Mattingly prevailing .343 to .340 (and also demonstrating a power stroke he'd never flashed in the minors, twenty-three homers, 110 RBIs). And while the same critiques that always haunted Berra reappeared—he was too soft with his players, too friendly, unwilling to rip them or burn them—Steinbrenner had to admit he'd done a hell of a job. He also knew Berra wasn't Martin. Yankees fans liked Martin, a lot.

But they *adored* Berra, who wanted one more year, this time with the most dynamic player in the sport, Rickey Henderson, before retiring to the golf course for good.

In late October, in one of the most sensible decisions he ever made, Steinbrenner announced Berra would be back in 1985. But he wouldn't—couldn't—stop there.

"I just can't understand all these teams changing managers the way they do," said the man who'd made at least one change in the manager's chair in eight straight years until this very moment. "The lack of stability is alarming. It's startling to me how many teams change managers now. It's getting to where you can't even make news anymore when you make a change."

Of course, if you thought *that* was funny, Steinbrenner had a genuine gut-buster waiting for folks the next February, the day the full team reported for spring training.

"Yogi Berra will be the manager this year," he said. "I said the same thing last year and I'm saying it again. A bad start will not affect Yogi's status. I have put a lot of pressure on managers in the past to win at certain times. That will not be the case this spring. I'm not going to worry if we lose a game to Boston or to the Mets."

Perhaps you've heard that one before.

CHAPTER 18

I have to admit there have been times this year when I've thought, "This is bullshit. Why take this? Let me go to a normal club where all they do is play baseball." And I want that. But I love this uniform. I wouldn't want to give it up.
—DON MATTINGLY

Yogi Berra knew, as well as anyone could, what he was walking into. He'd returned to the Yankees amid great fanfare after an eleven-year exile in 1976, he'd served as a faithful lieutenant/first base coach/bench coach to Billy Martin, Dick Howser, Bob Lemon, Martin again, Howser again, Gene Michael, Lemon again, Michael again, Clyde King, and Martin. Again. He'd survived mainly by being Berra: humble to a fault, loyal, gregarious, a walking baseball encyclopedia equally comfortable among Yankees legends (of which he was a charter member) and unknown spring training kids who were scared out of their minds. He'd seen up close the effect Steinbrenner had on his managers.

"You can't say I didn't know," Berra admitted in 2002. "Maybe you can say I should've been smarter, I guess. But how many times is someone going to ask you to manage the New York Yankees?"

He didn't have to wait long to discover what the job was really going to be. In the fourth game of the 1984 season in Arlington, with the Yankees and Rangers tied at 6–6, Texas shortstop Curt Wilkerson sent a routine grounder to Yankee shortstop Bobby Meacham, a twenty-three-year-old rookie who'd shown some promise in '83 and had a terrific spring. Meacham bobbled it, threw late to Ken Griffey at first, allowing Pete O'Brien to trot in with the winning run.

Meacham was unhappy but showed himself to be a pro by answering every question with unswerving confidence. "It came up on me a little bit," he said after. "I shouldn't have bobbled it, but it happens once in a while. I still thought I had time with a strong throw. The throw was right there."

George Steinbrenner was not as impressed with Meacham's composure. The next morning he called GM Bill Bergesch and demanded that Meacham be sent to the minors—and not to Triple-A Columbus, either. He'd be going to Nashville, in *Double-A*.

Meacham, again, took all of this well: "Mr. Steinbrenner believes it will help the team, and he wouldn't have done it if he didn't believe it. He wants to win more than anyone."

Others weren't as serene. Don Baylor, who'd quickly become a vocal leader in the clubhouse, seethed: "You wonder how something like this will affect a kid down the line. It could destroy his confidence. This could be very damaging." (Meacham wound up being recalled eight days later, but while he played 457 games in a six-year career, all with the Yankees, he never did match the stardom predicted for him.)

Berra was furious. Steinbrenner never even bothered to get his input. "It's not my decision," he snapped. "I had nothing to do with it."

That was the start. Steinbrenner's fury was muted as the Tigers ran away with the East, but his second-guessing was never put in a closet, not completely. And he had a wingman now to do a lot of his bidding. When the Yankees arrived in Seattle in May they were greeted by a familiar mustachioed face: Billy Martin's. Martin was trim and tan and looked ten years younger, the standard effect of his forced sabbaticals. Berra and Martin had been friends for almost thirty-five years; they'd been at the same table at the Copa on that infamous evening twenty-seven years before. But his presence made Berra uneasy. He knew he wasn't there simply to sample the Pike Place Fish Market.

"We all know why Billy is here," Don Baylor said. "We weren't born yesterday."

INTERLUDE: Losing affected Steinbrenner in odd ways. He threatened to start making the team fly commercial, "so they'll know what it's like to do a real job like real people." He threatened to force the Yankees out of the five-star hotels to which they were accustomed and see how they enjoyed big-time ballplayer life on the road at Howard Johnson's and Red Roof Inn. When he actually did announce he was shutting down the players' lounge at Yankee Stadium, that drew a laugh from Graig Nettles, now three thousand miles away playing for his hometown San Diego Padres: "George will take away the showers next. This way the players will stink just as bad off the field as they do on."

Just before the All-Star Game, with the Yankees seven games under .500 and twenty behind the Tigers, Steinbrenner decided to pay Berra and his coaches a visit.

"This is unacceptable," Steinbrenner said. "I've given you guys everything you asked for and *this* is what I get?"

Berra's coaches looked over at Berra, whose face began to redden.

More Boss: "This is the team you wanted and look at how they're playing! All of these guys, they're all stinking it up. *It's embarrassing!*"

The coaches looked again at Berra. Now he was forcefully crushing the butt of a Lucky Strike, having recently resumed a habit he'd quit years before.

More Boss: "And who's to blame for that? This is *your* team, and it's on *you guys* for the way they're playing."

Now the coaches noticed that Berra was gripping the arms of his chair so tightly, it was like he was riding the Cyclone roller coaster over at Coney Island.

"This," Steinbrenner said, "is *your* team, and . . ."

And now Steinbrenner, and his coaches, saw a side of Berra that even Berra himself might never have fully explored before.

"*I've heard enough of this shit!*" Berra roared.

"You keep saying this is *my* team but that's a fucking lie, and you know it's a lie. This is *your* fucking team. *You* put it together. *You* make all the moves around here. *You* get all the fucking players that nobody else wants. *You* put this team together and wait for us to lose so you can blame everybody else because you're a *chickenshit liar!*"

He rose, flipped the pack of cigarettes off his desk; they hit Steinbrenner in the chest.

"You want me to quit? I'm not quitting. You'll have to fire me."

He stormed out of the room. Steinbrenner let him go and smiled.

"I guess the pressure's getting to him," he said.

Then the Yankees had that remarkable second half, and they'd done it because Steinbrenner actually heeded Berra's pleas to call up some kids, let him have a crack at managing and developing them. Mattingly became a full-blown star. Mike Pagliarulo was handed third base and hit seven home runs in 201 at bats, playing elite defense. Meacham was called back up, and he shared shortstop with Andre Robertson. Both played well. Dennis Rasmussen won nine games. Steinbrenner was so impressed that on October 25 he welcomed Berra back for 1985.

Berra said, "Now we just have to pick up where we left off."

February 20, the Boss said Berra would get the whole year, *mark my words, read my lips, cross my heart and hope to die.*

On April 28, Steinbrenner fired Yogi Berra.

The record was 6–10, but Rickey Henderson had only begun to play, sidelined for the first two weeks of the season. There was no runaway team in the AL East; even at 6–10 the Yankees were only four and a half games behind the Tigers.

The players were ready to mutiny. Don Mattingly threw a garbage can against the clubhouse wall when he was given the news. Dale Berra, Yogi's son and the Yankees' backup third baseman, was weeping as he said, "It's

Mr. Steinbrenner's prerogative." The one outlier was Rickey Henderson, a Billy Martin favorite in Oakland who was about to be a Billy Martin favorite in New York.

Because welcoming the players when their plane touched down in Arlington, Texas, was their new manager. Billy Martin.

Billy IV, as the back pages declared it.

"It was a nice guy that got fired," Martin said, showing (and not for the last time) a stunning lack of grace regarding someone who was allegedly his friend, "but if the players like him so much, why didn't they play better for him?"

If any of this bothered Berra, he refused to show it publicly. He was photographed wearing a twenty-four-karat smile as he walked out of Comiskey Park for his flight home to Montclair, New Jersey. In a few days he'd be back on the golf course and doing as his wife had begged him to do eighteen months earlier: "Just be Yogi."

Quietly his anger festered. It wasn't the firing that bothered him.

"Hell," he said. "I'd already been fired twice."

But in 1964, he'd been told by the Yankees' outgoing owners, Dan Topping and Del Webb, that he was being let go. In 1975, M. Donald Grant had shown him the courtesy of personally delivering the bad news that the Mets were parting ways with him.

"But George," Berra said, "didn't have the stones to look me in the eye. He didn't have the courage to tell me man to man. Or even to call."

And that, to Yogi Berra, was unforgivable.

"I told Carm, 'I ain't ever going back there as long as that man owns the team.' She said, 'You'll be back in five years, tops. I'm betting less.'"

Berra laughed at that one, because he knew.

His wife should've taken the over.

BILLY MARTIN HAD one last burst in him. By now he was settled down with Jill Guiver (whom he would marry in 1988), and she had convinced him to go "two, sometimes three" days per week without drinking.

"It took me a while," he'd say, "to realize that it's harder to manage when you have a hangover that makes you want to die."

For most of Billy IV, he resembled the sharp, quick-thinking dynamo he'd been during Billy I, and at most of his other stops. He was energized by the fact that his favorite player, Rickey Henderson, was on his side again, and that Rickey was having the kind of year that made you wonder if he was playing a different game than everyone else. He hit .314. He stole eighty bases, a Yankees team record, and added twenty-four homers as a leadoff man. He scored an astonishing 146 runs in 143 games. A quintessential Yankees first inning looked like this: Rickey would lead off with a hit or a walk. He'd steal second. Willie Randolph would move him to third with a bunt or a groundout. Don Mattingly would drive him in with a hit or a sacrifice fly. Winfield would either double in Mattingly or hit a home run.

"It felt like every game we started out up two to nothing," said Lou Piniella, who'd retired in the middle of the '84 season and in 1985 was serving an apprenticeship as Martin's presumed heir and hitting coach.

It took a little while for all of that to properly jell. For one thing, when Martin returned to Yankee Stadium for his first game back the mood was decidedly different: Fewer than twenty thousand people came, and there were scattered boos among the cheers (security had confiscated a few pro-Berra banners to boot); the fans had finally grown weary of this odd serial drama. After the Yankees lost to the Brewers in early June to drop eight games out, Martin resumed his subtle critique of the way his predecessor conducted business.

"Yankees don't talk about Yankees in the press," Martin said one day, before saying this to the press about a Yankee: "I'm not knocking Yogi. But we need to correct a lot of things here that should have been done in spring training." He then went on to blast the team's lack of fundamentals.

The next day Martin said, "I wasn't criticizing Yogi."

Berra had a different take.

"It looked like they had pretty good fundamentals to me," Berra said about a stretch in May when they'd won twelve of fifteen.

It was around this point when Steinbrenner decided it was time to set his guns on Don Mattingly, with whom he'd gone to salary war in the spring (and won, renewing him at $325,000—less, Don bitterly noted, than his New York contemporary, Dwight Gooden, got from the Mets). Mattingly was the most vocal Yankee when Berra was dismissed. He didn't mind playing for Martin, but when the manager called for an off-day workout—an order Mattingly and everyone else knew had come from the Boss, since Martin hated off-day workouts more than they did—Mattingly, the future captain, spoke up on behalf of his teammates: "The guys need a day off. They need to step back and rest a day."

Steinbrenner reacted predictably.

"If he's upset at working out it's too damned bad," the owner snapped. "He ought to talk to the cabdrivers or the steelworkers about working hard, talk to the farmers around his Indiana home who are losing their farms. I'm fed up with his attitude."

Mattingly was in the midst of one of the great seasons in Yankees history, a .324 average, thirty-five homers, forty-eight doubles, 145 RBIs, and he was at his best in the season's home stretch. He won AL Player of the Month in August and September, a fifty-six-game period in which he drove in sixty-three runs and had twenty-two homers, hitting .357. By then, the Yankees were in the middle of an honest-to-goodness pennant race for the first time in five years.

It should have been a giddy time in the Bronx.

But all of this was muddied over. And George Steinbrenner seemed ever eager to add to the slop.

IT STARTED WITH a tinge of ugliness. Before the first game of a series against the Blue Jays, the crowd of 52,141 booed the playing of the Canadian national anthem. Steinbrenner, who would've attempted to declare war on Canada if Blue Jays fans ever booed "The Star-Spangled Banner" in Toronto, was understandably displeased, so before the next night's game he summoned Bob Sheppard, the Yankee Stadium PA announcer, to issue an apology to the Canadian fans.

Sheppard "appealed to the fans' good taste" and reminded them "of our two countries' long history as allies." It was, Steinbrenner agreed, beautiful. The fans cheered the announcement warmly.

Then booed the anthem again, across every word, from "O, Canada!" through "we stand on guard for thee."

By now, Steinbrenner could barely think straight. Luckily, before the third game on Saturday, the Yankees—though not Steinbrenner himself—hired a sweet-voiced professional named Mary O'Dowd to sing the anthems. The crowd didn't boo this time. They didn't have a chance. Poor Mary O'Dowd immediately forgot the words. Shaken, she retreated to the Yankees' dugout, where someone handed her the lyrics. She returned to the microphone. Began again. This time she had the words perfect.

Except she sang it to the tune of "The Star-Spangled Banner."

Steinbrenner, fully flummoxed, declared there and then that all future anthem singers would have to personally audition for him. The young Jays fought back. They beat Phil Niekro—trying for his three hundredth career win—on Friday, 3–2. They blasted the Yankees 7–4 on Saturday. And then, on Sunday, as the Jays surged to an 8–0 lead, Steinbrenner wandered into the press box.

Cleared his throat.

Then emptied his shotgun into the remains of his baseball team.

"We've been out-owned, out-front-officed, outmanaged and outplayed," he steamed. "We need the big performances from Winfield, Griffey and Baylor—the guys who are making the big money. My big-money players aren't playing like money players."

Then, the grand finale.

"Where is Reggie Jackson? We need a Mr. October or a Mr. September. "Dave Winfield," Steinbrenner said, "is Mr. May."

GEORGE STEINBRENNER DIDN'T realize it in the moment, couldn't have, but with those five words he'd launched a ground war that would nearly ruin him.

He and Dave Winfield had never been particularly close, and it started almost right away when Steinbrenner's accountants took a good look at the contract he'd bestowed. It was for ten years and $16.7 million, but cost-of-living escalator clauses meant the deal might ultimately approach $24 million, if not more. Steinbrenner always considered himself a master negotiator and now he'd been duped by Winfield and his agent, Al Frohman. He immediately insisted that the escalator clause be reduced. Winfield agreed to a few dollars in relief. But that was just the start.

Twice in Winfield's first four years with the club he sued Steinbrenner for the Boss's unwillingness to honor an important segment of the contact, an annual $30,000 donation from Steinbrenner to the David M. Winfield Foundation, which helped underprivileged kids in San Diego and, now, New York. Steinbrenner claimed he was never given access to the charity's taxes and hadn't been given, as promised, a seat on its board. Both lawsuits were settled out of court but the audacity of *Winfield* suing *him* . . . that didn't sit well. At all.

Nor did Winfield's 1-for-22 performance in the 1981 World Series. Nor did Winfield's unwillingness to fully respond to Steinbrenner's public harangues the way Jackson had. In 1982 Steinbrenner had declared, "Dave Winfield is not a superstar. He is a fine athlete, who performs all phases of the game well. But he does not have the ability to carry a team like Reggie Jackson could."

Jackson would've fired back. So, as it turns out, would Mattingly.

Winfield? He'd smile, shake his head, offer up something like, "I know how my teammates feel about me; that's all that matters," and be done with it.

Winfield laughed off "Mr. May" publicly. Eddie Lee Whitson, a Yankees pitcher days away from jumping into the crazy pool with a cannonball jump, found a copy of the May 1985 *Playboy*, hung the centerfold in Winfield's locker the next day. Winfield howled with delight. "Mr. May and Ms. May," he said. "A match made in heaven!"

But Winfield was privately peeved, and he was done serving as Steinbrenner's silent speed bag. Not long after, Steinbrenner came to the clubhouse to implore the Yankees to agree to voluntary drug-testing. Winfield interrupted him, told him it was a matter of collective bargaining.

"It's my responsibility as player rep," he said.

"Not for long," Steinbrenner shot back.

"Is that some sort of threat?" Winfield replied. "Because you and I both know I'm not going anywhere next year but right here."

"We'll see about that," Steinbrenner said.

"Yeah. We'll see," Winfield said.

This was the state of the Yankees after the Blue Jays left them for dead, and it only worsened, the losing streak hitting eight.

The eighth straight loss was a Friday night in Baltimore. Afterward, Billy Martin bellied up to the hotel bar at the Cross Keys Inn and struck up a conversation with a newlywed couple married that very afternoon. He bought them a bottle of champagne. He toasted them as they went upstairs. And was stunned when the groom—clearly wobbly—returned fifteen minutes later.

"Billy," he said, "we have a problem. My wife said you told her she has a potbelly."

"Well, she's wrong," Martin said, and pointed at another woman at the bar. "I said that *she* has a fat ass."

The resulting scuffle was quickly broken up, and by the time it became public there'd been a lot of witnesses willing to speak up that Martin had done nothing wrong other than be a little bit too much of a wiseass.

The next night would be different.

In the afternoon, the Yankees finally ended the losing streak, 5–2. Most scattered through the city for dinner before drawing back to the bar at the Cross Keys for a nightcap. It was a crowded room. At some point past midnight Martin became aware that one of his pitchers, Whitson, was involved in a heated argument with another patron named Albert Millus, a lawyer from Binghamton, New York. Whitson and Martin never hit it off, and lately Martin had taken to skipping Whitson in the rotation.

It's safe to say the last person Eddie Lee Whitson wanted to see as a peacemaker at this moment was Billy Martin.

And yet there he was.

"Eddie, you're drunk, you don't need this," Martin said.

Whitson turned, saw Martin, and his eyes filled with rage.

"Get the fuck away from me!" he screamed at his manager. And then he swung.

Martin might've come with diplomatic intent. But now he was wrestling with Whitson, a man thirty years younger. Whiston kicked him a few times, and a couple of those blows landed on Martin's right arm. They were separated.

"What's the matter with that guy?" Martin said. "Can't he hold his liquor?"

Whitson's rage doubled. He broke free, kicked Martin again, this time in the groin.

"Now," Martin shouted at Whitson, "I'm going to have to kill you."

Before he could reach his pitcher two separate gaggles of people carried both men away, taking Whitson outside the lobby door, keeping Martin inside.

"You've tried to bury me!" Whitson wailed. "You're trying to ruin me!"

Martin was finally talked onto the elevator by Lou Piniella, and he started to cool down. When the elevator reached the third floor they stepped out. At precisely the same time, the adjacent elevator door opened, too.

And out stepped—no shit—Eddie Lee Whitson.

For the fourth time, they charged each other although they were easily corralled.

"You're gutless!" Whiston yelled.

"They told me you were in trouble," Martin said. "I was only trying to help, Eddie."

The next morning, Martin reported for work at Memorial Stadium with a cast on his right arm, large sunglasses camouflaging the rest of the residue of a rough night.

One of the TV cameramen yelled, "What happened to your arm, Mr. Martin?"

"I hurt it bowling," Martin said. Later, he joked to the writers: "I can't fight feet."

Steinbrenner's phone rang around 1 a.m. and he was told his manager and big free agent pitcher had just gone four rounds in front of hotel guests, players, coaches and at least six of eight newspaper beat writers.

"Wait . . . did you say *four* rounds?" Steinbrenner asked.

The Yankees' season was on life support, and so was Billy IV. They made one last gallant stand, in game 160, Butch Wynegar tying a game in Toronto on a two-out ninth-inning homer, but they lost the next day when Doyle Alexander—a two-time Yankee whom Steinbrenner had twice angrily exiled—beat them 5–1. Three weeks later another ex-Yankee, Dick Howser, led a parade through downtown Kansas City when the Royals knocked off the Cardinals in a thrilling seven-game World Series.

By then, Martin was relieved of his duties. Steinbrenner insisted all month that he was staying out of the decision, that it would all fall on Clyde King's shoulders. That notion was funnier than Billy Martin's attempt to be a pacifist. Steinbrenner said he was pleased by the man that "Clyde King" had picked as Martin's replacement: Lou Piniella.

"I've played here," Piniella said, "I've coached here. I've sat in on meetings. I'm well attuned to what's transpired here. I've been here. I won't be surprised."

It was all so cute, so adorable, some of the writers almost wanted to pinch Piniella's cheeks, and ask him: "You have *met* your boss, right?"

CHAPTER 19

I will never let the Yankees be number two in this city.
—GEORGE STEINBRENNER

It was hard to imagine a worse-case scenario for George Steinbrenner. Beginning on the evening of Saturday, October 18, 1986, extending for the next ten days, the World Series would be fought between the two baseball clubs in which he'd invested thirteen years' of angst, worry, hubris and disdain: the Boston Red Sox, the Yankees' ancient blood rivals from the moment Babe Ruth was exchanged late in 1919 for $100,000 cash; and the New York Mets, with whom the Yankees shared a city and ever-shifting tides of consumer fealty.

When Steinbrenner boldly declared he'd never allow the Yankees to be second-best in New York, it was spring 1984 and the Yankees had enjoyed a distinct advantage over the Mets in on-field success, attendance and television ratings in every year since 1976.

But the sand under Steinbrenner's feet had already begun to shift. In 1983 the Mets traded for Keith Hernandez, the 1979 MVP with St. Louis who would become the Mets' first-ever team captain. Darryl Strawberry was called up in May, exactly the kind of swaggering slugger Steinbrenner coveted, and he'd won Rookie of the Year. The Mets did suffer a self-inflicted PR fiasco by allowing Tom Seaver to leave for a second time by senselessly keeping him unprotected in the free agent compensation draft;

that allowed a roster spot to be seized in spring 1984 by a nineteen-year-old named Dwight Gooden, who would become a sensation (and a box office bonanza) by winning seventeen games, striking out 276 batters in 218 innings.

By 1986 the gap was growing. There'd been the usual in-season drama when the Yankees, under rookie manager Lou Piniella, fell behind the Red Sox (thanks in large part to the hitting and leadership of Don Baylor, whom Steinbrenner couldn't wait to trade that spring). At one point, Steinbrenner ordered Winfield to the bench, after Winfield got off to his slowest start as a Yankee, sitting at .226 in July. Winfield, though furious, correctly surmised, "I don't think it's Lou who's doing it," and Piniella all but confirmed that for him by saying when he'd talked to Winfield, "I didn't make a point of yes or no, so you can interpret that as you wish." That set Steinbrenner off, too, and Piniella was pummeled with phone calls the next few days. Soon enough, Steinbrenner ripped Piniella, too.

"I've done everything for this guy," Steinbrenner said. "I gave him a chance to manage the Yankees without going to the minors. In retrospect, maybe that was a mistake."

Meanwhile, the Mets seized first place the second week of the season and never let up on the way to a 108–54 record. They set a single-season New York City attendance record by attracting 2,767,601, a half million more than the Yankees. The Mets would continue to outdraw the Yankees through the 1992 season, becoming the first-ever New York team to top three million in 1987 (and again in 1988).

The Mets weren't bashful about taking the town away, either.

"George doesn't want to admit it," Mets manager Davey Johnson said, "but we're claiming some of his fans, as well as Mets fans."

Steinbrenner ordered Mets games no longer be shown in the press box or in the media workroom. The Mets tweaked the Yankees by putting advertisements at the top of the stairs of the platform across the street from Yankee Stadium, at the 161st Street stop, with their slogan for 1986: "Baseball Like It Oughta Be."

"The subway is the best place to reach baseball fans," reasoned Jerry

Della Femina, still a Steinbrenner antagonist and the brains behind that placement. "And some nights, it's the best place to reach *disappointed* baseball fans."

After the resumption of the Mayor's Trophy Game for several years it was the Mets who decided to end that exhibition for good when they signed a two-year agreement in 1986 to instead play a home-and-home charity exhibition with—of all teams—the Red Sox.

So it was perhaps something of a shock when the *New York Post* announced a guest columnist for all Mets playoff games in October 1986:

George M. Steinbrenner III.

He had fun with the column—or as much fun as he could watching the Mets beat the Astros in six games for the National League pennant, capped by an extraordinary sixteen-inning classic in Game 6. He quoted Shakespeare. He quoted Milton. He quoted Dryden. He was quick to remind readers that he'd been sports editor of the student newspaper back at Williams College. And he conceded at the end of his column after the Mets' 7–6 clincher: "I am not sure the superlatives will not be exhausted—for with all of its periods of offensive frustration this was one hell of a ball game!"

> **INTERLUDE:** Steinbrenner quickly adapted to the New York tabloid style of get in quick, say what you want to say and get out. And also to the New York tabloids' eternal affinity for the slammer—otherwise known in the rest of the English-speaking world as an exclamation point!

Hard as he tried, it was obvious the seven-game World Series that followed made Steinbrenner want to jam his pencil in his eye; it was abundantly clear he would've preferred a way for *both* teams to lose the series.

After the Mets lost the first two, at home, Steinbrenner crowed on page one: "Welcome to the American League East!"

Following the Mets' epic comeback from near extinction in Game 6, when they'd rallied for three tenth-inning runs, Steinbrenner offered this counsel to Davey Johnson, reminding that the ancient Latin wordsmith Syrus had advised "it is a good thing to learn caution by the misfortune of others." And when the Mets finally took him out of his misery by winning Game 7, 8–5, he shared a paragraph with his go-to source: "For our neighbors at Shea . . . you are richly deserved and were so rewarded. And in the words of Milton: 'Well done! Well has thou fought the better fight.'"

It was Keith Hernandez, regular *Post* reader, who got the last word in with that one: "Look, George is the greatest thing that ever happened to the Yankees. He made them a winner. But when he said 'Welcome to the AL East,' that was my war cry. Welcome, George, to the New York Mets—the best team in baseball in 1986."

What could he do? The next day Steinbrenner called Yankee Stadium and ordered a message to be carried on the marquee outside: "Congratulations, Mets."

IT HAD TAKEN George Steinbrenner ten years, but by 1983 he'd rebuilt the Yankees, had lifted the brand beyond where it had ever been before. Starting in 1984, though, it wasn't just the emergence of the Mets that would help undo so much of this careful architecture. Through the end of the decade, the Yankees would annually find themselves battling two difficult opponents: the rest of the American League, and their own owner (a slide that wouldn't halt until the more destructive of those elements would disappear for two years).

For now, even as the Mets failed to duplicate their 1986 apex, Steinbrenner's Yankees could never seize back the city because he was incapable of crafting a full and balanced baseball roster. The Yankees offense—led by Rickey Henderson, Don Mattingly and Dave Winfield—would usually be fearsome. Their pitching was almost always circumspect. A different team every year would reach first place, stubbornly refuse to yield it to the Yankees—the Tigers, the Blue Jays, the Red Sox—who would win their share of games but not nearly *enough* games.

And George Steinbrenner would have his say.

Always, he would have his say.

In 1987, it actually seemed the Yankees might do the one thing that could keep the Boss quiet and quartered in Tampa: They started hot, and they kept it up through April, through May, through June. At the halfway mark they were 51–30 and led the East by five games. Piniella was being hailed as Manager of the Year. Dave Winfield, who'd driven in one hundred runs or better in five straight seasons, had sixty-three of them after eighty-one games. Henderson got off to a blazing start, ten home runs in the first two months (four of them leading off games), stealing twenty-three bases, hitting a robust .327.

Mattingly started slowly. Following a 1986 season that almost yielded a second straight MVP (.352, 113 RBIs, a remarkable eighty-six extra-base hits) he knew he'd be able to make a huge score in arbitration and most everyone encouraged him to ask for $2 million, a mark Steinbrenner repeatedly said "no player is worth." But Mattingly loved being a Yankee and only coveted tranquility, so he asked for $1.975 million, a symbolic olive branch to the Boss.

The Boss hadn't seen it that way.

"Arbitration," he sneered, "is the cancer of baseball."

He had a warning for his not-quite-two-million-dollar star: "I fully expect Don Mattingly to lead us to the World Series now and he'd better do it just like [Mets catcher] Gary Carter did after he got *his* big contract."

Steinbrenner stunned most of his audience by avoiding the temptation of a fifth walk down the aisle with Billy Martin, instead bringing Piniella back for a second year; more shocking was a few weeks later, when the time came to court free agents—usually the Boss's favorite time of the year. Everyone around the Yankees believed they were lacking one thing to put them over the top—an ace, a genuine horse to eat innings and anchor the pitching staff. As it happened, a perfect candidate was available: Tigers star Jack Morris. Even better: After negotiating with three teams—including his hometown Minnesota Twins—Morris and his agent, Dick Moss, gave Steinbrenner their terms.

One year, salary to be determined by an arbitrator.

"It's an offer George can't possibly refuse," Moss said.

George refused. Morris, stunned, went back to Detroit. And the case that the union had been building for years against the owners—charges that all twenty-six were colluding to drive salaries down—was at last fully in the open. Commissioner Peter Ueberroth had lectured them as a group since he'd taken office in 1984 to treat their baseball business as they would their other businesses.

"Baseball can't survive an ever-escalating salary structure," he'd warned.

Steinbrenner, in a staggering departure, went along with the plan. Instead of signing Morris—and, even better, taking him away from the Tigers—he walked away.

"It's evident Steinbrenner doesn't want to win," said Marvin Miller, by now retired as the head of the players' union but still a man who could spot collusion from a hundred paces. "Or that there are things he fears more than losing."

Ironic, then, that the Yankees' season died in Detroit, which started the season 11–19 but finished 98–64 and in first place in the AL East, thanks in no small part to an 18–11 season from Jack Morris, his 3.38 ERA and 208 strikeouts in 266 innings. On August 8, Tommy John threw a 7–0 shutout against the Tigers, and it moved the Yankees back into first place by a half game. It would turn out to be the last night the Yankees would go to sleep in first. Steinbrenner had already lit his blowtorch.

Five days earlier Steinbrenner, incensed after a shutout loss to Cleveland, told general manager Woody Woodward to instruct Piniella to be in his room at the Stouffer's Inn on the Square at two o'clock the next day to take a call. By this point, Piniella was on his last ribbon of rope with the constant harassment and relentless second-guessing. Piniella believed with all the injuries the Yankees suffered it was a miracle they were still even in the race. Henderson had twice been disabled with a bad hamstring. Mattingly hurt a disc, an injury that for a while had been rumored to be caused by some horseplay with little-used reliever Bob Shirley (Steinbrenner threatened to use lie detectors to get to the truth; Shirley was quietly released with no reason given).

Piniella laughed. "Some baseball teams, you don't think you'll ever hear words like 'polygraph,' and yet around here nobody blinks."

Piniella was easily talked out of sequestering in his room.

Steinbrenner called at two o'clock. And at two fifteen. And at two thirty.

It didn't help Piniella at all that his team was pulverized 15–3 that night, thanks in part to three passed balls by his catcher, Mark Salas. Piniella had begged for catching help for weeks (Salas had a remarkable *nine* passed balls), and when the team arrived in Detroit he approached Woodward about that.

"I'm sorry, Lou," Woodward told him. "I'm not allowed to talk to you."

"Excuse me?"

"I'm not allowed to talk to you."

Now, Piniella fully believed he was through the looking glass. He'd quit smoking in the offseason but was back up to three packs a day (a common malady for Yankees managers). Harvey Greene, the Yankees' PR chief, handed him two pieces of paper before the 7–0 win. It was a 743-word statement from the principal owner of the Yankees.

And it was a doozy. The Boss buried Piniella for insubordination—"I don't know of too many guys—even sportswriters—who if their boss told them to be available for a call at a certain time wouldn't be there!"

Worse, Steinbrenner said Piniella told him he was convinced Rickey Henderson wasn't as hurt as he claimed. Steinbrenner used a ballplayers' term—"Lou said he was 'jaking it.'" And with that Steinbrenner put his manager in danger of losing his clubhouse.

Still, the Yankees knew who was on the side of the angels in this one. After the game, Willie Randolph and Ron Guidry—named cocaptains when Graig Nettles departed for San Diego—summoned their teammates. Rick Cerone—back for a second of three tours with the Yankees—played the part of narrator. And three others—Claudell Washington, Gary Ward, Winfield—took the statement, held it over a trash can in the visitor's trainer's room at Tiger Stadium.

And lit a match.

And the 1987 Yankees laughed and rejoiced in burning the pages of George Steinbrenner's statement.

"They took the heart out of my team," Piniella said on the season's final day, his last day (for now) as manager of the Yankees. By then, it was an open secret that Piniella was going to be replaced, and just about everyone in New York City had the same reaction:

My gosh, is that Billy Martin's entrance music?

THIS TIME, EVEN Billy Martin was stunned at just how much of a madhouse the Yankees had become. Martin was used to the Boss getting on managers.

But now, Steinbrenner merrily went after his players, too.

Mostly, he went after the *best* of the players.

He'd gone after Dave Righetti good. Righetti had been the Rookie of the Year in 1981 and by '82 found himself in Columbus, sent there by Steinbrenner. He threw a no-hitter on Steinbrenner's fifty-third birthday, July 4, 1983. And while it displeased him, he willingly accepted an assignment as the closer in the bullpen beginning in 1984 when Goose Gossage fled. This, he soon realized, was tantamount to agreeing to sit about fifteen feet from Steinbrenner's duck blind.

"As a starter, you'd only be in danger once a week," he'd say with a laugh years later. "As a closer, it was two, three, sometimes four days a week. And the son of a gun was on point. Every time you blew a game, it seemed, you heard about it."

In 1986 Righetti set a major-league record by saving forty-six games. Across the last four months he'd been brilliant. But he'd struggled early, compounded by the inevitable critiques that followed every failure. The bottom came in Toronto, on June 20, when Righetti walked into the bottom of the ninth with an 8–2 lead and left with the game tied 8–8. When Piniella came to get him, instead of handing him the ball Righetti, in frustration, heaved it far over the distant outfield wall about 350 feet away. Piniella crowed, "I love the passion!" but Righetti admitted: "I have never felt that kind of anguish."

Afterward Steinbrenner—Hank Steinbrenner, George's twenty-eight-year-old son—declared "Maybe Alfonso Pulido could be the closer instead"—that would be Alfonso Pulido, who would pitch a total of thirty and two-thirds innings in the major leagues.

That one lit a fuse.

"We're not panicking like the guy upstairs," Righetti sneered after hearing the deep baseball thoughts of the guy upstairs' kid. "He's never played a fucking game for this team. What does he know?"

The oddest feud was with Mattingly. That one was complicated. As Mattingly rose, ultimately blossoming into the consensus best player in the sport according to his peers, Steinbrenner began to peddle a story that he'd been on an airplane thumbing through an issue of *Sports Illustrated* when he'd seen an item on Mattingly as a Reitz High player in its back-of-the-book "Faces in the Crowd" section.

"I told the scouts about him, because I read *Sports Illustrated*," he insisted. "It was my find."

Great story.

Except the item in *SI* ran in the edition of July 16, 1979. Mattingly had been selected in the nineteenth round of the MLB entry draft on June 6.

Now Mattingly was a star, the most popular Yankee since Mantle, and even working-class fans didn't begrudge him the checks he was cashing. Nobody did. Except the Boss.

Mattingly started 1987 slowly but, unsurprisingly, still had a remarkable year: .327, thirty homers, 115 RBIs. He'd also hit six grand slams that season and tied a record by hitting home runs in eight straight games in July.

He was the toast of the town. *Most* of the town.

"He was more concerned with the home run record than he was in helping us win games," Steinbrenner said, blissfully unaware of the irony that hitting home runs is, generally speaking, a *huge* help in winning games.

Mattingly normally let these observations pass like a slider down-and-away.

Not this time.

"For some reason, I just don't think it's going to work out," he said. "I think the owner will run me out of New York before it gets too late there."

"He might be right," Steinbrenner retorted. "It won't be the end of the Yankees if Don Mattingly leaves. I think he's frustrated."

Said Mattingly: "Frustration? What does he know? He never played the game."

Mattingly loved New York—loved the pinstripes—so much that when the Boss offered a three-year, $6.7 million deal, he signed. He said he could've held out for more, but felt like the Yankees were his family.

By this time the Boss signed for Billy V, and Lou Piniella was kicked upstairs, to general manager—an ill fit from the start. Piniella made no pretense about wanting to manage again—"but never here, not for *that* guy," he promised—and when friends asked why he'd stick around the zoo he was honest with them.

"I have kids," he said. "They'll be in college soon. They've lived here their whole lives. I can't walk away from that."

He'd walk in seven months, not long after Steinbrenner sent him and Gene Michael to Houston's Astrodome for a scouting mission. The Boss wanted his two closest protégés to be incognito so he recommended sunglasses, raincoats and umbrellas.

"Umbrellas in the *Astrodome*, George?" Piniella said.

"That's a true story," Michael said years later. "It sounds made-up. You want to know what it was like to work for George sometimes? *That's* what it was like."

All of it was starting to fry the nerves of even the stoic Indiana kid.

Late summer of '88, it was clear that another year of Mattingly's prime had come and gone, and while Steinbrenner had taken only subtle shots that year, they'd been heard. And on August 21, all of that bottled anger came pouring out.

"I think there are a lot of unhappy players," he said. "There's no respect. They give you money, and that's it. That's as far as it goes. They think money is respect. Call us babies, call us whatever you want. If you don't treat me with respect I don't want to work for you.

"They pay you the money," he continued, "and then they treat you like shit."

He never said the words "George Steinbrenner," not once.

But Steinbrenner sure recognized himself in the description. He fired off another statement, this time opting for the third person.

"The Boss," he said, "is really confused. I'm not making errors on the field. I'm not leaving men stranded in scoring position time and again . . . that is why Don Mattingly's statement doesn't bother me much. He's a young man who is upset and frustrated because he 'guaranteed a pennant' for the Yankees last winter and the team is playing poorly. . . ."

Mattingly knew he'd never win if he jumped in the sandbox. When he read the statement he smiled, shook his head and said, "Let's all move on."

BILLY V WAS a hit at first. The Yankees took over first place on May 3, stayed there for forty-seven straight days. Winfield had his finest season as a Yankee, despite Steinbrenner's daily attempts to trade him (Piniella and Michael's cloak-and-dagger mission to Houston was an effort to scout potential target Kevin Bass). Even as they coasted in first place, there was a problem.

Stunningly, it happened in a bar.

Actually, it *started* in a bar, at the Arlington Hilton. Martin was drinking to forget a 7–6 loss to the Rangers alongside Mickey Mantle, Mick's son Danny, and Mike Ferraro (who'd been hired by Steinbrenner for a third time, this time to be—no lie—third base coach). It was packed. Martin asked Mickey, who lived nearby, "Isn't there a quieter place than this?"

"I know just the place!" Mickey said.

So the four of them taxied to a windowless building with stucco exterior walls. The sign out front announced it as LACE; the throbbing music and plentiful G-strings confirmed it was a strip joint.

"You son of a bitch," Martin said to Mickey, laughing wickedly. "*This* is the quiet place?"

What happened next has never been fully determined. As in the past Martin was recognized. As in the past there were words, some of them sarcastic. Martin told Ferraro to take the Mantles home; Ferraro did as he was told. Martin went to the restroom. When he emerged he was a bloody mess. He said he was attacked. Others swore he fell. Martin somehow limped outside, found a cab, drove back to the Hilton, hoping he could sneak in quietly, get trainer Gene Monahan to tend to his wounds.

Good plan.

Only back at the Hilton, there had been an accident near one of the saunas. The fire alarms blared, and the entire building was evacuated. This included twenty-five Yankees, six coaches, eight traveling beat writers.

And George M. Steinbrenner III, wrapped in a silk robe.

"You've *got* to be kidding me," Martin said as he stepped out of the cab.

He was on the clock again, and time ran out June 23, with the Yankees at 40–28, still only two and a half games out of first. Steinbrenner told Martin he didn't blame him for what happened at Lace, he simply couldn't abide this kind of behavior; the New York papers had practically opened bureaus at Lace, keeping the story alive for weeks.

"He hurt me this time," a despondent Martin said a few weeks later.

Of course, he said this at Old-Timers' Day, to which he gladly accepted an invitation, happily drank in one more ovation, merrily donned his old number 1 jersey—which Steinbrenner had retired two years earlier, not bad for a .257 lifetime hitter with sixty-four lifetime home runs.

Yogi Berra kept his promise and his distance from the stadium that Old-Timers' Day; Piniella asked him to be his bench coach, and while Berra was touched, he told Lou he'd never set foot in Yankee Stadium as long as "that guy" owned the team. When the Yankees inducted Berra and Bill Dickey into the team Hall of Fame in 1988, adding the honor of a plaque in Monument Park, Dickey, at eighty-one, quickly accepted. Berra played golf. Four Old-Timers' Days passed without him, and he'd stay away for ten more. Martin? He trotted onto the field just twenty-three days after they axed him.

Applauding from the dugout was the new manager. Who was also the *old* manager.

"What the fuck are you doing here?" Dave Winfield asked Lou Piniella when he saw him sitting in his old office on June 24. Piniella, in truth, didn't have a good answer. And he admittedly didn't do a great job. Before the Yankees finished another fifth-place season at 85–76, Piniella all but begged Steinbrenner to fire him, once again vowed he wouldn't ever come back. This time, it took.

By now, the shining baseball city on a hill that Steinbrenner envisioned lay in rubble. Ten seasons had passed without a title, seven since a playoff berth, and many Yankees fans had grown weary of the slapstick. Fan groups organized across the boroughs, up and down the suburbs, demanding Steinbrenner sell the team.

If the Boss heard their pleas, he never let on. Besides, by now, he'd already made a decision that would nearly destroy him.

CHAPTER 20

I think George would agree that fans have every right to express their point of view.
—FAY VINCENT

It was an exhausting year for George Steinbrenner. His baseball team struggled in 1989, a fifth-place train wreck at 74–87 that exposed the franchise's stunning dearth of major-league talent to go with a farm system ransacked by years of malpractice. His feud with Dave Winfield reached its zenith, Winfield suing and Steinbrenner countersuing. Winfield missed the whole season thanks to back surgery. If there was one high point it came early: January 19, the last full day of his presidency, Ronald Reagan granted Steinbrenner a pardon for his 1974 conviction.

It was Christmas now, and with his family gathered at his Tampa home, grandchildren playing at his feet, the Boss could forget his troubles for a bit.

Just after dinner, his eldest son summoned him.

"You'd better see this," Hank said.

There, on the television, was an impossible bulletin interrupting the evening news: Billy Martin, sixty-one, five-time manager of the Yankees, had been pronounced dead at Wilson Memorial Hospital in Johnson City, New York, three miles outside Binghamton, about ten miles southwest of Fenton, where Billy and Jill Martin owned a farmhouse. After an afternoon of drinking Martin and his friend Bill Reedy drove back to the house, negotiating snowy, icy roads, missed a turn, lost control of Martin's Ford pickup truck and landed in a ditch mere yards from Martin's driveway. Reedy—who told authorities at the scene he was driving but later recanted, saying he was hoping to spare Martin legal trouble that would impede his career—suffered a broken hip, needed to be airlifted to a trauma center in Syracuse and survived.

Martin broke his neck. After a lifetime cheating death with endless bouts of saloon-aided misbehavior, what finally caught up to him was someone's decision to drive after spending Christmas Day quaffing beer and vodka at a restaurant named Morey's (many of Martin's friends, as well as his son, believed Martin was likely driving; it was never proven conclusively, and Reedy was later found liable).

Steinbrenner was left breathless.

Hal Steinbrenner, George's younger son and future heir, was home from Williams College for the Christmas holiday. He was stunned to see his father reduced to sobs, unable to believe the news, inconsolable even as Hal and Hank tried to offer comfort.

"I'd never seen my father react that way to anything before," Hal would remember. "It was as if he'd lost a brother. For all the bad times they'd had together, Martin was an essential part of the fabric of my father's professional life. And now he was gone."

Less than a week before, the Boss (dressed as Santa Claus), Martin and Yankees second baseman Steve Sax sang Christmas carols together before two thousand underprivileged kids at Tampa Performing Arts Center. Martin read *The Night Before Christmas* and joked with Steinbrenner that this particular Santa didn't need much pillow to fill his red suit. Steinbrenner laughed and then gave Martin the only holiday present he really wanted: If the Yankees got off to a poor start in 1990—and Steinbrenner knew the odds were good the Yankees would be *dreadful* in 1990—by May 1, the latest, he'd be restored to power for a sixth time.

To Martin—whose beloved mother had just died, leaving him in a profound depression—this wasn't just welcome news; it was a life preserver. As Steinbrenner watched the reports Christmas night, he remembered

Martin's smile six days earlier. Now he was dead. Steinbrenner assured Jill he would take care of all the arrangements. As a personal friend of Cardinal John O'Connor's, he convinced the cleric to allow the thrice-divorced Martin's service to take place December 29 at St. Patrick's Cathedral and arranged for him to be interred at Gate of Heaven Cemetery in Hawthorne, New York, not far from the final resting places of Yankee icon Babe Ruth and Yankee Doodle Dandy James Cagney.

"He gave us thrills and spills, ups and downs," Father Edwin Broderick said, eulogizing Martin before an overflow of three thousand. "We pray his is a safe slide into home plate."

Outside the church stood a throng of thousands, so many faces that when one of the funeral guests, Richard M. Nixon, saw Billy Joe, Martin's twenty-five-year-old son, weeping, he told him to lift his head.

"I want you to see all the people who loved your father," Nixon said.

A bad year reached its sad nadir for George Steinbrenner. Then, just nine days after laying his forever foil to rest, Steinbrenner assured that 1990 would be just as calamitous. Back on December 17, 1986, he'd reluctantly taken a call from a man who'd been pestering him for months, who for years was an annoying bee buzzing the ears of Yankees beat writers, always seeking an audience with the Boss. Steinbrenner assiduously avoided him, but on December 17 he took the call.

Into his life, Steinbrenner welcomed Howard Spira.

For the next few years, Spira would regale Steinbrenner with a wealth of stories and tales about Dave Winfield, for whose foundation Spira had once worked. The Boss, of course, was also in the shame-Winfield business, with both feet. Now, in January 1990, Steinbrenner sat down and signed two checks—one for $30,500, one for $9,500, made payable to the man who would replace Billy Martin as Steinbrenner's chief sparring partner for the foreseeable future.

Not long after, when he thought he'd rid himself of the nuisance with this ransom of $40,000, he received another message.

"He gave me the forty," Howie Spira told Phil McNiff, Steinbrenner's top security adviser. "I want another hundred and ten."

THE FORTY GRAND was handed over on January 7, 1990.

Exactly one year and one day earlier, Dave Winfield filed his third lawsuit against Steinbrenner for withholding funds to his foundation, as Steinbrenner was contractually obliged to do. The complaint asked for $1 million, said Steinbrenner failed to make the payments in an effort to get Winfield to agree to a trade. Steinbrenner never fully believed the charity was competently run. He intended to fight back. He put every cent allegedly owed into an interest-bearing escrow account, pending a deeper look into the books.

Two days later, Steinbrenner countersued. He charged Winfield, too, failed to make his full share of payments to the foundation, to which he was also contractually mandated, and asked the player to pay $380,000 to cover those costs.

That was just grist for the lawyers.

This was what caught everyone else's attention:

"Winfield has made large loans at usurious rates of interest (e.g., over 700 percent in one instance!) to an individual he knew was engaged in heavy gambling on the outcome of baseball games and other sporting events."

That individual was Howie Spira.

Now the army of reporters who'd spent years begging Spira to stop calling at crazy hours of the night . . . well, suddenly they were scrambling to find Howie Spira's phone number, and the address for his parents' house in the Bronx, near Van Cortlandt Park.

Spira waited a long time for these fifteen minutes of fame (that would ultimately yield two and a half years inside federal penitentiaries in West Virginia, Texas and North Carolina). Spira, who'd worked for the Winfield Foundation as a gofer from 1981 to 1984, still had photographs of a canceled check for $15,000, made out to Spira and signed by Winfield. Spira said Winfield gave it to him to settle a gambling debt; Howie was *always* swimming in gambling losses.

There was more. Back in 1981, during Winfield's nightmarish

1-for-22 World Series, Winfield's rep, Al Frohman, hatched an idea and scribbled on a piece of paper: *N———, if you play tonight, you are going to be shot and killed right on the field.* Then he gave it to Spira and instructed him to mail it to Frohman or else Frohman would alert every wiseguy in New York to his whereabouts. Since Howie owed almost all of them, that could be hazardous to his health. Howie claimed he did that one gratis, dropping the fake death threat in the mail, then took the letter once Frohman plucked it out of his mailbox and passed it along to his friends in the media.

Steinbrenner took great delight in all of this. He'd been ransacked in the papers for years over the way he treated Winfield, and now, thanks to his new friend Howie Spira, he'd toppled Winfield from the sanctimonious high ground. He thanked Spira, made what were either promises of a cash windfall, a job and a place to live at Steinbrenner's hotel in Tampa (that was Howie's take) or the Boss's eternal thanks and the promise of box seats at Yankees games whenever he needed them (that was George's).

In late January Mike Lupica, then the most influential sports columnist in the city, suggested in the *Daily News* that the men save themselves a lot of money and the Yankees a season of outright civil war by agreeing to binding arbitration. Steinbrenner, who already believed he'd won the PR battle, readily agreed. It took Winfield a few days, but he saw the wisdom of avoiding a ruinous court fight. It took arbiter Michael Armstrong more than eight months to sift through all the documents, to interview the relevant parties and, hardest of all, to keep any of this from leaking to the press. But on September 6, the matter was settled when Steinbrenner agreed to free up $600,000 sitting in escrow and Winfield agreed to make a delinquent $229,667 payment of his own, in addition to $30,000 "inappropriately expended by the foundation."

Steinbrenner could barely contain his glee: "It's difficult for a man to admit he's made mistakes, but David is doing that, and that makes him a bigger man in my eyes. I will be most happy to have him back with the Yankees next season."

Winfield wrapped his arm around a beaming Steinbrenner, his own fully bearded face brightened with a smile. The TV cameras whirled. The newspaper cameras clicked. Back at his apartment by Van Cortlandt Park, Howie Spira saw these two men he hated mugging for the cameras. He seethed, and he stewed, and soon he would call Steinbrenner, and call him again, and call his family, again and again, until the day the Feds came storming through the front door.

BEATING WINFIELD WAS a rare win for Steinbrenner. The Boss hired Dallas Green to manage the Yankees in 1989, and for a short while was smitten—for a short while. Green was, in almost every way, Steinbrenner's blueprint for a manager. He had a track record, winning the 1980 World Series with Philadelphia, the first-ever championship in that franchise's ninety-eight-year existence. He was unafraid of millionaire ballplayers, seemed to relish publicly challenging his superstars: Mike Schmidt, Pete Rose and Steve Carlton. He was six-foot-five and by now a good 240 pounds, imposing as hell, big enough that you could almost fit two Billy Martins in his pinstripes. He'd enjoy a drink with his coaches after the game, but he was never going to wind up on the front page with a black eye or a missing tooth.

"I think I bring something to the table that puts us over the hump," Green said the day he was hired. "I intend to instill team discipline to get things done."

Steinbrenner marveled at the tight camp Green ran in Fort Lauderdale. He was especially delighted when he picked up a newspaper during the Yankees' first western swing of the season and saw Green's succinct description of the team: "We stink."

There was one problem.

Green was right. The Yankees *did* stink. Losing Winfield was a killer. In what would become a sad ritual from now on, Don Mattingly's back began to bark. When it was obvious they would struggle, Steinbrenner sent Rickey Henderson back to Oakland. The pitching staff was a mess, the lineup worse. One exception was a twenty-one-year-old speedster the Yankees took as a flier in the '88 draft who seemed destined for greatness as a football player. The first time Deion Sanders walked into Green's spring training camp he asked for a single-digit number—"I always wear a low number," he said, unaware that around the Yankees most of the single digits were already retired. He settled for 44, Reggie Jackson's old number, which seemed exactly right.

"I like the kid's confidence," Green said.

There was little else to like, though, and soon even Steinbrenner got tired of hearing Green bitch about his players.

"I think this team is better than the way we're playing," Steinbrenner said at last, in August, and the reporters who'd been around a while understood they'd better not make Jersey Shore plans the next few weeks. Steinbrenner knew Green would see that little shot and respond exactly as he did.

"The statement that Manager George made about the game is a very logical second-guess," Green said, replete with shit-eating grin, "and hindsight being twenty/twenty, that's why managers go gray. It's always easier to piss from above."

Manager George.

"You had to give Dallas this," Don Mattingly laughed. "He had officially run out of fucks to give."

Steinbrenner waited two weeks, then reached back to happier times by calling Bucky Dent up from Columbus.

More and more, fans and commentators called on Steinbrenner to sell the team, but they had little idea the force they were up against. In 1982, while shopping the Yankees' TV rights, Warner Communications head Steve Ross half jokingly asked Steinbrenner if he'd take $100 million for the team.

Steinbrenner just laughed.

Not long after *that* he took a call from a young New York millionaire with whom he'd grown acquainted, eager to buy a franchise, so he floated a figure for the Yankees.

"How about $150 million?" Donald J. Trump asked.

Steinbrenner said no. Trump bought the New Jersey Generals of the United States Football League instead.

The whole landscape of sports had become a louder and more wrathful space. In 1987, WFAN radio debuted, a twenty-four-hour haven for hot takes and all manner of sporting anguish. In 1989, the Yankees made an ill-fated decision to hold a Banner Day, and the results were predictably ugly, dozens of bedsheets sacrificed in the name of vulgar frustration, much of it aimed at Steinbrenner. On June 27, 1988, Mike Tyson knocked out Michael Spinks at Atlantic City's Convention Hall, the most anticipated boxing match of the year. Introduced ringside to the overflow crowd, Steinbrenner was booed lustily. The fight itself lasted only ninety-one seconds; Steinbrenner's greeting dragged at least twice as long.

> **INTERLUDE:** It was on July 21, 1988, when Steinbrenner would execute perhaps his most famous failed trade. We'll fast-forward to 1996 and a *Seinfeld* episode entitled "The Caddy" to explain. We pick it up with George Costanza AWOL from his position as Yankees traveling secretary. Steinbrenner [voiced by Larry David] tells George's parents the sad news.
>
> **STEINBRENNER:** Well, he'd been logging some pretty heavy hours. First one in in the morning, last one to leave at night, that kid was a human dynamo. . . .
> **FRANK:** What the hell did you trade Jay Buhner for?! He had thirty home runs, over a hundred RBIs last year; he's got a rocket for an arm . . . YOU DON'T KNOW WHAT THE HELL YOU'RE DOING!
> **STEINBRENNER:** Well, you know he was a good prospect, no question about it. But my baseball people loved Ken Phelps's bat. They kept saying, "Ken Phelps! Ken Phelps!"

Soon it was clear the fans weren't the only ones who were rankled.

FAY VINCENT KNEW George Steinbrenner long before he *knew* the man. Vincent graduated from Williams College in 1960, eight years after

Steinbrenner. He'd watched Steinbrenner's rise from a distance as Vincent built a successful career in law, then as the director of finance for the Securities and Exchange Commission, later as the chairman of Columbia Pictures and senior vice president at Coca-Cola. When his longtime friend Bart Giamatti succeeded Peter Ueberroth as baseball's commissioner in 1989 Vincent joined as his deputy, and it was his sad duty to replace him when Giamatti died suddenly September 1, 1989. Now he saw, up close, Steinbrenner's vast array of quirks and tics, and it appalled him the way Steinbrenner so often resorted to bullying and bluster.

It's easy to understand why Vincent might've cocked an eyebrow when he read the *Daily News* on the morning of Sunday, March 18. There, it was revealed that Howie Spira hadn't just received a $40,000 payment from George Steinbrenner; he'd been smart enough (or mousy enough) to record the conversation, and dozens of others with Steinbrenner, his associates and his family over the next few weeks.

On that fateful December 17, 1986, Spira began his day trying to reconcile with Dave Winfield, who'd spent the better part of two years hoping Spira would lose his number. Spira asked for a job. Winfield turned him down flat, and when Spira wouldn't let it go, Winfield threatened: "Howard, I'm going to hang up on you in a minute."

"Don't bother!" Spira snapped, and slammed the phone.

Then he dialed George Steinbrenner.

"You should only know how much money they stole from you," Spira said.

He knew a lot more, and happily shared: the $15,000 check, and why Spira so desperately needed it; the fake death threat; Winfield's less-than-type-A work ethic when it came to the foundation. Steinbrenner gobbled it all up and would soon use it to kneecap Winfield. Somewhere along the way, Spira believed Steinbrenner agreed to take care of him the rest of his life. If that conversation ever happened, Spira forgot to turn his tape recorder on. He changed course. He became a nuisance. He called Steinbrenner every day, and when the Boss finally realized he needed to stop taking those calls Spira moved on to his associates, his lawyers, his children . . . even his wife, Joan, to whom Howie said his life was in imminent danger thanks to his gambling debts.

"I don't understand why you keep bothering this house," Joan Steinbrenner said on one recording. "I have nothing to do with anything in his life except his children. It couldn't have been that bad, you're still alive and walking."

"Barely, ma'am," Spira said.

"Do you have a job? Do you work?"

"No, ma'am. I was supposed to work for your husband."

"There are millions of people who are 'supposed' to work for my husband who don't work for my husband. That happens with every big company."

Spira kept at it.

"Howard," Joan said, "I think you need to see a doctor, I really do."

"That's not very nice," Spira said. The conversation grew more heated. Spira said, "Why are you yelling at me? I didn't do anything."

"You're a young man," Joan said. "Get out and work."

Then she hung up.

By January—after Steinbrenner paid the forty large, after Spira demanded he make it a nice round one fifty, after he'd threatened Phil McNiff that he'd take his story to the papers, that he thought about suicide "every day" and when he did it the "blood will be on [Steinbrenner's] hands"—Spira managed to get through to Steinbrenner one last time, begging for money.

"I'm telling you: no more," Steinbrenner said. "Don't bother my people anymore."

Said Spira: "I'm forced to slit my throat, but before I do I'm going to make everything I've been through made public to the whole world. There's nothing wrong with that, right?"

"Howard," Steinbrenner snapped. "That's extortion in its purest form!"

Six days after that friendly little chat, four FBI agents knocked on Spira's door. They had warrants for all of Spira's tapes, diaries, phone records, all correspondence with Steinbrenner. That's how, a few months later, the tapes came into the possession of *Daily News* reporter Richard T. Pienciak.

How Fay Vincent read all about it over his Sunday-morning coffee.

IT WAS BAD enough that Steinbrenner's baseball empire was lying in state. The 1990 Yankees were destined to finish in last place for the first time since 1966, only the second time since 1912. They'd lose ninety-five games, the most in seventy-eight years, a roster that included Mel Hall—who terrorized young players (notably, and most egregiously, a shy rookie outfielder named Bernie Williams), who once brought a live tiger to the clubhouse, who lived (somewhat openly) with a teenaged girlfriend and who, by 2024, was fifteen years into a forty-five-year prison sentence for rape and sexual abuse. The Boss's big free agent pickup was pitcher Pascual Perez, best known for getting lost on his way to the ballpark on a day he was pitching and also for dabbling in cocaine; he would suffer an arm injury and a drug relapse and would win a total of three games for the 1990 and 1991 Yankees before being thrown out of the game for good.

Before the season, at a dinner at 21 with Bucky Dent and the Yankees' beat writers, Steinbrenner said this about his manager, somehow doing so without collapsing into hysterics: "Bucky Dent will be my manager all year."

The writers didn't laugh, either, and didn't even bother to write it down.

The Yankees were dreadful from day one, and Steinbrenner jettisoned Dent at Fenway Park—scene of his home run in the 1978 one-game playoff with the Red Sox, his greatest professional triumph. Tough room.

Steinbrenner elevated his manager at Columbus, Carl Harrison (Stump) Merrill; more important was a move later that day that would have longer-lasting impact: Steinbrenner promoted Buck Showalter, who'd been serving as Dent's "eye in the sky" scout, to third base coach. For Showalter, who'd never earned even one cup of coffee in the Show, his first day working for Merrill was his first day wearing a major-league uniform.

Steinbrenner also rid himself at last of Winfield, who returned from his year off with a 1-for-29 spring and an 0-for-20 slump in April. He was finally shipped to the Angels for pitcher Mike Witt, a former All-Star who was clearly on the back nine of his career.

"I was assailed, vilified, stabbed in the back and thrown off a cliff," Winfield said on his way out. "Everything possible was done to attack my credibility and my career. And I survived. Steinbrenner said he always wins. Well, he didn't beat me."

By then Fay Vincent had already begun to close in on Steinbrenner, his interest in Howie Spira's story sparking as an inquiry and developing into a full-blown investigation spearheaded by John Dowd. A year earlier, Dowd lent his name to the report that effectively kicked Pete Rose out of baseball.

Vincent announced he would begin a hearing to determine consequences for Steinbrenner's Spira association on July 5—a day after the Boss's sixtieth birthday. That bulletin was greeted with great delight by a preponderance of Yankees fans.

But as the day drew close, a lot of odd things happened. A week before, Steinbrenner's lawyers asked to see a copy of Dowd's report, which he'd already submitted to Vincent. It was a simple case of due process, allowing Steinbrenner to see the case built against him. But Vincent, quite adamantly, refused to do so. "I don't think there's any particular purpose to that."

Well *that* didn't smell quite right.

Also, during Dowd's investigation, Steinbrenner spent several days providing testimony, and the exchange was feverishly transcribed by a court stenographer named Philip C. Rizzuti. But when that transcript was delivered to Steinbrenner's lawyers, entire passages were deleted or altered. One of Steinbrenner's attorneys, Bob Gold, contacted Rizzuti, who was shaken, and admitted: "Dowd made me do it. I can't discuss it."

Well, *that* was a little off, too.

Was Vincent putting his thumb on the scale of a baseball justice system over which he presided like a Star Chamber? Vincent long insisted that wasn't the case.

When Steinbrenner met with Vincent, the commissioner had a simple question.

"Did anyone say to you, 'George, suppose this guy takes the money and pays off gambling debts? You are now an owner in baseball financing a gambler.'"

"Well, I didn't," Steinbrenner insisted. "I never thought of that. Nobody ever mentioned that to me, Commissioner."

"I am saying to you: Why didn't you call *me*, get help from other people, before you did something which your advisers told you not to do?"

Steinbrenner was flustered. He asked Vincent why he hadn't taken a similar leap with Dave Winfield about bankrolling a gambler. He let slip that part of the reason he paid Spira off wasn't just to protect his own interests but also Lou Piniella "and his sports betting habits." (Piniella, known to place a wager or two at a racetrack, admitted that freely, but insisted he had never even met a bookmaker in person, let alone engaged with one.)

Vincent shook Steinbrenner and knew it. But Steinbrenner's lawyers figured they could blunt the damage by calling witnesses on their own behalf.

But Vincent decided zero of Steinbrenner's witnesses were relevant. One more time, the commissioner seemed amused at the notion of due process.

In time Vincent's power play would be exposed, and he would suffer the consequences. For now, he retreated to his summer home on Cape Cod to deliberate, and Steinbrenner began to realize Vincent was only doing this so he couldn't be accused of having his mind already made up. Which it was.

It came as little surprise to anyone in the commissioner's office at 350 Park Avenue when Vincent told Steinbrenner that he was prepared to suspend him from baseball for two years. The commissioner would have loved nothing more than to boot him out permanently, but he knew if he did someone, somewhere, would discover that Dowd's investigation—and his own jurisprudence—hadn't exactly been models of fairness. He actually felt Steinbrenner would be getting off light with two years.

He was stunned when Steinbrenner refused the deal.

"I can't have the word 'suspension' attached to any of this," he said.

Vincent was stupefied, no more than Steinbrenner's own lawyers, who understood that behind door number two was Vincent's only other option, a place on baseball's ineligible list. In case there was any doubt what that meant, Vincent quickly laid it to rest.

Steinbrenner said, "You know, Fay: this ineligible-list stuff—how long am I on it?"

"George," Vincent said, "try forever."

He was opting for a lifetime ban. Steinbrenner had waited fourteen long years to get the stain of the Watergate conviction bleached off his record. But he had just been granted a place in the hierarchy of the US Olympic Committee (USOC) and feared a second suspension from baseball might imperil that. The sides negotiated eleven hours. Vincent couldn't believe his good fortune: Steinbrenner was *volunteering* for the lifetime ban—which, as a bonus, forbade anyone on the ineligible list to ever sue baseball. Steinbrenner's lawyers filibustered, but by eight o'clock—three hours after the Vincent-imposed deadline—Vincent snapped closed his briefcase and headed for the elevator. He wanted to alert the press of his decision. One of the Boss's lawyers, Paul Curran, said, "See you in court."

"He's disruptive, corruptive, corrosive, boorish and embarrassing," Vincent would write of Steinbrenner years later, in an unpublished memoir. "If George wanted out, I was happy to show him the door."

He stepped onto the elevator. As the doors closed, an arm shot in, nudging them open. It was Steve Kaufman, Steinbrenner's other lawyer.

"George will sign," Kaufman said.

And he did.

Just before 8:30 p.m. on July 30, 1990, Vincent stepped before a swarm of reporters at the Helmsley Palace Hotel on Madison Avenue, not far from MLB headquarters. When he announced "George Steinbrenner . . . has agreed to be treated as if he has been placed on the permanent ineligible list," an audible gasp rose from even this seasoned band of media. He cited the commissioner's always-helpful "best interests of baseball" powers.

"This sad episode is now over," Vincent said. He couldn't resist spiking the football: "My decision in this case and this result will serve, I trust, to vindicate once again the important responsibility of the commissioner to preserve and protect the game."

Within seconds, word of Steinbrenner's ban was on the radio, and the news wires, and local TV programming in New York was interrupted. It didn't take long for the news to reach Yankee Stadium, where 24,037 people were gathered to watch the Yankees play the Tigers. A buzz began to build, which became loud cheering and finally became a roar—or as much a roar as a half-filled stadium in the middle of a lost summer can generate. Later, in the seventh-inning stretch, after singing "Take Me Out to the Ball Game," the crowd updated its longtime mantra and let loose; those who were there swore it was loud enough to be heard at the Helmsley Palace Hotel.

"NO MORE GEORGE!"
"NO MORE GEORGE!!"
"NO! MORE! GEORGE!!!"

CHAPTER 21

Steinbrenner was railroaded out of baseball on charges so flimsy it's impossible to imagine his being taken to court on them.
—MARVIN MILLER

If a polling service tried to put a number on Fay Vincent's approval rating on August 1, 1990, it probably would've been right around the 89 percent peak George H. W. Bush reached a little over six months later, in the wake of the first Gulf War. In the same way it would've seemed impossible Bush would be voted out of office twenty-one months later, the notion Vincent would similarly be out of a job would've been equally preposterous.

Vincent catapulted to prominence less than two months after assuming office, when a shattering earthquake devastated the San Francisco Bay Area on October 17, 1989, the initial tremors arriving minutes before the first pitch of World Series Game 3 between the Giants and Athletics, neighboring ball clubs in that stricken zone. Vincent's calm but forceful leadership was universally lauded. His profile soared. His power inside the game quickly became absolute, virtually unassailable.

Now, he'd actually kicked George Steinbrenner—*George Steinbrenner!*—out of the game. Forever, if you believed such things. The rejoicing was emphatic in New York City, specifically among Yankees fans who'd wearied of Steinbrenner. Years later, many of those same fans would contract convenient amnesia, but in the days after July 30, 1990, almost all were boundlessly elated.

Vincent gave Steinbrenner until August 20 to get his affairs in order, name a replacement as managing general partner and a point man to conduct all baseball business in his absence. He wasn't forced to divest what by now had grown to a 55 percent stake in the club, more like 60 percent when all family members' shares were counted. Vincent warned Steinbrenner he wouldn't be as disinterested in the details of his ban as Bowie Kuhn had been sixteen years earlier—especially when Gabe Paul, now eighty and living a peaceful retirement in Tampa, turned up in the newspapers admitting, "Yeah, I talked to George more than a few times in those days."

Steinbrenner soon realized what a foolish deal he'd struck. He'd been so worried about the USOC reacting to the word "suspension" he'd never pondered it might not be delighted by the word "expulsion," either, so he resigned from the USOC—for the moment—while plotting a path to getting his sentence commuted.

That would take hundreds of days, thousands of billable hours.

His first choice was to hand the team over to thirty-three-year-old Henry George Steinbrenner III, eldest of the four children of George and Joan Steinbrenner, named for his paternal grandfather, nicknamed "Hank." He'd spent some years apprenticing with the Yankees but had since retreated to Ocala, Florida, where he ran Kinsman's Stud, the family horse farm. The elder Steinbrenner knew Hank might be reluctant and already believed that if one of his offspring were going to run the Yankees one day it would be his younger son, Harold—Hal—but Hal was a junior at Williams College and nowhere near ready for such responsibility.

The eighteen limited partners assured Steinbrenner that they'd happily nominate Hank, and Vincent pledged he wouldn't stand in the way as long as the owners approved him, even though he knew Hank would never cut communication with his father. As Yogi Berra quipped, in the days after Steinbrenner's punishment, when he was asked if this might end his boycott from Yankee Stadium, now in its fifth year: "I mean, I'll have to see. Don't you think the two of them will get together for holiday dinners?"

Hank spent a few years coaching high school soccer. Bernie Dickman, the editor of *The Florida Horse* magazine and friend to both father and son, saw a few games and was amazed at Hank's demeanor. When George was Hank's age, running the Cleveland Pipers of the ABL, he regularly stormed into locker rooms to berate players and coaches, was a loud presence in the stands.

This was Hank: "He never raised his voice, not once," Dickman said. "People who expect Hank to be George couldn't be more wrong."

Hank was happy where he was. He didn't have much of an appetite for New York, or running the Yankees, but he was willing to be a dutiful son. George appreciated that.

Soon he hatched a different succession plan with the help of his legal team. They suggested Steinbrenner nominate Yankees CEO Leonard Kleinman despite knowing Vincent was sure to instantly reject that name because Vincent was still investigating Kleinman's possible involvement in the Howie Spira mess. Kleinman, the man who did most of Steinbrenner's unpleasant business when it came to the Yankees, was accused by Spira of expediting payment of the $40,000 payoff because he'd arranged a bank account for Spira even though he didn't have enough money to open one. Vincent wanted Kleinman off the Yankees payroll.

Steinbrenner thought it folly to nominate Kleinman, but his lawyers patiently explained that when Vincent inevitably rejected Kleinman, Kleinman could sue.

"Why don't *I* just sue him?" Steinbrenner asked.

For the hundredth time, his lawyers explained he *couldn't* sue, that part of the agreement he'd signed forbade him from suing baseball. Kleinman wasn't bound by that. And if *he* sued, then Vincent would be forced by discovery to hand over the information he'd withheld about Dowd's investigation. That would be ruinous. All Steinbrenner had to do was give Kleinman a fraction of a percentage point—a one-time payout of about $1 million—and make him a limited partner.

That, the Boss was advised, would set the wheels in motion.

Steinbrenner agreed. Robert Nederlander—brother of Jim, one of Steinbrenner's original partners, now president of the family's theater company—was prepped to replace Kleinman once Vincent took the bait.

On August 20 Steinbrenner visited the stadium one last time, enjoyed a lunch in his honor, said his goodbyes. He and Don Mattingly had gone fifteen rounds time and again, but now Mattingly requested a brief visit and afterward said, sadly, "I've been privileged to see the other side of George Steinbrenner. I probably have a different perspective."

Steinbrenner drove away from the stadium weeping. But his last order of business before putting a two-paragraph letter of resignation in an envelope bound for 350 Park Avenue was one of the most inspired things he ever did. There were few people he ever trusted more than Gene Michael—even if it was hard to tell during Michael's two stints as Yankees manager. Now he was entrusting Stick with his baseball team.

"Do it your way," Steinbrenner told his new GM.

"This is a challenge, to bring back the Yankees," Michael said. "I'm confident I can do it well."

Sixteen years earlier, Gabe Paul seized a similarly thin window of opportunity nudged open when Steinbrenner was banned by Bowie Kuhn. Paul immediately set about the task of building the core of a champion—with minimal interference, despite all those calls he now admitted receiving. The same opportunity awaited Michael. He knew he'd have to tiptoe through a minefield of Steinbrenner "counsel"—off the record, of course—but there would ultimately be no way the Boss could, say, insist on trading blue-chip prospect Bernie Williams (which he'd already come perilously close to doing) without inviting the commissioner to tighten the vise.

"I'll make the decisions," Michael said, and all that would do was alter the arc of Yankees history forever.

ON SATURDAY, OCTOBER 20, 1990, just past 11:30 p.m. on the East Coast, the cold open for the third episode of the sixteenth season of *Saturday Night Live* was a funny one: George Steinbrenner asleep on a couch in a locker room. Then we saw what he was dreaming about: playing all nine positions for the Yankees, and also every player sitting in the dugout. Announcer Don Pardo soon recited the cast members, a group that featured Dana Carvey, Mike Myers, Dennis Miller and Jan Hooks, among others. Pardo then introduced the musical guest that night, the Time.

And then . . .

"And starring . . . George Steinbrenner!"

The audience roared. Tom Shales, the longtime TV critic for *The Washington Post*, suggested wryly "they must've filled the room with Mets fans."

It seemed an odd zag for someone who'd fallen on his sword in the public square just two months before. He gave a credible performance (though, if he'd actually still had a day job, he probably wouldn't have been urged to give it up). His most memorable scene was a skit in which he played a store manager incapable of firing anyone—"How do you fire a man?" he asked. "I just can't fire people. It's not in my nature."

One skit he probably wished he could have back he played himself, welcoming a female sportswriter from the *New York Post* named Meghan (played by Hooks) to his office, there to lodge a complaint. When she enters he comes out from behind his desk wearing skivvies and socks, no pants. (It remains every bit as painful to watch as it sounds.)

Yankees fans had other things on their mind that night.

Exactly sixteen minutes before NBC clicked on to *SNL*, over on CBS, a Cincinnati Reds pitcher named Randy Myers induced Carney Lansford of the Oakland A's to pop up in fair territory to Reds first baseman Todd Benzinger. With that, the Reds cinched a sweep in the 1990 World Series with a 2–1 win. It was one of the most stunning upsets in the eighty-seven-year history of the series, a dizzying moment of triumph for the Reds.

And for their manager, Lou Piniella.

In his office, his hair still soaked with champagne, Piniella was asked if he'd gotten a phone call yet. He smiled.

"George? No. Not yet. I hear he has another job tonight."

INTERLUDE: Piniella was just the latest ex-Yankee to find championship glory away from Steinbrenner. The most striking was 1985, when Dick Howser led the Kansas City Royals to their first title. Less than two years later, Howser died at age fifty-one from a malignant brain tumor. Steinbrenner was shaken. "Firing Dick Howser and not re-signing Reggie Jackson were the two biggest mistakes I ever made," he said the day Howser passed, June 17, 1987. "We may not have had the right chemistry but I admired him greatly."

Steinbrenner could still share opinions about the Yankees. Throughout his exile, he'd occasionally take his familiar place on the back page. Though he was wary of taking calls at first, convinced Vincent was tapping his phones, he ultimately couldn't help himself. He said Vincent told him he could take part in free agent signings (Vincent maintained he most certainly had not). He said he and Michael agreed Michael would run all personnel ideas by him first (Michael wasn't familiar with that conversation).

Michael fully understood how hard a task the rebuild would be. The Yankees finished 1990 67–95, barely avoiding the ignominy of losing one hundred games, still finishing last for just the second time since the *Titanic* collided with the iceberg. While Michael gave Stump Merrill another crack at managing in 1991, the talent level was still egregious—and Merrill was never going to be confused with Earl Weaver, either. They crept up to fifth at 71–91, but Michael knew he had to make changes. Soon after the season, he fired Merrill and all his coaches—including third base coach Buck Showalter, who'd previously won three minor-league championships managing Fort Lauderdale and Albany. Showalter was considered a rising star in the organization, but Michael was determined to hire a manager with experience. He told Showalter directly he should look for another job in baseball.

"I tried to wreck the whole thing quick," Michael described it years later, laughing.

But Michael was lucky and so, it turned out, was Showalter. Michael was close with one of Steinbrenner's limited partners, Marvin Goldklang.

"Stick called me up," Goldklang said in 1994. "I said, 'Look, you've forgotten more baseball than I'll ever know. But don't you think we should look for something other than guys who've already been fired by other teams?'"

"Who do you have in mind?" Michael said.

Goldklang pitched Showalter: thirty-five years old, who to that point had cashed only one paycheck in his life that wasn't issued by the Yankees (when he'd been hired to clear some land when he was playing in Nashville for $5 an hour one off-day). Michael called Showalter. Showalter sold himself brilliantly. Michael took a chance. The selection drew praise from one especially invested Yankees fan.

"I would say this young man is as bright and hardworking and detailed a guy as you're ever going to find," George Steinbrenner said.

Installing Showalter was just one essential piece to an intricate puzzle few could quite see yet. A project like this wasn't done quickly; though the Yankees started 6–0 under Showalter in 1992, they won only five more games for him than they had for Merrill in '91, finishing fourth. There was little doubt if someone other than Gene Michael was in charge, someone else would have been the Yankees manager in 1993.

"But honestly, the first week of spring training I watched Buck with the players, saw how beautifully he ran camp, saw how hard he worked, and I knew right away that this guy was something special," Michael said.

"Stick gave me a shot," Showalter said in 2021. "And then he decided to stick with me. Not a lot of guys would've done that."

Michael still had to deal with the shadow government of an absent boss growing restless as his team kept losing. The benefit of finishing last in 1990 was the Yankees earned the first pick in the entry draft, and there was a five-star blue chip that everyone in baseball coveted: Brien Taylor, a flame-throwing nineteen-year-old who reminded every scout who saw him of a young Dwight Gooden. Taylor struck out 213 hitters in eighty-eight innings at East Carteret High School in North Carolina, walked only twenty-eight. His adviser, a ruthless agent named Scott Boras, engaged Michael in a protracted negotiation that stretched into August.

It was then Steinbrenner decided to pop off to two reporters from *Newsday*: "I just don't know what my people are doing or what they're thinking. If they let him go, they ought to be shot!"

Armed with that fiery quote, Boras dug in even deeper until finally, on August 26, the sides agreed on a record $1.55 million deal. The *Newsday* reporters called Steinbrenner back. *This* time the Boss railed, "Never in my wildest dreams would I have paid a kid a million and a half. I said I'd love to see us sign him. I never said 'go spend a million and a half.' No goddamned way. I'm getting damned tired of people spending my money like this."

In the moment, for the public, Michael said, "George might've handled that with a little more style than me, because he's good at that. But he would've done the same deal."

Privately, Stick seethed, fried by the second-guess and because it was *Steinbrenner* who'd handed Boras the leverage to keep the fight going by threatening to metaphorically murder his own GM. He also knew Steinbrenner wouldn't let this go. Sure enough, at the next quarterly meeting of the partners—Vincent signed off on Steinbrenner taking part in these—the Boss started to bitch about the Taylor signing, and Michael saw his opportunity.

"You don't know what the *fuck* you're talking about, George," Michael snapped. "If it wasn't for you in the papers we could've had the kid for a lot less."

Taylor never pitched an inning in the major leagues, his can't-miss career sidetracked in December 1993 when he hurt his shoulder in a fistfight defending his brother. But for Michael, standing up to the Boss changed everything.

"That impressed the hell out of us," Goldklang said. "There was no question who was in charge."

Michael's position was solid. Even as he stepped up his renovation, Steinbrenner was already inching closer to being back in the building.

FAY VINCENT, AS expected, took about thirty seconds to deny Kleinman's nomination as managing general partner. It took Kleinman even less time to file a $22 million federal lawsuit against Vincent and John Dowd. Vincent figured this was just another poisoned dart from Steinbrenner, and treated the story as white noise.

Vincent's hubris remained intact even as he realized his ideal of making Steinbrenner disappear forever was probably never going to happen. Vincent agreed to allow Steinbrenner to build a case for himself for reentry, but he intended to make the Boss sweat as long as he could.

Vincent made a point of attending the Yankees' home opener April 15, 1991, made sure he was assigned the owner's box—a seating assignment George Steinbrenner, still the Yankees *nominal* owner, could no longer occupy; if he wanted to see the Yankees in person, he needed approval from the commissioner's office and could buy only a general-admission ticket. Steinbrenner sat in that box for every home opener since 1976; it had become a must-have among New York's glitterati to earn an invite, where they could rub shoulders with Cary Grant, Richard Nixon, Ed Koch, Donald Trump, Barbara Walters, Jimmy Cagney—they all made the pilgrimage. It was said Vincent enjoyed the view just fine, even if he didn't have any Page Six company.

When Steinbrenner started sniffing for ways back in, hinting Vincent's power wasn't as absolute as he believed, the commissioner struck right where it hurt most, in Steinbrenner's eternally red-white-and-blue-tinted soul: "I can't think of anyone other than Saddam Hussein I'd rather have making these complaints."

Steinbrenner countered: "It only underscores the question many people in baseball have raised recently regarding [Vincent's] ability to be commissioner and act rationally."

Howie Spira was convicted of blackmail in federal court on May 8, 1991. The most poignant moment of the trial came with Steinbrenner on the stand. US Attorney Gregory Kehoe showed him a list of phone numbers the Feds seized from Spira's apartment. Steinbrenner's own lawyers knew the names but hadn't briefed Steinbrenner; they had an idea how he'd react.

"Joan, that's my wife," he said in the witness box. "Henry, that's my son. Rita . . ."

Steinbrenner began to cry.

"Are you all OK, sir?" Kehoe asked.

"I'm all right," Steinbrenner choked. "Rita . . . that's my mother."

Spira was as good as done as soon as Steinbrenner began to sob. He was sentenced December 10 to two and a half years, and as he was led away screamed, "I hope Steinbrenner never gets his team back. And I hope God knows what he did to me." This capped a four-month tour where Spira had been everywhere, bashing Steinbrenner at every turn, infuriating Vincent, who realized the more Spira opened his mouth the more his case would suffer. Spira was recognized often in his travels, and when someone would ask "Are you . . . ?" he would happily identify himself.

"I'm the guy who got rid of Steinbrenner!" he'd crow.

Every time one of these stories got back to Fay Vincent he'd die a little more inside. Howie Spira did the impossible. He'd actually made people feel *sorry* for George Steinbrenner.

Alas, so would Vincent.

He and Steinbrenner played a game of chicken for weeks. The idea of bringing Steinbrenner back March 1, 1993, was floated—but only if Kleinman dropped the suit. He did. The men scheduled a face-to-face. Steinbrenner flew from Tampa and was driving to 350 Park Avenue when he received word: Vincent postponed the meeting indefinitely; *The New York Times*—by now Vincent's fiercest, and lone, ally—was doing its own investigation of Steinbrenner's behavior during his suspension. That was the appetizer.

What followed that summer of 1992 was the main course that ended Vincent. The Yankees had a relief pitcher, Steve Howe, who'd been suspended seven different times for drug violations. Vincent handed him a lifetime ban, pending a hearing in front of arbiter George Nicolau. Gene Michael was summoned and told he wouldn't be allowed to have a lawyer present. Specifically, Vincent didn't want *Michael's* lawyer—Robert Costello, one of the masterminds behind Steinbrenner's side of the chessboard. A few weeks later, both Michael and Showalter were subpoenaed by Nicolau and asked their opinions about Vincent's ruling. Both agreed there needed to be consequences for recidivist drug users in baseball but also said what Howe needed most was professional help for his addiction. Jack Lawn, the vice president of operations who, with some irony, was a former chief of the Drug Enforcement Agency, also testified. He said much the same as Michael and Showalter.

A few days later, Michael received a call at home.

"Be at the commissioner's office at eleven o'clock sharp. No lawyers."

Lawn got the same message, as did Showalter, especially concerned since the Yankees had a one o'clock game that afternoon against Kansas City.

The trio arrived on time, immediately confronted by an irate Vincent.

"You have effectively tendered your resignation from Major League Baseball," they were told. "The moment you all testified, you quit the game."

Vincent was upset the men honored the subpoena and hadn't simply agreed with his ruling. Michael and Showalter were terrified. To them, specifically, Vincent sneered, "I'll let you sweat through the weekend before you know if you still have jobs or not."

Lawn, who still looked like he could take down Pablo Escobar all by himself, was less cowed and far more outraged. To Lawn Vincent said, "I could not believe you would testify because of your interest in seeing Steve Howe in a Yankees uniform."

"That's not why we testified," Lawn replied. "We testified to tell the truth."

"Then why would you want to testify?"

"Because a month from now if I pick up the paper and see that Steve Howe killed himself, at least I would know I tried to help. As I learned in the Marine Corps, you don't abandon the wounded."

The men returned to Yankee Stadium five minutes before the first pitch. Slowly, methodically, they helped reconstruct their two hours with Vincent, and the resulting firestorm—everywhere except the *Times*—excoriated the commissioner. There was more. A few days later it was leaked that on June 18, Vincent sent a letter to all twenty-eight owners informing them he was revoking baseball's Rules of Procedure, created by previous commissioners to establish protocols for matters of dispute—a safeguard against exactly the type of behavior Vincent and Dowd exhibited in investigating Steinbrenner.

Vincent turned baseball jurisprudence into a kangaroo court.

And now, a lot of owners realized: *If Vincent can poke Steinbrenner with a stick like this, what's to prevent him from doing the same to* us?

As Chicago White Sox owner Jerry Reinsdorf told Bill Madden of the *Daily News*: "I don't know why Vincent didn't just rescind the Bill of Rights while he was at it."

In the *Post*, columnist Mark Kriegel reported not only had Vincent assured Howie Spira at the outset, "You'll never see the inside of a jail cell," but also the genesis of the whole mess was when Vincent himself urged Spira to, in essence, set Steinbrenner up. Spira, ever helpful, had taped that conversation, too.

Vincent was finished. The owners waited until the commissioner tried to unilaterally impose division realignment to strike: By a count of 18–9–1 they issued a no-confidence vote. Vincent—who'd piously insisted for years "nobody is allowed to sue baseball"—briefly threatened to take the case of his dismissal to the Supreme Court if necessary, but September 7, 1992, he finally resigned.

"Resigning, and not litigating, should be my last act on behalf of the 'best interests of baseball,'" said Vincent, who died February 1, 2025, still convinced he'd been in the right in the Steinbrenner matter.

George Steinbrenner waited a respectful hour after hearing the news.

Then asked, none too subtly, "So . . . when do I get to come back?"

His fellow owners nominated Bud Selig, owner of the Milwaukee Brewers, to serve as temporary commissioner. Selig felt compelled to honor at least a degree of Vincent's ruling and told Steinbrenner he would be welcomed back March 1, 1993.

"But what about free agency?" the Boss asked. "That's my favorite time of year."

"March 1, 1993," Selig repeated.

Steinbrenner had already endured twenty-five months of exile, and he'd already pulled off—Reinsdorf's words—"the greatest resurrection in two thousand years."

He could wait another six months.

MICHAEL SAW UP close the full extent of damage Steinbrenner's long-term dismantling of the Yankees brand rendered. The free agent season of 1993 was crackling with franchise-altering talent, and the Yankees fixed their eyes on the three brightest available stars: David Cone, Greg Maddux and Barry Bonds. Maddux and Bonds—reigning Cy Young and MVP of the National League—played hard-to-get immediately. The Yankees offered to make Bonds the highest-paid Yankee in history. Michael wined and dined Maddux, took him to see *Miss Saigon* on Broadway. He appealed to Cone's love of New York City, and his clear desire to stick it to the Mets for trading him the year before.

They went 0-for-3. Maddux took less money to sign with the Atlanta Braves. Bonds went to San Francisco to play for the Giants, for whom both his father, Bobby, and godfather, Willie Mays, played. And Cone—seeing the looming labor calamity around the bend—took an $18 million deal with his hometown Kansas City Royals in which half was paid up front as a bonus, making it strike-proof. These high-profile swings and misses immediately brought heat and questions that weren't entirely unfair: If Steinbrenner had been sitting next to Maddux and his wife during *Miss Saigon* would he have been able to close the deal? If George had done the wooing of Bonds would he have channeled the charm from sixteen years before when he'd simply refused to allow Reggie Jackson to sign anywhere else?

Michael also had a belief system he insisted on honoring. He'd already made a high-risk trade, swapping Roberto Kelly (whom the Yankees had waited to blossom into a star; they were still waiting) for Paul O'Neill. In 1992 he signed Mike Stanley and Mike Gallego, low-profile free agents who brought instant professionalism to the clubhouse. Also in 1992 he gave final approval to selecting a skinny shortstop out of Kalamazoo, Michigan, with the sixth-overall pick in the draft, a seventeen-year-old named Derek Jeter.

More important, long before Billy Beane became a household name thanks to *Moneyball*, long before analytics seized control of the sport, Michael saw where the future of the game was headed. One day he invited the young beat writer for the *Post*, Joel Sherman, into his office and showed him a list of players with numbers next to their names. Sherman quickly realized the numbers were on-base percentage. And they were all low.

"Our offensive innings go too fast," Michael explained. "We make it too easy on the pitcher. We have to have better at bats."

With those twenty-one words, a new Yankee way was founded. It was why Michael insisted Bernie Williams be kept around, even as Steinbrenner raged at a variety of Williams errors of both commission and omission. It was what made even a teenaged Jeter so appealing, and all the quiet acquisitions. Michael wasn't perfect; he exposed third baseman Charlie Hayes in the 1992 expansion draft, and he caught hell from Steinbrenner when the Colorado Rockies selected him. But even that had a positive effect. Steinbrenner deputized his son-in-law Joe Molloy, and when Bob Nederlander wearied of the job Molloy replaced him as managing general partner. Suddenly, the Yankees were in play for Wade Boggs, a five-time AL batting campion who'd compiled a .338 lifetime average through eleven seasons, all with the Red Sox. Molloy was the point man—he swore up and down he wasn't being advised by anyone else—and while it was reported Showalter and Michael were less than pleased with the move, Boggs and his .428 lifetime on-base percentage were locked down to a three-year, $11 million deal.

Once Michael signed Jimmy Key away from the Blue Jays, the sting of losing out on Maddux and Cone faded, and for the first time in five years the Yankees headed for Fort Lauderdale with legit, genuine postseason hopes. They would soon be joined by an old friend. As if anyone could have forgotten, the March 1 issue of *Sports Illustrated* heralded the news with a picture of George Steinbrenner astride a white horse, wearing a Napoleonic uniform, his right hand tucked between the second and fifth buttons of his tunic, the headline reading:

GEORGE II: GEORGE STEINBRENNER RIDES BACK INTO BASEBALL

CHAPTER 22

I always knew the job description in New York.
—BUCK SHOWALTER

The day before Steinbrenner's *Sports Illustrated* issue released, February 28, felt like the last day of freedom before new recruits take a military oath, have their heads shaved and get thrown before the drill sergeant for the first time. It was a lazy Sunday at Fort Lauderdale Stadium. A Yankees official was spotted with his eyes closed, catching twenty winks in the home team dugout. A security guard sat on a stool, breezily thumbing through a newspaper. A young player who didn't know any better showed up in the locker room in work boots and a flannel shirt, like he'd just finished a jam session with Soundgarden.

A day later, two of those men would have been fired and the third released. Because a day later, George M. Steinbrenner III would officially be reinstated, restored to power, and a new sheriff—actually, the old sheriff—would roam the town. And he was eager. At exactly 12:01 a.m. on March 1, Steinbrenner appeared on the groundbreaking sports-talk station WFAN in New York and granted a ninety-minute interview to the station's Yankees reporter, Suzyn Waldman.

"I'm not talking; I'm not talking," Steinbrenner told Waldman. "I've had two and a half years to be quiet, and I don't know how to talk anymore."

Later that morning, at ten fifteen, Steinbrenner stepped off a small airplane at Fort Lauderdale Executive Airport and walked by himself the quarter mile from the tarmac to the ballpark next door. When he reached the parking lot at 10:32 he was besieged by 250 media members. The throng moved as Steinbrenner did, through the lot, through a tunnel into the stadium, into the Yankees' clubhouse, and then, at last, at 11:33 a.m., out of the Yankees' dugout and into the bright South Florida sun. Don Mattingly and Paul O'Neill were taking their regular turns in the batting cage, oblivious to the gathering din, but even they took pause when the Boss stepped onto the field for the first time in three springs. A smattering of boos cascaded from the crowd of two thousand spectators, and a brief reprise of the "George must go!" chant. All of that was quickly drowned by a thunderous roar. When Steinbrenner approached the chanters and shook their hands, they quickly changed their mantra: "Go, George, go!"

"The Boss," Mattingly mused, "is back."

"You can't have something that means so much taken away and not have it mean a lot," Steinbrenner said. "But the juices are flowing. I want back in the fray."

He was asked how much of an impact his return would have on the club.

"Certain things will change and certain things will never change," he said. "Hopefully I've learned from my mistakes. I'm going to be different. You'll see."

One wise guy with a camera asked, "Have you fired anyone yet?"

Steinbrenner waved at the horde around him.

"Not yet," he said. "I can't get to any of them."

THE QUESTION WAS designed to draw laughs, but two men who weren't terribly amused were Gene Michael and Buck Showalter. Much like Gabe Paul in 1974–75, Michael had been allowed to rebuild a roster without much interference.

That slice of nirvana was about to vanish.

The Boss was quick to give the duo their due on day one. "The players they got were perfect," he gushed. "This team can win it."

But as if to remind them they weren't in the company of a kindly, aloof uncle, he also stressed to the players: "I saw you guys on TV a lot last year. Too many mental mistakes. Those have to stop right now."

Stick called his first meeting with the Boss "very positive." He, maybe more than anyone who ever worked for Steinbrenner, knew that would be a fleeting feel-good spark.

"Those lessons would last," Michael said, "until the first three-game losing streak."

Opening Day at Yankee Stadium was just as satisfying for Steinbrenner as March 1 had been. He spent the morning playing with a chimpanzee on *Live with Regis and Kathie Lee*, zipped over to the stadium, filled his owner's box with the old eclectic assortment of Page Six names: Donald Trump and Marla Maples, Regis Philbin, Rudy Giuliani, Gay Talese.

"I haven't had a feeling about a team like this since 1977," Steinbrenner declared to his guests, as he watched the Yankees beat the Royals, 4–1, in front of a packed house of 56,704. Later, he wandered into Showalter's office.

"Not bad," he said. "Just a few things . . ."

Again there was laughter. Again Showalter refrained from it. He and Michael understood the best way to avoid the Boss was to make themselves bulletproof—that meant winning. For the first time in five years, the Yankees were winning lots of baseball games in 1993. On July 17 they crept into a first-place tie with the Blue Jays. Better, every big offseason acquisition worked out perfectly. Paul O'Neill was hitting .331, and had twelve homers thanks to a lefty swing custom-built for Yankee Stadium. Jimmy Key was even better: 12–2 with a 2.25 ERA. After a slow start Wade Boggs hit .310 for two months.

New York was officially a Yankees town again. In 1992 the Mets outdrew the Yankees for the ninth straight season. Starting in '93, they've never done that again.

Steinbrenner was mostly true to his word. In late July, at the trading deadline, he'd aired out Michael when the Jays acquired Rickey Henderson from the A's. That transaction helped Toronto win a second straight title, but Michael had called the A's several times and tried to see what it would take for them to ship Rickey back to New York. Every time they came back with a list that included at least one or more of the same names.

Derek Jeter.
Bernie Williams.
Mariano Rivera.
Jorge Posada.
Andy Pettitte.

Only Williams's name was familiar to Yankees fans and then only as a talented but scatterbrained and mistake-prone kid still finding his way in the big leagues. For two and a half years Michael could protect the crown jewels without fear of the Boss going behind his back to ransom them.

The storm passed. The Yankees kept winning. On September 4, Jim Abbott—a left-handed pitcher forced to throw that way because he was born without a right hand—tossed a no-hitter against Cleveland at Yankee Stadium. Abbott was a clever acquisition by Michael, and Steinbrenner used one of his favorite terms to describe him all year—Jack Armstrong, the All-American boy—and the next day, the Yankees won again to join Toronto atop the AL East with twenty-four games to go.

It wasn't until September the slumbering giant grunted awake. When he did he went medieval on his team. After Abbott's no-hitter the Yankees lost five of their next six and the Blue Jays began to pull away from them. After meeting the team in Milwaukee Steinbrenner cleared his throat. He spent twenty minutes with his team. When he left the clubhouse he snarled at reporters, "I have nothing to say."

And then had plenty to say.

"I'm getting to the point where I'm going to be a little disappointed in people," Steinbrenner said. "I don't want to say it right now. Let's see if they rise to the challenge. They're going to go one way or another. Let's see if they want it bad enough. It's nut-cracking time."

He accused some of his injured players of "jaking it," still the worst slur a professional athlete can hear. "Hurt is related to character," he insisted. "I can remember Thurman Munson with half his body black and blue, going out there in 1977."

These Yankees mostly shrugged off the Boss's berating, and completed what in just about every baseball circle was a wildly successful 88–74 season trending the right way.

"I can't wait to get to Fort Lauderdale," Don Mattingly said after the season's final game. "This team is ready to do some very special things."

Mattingly had been named captain of the Yankees early in 1991, and though quiet by nature he'd taken to the role effortlessly and seriously. One spring day he was on a back field at Fort Lauderdale. When he finished up he and the Yankees' shortstop of the future, Derek Jeter, began to walk back to the clubhouse. Before they did, Mattingly glanced up at the glassed-in area high in the main stadium where the owner's office sat.

He turned to Jeter—the present captain addressing the future one.

"Let's run it in," he said. "You never know who's watching."

BUT THE YANKEES' full renaissance would have to wait. Once again, tensions reached a boiling point between the owners and the Players Association, and this time the owners were prepared for nuclear winter.

This left George Steinbrenner in a peculiar predicament.

For the first time in fourteen years, the Yankees were the best team in baseball. When Jimmy Key beat the Twins 12–3 on August 5, 1994, the Yankees moved to 69–38, the best record in the sport, ten games clear of the Orioles. Everything Gene Michael envisioned the Yankees to be was in full bloom. They were a lineup of patient hitters, logging long at bats, exhausting starting pitchers. A few years later, Hall of Fame pitcher John Smoltz would summarize the Yankees perfectly after losing a 1–0 game to them in the World Series: "The team that wouldn't swing."

Actually, they swung plenty, just rarely at anything but smashable pitches. Paul O'Neill flirted with .400 for three months and was still at .361. Wade Boggs was at .342. Bernie Williams had become a star. Key's win over the Twins was his seventeenth of the season, putting him on track for the most wins by a Yankee since Ron Guidry's twenty-five in 1978. Buck Showalter, who spent more than a few nights sleeping on a folding cot in his office, the better to maximize his time figuring ways to give the Yankees an edge, was on his way to winning Manager of the Year.

They did all of this with an ominous clock ticking toward a 232-day strike that would wipe out the World Series for the first time since 1904.

It was a dark time for the grand old game.

A darker time for Steinbrenner.

It wasn't just the possibility of losing a chance for his third World Series title. Every game missed cost Steinbrenner close to $300,000 in television revenue.

The Yankees began a long association with WPIX/Channel 11 in New York in 1951. That network aired between ninety and one hundred games every year on "free" TV, and offered the Yankees a reasonable annual income based on advertising revenue. Channel 11 made a star of Phil Rizzuto (who would at last earn induction to Cooperstown that summer of '94). It was the same deal the Dodgers, and later the Mets, had with WWOR/Channel 9. Year after year, that was the rhythm of the baseball summer: Mets on 9, Yankees on 11, and when remote controls became popular in the 1970s it became even easier to watch both teams at once if you were so inclined.

In 1979, both the Yankees and Mets signed contracts with Cablevision, a Long Island–based cable company run by Charles Dolan, who'd invented HBO a few years earlier and was among the pioneers in the cable-TV revolution. For about $250,000 a year, Cablevision agreed to telecast games that weren't committed to the over-the-air channels, shown on another Dolan invention called "SportsChannel."

Steinbrenner, faster than most, realized in the same way baseball players could make fortunes shopping their wares every few years as free agents so, too, could franchises. That could mean scaring up what amounted to an open-air auction on what ballpark—and city—that team chose to play its home games. But it also meant nothing was forever in television, either. By 1982 he was welcoming suitors to bid for his cable package.

In 1984, Steinbrenner began a regular game of playing WPIX against SportsChannel, decreasing the games available on Channel 11. This made a lot of Yankees fans unhappy, because there were still large chunks of the outer boroughs that weren't yet wired for cable. His reply: "If we want to have the horses, we have to be able to pay them."

In 1986 Steinbrenner was spotted taking lunches around town with various executives from Gulf + Western, which owned the Knicks and Rangers as well as Madison Square Garden. Initial buzz was that Steinbrenner was interested in buying MSG, a rumor that had regularly been tossed around ever since Steinbrenner bought the Yankees. Steinbrenner had no intention of that; he was interested in what MSG's cable arm could offer. His latest deal with SportsChannel would expire in two years. He was open for business.

MSG was a more-than-willing dance partner. The Yankees would receive $6.7 million from Cablevision for 1988, but Steinbrenner had an out clause for 1989. Now the two cable networks were arm-wrestling over the Boss. On December 9, 1988, came the bombshell: twelve years, $500 million, an average of $42 million a year, six and a half times what the Yankees were getting from Cablevision. Across baseball, the effect was palpable: The richest team had now gotten an infusion of a half-billion dollars. Now Steinbrenner couldn't just afford the priciest players; he could correct his personnel mistakes, too, without feeling near as much pain.

> **INTERLUDE:** Steinbrenner insisted MSG would be state-of-the-art when it came to baseball broadcasts. He was true to his word. He approved MSG's preference to hire Tony Kubek, a former Yankees All-Star shortstop who'd become a star on NBC's national broadcasts but incurred the Boss's wrath with regular and pointed criticisms. As far back as 1978 Steinbrenner had tried to have Kubek removed from Yankees games on NBC. And during Kubek's five years at MSG he regularly offered stinging critiques on-air, and Steinbrenner lobbied MSG not to renew his contract. MSG refused. When Kubek retired, MSG brought in Jim Kaat, a Hall of Fame pitcher who'd played briefly

for the Yankees and was every bit as candid as Kubek. In fact, when *Sports Illustrated* had the cover of Steinbrenner dressed as Napoleon in 1993, Kaat had a letter published in the magazine two weeks later that said, in part: "There are so many classy owners, executives and players who could have kicked off the 1993 season by appearing on your cover. If baseball... represents a lot of what is good in America—reaching the top of one's profession through hard work, regardless of education and family background—then Steinbrenner represents the opposite. Please do not fall into the trap... of publicizing the few who gain notoriety through phony bluster."

Kaat would announce Yankees games for twelve seasons.

The strike caused the first friction between Steinbrenner and his star manager. As it became apparent scabs would be welcome to spring training, Showalter struggled with the idea of working with them, given how much loyalty he demanded from his regular players. That spring, the Detroit Tigers agreed to let Sparky Anderson stay away from camp for as long as replacement players were there. The Blue Jays did the same with Cito Gaston. Orioles owner Peter Angelos, who'd made his fortune repping labor unions, refused to field a replacement team at all. In early February Showalter admitted he was conflicted.

Steinbrenner was unsympathetic.

"They can do whatever they want," the Boss said of Showalter and his coaches. "This is a free country. But when you're under contract, and accept funds from the person paying you all this time while others are on strike, we expect them to honor their contracts."

Showalter reported, and was miserable all spring, as was everyone else associated with scab baseball as the league marched toward Armageddon. But on March 31, 1995—the day before the season was to start—US District Court Judge Sonia Sotomayor granted an injunction requested by the National Labor Relations Board on a complaint of unfair work practices. There was no deal in place yet, but the players and owners agreed to go back to work on a 144-game schedule.

Steinbrenner had gone rogue in the final weeks of the strike, allowing players who lived near Tampa to use the team's minor-league facility. He'd also hired Steve Howe to work the team's minor-league ticket office as part of his drug rehab aftercare program. Both moves angered the other owners, but Steinbrenner ignored them. If the 1995 season happened at all, he wanted the Yankees to be ready for it.

THEY WEREN'T READY for it.

They should've been better than '94. Steinbrenner traded for a high-end starter (Jack McDowell) and a high-end closer (John Wetteland). But in late May and June they lost fifteen out of eighteen to fall to 15–24, already ten and a half games behind the Red Sox.

The Boss began to percolate.

For the better part of three years, Steinbrenner had seethed watching Danny Tartabull underachieve. Tartabull was Steinbrenner's answer to the Mets signing of Bobby Bonilla in the offseason of 1991–92.

"I'm very disappointed in Tartabull," he snarled in May. "He has to do a better job. He's supposed to be a cleanup hitter. He's under .200 with runners in scoring position. That's not helping the team."

Michael was already tired of the Boss's nagging, and while he finally did rid himself of Tartabull—sending him to Oakland in exchange for Rubén Sierra, who would bring his own various dysfunctions to the Yankees—Steinbrenner soon brought another unwanted distraction. Steinbrenner had long coveted Darryl Strawberry, who at one time in the eighties was neck and neck with Don Mattingly as the city's biggest star. He'd moved on to Los Angeles and San Francisco and was now out of baseball altogether because of drug problems but swore he was clean, and Steinbrenner believed him. He wanted to sign him.

That transaction fed Steinbrenner's ever-active fascination with ex-Mets stars. Michael would soon add to it by acquiring David Cone from Toronto for three minor-league pitchers. Strawberry's impact would be minimal: three homers in ninety-nine plate appearances. Cone's would be profound: 9–2 in thirteen starts, as the Yankees—left for dead at 53–58 on

August 26—suddenly rediscovered some of the magic from 1994, winning twenty-six of their final thirty-three.

They clinched the first-ever American League wild card on the season's final day in Toronto. Don Mattingly hit a home run, and after the final out he knelt and punched the ground triumphantly with his left hand before he was mobbed by teammates. Finally, in his fourteenth year of pinstriped service, he'd get a few innings, at least, of postseason. It had been a difficult season for Mattingly, and there'd been increasing speculation that the Yankees were prepared to move on. Mattingly suspected Steinbrenner was behind the talk.

"You just don't kick a guy and spit on him and 'go get out the door' type thing," he said in late August. "I don't like the way it's been handled, to tell you the truth. The way I've been treated. I feel this might be my last twenty games with the Yankees."

If that was so, Yankees fans were prepared to savor every last at bat. In the sixth inning of Game 2 of the ALDS with the Seattle Mariners, Mattingly rocketed a Tim Belcher changeup deep over the right-center field wall.

On TV, broadcaster Gary Thorne yelled "Hang on to the roof!" and inside Yankee Stadium, 57,126 delirious fans tried to blast that metaphorical roof into outer space. There would be a lot of earsplitting moments in that building over the next five years, none quite as sublime as that one. Mattingly played brilliantly, hitting .417 with six RBIs, though the season ended bitterly when the Mariners—managed by old friend Lou Piniella—roared back from an 0–2 deficit and won three straight in Seattle. Edgar Martinez's two-run double in the bottom of the eleventh inning of Game 5 eliminated the Yanks.

Steinbrenner had one glorious throwback moment during Game 2 at Yankee Stadium. After barking privately about what he perceived as poor umpiring, and after home plate umpire Dale Scott called a borderline strike three against the Yankees' Dion James, suddenly Steinbrenner parked himself at the back of the press box. The Yankees were playing their second playoff game in fourteen years, but now most of the sportswriters had their backs to the game as Steinbrenner held court.

"This crew is a disgrace!" he raged. "Where is the home plate umpire from, Oregon? [Scott was—from Eugene.] My geography teacher told me that's right by Washington." Steinbrenner, in essence, was accusing Scott of taking a dive for Seattle.

It went on for ten minutes. Reporters couldn't help laughing as they furiously transcribed the tirade. "Can any of you tell me Scott is a good umpire?" he asked. It cost him $50,000 once AL president Gene Budig stopped pounding his head against his desk.

Everything old was new again.

Four days later, as the raucous celebration inside the Kingdome bled through the walls of the visiting clubhouse, Steinbrenner walked into a clubhouse whose occupants looked and felt like a high school football team who'd just lost State. You don't see many pro locker rooms like this. In the manager's office, Showalter held his head in his hands. The players looked broken. Some had red eyes. Steinbrenner was moved.

"You guys made me very proud," he said. "And you made yourselves proud."

Later, to reporters, he said, "This group made the Yankees the Yankees again."

CHAPTER 23

You know how they say a "dog year" is like seven for a human? If you calculated "George years" I'd probably be celebrating my bicentennial soon.
—GENE MICHAEL

Sometimes, when you worked at a tabloid when the *Daily News/Post/Newsday* war was at its most intense, you woke up with an unshakable sense of dread. This was before the internet, before social media, when an exclusive story lasts only as long as it takes to confirm with your own sources. In those days, if you got beat on a story, the misery lasted—best case—a full day. It caused a lot of dread and a lot of dyspepsia among the rank and file on the Yankees beat.

Every now and then, though, there'd appear something in one of the competing papers for which even rivals had to pause for a moment, smile, throw a quiet salute.

Such was the case on the morning of Friday, November 3, 1995.

There, on the back page of the *Daily News*, was a photo of Joe Torre, minutes after his introduction as the new Yankees' manager, smiling broadly in front of the Yankees' Uncle-Sam-hat-on-a-bat logo. And over this image was a headline dreamed up by a young desk man named Anthony Rieber (later a fine baseball writer for *Newsday*):

CLUELESS JOE

Inside the paper, columnist Ian O'Connor led his piece thusly: "He thinks he knows, but he has not a clue. Joe Torre described George Steinbrenner in rational terms yesterday, calling him an unyielding competitor and demanding boss. He just wants a winner on the field, and my job is to give it to him. New day, old song. Torre's smile belied the moment. It is always a sad occasion when a man becomes a muppet."

Across the next thirteen years, that back page would be cited more than DEWEY DEFEATS TRUMAN as the Yankees became a modern-day dynasty under Torre. Of course, in the moment, it was 100 percent accurate, as was the column. Nobody was accusing Torre of being a clueless baseball man, just naive in the ways of George. And who could argue? In the twenty-two years Steinbrenner owned the Yankees he had now changed managers twenty-two times.

The most recent one had nearly caused a mutiny.

As his sadness over the Yankees' loss to the Mariners in the 1995 ALDS morphed, inevitably, into anger, the Boss convinced himself the reason the Yankees' had blown a 2–0 lead in that best-of-five series was due, in part, to complacency that Steinbrenner—and only Steinbrenner—could plainly see had crept into the organization. People performed better when they worked on edge. There would be change. The first one was easy: He told Gene Michael he wanted him back as GM but he'd need to accept a $200,000 salary cut.

Michael said, "There's no way I'm doing that, George."

The men agreed that Stick would become something of a combined adviser/superscout/sounding board—he would soon be affectionately referred to as a "designated guru"—for a modest low-six-figure salary and the ability to get his voice (to say nothing of his golf game, and his sanity) back again. Steinbrenner charged Michael with the task of finding his own replacement. He did so merrily.

Buck Showalter was a different matter.

The Boss was antsy.

"I want you back," he said in their first conversation after Seattle. "But you need to change up your coaching staff."

Specifically, he wanted hitting coach Rick Down gone.

"If you fire my coaches, George," Showalter said, "that's as good as firing me."

Showalter played golf after that conversation, figured there'd be another. He returned home to discover the Yankees had issued a statement saying he had resigned.

"I tried to dissuade him," Steinbrenner insisted.

What resulted was an outcry unlike any Steinbrenner had ever experienced.

"It's never been like this before," he told Michael. "Not even close."

"I tried to warn you, George," Stick said.

In the meantime, Michael hired Bob Watson, the ex-Yankee first baseman who'd done a fine job as GM of the Houston Astros, for his old job. After a strong recommendation from close Steinbrenner adviser Arthur Richman, who'd worked for the Mets from their inception before switching sides, Torre was also hired.

Steinbrenner called Gene Michael. He was frantic.

"Are you sure Torre can do the job?" the Boss asked.

"He's very good," Michael said. "And he's a New York guy."

"But is he the *best* man for the job?"

Michael held the phone away from his face for a second. He no longer had to take bullets for his boss, not anymore.

"I told you who the *best* man was, George. I told you to keep Buck."

There was silence for a beat.

Then: "What if I get Buck back?"

Steinbrenner called Jim Krivacs, Showalter's agent. Krivacs told him Buck was about to sign on with the expansion Arizona Diamondbacks, who wouldn't begin play until 1998 but were offering to essentially give Showalter free rein and at a steep raise.

"Don't you already have a manager?" Krivacs asked.

Details, details. Steinbrenner already figured that part out: He could just stash Torre on top of his pile of advisers; at a half million a year, who would argue? A few days later, Showalter shook hands with Arizona owner

Jerry Colangelo on a seven-year, $7 million deal. He walked into his house in Pensacola.

And found Steinbrenner in the living room.

He was eating cookies baked by Buck's wife, Angela.

Soon he would eat the slightest morsel of crow, realizing he'd changed his mind too late. The men shook hands. They figured they would keep this as their own little secret. That lasted a few weeks, until Jack Curry of the *Times* caught wind of the rumor, confirmed it and splashed it at the top of the paper's Sunday Sports section on December 3.

O'Connor had gotten it exactly right.

New day, same song.

OF COURSE, WHAT we know now is this: It may have been impossible for Steinbrenner to have identified, and hired, a more perfect manager than Torre, whose personality was ideally suited for the job, far better than any one of the thirteen men who'd preceded him.

"Nothing bothered him," said Willie Randolph, his third base coach. "Certainly not George. Not that he ever let anyone see."

It helped that the '96 Yankees made the transition easy. They moved into first April 28 and stayed there the rest of the season's final 154 days. The tone was set opening day, in snow-blown Cleveland, when rookie Derek Jeter, twenty-one years old and freshly installed as the everyday shortstop, hit a home run and made a spectacular over-the-shoulder catch to help David Cone shut down the defending AL champions. Bernie Williams bloomed into a full-blown star. Andy Pettitte, twenty-four, won twenty-one games.

Two unwanted imports also helped the cause. One was Joe Girardi, acquired from Colorado at the behest of new bench coach Don Zimmer. Girardi was given the job over über-popular Mike Stanley, exiled to Boston because Torre favored Girardi's defense (and Steinbrenner didn't like that Stanley was one of Showalter's loyal lieutenants). The other was Tino Martinez, a slugging first baseman who'd helped Seattle tame the Yankees in the playoffs. His chief sin: He wasn't Don Mattingly, who'd chosen to take a year off to evaluate if he wanted to further his career. Both transactions were greeted with such public malice that at the home opener on April 9 the Yankees canceled the tradition of introducing the whole team to stand along the first base line because they feared the ugly greeting the fans might give Girardi and Martinez (to say nothing of Joe Torre). Both would hear boos—and worse—ringing down from the grandstands at the bleachers at Yankee Stadium.

Both eventually won the fans over. It helped that the Yankees, at last, had assembled a team built to survive the 162-game test of a regular season. Jeter was named Rookie of the Year. Martinez became an RBI machine, driving in 117 runs. Bernie Williams blossomed into a full-blown star (.305, twenty-nine homers, 102 RBIs). The Yankees held off a late charge by the Orioles to finish in first place in a full season for the first time in sixteen years. They promptly dispatched the Rangers in the ALDS and the Orioles in the AL Championship Series, losing only two games along the way.

They were the first two postseason series Joe Torre ever won, either as a player or as a manager. Finally, he would get a taste of the World Series, a destination he'd grown to believe he'd never reach. And at first, it didn't go well. The Yankees entered the series heavy underdogs to the defending-champion Atlanta Braves, and the Braves proved equal to the betting line, pounding the Yankees in Game 1 at Yankee Stadium, 12–1. Then Torre delivered what proved to be one of the defining moments of his professional relationship with Steinbrenner.

The next day, as Torre filled out his lineup card for Game 2, there was a knock on his office door.

Steinbrenner bypassed hello.

"This is a must-win!" he barked. "I hope you have the guys ready!"

Torre stood up and greeted the Boss with a smile.

"I got news for you, Boss," he said. "The Braves have Greg Maddux on the mound, and he's the best pitcher in the world. Our guys have been scuffling with the bats. We're probably going to lose tonight, too." (Which they did, 4–0.)

Before Steinbrenner could answer, Torre continued.

"But Atlanta's my town [he'd played there from 1966 through 1968 and managed the Braves from 1982 to 1984]. We're going to go down there, win all three, and then next Saturday we're gonna come back here and win Game 6. How do you like that?"

With that Torre patted Steinbrenner on the shoulder, walked out of his own office and left the Boss speechless.

The fact that the Yankees did just that was one last tribute to the calming waters that Torre's presence brought.

In Game 3, the key moment came when Torre visited the mound to talk to Cone, who was clearly leaking gas and had loaded the bases with one out, the Yankees leading 2–0. A year earlier, in a similar predicament in Seattle, Game 5, Buck Showalter had trusted Cone's heart but been betrayed by his arm: Cone walked in the tying run. This time Torre told Cone, "I want you to level with me. Look me in the eye."

Cone did.

"How do you feel?"

Five months earlier, Cone thought his career might be over when he was diagnosed with an aneurysm in his pitching shoulder. Now he looked into Torre's eyes. He knew the manager wanted the truth. But also knew he preferred a certain answer.

"I'm good," Cone said. And proceeded to get out of the inning with a 2–1 lead. The Yankees won that night, and would sweep all three games in Atlanta.

Now it was time for the Hollywood stuff.

In the summer, Torre had lost his oldest brother, Rocco, who suffered a fatal heart attack while watching a Yankees–Indians game on TV. The day before Game 6 his other brother, Frank, himself an ex-ballplayer, received a heart transplant. Steinbrenner hadn't left Torre completely alone on the way to the Canyon of Heroes, especially when the Orioles cut the Yankees' lead to two and a half games in September. But Torre always kept him at arm's length. And now Torre was on the verge of repaying that fragile trust.

"He couldn't kill me," Torre recalled years later. "He couldn't hurt my family. All he could do is fire me, and guess what? I'd already been fired three times and lived to tell about it every time. Nobody *wants* to be fired. But you can't let it consume you."

IF ONLY TORRE could've transferred some of his zen to poor Bob Watson. With Michael out of the way, there was nobody close to Steinbrenner who could blunt his worst impulses. There had long been floods of stories emanating from the corridors of Yankee Stadium as well as the Boss's Tampa headquarters about what a tyrant Steinbrenner could be: a string of secretaries fired on whims, an even longer list of interns and junior executives and PR staffers who'd made seemingly minor mistakes—or simply turned the wrong corner at the wrong moment when Steinbrenner was in the wrong mood—and wound up fired. Sometimes they'd show up for work the next day and the Boss would forget the whole thing; sometimes they'd find someone else in their parking space. From the start he'd been prickly, and sometimes worse, and would often justify this by saying, "If you think I'm tough, you should have worked for my father...."

There was a fairly public glimpse of all of this a few days before Christmas 1995. Steinbrenner engaged in a protracted negotiation to re-sign David Cone, and finally the deal was completed on December 21. Steinbrenner wanted to have a press conference the next day and reached out to his PR director, Rob Butcher. The problem was, Butcher was in Wilmington, Ohio, when the news broke, together with his parents and nine siblings for the first time in six years. He'd cleared the trip with Steinbrenner repeatedly; even then, when he landed in Ohio and saw the news, he called back to New York and said he'd jump on the next plane and be there to conduct the news gathering.

"Don't bother," he was told. "He just fired you."

Butcher got on the plane anyway, got to the stadium in plenty of time, sought out Steinbrenner, tried to apologize.

"Finish out the year," the Boss said. "And find another job."

Butcher called home. He told his mother he'd been fired.

"You got fired on Christmas weekend?" she asked.

"Yes."

"Why would you want to work for someone who would do something like that?"

That one landed Steinbrenner on the back pages, but not the way he preferred; the *Daily News* screamed SCROOGE! with a cartoon George as Ebenezer himself, replete with cane and top hat. Steinbrenner later offered Butcher his job back but Butcher, to the eternal delight of hundreds who'd similarly ran afoul of the Boss's moods, chose instead to do PR work for the Atlanta Olympics; a year later he became media relations VP for the Cincinnati Reds, until his retirement in 2024.

> **INTERLUDE:** There was one giddy Yankees fan who was able to turn the tables somewhat on the Boss. Larry David had hilariously portrayed Steinbrenner on *Seinfeld* (from the back, and always with an exaggerated voice impression) for years, and as the show's chief producer thought it would be great to get the actual Steinbrenner to appear. The Boss flew to LA, did a scene with Elaine (Julia Louis-Dreyfus) at a restaurant and then triumphantly talked about it everywhere the moment he landed back in Tampa. That annoyed David. But that's not why the scenes never ran.
>
> "He sucked!" David said. "He was awful!"
>
> The scenes survive on YouTube; you can judge for yourself if the Boss's acting chops improved since *Saturday Night Live*.

Bob Watson, he never got used to the constant belittling, the ceaseless badgering, the uninterrupted second-guessing. Steinbrenner himself made many of the moves that filled out the 1996 champs. He'd acquired Tim Raines. He'd retained Cone. He gave Darryl Strawberry another chance, and this time Strawberry delivered eleven homers in 202 at bats. He signed yet another faded Mets hero, Dwight Gooden, who stunningly repaid the gesture by throwing a no-hitter at the Mariners on May 14. Watson acquired slugger Cecil Fielder at the deadline (with the Boss's approval of his $7 million salary), but he also traded for lefty relief pitcher Graeme Lloyd, who was initially terrible and then admitted his arm was hurting.

Steinbrenner became unhinged as he watched Lloyd struggle and ripped Watson with such ferocity that it quickly got back to the GM, who was unnerved by it.

"If he has a problem, he should talk to me," Watson said. "I'm a man. I can handle it."

Steinbrenner had already sent an unmistakable message. Even as the Yankees' lead shrank against the Orioles, he delivered a vote of confidence for Torre; he did no such thing for Watson, whom he made sweat for several weeks *after* they all won a championship together. That was no favor to Watson, who continued to boil at Steinbrenner's perceived disrespect. Even as the Yankees cruised to ninety-six wins and a return to the playoffs in 1997, Watson's health deteriorated. He gained weight. He was hospitalized when his blood pressure spiked. After a while, he simply locked himself in his office, far away from the maddening crowd; when he finally quit in February 1998 the consensus was his departure was something of a merciful termination.

Stepping into the breach would be a bookish thirty-year-old who'd played second base at Catholic University in Washington, DC, for four years and had joined the Yankees as an intern in 1986. When he graduated college three years later he'd been hired full-time in baseball operations. Brian Cashman's father, John, was the manager at Castleton Farm in Lexington, Kentucky, and had long been friends with Steinbrenner, but if there was any trace of concern about Cashman's "hook" with the Yankees he quickly made them vanish with years of seventy-hour workweeks. He was a grinder, he was smart and he'd become a top assistant to both Michael and Watson, so when the time came to promote him the Boss offered him a multiyear contract.

Cashman turned him down.

Steinbrenner was perplexed.

"I want a one-year contract," Cashman said. "I want to prove I'm correct for the job."

Steinbrenner couldn't argue with that logic. He snapped Cashman up: one year, $150,000. To that date, he had hired eleven general managers in twenty-five years. He would never hire another.

•

STEINBRENNER HAD LONG been fascinated by David Wells, a roly-poly lefty with a rubber arm who'd mostly underachieved across a ten-year career, compiling a 90–75 record with a 3.99 ERA while pitching for the Jays, Tigers, Reds and Orioles. To that point he'd never received even one vote for Cy Young, but Wells, a Yankees fan, had purchased for $30,000 a game-used cap worn by Babe Ruth, whose nutritional plan Wells also seemed to favor.

After Steinbrenner signed Wells to a three-year, $13.5 million contract Wells hinted he might be every bit the handful that Jackson used to be, for different reasons. He hurt the pinky finger of his pitching hand in a late-night encounter in his native San Diego in January, and while he was cleared of wrongdoing, when Steinbrenner offered a helpful piece of advice—"Stay out of bars"—Wells had a retort for his new benefactor with what amounted to his philosophy on problem-solving.

"If it's beer, then go to whiskey," Wells said. "If it's whiskey, then go to vodka."

Steinbrenner tried to make light of it when Wells showed up to camp with a painful case of gout—which the tabs were more than happy to report was also known, colloquially, as "fat man's disease."

Torre did his best to keep the peace. When Wells reported at 248 pounds he laughed.

"That's a few pounds over acceptable weight, maybe five pounds," said Torre, who himself had struggled with weight early in his playing career. "But let's face it: at 243 he'd still look a few pounds overweight."

As long as Wells could take the ball every fifth day he wasn't going to find issue with Torre, and through mid-August 1997 Wells was the ace of Torre's staff, 14–5 with a 3.60 ERA. But the dog days got to Wells, and he fell apart over the next few weeks, getting slapped around to the tune of a 7.71 ERA. To Steinbrenner's eyes, it seemed he was starting to gain three or four pounds between every appearance. One day in early September, the two men ran into each other in the Yankees' clubhouse. A day earlier, a fan lunged over the right field wall to take a ball away from Paul O'Neill, who thought he could have caught it. It was ruled a home run.

"Hey, George, you need to get some new security out there," Wells said. "Build a wall or something." He was smiling.

George was not.

"Never mind about the fucking security," he snapped. "Just worry about pitching. You better start winning some games because you're not the pitcher I thought you were."

Wells was no longer smiling, either.

"Is that right?" he said. "Well, you can go fuck yourself. If you don't like it, you can trade me."

"Believe me, I would, but nobody wants your fat ass."

"You better get the fuck out of this room before I fucking kick your ass."

"Go ahead, do it. Try it. You think I'm afraid of you?"

When they finally walked away from each other Steinbrenner was heard to mutter, "I paid fourteen million dollars for *this*?"

THE YANKEES' DEFENSE of their first championship in eighteen years ended quickly in the 1997 playoffs, the Indians rallying from a 2–1 deficit to beat the Yankees in five games after the Orioles had outpaced the Yanks to win the AL East, New York having to settle for a wild card berth. Afterward, Steinbrenner vowed: "We'll win it all next year. Mark my words."

Cashman's first job as GM was to finalize a blockbuster deal that made four-time All-Star second baseman Chuck Knoblauch a Yankee, and soon he added veteran slugger Chili Davis. Later, the Yankees would add a thirty-two-year-old rookie named Orlando Hernandez, a legendary Cuban pitcher who'd boarded a rickety raft to seek freedom in 1997, and when he landed ashore on US soil found himself in a bidding war; El Duque would be a Yankee by summer.

Before that, though, the Yankees began the 1998 season on the West Coast, and it was disastrous. They started 1–4. They were already three games behind the Orioles, and the season wasn't even a week old, and the only question seemed to be if Joe Torre might make it as far as Bob Lemon had in 1982 (fourteen games) or as far as Berra had in 1985 (sixteen). Steinbrenner wasn't bashful about planting that particular flag, either.

"I'm worried our guys are reading their own press clippings," Steinbrenner said. "You still have to go out on the field and do the job. Nobody's going to hand anything to them. They haven't won a thing yet."

At the time, the Yankees' record stood at 0–1.

They would recover fine, despite the fact that on April 13, at Yankee Stadium, a 350-pound expansion beam fell onto an empty seat—Section 22, Row 2, Seat 7—and obliterated the chair. It was hours before the stadium was set to open, so a catastrophe was averted, but while the Yankees' owner had for years absorbed criticism and lampooning when he'd hinted—if not said outright—that his seventy-five-year-old ballpark was falling apart . . . *it was now literally falling apart.*

And George Steinbrenner couldn't possibly have been happier about that.

CHAPTER 24

> MOOGIE: Hey, lemme ask you a question. In the legal sense, can fuckin' Steinbrenner just move the Yankees? Does he have the fuckin' right to just move them?
> MIKE MCD: I don't know. How should I know that?
> MOOGIE: You didn't learn that yet?
> MIKE MCD: No, we get to Steinbrenner in the third year of law school.
> —ROUNDERS

One of the reasons William Paley found George Steinbrenner's partnership group so enticing in late 1972, despite the fact that it wasn't the high bid, was Steinbrenner's insistence he'd keep the Yankees in New York. Paley didn't want as part of his legacy to be responsible for the most famous franchise in American sports to move to Denver, or New Orleans, or—horror of horrors—New Jersey. Paley asked Steinbrenner if he was planning on making a go of it long-term in New York City, and he'd looked the young man square in the eye.

"Yes, sir, I am," Steinbrenner said.

Right from the start, Steinbrenner realized there were problems in the Bronx. The city had given Yankee Stadium a $167 million facelift in time for the 1976 season but certain things couldn't be so easily bought, like foresight: The coming ballparks of the eighties and nineties would all be overrun with luxury suites, which turned them into virtual ATMs for owners seeking to compete with the Yankees for the best talent; Yankee Stadium could only squeeze twenty of them, even after the renovation. Of equal disquiet was the neighborhood around the ballpark, which in 1973 was concerning and within a few years ruinous.

It wasn't long after that "Bronx is burning" era when Steinbrenner began a twenty-five-year on-again, off-again affair with New Jersey, which already built a stadium for New York's football Giants, was about to build an arena for the Long Island–based Nets basketball team, and was shortly to lure the Jets away from Shea Stadium. The Yankees were the desired plum all along, and beginning around 1984 the dalliance turned serious. A state-of-the-art stadium neighboring Giants Stadium was proposed, and the state was (in theory) willing to guarantee 2.2 million in annual attendance and hand over all parking and concessions if the Yankees agreed to flip sides of the Hudson River. At first this was simply a rumor wafting in the wind. But it never went away. By 1986, there was talk New Jersey might be willing to buy out the rest of the Yankees' lease with the city, which expired in 2002 (although they'd need the taxpayers to OK that).

Publicly, Steinbrenner played it coy: "We sure like New York," he said in 1987. "We don't want to move anywhere else." Then he'd talk about how little parking there was around the ballpark. He'd speak of the need for a new train stop adjoining the property. He also, in essence, stopped paying his rent, which was supposed to be $1.5 million annually, from which he was allowed to deduct all maintenance costs—which, often as not, amounted to just around $1.5 million. It was Jim Dwyer, the Pulitzer Prize–winning cityside columnist for *Newsday*, who revealed that between 1986 and 1992 the Yankees paid about $136,000, total, in rent.

"The wealthiest sports franchise in the nation paid less in rent over the last decade than the working poor of any six-story apartment house on the Grand Concourse," Dwyer wrote in 1993. "These are the same people who Steinbrenner blames for frightening away the customers from his ballpark. Yet they pay rent. He doesn't."

By then, New Jersey's aggressive efforts were cooled off by the voters, who overwhelmingly rejected a referendum to use tax dollars to build a stadium there. But Steinbrenner was still restless. When Rudy Giuliani became mayor of New York City, he proposed a couple of Manhattan locations—one on the West Side, one near Madison Square Garden—that quickly yielded hoots of protests from NIMBY residents and environmentalists. Governor Mario Cuomo talked about an arena not far from Yonkers Raceway. The day before the beam fell at Yankee Stadium, another faction of Jersey politicos announced they might try to relaunch the Garden State's recruiting efforts.

Whenever the Jersey/Steinbrenner flirtations resumed every few years he invariably stoked fury among Yankees fans who looked at Yankee Stadium as Catholics saw St. Peter's Basilica. Steinbrenner's last attempt to negatively paint the stadium neighborhood was met harshly by a loud voice belonging to filmmaker Spike Lee.

"He's a greedy asshole who is trying to hold up New York City, and it's disgraceful," Lee said. "He's drawing on white hysteria; he's afraid of the Blacks and Puerto Ricans in the Bronx and is basically saying, 'If we don't stop them from taking over, New York is going to be like Detroit.' All he cares about is stuffing his pockets and catering to suburbanites. The Yankees in New Jersey? *The New York Yankees* in New Jersey? That's unthinkable."

Then the beam fell.

The Yankees moved one home game to Shea Stadium, where they beat the Angels, 6–3. They swapped a series with the Tigers so workmen could repair the area while they played in Detroit, and engineers could do a comprehensive study that declared the stadium sound and fit for public consumption. When the stadium opened back up for business on April 24, fans walking to their seats in Section 22 found George Steinbrenner there, seated for the night not far from where the beam destroyed Seat 7 in Row 2. He bought hot dogs for everyone and declared: "I'm not scared. Are any of you?"

He was a man of the people. For a day, anyway.

HIS BALL CLUB certainly helped scrub whatever hard feelings the fans might've had about the owner. They seized first place on the last day of April. By the end of June the record was 56–20, and there started to be real talk that these Yankees might break the franchise record of 110 wins set by the fabled '27 Yankees, dubbed Murderers' Row, and also the 1906 Cubs, who'd won 116 games in a 154-game season. That speculation turned out to be half right. They won 114 and never did stand on the brakes, winning seven in a row to close out the season long after they'd cliched. Steinbrenner's old sparring partner David Wells, enjoying his finest season, even pitched a perfect game against the Minnesota Twins on May 17.

The '98 team discovered the secret for avoiding the "George-ing" that waylaid so many other teams through the years: They won. A lot. Almost every day. He had nothing to say about Torre's managing, or about the team Brian Cashman had assembled (with the Boss's help and also with his approval for a record $72 million payroll). The Boss did talk to his friends at Page Six and planted a story that perhaps Derek Jeter's burgeoning romance with pop star Mariah Carey might be causing him a few off-field distractions; whether it was Jeter being a loyal employee (or just a famous single guy with an eye toward making his way through as much of the *Maxim* magazine Hot 100 as possible), that flame flickered out soon enough. Jeter finished third in the MVP vote.

Steinbrenner also issued a challenge for Yankees fans in 1998: pack the stadium three million strong for the first time, he'd never talk about New Jersey again. They would set an all-time Yankees attendance record but fall 44,807 shy of Steinbrenner's task. Still, there was already a sense the Boss was softening, that his wandering eyes were finally content, at least for the time being. He had a friend in Mayor Giuliani, and there was momentum building to replace both Yankee Stadium and Shea Stadium. In 1999, the Yankees really would top three million for the first time, and by 2005 that would reach four million, a feat repeated four years in a row. New Yorkers confirmed an age-old truth: If you win—a lot—they will come. And the

Yankees won. A lot. Their run to the 1998 championship consisted of only one day of stress—the Indians took a 2–1 lead in the best-of-seven ALCS—but the Yankees proceeded to win seven straight games, including a sweep of the Padres in the World Series. When the carnage was complete, the Boss wept as he accepted the Commissioner's Trophy from Bud Selig.

"They've got to rank among the greatest ever—not just greatest Yankees teams, but greatest ever teams," he said. "The old Yankees, each year they would get bigger in people's minds. This team will be the same way. How can you do any better than they have?"

Just eight years earlier, that crowd at Yankee Stadium stood and roared when it was announced Steinbrenner had been tossed out of baseball a second time. Now, there were a few thousand Yankees fans who'd made the pilgrimage to Qualcomm Stadium to watch the Yankees tie a bow on a 125-win season, and when they spotted Steinbrenner on the field they made him cry all over again.

"Thank you, Boss!
"Thank you, BOSS!!
"THANK YOU, BOSS!!!"

Even in this moment of unfiltered triumph, a new seed of contention had been planted. Prior to Game 1, Padres CEO Larry Lucchino had taken a tour of Yankee Stadium's Monument Park. He and Steinbrenner had already gone a few rounds on a couple of occasions, Lucchino always making sure to remind the world the Padres and Yankees existed in entirely different economic spheres. Each time, that irked Steinbrenner. Now, Lucchino thought it a good time to quote Dean Acheson, Harry Truman's secretary of state, after saying, "Tell George we still respect the Yankees."

"There are no permanent friends," he said. "There are no permanent enemies. There are only shifting alliances."

Lucchino annoyed Steinbrenner to no end, and he couldn't just let it go unanswered.

When the Boss saw the sorry condition of the Padres' ballpark he sneered, "Tell Lucchino his stadium looks like a cow pasture."

It would take a few years. But Lucchino would be heard from again.

LUCCHINO WAS ONLY lending voice to what a lot of people inside baseball believed: The Yankees were enjoying the perks of playing on an uneven playing field. There was their near-half-a-billion-dollar TV deal. In 1997 Steinbrenner signed an agreement with Adidas, and that landed him not only a cool $100 million contract but also in court with his fellow owners, who believed all such revenue was supposed to be divided evenly by the clubs. Steinbrenner sued them back. It cost him a seat on the sport's executive council, and it further alienated him from the others, who kept watching Steinbrenner's payrolls inch closer and closer toward $100 million annually.

This was underlined by the rosters he kept green-lighting for Cashman. In the spring of 1999, Steinbrenner authorized a trade for Roger Clemens, the two-time reigning Cy Young Award winner. The swap cost the Yankees David Wells, a blow to the fanbase and to most of the saloon owners all across Manhattan. Baseball fans in Pittsburgh and Kansas City howled at the unfairness of the winningest team in history adding the game's best pitcher; if Steinbrenner heard them he didn't let on.

Meanwhile, Cashman was exploring nontraditional sources of talent. Orlando Hernandez was an instant sensation after emigrating from Cuba, going 12–4 in 1998 and finishing fourth in the Rookie of the Year balloting (at age thirty-two). A year earlier, the Yankees conducted a full-court press securing Hideki Irabu, a twenty-eight-year-old fireballer who'd been dubbed the "Nolan Ryan of Japan." The Padres were awarded Irabu's rights, and it was while negotiating with them that Steinbrenner remembered just how profoundly he disliked Larry Lucchino, who ultimately demanded a host of young prospects before sending Irabu east.

Irabu was good for business initially, but he never did adjust to American baseball. He would go 34–35 in a six-year career (29–20 with the Yankees) and pitch to a 5.15 ERA. He also rarely kept himself in shape and wasn't keen on fundamentals. The height—and depth—of Irabu-mania arrived on April Fool's Day 1999. Pitching in the top of the ninth of an exhibition game against Cleveland, he failed to cover first on a grounder to first baseman Clay Bellinger. It had been a nightmarish spring for Irabu, who that morning weighed in at 253 pounds and then insisted just a day earlier he'd tipped the scales at 242.

"My weight goes up and down," he said through a translator, and the writers who dutifully jotted that in their notebooks tried not to burst out laughing because *that* would've needed no interpretation.

Steinbrenner had seen enough.

"He looks like a fat pussie toad out there," Steinbrenner said.

INTERLUDE: And thus began one of the great days in the history of American journalism: How, exactly, were you supposed to spell the word between the "fat" and the "toad" in that sentence (which the Boss had intended as the thick, green ooze that sometimes emanates from an infection)? The *Daily News* just eliminated it. *Newsday* opted for ellipses where the word in question once stood. The *Post*? The *Post* went with "pus-ie [rhymes with 'fussy']." The *Times* opted for "pus-sy," but only after baseball columnist Jack Curry fought his desk about it. Me, I was at the Newark *Star-Ledger* then, and we were a few months into a fairly tight relationship with the producers of *The Sopranos*. The *Ledger* was the paper Tony retrieved at the end of his driveway in many episodes. And we had already demolished one door of decorum by regularly printing the name of one of Tony's closest associates on the show: Salvatore Bonpensiero—a.k.a. "Big Pussy."

"Use something other than that spelling," we were told. I consulted with Tim Brown, our Yankees beat writer, and after some minutes of debate concluded we should go with "fat pussie toad."

Irabu had been a rare miss. There were few others. No team since the Oakland A's of 1972, 1973 and 1974 had won three straight championships before the 1998, 1999 and 2000 Yankees came along. No team had ever come close to winning four in five years since the Yankees of 1949,

1950, 1951, 1952 and 1953 had won five in a row. Recall that two days after he'd completed his first suspension from baseball, on March 3, 1976, Steinbrenner said this:

> We're going to restore the Yankees to what they used to be, the greatest name in sports. I don't mean we're going to win five World Series in a row. Nobody will ever dominate that way again. The talent is spread out too evenly . . . but we're going to be up here all the time, right in there.

Remarkably, it turned out he'd underestimated his own wildest dreams and came as close as possible to four in a row and five out of six, the Yankees only losing the 2001 title because of an epic ninth-inning comeback by the Arizona Diamondbacks in Game 7 of the World Series.

He'd built one champion, fallen as far as a man can tumble, then built up another, and he'd done it this time by mostly staying off the back page, allowing Joe Torre to do his job and Brian Cashman to do his, content with signing checks and occasionally ripping an umpire. Somehow, he'd gone from belittled pariah to beloved patriarch.

He was alone at the top of the heap, as his idol, Frank Sinatra, sang.

Now it was time to right an old wrong.

IN THE SUMMER of 1998 George Steinbrenner began to let go a series of old antipathies. One he'd inherited. Jim Bouton was a terrific Yankees pitcher in the early sixties before arm woes shortened his career; toward the end, he authored *Ball Four*, a book cowritten with *Post* writer Leonard Shecter, in which he gleefully shared a buffet of clubhouse secrets.

Specifically, Mickey Mantle—whom Bouton outed as a drinker and a carouser—disliked the book, and its authors. His unhappiness made Bouton persona non grata in the Bronx when Old-Timers' Day invites were handed out, and when Steinbrenner bought the team, he dutifully honored what he assumed were Mantle's wishes.

By June 1998, Mantle had passed three years before and Bouton was grieving the loss of his daughter, Laurie, to a car accident the previous August. Bouton, who'd become a New York sportscaster in the wake of his book's success, had always been detached and irreverent about his Old-Timers' Day ban. Things were different now. He was almost sixty. Moved by a letter from Bouton's son Michael that appeared in *The New York Times* on Father's Day, Steinbrenner invited Bouton personally.

Bouton cried during the call—after he realized it wasn't a friend pranking him. And when he was introduced July 25, he received one of the loudest ovations of anyone.

Yogi Berra was a whole different category. Berra remained stubborn and steadfast in his refusal to darken the stadium's door as long as Steinbrenner was sitting in the owner's office. His resolve had actually stiffened, even as Steinbrenner's public image seemed to soften. On June 26, 1998, the Mets asked Berra to throw out the ceremonial first pitch before a Subway Series game at Shea Stadium. Berra happily accepted and enjoyed a loud ovation from Mets fans when he threw a strike to Mike Piazza. Of all the things Berra had chosen to miss over the years—his own plaque dedication, a day devoted to his old roommate Bobby Brown, open invites to throw out the first pitch to any of the sixteen home playoff games the Yankees had played between 1996 and '98, all those Old-Timers' Days—the sight of him getting a standing O in Queens devastated Steinbrenner the most.

"He has no interest in tweaking George," Dale Berra insisted of his dad.

Two important things happened in the months to come. Before Game 2 of the '98 ALCS, a most unexpected guest walked out onto the field at Yankee Stadium. Dave Winfield waved his arms, smiled at the crowd, threw the first pitch to Jorge Posada's glove and later said, "To come back and be recognized as a significant Yankee is much appreciated."

If Dave Winfield—whom Steinbrenner had spent the better part of a decade trying to destroy—could make peace, wasn't détente possible with Berra?

It was a visit to the hospital room of Joe DiMaggio that finally pushed the Boss to action. The eighty-four-year-old DiMaggio was suffering from pneumonia, which would later reveal lung cancer and would kill him within a few months. When he saw Steinbrenner, DiMaggio immediately made a plea.

"This thing with Yogi, it shouldn't be a personal thing," DiMaggio said. "It should be first for the fans, then for the game, then for the Yankees. That should be more important than two men having a feud."

In early December, Mark Chernoff, the program director for WFAN radio, dreamed up a remote show for the next month, to take place at the Yogi Berra Museum & Learning Center in Montclair, New Jersey. Not long after securing the date, he reached out to Suzyn Waldman, who'd had a long association with Steinbrenner, knew him well and would host the event.

She called Steinbrenner. "George, I want to talk to you about Yogi."

Steinbrenner was alarmed, fearful something had happened to him. When he was assured Berra was fine, he kept thinking about what DiMaggio had told him.

That's when Waldman first thought, *This might work.*

George was the easy part.

It was Berra who was holding the grudge. Waldman called Dale Berra, told him Steinbrenner would fly up from Tampa, take a car to the museum late in the afternoon of January 7. Dale, who like most of Berra's family members respected his father's pride but also yearned for him to return to Yankee Stadium so he could enjoy a few more moments in the sun, was nevertheless skeptical.

"How do you know he's going to apologize?" Dale asked.

"The man isn't flying two thousand miles in the dead of winter to come in and say 'Fuck you,'" Waldman reasoned.

On the day in question, Berra and his family waited in the lobby. Traffic kept Steinbrenner from arriving at the appointed hour of 5 p.m. sharp.

"You're late," Berra said when Steinbrenner finally showed.

They retreated to a private room, and Berra heard the words he'd waited fourteen years to hear. Steinbrenner apologized, admitted he'd handled the firing sixteen games into the 1985 season terribly.

Berra's signature expression in a lifetime that produced more quotes than *Bartlett's* had always been "It ain't over till it's over," which was how he'd described his '73 Mets when they were still in last place on August 31. Now, as Waldman asked him about the most famous vendetta in American sports, he borrowed from it.

"It's over," he said.

CHAPTER 25

*Everybody on the Yankees has played so well,
George Steinbrenner doesn't know who to fire.*
—DAVID LETTERMAN

They came after him with money, figuring he was an easy mark. It wasn't a ridiculous play. By 1998, George Steinbrenner was sixty-eight years old. Twenty-five years earlier, he'd invested $168,000 of his own money as part of the $8.8 million that took the Yankees off CBS's hands. Now the men in the limousines were offering him more than half a billion dollars for his share. He'd won four championships but, more: He'd *won*; the men in the limos were eager to ensure he'd earn a 342,162 percent return on his initial investment.

Winning?

They'd be talking about him in business schools for eternity.

"George," Charles Dolan said at their first meeting, "you're a giant."

Dolan was himself a self-made business behemoth, also a product of Northeast Ohio, just like Steinbrenner. He dropped out of John Carroll University and founded a company in his mid-twenties that focused on the packaging, marketing and distribution of sports and industrial films. At twenty-five, he sold his business to a Cleveland company called Teleguide in exchange for a full-time job with benefits, and a year later moved to New York to seek his fortune. He found it in cable television. In 1972 he created Home Box Office (HBO), quickly built that into an unlikely powerhouse featuring live sports and first-run uncut movies. After selling HBO to Time-Life he focused on his other company, Cablevision, which dominated the cable-TV market on Long Island. It made him a billionaire. And when he further expanded his empire by purchasing Madison Square Garden in 1999, he at once became the dominant sports executive in New York with the Rangers, Knicks and a money-printing sports television network whose flagship programming was Yankees games.

"Chuck Dolan is a Clevelander," Steinbrenner said, "and an idol of mine."

Now Dolan wanted the Yankees.

Steinbrenner was eager to listen. Half a billion dollars is half a billion dollars, after all. But there was something no amount of money could buy. Soon enough, Steinbrenner recognized that.

"They tried to tell my dad they could work it out where he'd still be in charge of the Yankees, they'd pay him a seven-figure salary and he'd allegedly call the shots," Hal Steinbrenner said. "But look who they were talking to. My father knew better than anybody you couldn't be *appointed* the boss. You had to *be* the boss. If you had to look at a corporate directory to determine who the boss was, then that's not really a boss."

Someone should have told Dolan. Someone should've warned him he'd never get his hands on the Yankees as long as Steinbrenner had a say. Nothing personal, of course. *Nobody* would.

Not even his idol.

THE BOSS WOULD still rage behind closed doors. He would still vent his anger at secretaries, at office staff, at his so-called "baseball people," at his PR guardians, at Brian Cashman. Occasionally he would pick up the paper and see the Yankees had lost six out of nine, something like that, and he'd dial the telephone and gently prod Joe Torre, but before he could even think about igniting his blowtorch Torre would calm him.

Slowly, imperceptibly, George Steinbrenner began to fade from the back pages. Oh, he'd wake up on the wrong side of the bed some days and call Bill Madden of the *Daily News* or Joel Sherman of the *Post* or Jack Curry of the *Times* or Jon Heyman of *Newsday*, and there would be a brief string of throwback "woods," which is what the headlines on both the front and back pages are called in tabloid vernacular.

BOSS UNHAPPY WITH KNOBBY

BOSS WANTS TO SEE FIRE IN YANK BELLIES

BOSS: THE METS ARE SECOND-RATE

But as 1998 bled into 1999, which gave way to 2000, which ceded to 2001, more often when Steinbrenner had something to say he'd filter it through his outside PR man, Howard Rubenstein. Plus there was very little for the Boss to be mad about. Once the Yankees broke the three million attendance barrier in 1999 they've never drawn less, with the exception of the COVID-19-affected seasons of 2020 and 2021. Within a few years of turning Dolan away the Yankees' value doubled, meaning Steinbrenner was now sitting on a billion-dollar asset, and once the Yankees' TV deal with MSG expired after the 2001 season he and his advisers put together plans for their own TV network.

To fill programming hours, Steinbrenner entered into an agreement with the owners of New Jersey's Nets of the NBA and Devils of the NHL, dubbed the partnership YankeeNets, and whether it was coincidence or not the Devils won Stanley Cups in 2000 and 2003 and the previously woebegone Nets made back-to-back appearances in the NBA Finals in 2002 and 2003. He was printing money.

For a time, Lou Lamoriello, architect of the Devils, became Steinbrenner's most trusted adviser, a right-hand man supervising both the Nets and the Devils and offering opinions when asked about the Yankees.

"Mr. Steinbrenner was easy to work with," Lamoriello said a few years later. "We won, and won a lot, and so there wasn't a lot he could find fault with."

It was the same with his baseball team, which had not only completed the sport's first three-peat in twenty-six years by adding the 1999 and 2000 World Series to 1998 but also did so with style and grace and panache.

He'd always been partial to stars, and now he had a boatload: future Hall of Famers Derek Jeter and Mariano Rivera; borderline Hall of Famers Paul O'Neill, Bernie Williams, Andy Pettitte and Jorge Posada; Roger Clemens, who would've surely been a Hall of Famer had he not gotten caught in the steroid dragnet of the mid-2000s. Best of all: They all performed. In October. Under the brightest lights. Year after year after year.

Yankees games now became a gathering spot for the bold-faced names who regularly filled Page Six and *US Weekly* magazine and TMZ.

> **INTERLUDE:** One particularly crazed day was the morning of August 12, 1998. Steinbrenner granted Spike Lee one day to film a scene of his movie *Summer of Sam* at Yankee Stadium, so Lee had directed Reggie Jackson—playing a version of himself twenty-one years younger, stuffed into his old number 44 uniform—on a steamy morning in right field. When they returned to the clubhouse both men were mobbed by reporters; I was the only one who noticed another clubhouse stranger wearing blue jeans, brown work boots and a painter's cap. He had his eight-year-old son with him. I was working at the Newark *Star-Ledger* at the time, and spotting Bruce Springsteen was the equivalent of the columnist of the *Vatican City Times* noticing the pope. He was there to swap guitars with Bernie Williams. He pointed at Jackson and told his son, "See that man? He used to be the best home run hitter in the world." To which Evan Springsteen replied, "The bald guy?"
>
> The column the next day was headlined: THE BOSS—NO, NOT GEORGE—HAS YANKEES ROCKIN'.

STEINBRENNER WOULD QUICKLY tire of his alliances with the Nets and Devils. Signs were evident early when he grumbled his new partners with the Nets, Lewis Katz and Raymond Chambers, seemed a bit too concerned with the philanthropic aspect of the job as opposed to winning as many games as possible. One day, David Cone was told the Nets' ownership philosophy broke down this way, and in order:

1. Charity
2. Dignity
3. Victory

Cone laughed at that.

"Charity and dignity," he said, "don't get you a recurring character on *Seinfeld*."

The Nets would be sold to New York developer Bruce Ratner, who would move the club from North Jersey to Brooklyn, but the team would still follow Steinbrenner when he announced the formation of the Yankee Entertainment and Sports Network—YES—late in 2001. The Yankees' twelve-year association with the MSG Network was a boon for both parties, and by the time YES came into existence the two had most of New York's baseball, basketball and hockey teams carved up; within a few years, the Mets would establish their own regional cable network, SportsNet New York (SNY).

Steinbrenner's empire was expanding rapidly. He'd already overseen the construction of a state-of-the-art spring training facility on Dale Mabry Highway in Tampa, and in 1996 he moved all operations from Fort Lauderdale to his adopted home. The network gained momentum even as Dolan, always a sore loser, vowed he'd never allow Cablevision to carry Yankees games. Steinbrenner's idol was now his rival, and Steinbrenner knew with the Yankees in his pocket he had an unbeatable hand. When the Boss wrote a $30 million check to Dolan to officially end the Yankees' stay on MSG, Dolan couldn't yet see he'd been usurped by his erstwhile protégé.

"We'll never put you on the air, George," he vowed. "Mark my words."

"We'll see about that, Chuck," Steinbrenner replied, with a smile. Dolan did manage to keep Yankees games off his system for all of 2002—as he stubbornly watched Cablevision's stock plummet—but by '03 he'd wearied of the fight and gave in.

The last order of business in completing the Steinbrenner dynasty was finding a new home for his baseball team. For all the threats he'd posited through the years New Jersey had never actually come close to passing the kind of public backing such a facility would require. Manhattan's doors never really opened for him. Yonkers was available . . .

"The *Yonkers Yankees?*" Gene Michael laughed in 2016. "Really?"

Whatever concerns lingered about the safety and viability of the South Bronx had vaporized by now. Crime citywide was down under the auspices of the Yankees' most visible fan, Mayor Rudolph Giuliani. Attendance was more robust. Late in his administration, Giuliani announced an agreement between the city, the Yankees and the Mets whereby two new retractable-roof stadiums would be built (though ultimately the roofs would vanish by the final blueprints). For the Mets, their new home would be in the parking lot next to Shea Stadium; for the Yankees it would rise out of Macombs Dam Park, across 161st Street from the stadium. The cost would be $800 million (and would swell to some $1.7 billion before the doors opened; Citi Field's final number was $930 million), with the city picking up the tab for half, the teams the other half. Giuliani left office in January 2002, but these ballparks, he believed, would be his grandest legacy. That turned out not to be the case because of simple politics and because of something that would have been unimaginable on the day of the announcement.

STEINBRENNER WOULD NEVER rank his championships. For one, he fully expected to win one every year. There was also an unwillingness to lessen the achievements of any of the teams that came before, or the ones that would come later.

In the year 2000, he enjoyed his more triumphant hour.

The Yankees and Mets only made the postseason together once in their shared history going back to 1962. In 1999 they'd come achingly close to meeting in what would be the first World Series Subway Series since 1956. The Yankees and Dodgers tangled seven times in the Fall Classic between 1941 and 1956, the Yankees winning six. The Yankees and Giants met six times between 1921 and 1951, the Yankees winning four. In '99 the Mets lost in six games to the Braves in the National League Championship Series (NLCS), blowing two late-inning leads in Game 6, and it began to feel like the only interborough clashes the city could expect were the two annual interleague series built into the 162-game regular season.

There was something different about that 2000 season. Both teams were *good*, the Mets securing a wild card with ninety-four wins, the Yankees winning another AL East title despite surviving a late-season losing streak that kept their win total at a modest eighty-seven. Together they'd drawn nearly six million fans to their aging ballparks. And on the afternoon and evening of July 8, a whiff of foreshadowing filled both boroughs.

An earlier rain delay required the teams play a split doubleheader. The afternoon game was at Shea Stadium, and in a remarkable twist Doc Gooden was brought back out of mothballs to make a start in the building for which he'd once all but owned the deed. He pitched well, too: five innings, two runs, credited with a 4–2 win. At night, the action shifted to Yankee Stadium and in the top of the second inning in a scoreless game Roger Clemens threw a 97 mph fastball that hit Mets All-Star catcher Mike Piazza square on the helmet. Piazza had a long history of wearing Clemens out; there wasn't a soul on either side who believed this was an accident.

Well, with one exception.

"I don't blame Mike Piazza for thinking what he wants to think because he's the one who got hit in the head," Steinbrenner said. "But if anyone thinks Roger Clemens was trying to hit Mike Piazza in the head, I don't believe that. He wouldn't try to hurt anyone."

Steinbrenner hinted the Mets' emotional and angry reaction to Clemens was a "PR stunt" by the Mets to draw attention away from the fact they'd lost three out of four that weekend (including the Clemens game). It was ex-Yankee Al Leiter who took the lead on the Mets' rebuttal.

"I'm not trying to undermine George here or anything, but if he thinks our reaction has anything to do with PR he has no idea how angry we were at Roger," he said. "I don't know what the organization had to do with teammates standing on the top step of the dugout yelling every cuss word ever invented at Roger after he hit Mike."

Sure enough, the Yankees and Mets both survived to the World Series three and a half months later. As impossible as it was to believe, in Game

2 Clemens and Piazza actually had a rematch. Clemens broke Piazza's bat with a pitch, and the barrel rolled out toward Clemens. He picked it up and instead of discarding it . . . *he (holy shit!) threw it at Piazza!*

There were 56,059 inside Yankee Stadium, and for a beat or two nobody knew how to react. In a moment, it became WrestleMania. No punches were exchanged but plenty of hard words were, in addition to 56,059 voices sending boos and catcalls descending on the combatants—most of them, given the venue, landing on Piazza.

Again Steinbrenner had Clemens's back even as the consensus of opinion—even from Yankees fans—opted for words like "off" and "not right" and "'roid rage" to describe what Clemens had done.

"I don't think for one minute that Roger Clemens picks up a bat to throw it at Mike Piazza," said Steinbrenner, expressing a very lonely opinion. "Emotion played a lot in it, but nothing more."

He was enjoying himself. This was something he'd both dreaded and coveted for years, a chance to beat the Mets on the sport's grandest stage. After the Yankees' lone loss, Game 3 at Shea Stadium, he walked restlessly around the sparse visitor's clubhouse. He heard Mets manager Bobby Valentine say, "I never thought we could make the Yankees feel uncomfortable, that's an encouraging sign."

So on the spot he made a snap decision: He ordered club officials to fill an eighteen-wheel Ryder truck with furniture from the Yankees' home clubhouse on the other side of the Triboro Bridge. Off the truck before Game 4 came a pile of comfortable high-backed chairs to replace the hard wooden stools in front of every locker. Off came a large couch. Off came two trainer's tables.

The players all appreciated the gesture. And maybe this was coincidence, but they won Games 4 and 5, wrapping a third straight championship, the twenty-sixth in team history, the sixth on the Boss's watch, and for the third straight year Steinbrenner wept unabashedly as he accepted the Commissioner's Trophy from Bud Selig.

"Why shouldn't a man cry when he's this happy?" the Boss asked.

A year later, the Yankees would do their part to help heal their city after the terrorist attacks of September 11, 2001. They won a thrilling five-game series with Oakland (highlighted by Jeter's signature "flip throw"), they crushed the 116-win Seattle Mariners in six and they seized a 3–2 lead on the Arizona Diamondbacks after back-to-back games at Yankee Stadium, where first Tino Martinez and then Scott Brosius rescued them with two-out ninth-inning home runs. The Diamondbacks ransacked Andy Pettitte in Game 6, 15–2, and then did the unthinkable, rallying for two in the bottom of the ninth against Mariano Rivera, who'd become the sport's most fearsome closer. When Luis Gonzalez dunked a bloop over Derek Jeter's head, the celebration was so loud, so raucous, it bled into the Yankees' clubhouse.

Row after row of players sat in sad silence. This was different from the scene inside the Kingdome six years earlier. The core of this team had won multiple championships together, and they'd just missed making it five out of six. They'd bled every ounce of satisfaction they could. They knew that. Steinbrenner probably did, too.

But he was also less emotional than he'd been at the Kingdome. He distributed fewer hugs. He was legit *angry*. He'd watched Game 7 in the Yankees' clubhouse at Bank One Ballpark, watched as workers prepared the room for a celebration that never came, and was quick to rip MLB for stealing his mojo.

Steinbrenner looked grim. "There's going to be changes," he said. Then he went to one of his go-to sources, Ernest Hemingway.

"The way to be a good loser is to practice it," he said. "And I am not going to be practicing."

By the time they boarded the long flight home, most of the men who worked for Steinbrenner were in agreement: It's much, much better when the old man has himself a good cry.

CHAPTER 26

We realize the Evil Empire is always out there, willing to do what's in their best interests. We can't control that. We recognize the threat is always there, and the Force will be with us.
—LARRY LUCCHINO

The emergence of Larry Lucchino as the last great foil of his life—along with the corresponding revival of the Boston Red Sox, and that franchise's boundless determination to reverse the stubborn tides of history—provided the last eruptions of Old Mount St. Steinbrenner, a volcano that had started to lay dormant.

He was still a demanding Boss—still earned the capital "B" to those who really did work for him—but he found less and less need to feed the tabloids, and scream across the back pages. More and more, if something was bothering him, he'd call Howard Rubenstein, who fifty years earlier founded Rubenstein Associates, the most notable public relations firm in New York City. Rubenstein's high-profile client list included Donald Trump and Rupert Murdoch, the Metropolitan Opera, and Michael Jackson. Rudolph Giuliani once dubbed him "the dean of damage control."

Through Rubenstein, the Boss's colorful commentaries became so cliché-ridden and perversely purple that it became a regular bit on talk radio in New York to read them while fife-and-drum music played in the background.

One example, just after the Angels eliminated the Yankees from the 2002 American League Division Series:

> *There is an old Scottish proverb that says, "I am wounded, but I am not slain. I shall lay me down and bleed a while, then I shall rise and fight again." That should be the feeling of all Yankees today. As for me, my chin is not on my chest. And I don't want anyone on my team to have his chin on his chest. . . . The Yankees have come to symbolize the spirit, strength and resilience of New York. . . .*

You weren't getting "My gutless team spit the bit," anymore.

The papers tried. Every time Steinbrenner was spotted anywhere near a Yankees game, they dispatched reporters to stake out the Boss's favored entrances and exits. A twenty-two-year-old news clerk for *The New York Times* who'd been covering "mostly low-end shit, helping reporters on murders in the Bronx or in Brooklyn" received a call one day from the *Times'* baseball editor Jay Schreiber.

"You're on Steinbrenner duty," Schreiber said.

Soon, it would be redubbed "Boss Watch," and it was a distinctly unglamorous assignment: You'd stake out the front of the stadium. You'd throw questions at Steinbrenner; usually the most you'd get was a smile or a wave. You'd go up to the press box, watch the game, and, as soon as the traditional eighth-inning song—"Cotton Eye Joe"—played you'd hustle back down, wait for the Boss to leave, fire a few more questions. Sometimes he'd have something to say.

"Mostly," Michael S. Schmidt says, "it was about playing defense. On the rare occasions he did have something on his mind, the *Times* wanted to make sure it wouldn't only appear on the back pages of the tabloids."

Across the next twenty years Schmidt would win two Pulitzer Prizes and become one of the most decorated reporters in the country. Long before he covered presidents, he was sent out on Boss Watch thirty or so times to yell "How do you feel about the Yankees?" and hope for something in return like "We stink!"

"He still held a lot of currency," Schmidt says. "It was also increasingly clear, as we were stuck behind barricades, that nobody wanted him to say much of anything anymore."

Larry Lucchino could still relight the smoldering embers of the Boss's rage, however.

The two had been at odds for years, ever since Lucchino became president of the Baltimore Orioles in 1988, working under Steinbrenner's old Watergate attorney Edward Bennett Williams. They were dishwater and motor oil. One time at an ownership meeting, as a goof, Lucchino convinced the other attendees to show up wearing a white turtleneck and a blue blazer—Steinbrenner's standard "uniform" by the early nineties.

Everyone thought that hilarious. George thought it infantile.

"I don't think George even got the joke," Lucchino said.

When John Henry—once a limited partner with the Yankees and an old Steinbrenner friend—bought a controlling interest in the Red Sox in 2002, he hired Lucchino as team president. Steinbrenner's simmering animosity toward Lucchino percolated.

"I mean, look at me: a kid from Pittsburgh, president of the mighty Boston Red Sox. Are you kidding me?" Lucchino said. "If I can't have fun with this job it's a sin and a crime."

When Lucchino dubbed the Yankees the "Evil Empire" that made the Boss, by association, Darth Vader. Lucchino used the term for the first time, in October 2002, and it barely made a ripple.

"My guess," Lucchino said, "is George never saw *Star Wars*."

The second time, though, it was the baseball equivalent of firing on Fort Sumter. The Yankees and Red Sox were both pursuing an exiled Cuban pitcher named José Contreras, who was greeting suitors at the Hotel Campo Real in Acoyapa, Nicaragua. The Sox put on a full-court press, renting all fourteen rooms so no other team could get close to him. The recruiting party Lucchino sent included his freshly hired twenty-eight-year-old GM, Theo Epstein, and a contingent of four Latin Red Sox front-office workers led by Luis Tiant, a great Sox pitcher of the seventies, who himself fled Castro's Cuba. It seemed a brilliant flooding of the zone.

Contreras signed with the Yankees anyway, Steinbrenner approving a $32 million deal.

Epstein, in the early hours of a surefire Hall of Fame career, threw a tantrum in his hotel room. Lucchino led with his lip.

"The Evil Empire," he said, "extends its tentacles even into Latin America."

This time, Steinbrenner paid attention. This time he read those words on Christmas morning in *The New York Times*, and he detonated.

There would be no call to Rubenstein Associates this time.

This time it would be Boss, Unplugged.

"That's *bullshit*!" he raged. "That's how a sick person thinks. I've learned this about Lucchino: He's baseball's foremost chameleon. He changes colors depending on where he's standing. He's been at Baltimore and he deserted them there, and then went out to San Diego and look at what trouble they're in out there. When he was in San Diego, he was a big man for the small markets. Now he's in Boston and he's for the big markets.

"He's not the kind of guy you want in your foxhole. He's running the team behind John Henry's back. I warned John it would happen, told him, 'Be careful.' Lucchino talks out of both sides of his mouth. He has trouble talking out of the front of it."

Remember when everyone thought John Travolta's career was over and then, out of nowhere, *Pulp Fiction* happened? This was the Boss as Vincent Vega. He was back. Who knew how long it would last, but for now, the bard of the back page cleared his throat and was fully reengaged.

WHENEVER STEINBRENNER DID go solo, on the record, he could still be counted on to keep his team on its toes—even its best player. After six years of brilliant play Derek Jeter earned a $189 million contract extension from the Boss—the richest in team history. The Yankees shortstop had a fine year in 2002, the first of his new deal—.297, eighteen homers, 124 runs scored—but it marked the fourth consecutive year his batting average and OPS dipped. Few in New York noticed, fewer still complained.

One man noticed.

"How much better would he be if he didn't have all his other activities?" Steinbrenner asked Wayne Coffey, the elegant feature writer for the *Daily News*, in a long sit-down in December 2002 in advance of his thirtieth year on the job. "I tell him this all the time: You can't be everything to everybody. You've got to focus on what's important."

Then, the money shot:

"When I read in the paper that he's been out until three a.m. in New York City going to a birthday party, I won't lie. That doesn't sit well with me. That's the focus I'm talking about."

Steinbrenner had taken his sledgehammer to Billy Martin before, to Reggie Jackson and Thurman Munson, to Dave Winfield, even to Don Mattingly.

But Jeter?

That was like . . . well, it was unlike anything you might compare it to. Plus, Jeter always went to great lengths to keep this highest of public profiles in check. Once, in 1999, during a chat with a few trusted reporters, he'd said, "Look, I don't ever want to see my name on Page Six, let alone page one."

Jeter kept an even lower profile than usual until he arrived at spring training. It was clear the Steinbrenner comments stung; it was also obvious he'd been paying a good deal of attention to the way Joe Torre expertly deflected so many Boss broadsides the past seven years.

"He's the boss and he's entitled to his opinion . . ." Jeter said. "But what he said has been turned into me being this big party animal. He even made a reference to one birthday party. That's been turned into that I'm Dennis Rodman now."

INTERLUDE: As usual, Steinbrenner managed to spin this perfectly. An executive from the advertising agency Batten, Barton,

Durstine and Osborn approached Steinbrenner and Jeter about doing a commercial for Visa. The result was priceless—Steinbrenner summoning Jeter to his office, saying, "You're our starting shortstop. How can you possibly afford to spend two nights dancing, two nights eating out and three nights just carousing with your friends?" and ending with Steinbrenner at the back of a conga line after Jeter shows him his Visa card by way of explanation. The ad ran on endless loop for months.

Maybe it was coincidence, maybe not, but Jeter bounced back to hit .324 despite missing a month and a half after dislocating his shoulder. In June George Steinbrenner decided to add a little weight behind the expectations: He made Jeter the eleventh captain in team history, the first since Don Mattingly almost eight years earlier.

IN THE RED SOX, the Yankees now had a foe unlike any they'd ever encountered. For decades, Sox ownership—at first Tom Yawkey, then those entrusted with his estate—operated the team with the hope they'd be regularly competitive, they'd always have a deep supply of right-handed bats to take aim at Fenway Park's famed wall and they'd keep drawing customers to the aging bandbox . . . and, every few years, have a team good enough to take a shot at first place. Under the three-headed leadership (and astride the deep pockets) of John Henry, Tom Werner and Larry Lucchino, with Theo Epstein tirelessly looking to upgrade the roster, the Sox announced a new chapter of this feud, which dated to 1920, when Sox owner Harry Frazee sold Babe Ruth to the Yankees.

"We are going to win a championship," Henry declared early in the 2003 season.

"I look forward to seeing them try," Steinbrenner replied.

What followed was two years of the most extraordinary baseball conceivable. Both sides loaded up on stars—Manny Ramirez, Pedro Martinez, David Ortiz, Curt Schilling and Nomar Garciaparra in Boston; Gary Sheffield, Roger Clemens, Hideki Matsui (the best player in Japan, dubbed

"Godzilla") adding to the Yankees' core that won four championships. In the winter of 2004, both teams went full-throttle after the best player in the game: Texas Rangers shortstop Alex Rodriguez.

The Sox thought they'd made a deal for Rodriguez, a three-way trade that would've meant shipping away both Ramirez and Garciaparra. Rodriguez agreed to restructure the rest of the ten-year, $252 million deal he'd signed with the Rangers. At the last minute, the players' union disallowed it and the deal was dead. Unknown to the Sox, their October tormentor—Aaron Boone, whose walk-off home run in the bottom of the eleventh inning of Game 7 of the ALCS clinched the '03 pennant—blew out his knee playing pickup basketball. The Yankees needed a third baseman. They reached out to gauge A-Rod's interest, which was high. Things moved quickly. And on February 17, 2004, Rodriguez was introduced wearing number 13 in pinstripes.

"I keep waiting for someone to pinch me," Rodriguez said.

The Sox did, too. Henry cited an ESPN poll after the deal that said 57 percent of baseball fans characterized the Yankees/Rodriguez deal as "disgusting" or "sad."

"Although I've never been an advocate of a salary cap in baseball out of respect for the players," Henry said, "there is really no other fair way to deal with a team that has gone so insanely far beyond the resources of all the other teams."

Steinbrenner, staring at a payroll of near $180 million at a time when two-thirds of the league was under $100 million, took great delight in Henry's bitterness, even greater enjoyment in volleying back.

"We understand John Henry must be embarrassed, frustrated and disappointed by his failure in this transaction," he said. "Unlike the Yankees, he chose not to go the extra distance for his fans in Boston."

This all transpired just four months after the latest twist in the near-hundred-year struggle between the Yankees and the Sox. The 2003 ALCS was hard-fought—and in Game 3 that had been literal, when a benches-clearing brouhaha resulted in Yankees coach Don Zimmer charging at Pedro Martinez and taking a half punch before Martinez swung Zimmer to the ground. The teams were locked up 3–3 after six games, and the Sox took a 5–2 lead into the eighth with Pedro on the mound. But he tired, manager Grady Little inexplicably chose to keep him on the mound, the Yankees tied it at 5, and finally Boone unloaded on a Tim Wakefield knuckleball to send the Yankees to the World Series.

It was a glorious series, and the jubilation in the Yankees' clubhouse was met by a mirrored display of torment in the Sox's room, where players hung on to each other and wept in the aftermath of this emotional bloodbath of a series.

Steinbrenner couldn't help himself. This time, when the gaggle of reporters greeted him after the Yankees' 6–5 win, he praised everyone: Jeter, Rivera (three innings of shutout relief), Boone, Torre. Then the conversation turned to his freshly vanquished opponent.

"Go back to Boston, boys!" he said. "Goodbye! They didn't treat us very well in Boston, you know. But we got the last laugh."

A year later, the Boss was fixing to smile again, to tweak Henry and Lucchino again. They were still the two best teams in the American League, and unsurprisingly hooked up again in the ALCS. This time, it was going to leave a mark. The Yankees swept the first two games at Yankee Stadium, then stomped the Sox 19–8 in Game 3. No team in baseball history had ever come back to win a best-of-seven series after trailing 0–3; no team had ever even *forced a Game 7* out of that ditch. To make it all sweeter, the Yankees took a 4–3 lead into the bottom of the ninth of Game 4, three outs away from another conquering, with Rivera on the mound. Fenway was quiet as a crypt.

But Rivera walked Kevin Millar leading off. Pinch runner Dave Roberts stole second—barely—and Bill Mueller tied the game with an RBI single. In the twelfth, David Ortiz hit a two-run walk-off home run off Paul Quantrill. The Sox were alive.

In Game 5, trailing 4–2 in the eighth, the Sox scored twice to tie. Again Ortiz came up in a huge spot, bottom of the fourteenth, man on second. Again, on the last of ten pitches from Esteban Loaiza, he hammered an RBI single. Now the Sox forced a Game 6.

George Steinbrenner, seeking to ladle out blame, found a target.

A year earlier, unhappy at how the playoffs were starting, the Boss cornered his GM, Brian Cashman, and unleashed on him.

"You're horseshit, and you're overpaid!" he lashed. "No one will take your contract off my hands! Maybe the Mets will take you. You have my permission to talk to the Mets."

Steinbrenner would outflank Cashman, deciding a few days later to pick up his option for 2004 so Cashman *couldn't* talk to the Mets. Cashman grew used to this after six years on the job, but it still unsettled him. Now, with Ortiz singularly trying to reverse a curse that had merrily motored unencumbered for eighty-six years, it was hard not to remember a classic bit of revisionist history authored by his boss the Boss. Back in September 2003, when Ortiz was first starting to treat the Yankees as his personal punching bag, Steinbrenner invited Joel Sherman of the *Post* into his office.

"I told Cashman in the offseason to sign Ortiz," Steinbrenner said, referring to the previous winter, when the Minnesota Twins opted not to tender Ortiz a contract. "But he told me we already had two first basemen. I said, 'Find a way!'"

Cashman had his reasons, good ones, for staying away, starting with the Yankees eight-year, $135.4 million commitment to Jason Giambi, and Giambi was coming off a forty-one-homer, 122-RBI year in which he'd finished fifth in the MVP vote. His backup, hard-hitting Nick Johnson, was their top prospect. The Yankees *did* have two first basemen. Ortiz? He'd yet to distinguish himself as a player or even gain regular playing time as a Twin.

Cashman confirmed Steinbrenner's story to Sherman, but neither Sherman nor any of New York's other two dozen full-time baseball writers could ever remember the Boss pining for Big Papi until he started tormenting them.

And he was torturing them now.

By the first inning of Game 7, after the Sox evened the series at 3 with a 4–2 win in Game 6, with most of New York braced for the impossible, which now seemed ever so inevitable, Ortiz walked to the plate in the top of the first, one on, two out. Baseball isn't supposed to be this easy—this predictable—but by now all bets were off. Ortiz launched one into the seats in right. Cameras captured Steinbrenner shaking his head ruefully. It was 2–0, Sox. It would end 10–3, Sox. Eighty-six years later, the Sox finally punched back.

Larry Lucchino couldn't wait to flex.

"Somebody sent me a hat recently that said, 'All Empires Fall,'" he said, champagne dripping off his topcoat. "I refused to wear it. But I might wear it a few hours tonight."

Everyone in the employ of the Yankees quietly waited for the tornado to strike. The Yankees had authored the worst collapse in baseball history. After writing so much of baseball's history going back to 1920—almost all of it superb—this would be a permanent mark on their record, no getting around that. Surely Steinbrenner would blow his stack, if he hadn't already.

But a curious thing happened.

The Red Sox fans in attendance at Yankee Stadium, so overwhelmed all night, engineered something of a palace coup, commandeering the lower bowl of Yankee Stadium just behind the Sox's third base dugout. For a time, they tried in vain to drown out the final few replays of "New York, New York," and when the Yankees finally pulled the plug on that, you could hear the Boston fans lift their voices to the sky.

"Thank you, Red Sox!"

"Thank you, Red Sox!"

"Thank you, Red Sox!"

A few of Steinbrenner's underlings started to fume and began to fret the Boss might be on the verge of meltdown. They cautiously visited him in his office. They lodged their formal complaints, and Steinbrenner listened very carefully to each one.

"They won't go home, Boss," they said.

"They keep spraying champagne, Boss," they argued.

Steinbrenner nodded. Then shook his head, leaned back in his chair.

"Keep the lights on as long as they want to stay," he said quietly. "They've earned it."

CHAPTER 27

*If you don't want to play for Mr. Steinbrenner,
you've got problems. You don't want to win.*
—DEREK JETER

There were eighteen dignitaries and VIPs gathered in front of a wall across the street from Yankee Stadium the afternoon of August 16, 2006. It happened to be the fifty-eighth anniversary of the day Babe Ruth died, and when he'd been waked a few days later in the stadium vestibule there'd been a line four hours long wrapped around the familiar secular cathedral at 161st Street and River Avenue, thousands of fans wishing to pay their final respects for the man who'd lent his name to the House that Ruth Built.

Now, they were breaking ground on the House the Boss Built.

(Or, as a few cynical wags put it: "The House that Ruthless Built.")

The press and members of the Yankees faithful had gathered again, this time on a sunny, hot day, this time to commemorate a new chapter in Yankees history, one George Steinbrenner had been pushing for almost as long as he'd owned the team. Steinbrenner was one of the eighteen with silver shovels in their hands, the handles shaped like baseball bats, to officially break ground on this new Yankee Stadium. The Boss was the only one not wearing a protective hard hat.

"I'd rather not," he said when handed one.

He was still the Boss.

One by one, twelve politicians walked to a rostrum and addressed the crowd, capped by Mayor Michael Bloomberg, who said, "I can't think of a better time to do this. It ties together old and new. I think Babe must be looking down and saying, 'You go, guys.'"

Then the featured speaker walked slowly to the microphone. As he stepped to the podium he bumped into a chair and seemed for a terrible second to be on his way down; John Sterling, the iconic Yankees broadcaster serving as master of ceremonies, caught him, steadied him, and guided him to the stand.

"It's very hot sitting up here," George Steinbrenner said. "But I get a good feeling. Enjoy the new stadium. I hope it's wonderful."

To the end, there'd been howls of protest. Upon taking office Bloomberg halted the plans Giuliani laid to build ballparks for the Mets and Yankees. Each would have matching $800 million price tags with half the tab picked up by the city. Bloomberg called that plan "corporate welfare," and was cheered by fiscally minded officials who'd been steamrolled by Giuliani's ambitions. Five years later the city's finances were in better shape and the need to replace the aging ballparks in Queens and the Bronx was even stronger. The Mets and Yankees were also allowed to use money spent on the stadium to defray revenue-sharing taxes, a new provision of baseball's latest collective-bargaining agreement.

Still, Yankee Stadium was going to cost taxpayers in excess of $400 million, and this time it sped through the city council without even a public hearing. The team wouldn't have to pay for the cost of tearing down the old stadium and would no longer be on the hook to pay rent. It was one final example of just how remarkable an investment the Yankees had been; if, in 1973, Steinbrenner's group had put their $8.8 million in a fund that mirrored the Dow Jones Industrial Average, they would've turned that into a tidy $109 million.

Instead, the Yankees were now worth $1.2 billion.

And growing every year.

"It's a pleasure giving this to you people," Steinbrenner said as he concluded his remarks, which took less than a minute. They were the last words Steinbrenner would ever say before a public crowd.

STEINBRENNER'S DECLINING HEALTH was an open secret for years. A few months after his seventy-third birthday one of his boyhood heroes, ex–Cleveland Browns quarterback Otto Graham, died at age eighty-two on December 17, 2003. Steinbrenner had grown close with Graham through the years and took his passing hard, an unwelcome reminder of his own mortality. Eleven days later Steinbrenner sat in a pew at Church of the Palms on Bee Ridge Road in Sarasota, Florida, watching a slideshow presentation of Graham's life when he suddenly was struck by a hot flash. He labored to breathe. When Graham's daughter-in-law started a eulogy, Steinbrenner began to lose consciousness and, according to someone sitting near him in the pew, turned "pasty white." Then he toppled to the church floor.

Paramedics were summoned. Horrified mourners raced to his side, loosened his tie and were greeted with "I'm all right, dammit!" as Steinbrenner regained consciousness and asked he not be lifted onto a stretcher; he was, anyway, and was rushed to Sarasota Memorial Hospital for tests. He stayed overnight. The next day, as word leaked out, Steinbrenner's personal physician, Dr. Andrew Boyer, declared, "It was nothing more than a fainting spell. He's feeling well, and his general health is excellent."

A few days later—through Howard Rubenstein—the Boss tried to make light of the incident: "I didn't faint. I was just practicing my slide into second base."

More and more, though, the pithy comebacks filtered through Rubenstein bore little resemblance to the short, sometimes ill-tempered and often stilted remarks he would offer when walking past reporters on Boss Watch before and after games. After the Yankees blew the 2004 AL Championship Series to the Red Sox, with most of New York eagerly awaiting a classic Boss rant, he said nothing.

He was being kept farther and farther from the fray, and with reason. In the summer of 2003, after Pedro Martinez sent both Derek Jeter and Alfonso Soriano to the hospital with inside brushbacks, he wept while talking about how the team battled back to win the game, 2–1. At the home opener in '04, he broke down crying when interviewed on the pregame show by sportscaster Warner Wolf. He'd already made a habit of crying after the Yankees won all those important games from 1995 to 2001; now, it seemed, he would be moved to tears by just about anything.

"Maybe he's acting," Yankees pitcher Mike Mussina said wryly, after he'd outdueled Martinez that day in '03.

Soon, it became hard to hide. In May 2005 Steinbrenner agreed to appear on the YES Network program *CenterStage* hosted by longtime Yankees broadcaster Michael Kay and asked that it not be taped before a studio audience, as the show always was. He appeared distracted and confused, often simply repeating Kay's questions as his own answers. For anyone who had ever been on the other side of a Steinbrenner interview, scribbling furiously in your notebook so you could keep up, it was heartbreaking to watch.

Not long after, there was a gathering at Yankee Stadium to announce plans for the new stadium had officially been green-lit. He offered a few remarks that day, too, but they were so halting that when the groundbreaking was announced for August, a number of Yankees officials fretted about letting Steinbrenner talk at all—and were visibly relieved when he got through it fine.

But in early November 2006, he suffered another incident. He traveled to Chapel Hill, North Carolina, along with his wife, Joan, and his daughters, Jessica and Jennifer, to see his granddaughter, Haley Swindal, a drama student at North Carolina, perform as Sally Bowles in *Cabaret*. Midway through the show, Steinbrenner felt chest pains and began to black out again. The performance was halted at intermission, and once again he was loaded into an ambulance and taken to a local hospital for tests. Again he returned to Tampa and allegedly went back to work.

"George Steinbrenner is well and raising hell," Rubenstein insisted. "He is just fine."

George wasn't fine, and was less fine every day, and it was now that he recognized the need to tend to the Yankees' future with a lot more urgency than he ever had before. He needed to put the House of Steinbrenner in order. Fast.

BACK WHEN HE needed a trusted surrogate in that awful summer of 1990, when Fay Vincent threw him out of baseball for life (for the time being, anyway), George Steinbrenner turned to his elder son, Hank, who'd spent time in the 1980s learning the baseball business but quickly retreated back to Florida to run the family horse interests.

Hank was the Steinbrenner sibling who best remembered his father before he became famous. He was fifteen when George fronted the group that bought the Yankees from CBS. He remembered distinctly his father coming home to suburban Cleveland one night just before Christmas, brimming with good news. Hank was hoping maybe he'd gotten a chance to buy the Cleveland Indians again.

"Nope," the father said. "It's the Yankees."

Hank was floored. He was a baseball freak, old enough to appreciate precisely the adventure his family was about to embark on. His brother, Hal, had just turned three; Jessica was eight, Jennifer thirteen. Hank was a devoted son but of a different makeup than his father. He was always quick to point out, "I don't fly off the handle like my dad does," and quicker to report he'd often made trade suggestions to his father. The one he'd proposed that George actually listened to—according to Hank anyway—was the 1976 blockbuster with Baltimore in which the Yankees got Ken Holtzman and Doyle Alexander in exchange for Rick Dempsey, Tippy Martinez, Rudy May and Scott McGregor.

"I told Dad, 'You have to get Alexander,'" Steinbrenner insisted in 1986, and since by then that trade was already considered among the worst in the Steinbrenner Era, it's hard to believe Hank would own it if it wasn't at least a *little* true. Of course, by '86, he really did have his father's ear, and even the old man had to dismiss him one day when Hank insisted Dave Righetti could easily be replaced as the team's closer by a junk-balling journeyman left-hander named Alfonso Pulido.

Once the press started writing down this stuff, it was delighted. Once, when a late Yankees rally fizzled, Hank roared, "This team has the killer instinct of a Quaker!"

The Boss had laughed at that one.

But Hank quickly grew tired of being a back-page punch line, and much as he'd loved baseball as a kid he'd fallen out of love with the sport as an adult. He told his father he'd do his duty as a son and take over in 1990, but George could see Hank's heart wasn't in it. They agreed he'd be more useful as a horseman than a henchman. By 2007 Hank was still happy where he was.

So . . . who?

Joe Molloy became a trusted Steinbrenner lieutenant soon after marrying Jessica, the Boss's youngest daughter, and he was a key advocate for Gene Michael when he ran the team in Steinbrenner's absence. He'd been a former high school basketball coach and was well-liked and for a time seemed to be a likely successor. But Molloy found the pressures of the job overwhelming and in 1997 took a one-year leave of absence; before he could ponder whether he wanted to return or not, he and Jessica had broken up and Molloy happily returned to teaching.

Into the breach stepped Steve Swindal, Steinbrenner's other son-in-law, married to Jennifer. He joined the Yankees in 1995, became a general partner and quickly became the secondary face of the team, behind the Boss. By 2005 Steinbrenner anointed him his eventual business heir, and it was a popular choice. Swindal was smart, well-liked, and promised that when the time came, he'd be just as committed to winning as his father-in-law. Like Joe Molloy he also had an everyman side to him.

"You think about it," Swindal said in 2006, speaking about the enormity of following in Steinbrenner's loafers. "But then you say, 'God, it's the *New York Yankees*. What guy wouldn't love to be involved in a major sport with the best team in all of sports? Go for it. See what happens. What's the worst that can happen?'"

Well, since he asked . . .

February 15, 2007, can happen.

That night, Swindal was driving his Mercedes-Benz 61 mph on a 35 mph road in St. Petersburg. When a police car followed the officer noted he was drifting out of his lane. Pulled over, Swindal failed a field-sobriety test when the officer noted he was "swaying, stumbling fumbling," and added his "staggering motor control, watery eyes, and a strong odor of an alcoholic beverage coming from his breath." Swindal was also described thusly: "slurred, mumbled speech [and] a blank, dazed, uncomprehending facial expression."

Swindal refused a Breathalyzer but was booked for driving under the influence and had his mug shot snapped, which dutifully appeared in hundreds of newspapers the next day. It turned out that was only part of a really, *really* bad day for Swindal: Hours before he'd gone on his bender, Jennifer informed him she wanted a divorce.

So that was the end of Steve Swindal, heir apparent.

That left Harold—Hal to everyone—who followed in his father's path at both Culver Military Academy and Williams College and took his first job with the Yankees the summer after he graduated college, working in Tampa at the lowest rung of the organization. He was quieter than Hank, *much* quieter than his father.

Hal first impressed his old man when he was twelve. Burger King produced a set of Yankees cards to distribute along with cheeseburgers and fries and milkshakes. Hal picked up his set along with a Whopper one day, flipped through it, and noticed that Lou Piniella—his father's favorite—wasn't included. He called his dad. His dad made a call. In a couple of days, Piniella's card was added to the set as a bonus—and, because they were printed so late, there were only a limited number of Piniellas available. By 1986, you could fetch as much as $50 for a Burger King Lou. That caught the old man's eye.

So, too, did his son's introversion.

"I wouldn't push him if I thought he'd be intimidated by this life," the Boss said just before he began his second suspension. "Hal is very independent. He has absolutely no fears."

Hal confirmed that.

"It is very uncomfortable to be in a situation when you are so privileged and it makes you stand out," Hal said in November 1990, still but twenty years old and a senior at Williams. "To see other [students] just worried about getting jobs right now, especially during a recession, kind of makes me feel guilty."

Eventually George would have to pick Hal or Hank as his successor. For now, in September 2007, he named Hal chairman of the board. All four of his children held the title of general partner. George was still boss, still managing general partner. In time he'd have to surrender that title, and only one of his kids could hold the job. For now, Hal was in pole position.

AND YET . . .

Every now and again, the old lion would emerge from behind the protective curtain, and he would roar—perhaps not as loudly as before, perhaps absent the fire that always made his words resonate when they truly emerged from his own voice box.

There was the day in spring training 2005 when the Boss walked onto the elevator at Legends Field in Tampa, fresh from an aggravating meeting with Arn Tellem, one of the powerful player agents of the time. Tellem was talking to Steinbrenner about a contract extension for Hideki Matsui, but Steinbrenner was eternally peeved about another of Tellem's clients, Jason Giambi, who'd not only hit an anemic .208 the year before but also was becoming one of the faces of the steroid controversy now blanketing baseball.

Steinbrenner was in a foul mood when he stepped on the elevator.

The presence of a couple of reporters—including this one—didn't brighten his day any. Especially when one asked about the Matsui talks.

"Fuck the agent," Steinbrenner barked. "He's no good."

BOSS BLOWS! blared the *Post*.

FURIOUS GEORGE! countered the *Daily News*.

GEORGE GIVES AGENT AN "F"! was how *Newsday* checked in.

It was glorious! It was throwback Boss! Perhaps reports of the demise of his feisty side really were exaggerated!

Except the next day, when the media reported to Legends Field, they discovered one of the two elevators was suddenly off-limits to them and anyone else besides those requiring access to the owner's office on the fourth floor.

By the time the Yankees were engaged in the 2007 Division Series with Cleveland, it had been months since Steinbrenner had been heard from anywhere other than a press release. The Boss Watch was still on, but that was an increasingly soul-crushing assignment. The Yankees came home to play the Indians in Game 3 having dropped the first two, the latter of which was marred when swarms of gnat-like insects known as midges wandered in from Lake Erie to torture Yankees reliever Joba Chamberlain as he tried to protect a late lead.

On the off-day, a Saturday, Ian O'Connor, now a columnist for the Bergen *Record*, took a shot calling Steinbrenner at the Regency Hotel on Park Avenue, his usual residence in New York. O'Connor called the main hotel operator, who transferred the call to Steinbrenner's personal assistant. This is where, about 100 percent of the time by October 2007, a reporter's pursuit died. O'Connor understood the odds. He called anyway.

Before he knew it, the Boss was on the line.

He had stuff on his mind, too.

"His job is on the line," Steinbrenner said, referring to Joe Torre, managing in his twelfth straight postseason in twelve years as Yankees skipper. "We're paying him a lot of money. He's the highest-paid manager in baseball. I don't think we'd take him back if we don't win this series."

In the old days, Steinbrenner would've stormed into the press box while the midges were still attacking Chamberlain, raised hell with everyone: writers, league president, commissioner. A day later, the only one who'd said (correctly) the umpires should've halted the game until the bugs could be cleared was Roger Clemens, the Game 3 starter. That infuriated the Boss.

"The umpire was full of shit," the Boss raged.

He said he'd complained to commissioner Bud Selig.

"Bud just said, 'That's in the umpires' hands.' But Jesus Christ, it was terrible. It messed up the whole team, Jeter, all of them."

Steinbrenner had one last message.

"I have full control," he said. "I'm doing all right. I'm fine."

For a few days, New York was electrified. O'Connor's competitors in the papers and talk radio were incensed, certain he'd been set up with the Boss by factions of the team's leadership eager to part ways with Torre. All flatly denied that. O'Connor insisted he'd simply done what every journalism school student learns on the first day of Reporting 101: pick up the phone, make the call, ask some questions.

> **INTERLUDE:** By now, the public really did seem nostalgic for the Old Boss. That summer, ESPN broadcast an eight-part limited series, *The Bronx Is Burning*, dramatizing the fabled Bronx Zoo Yankees of 1977. Oliver Platt, a much-acclaimed Canadian actor, portrayed Steinbrenner, and he didn't hold back even a little bit in his admittedly hammy performance.
>
> "I was a Red Sox fan who'd hated the Yankees, mostly because of Steinbrenner," Platt told me that July. "I used to think they won despite him but I learned it was quite the opposite, and I wanted to bring that to the character. It's a challenge to play someone who's already larger-than-life."

That was the last cloudburst from the old hurricane. A year later, three months shy of a date with a wrecking ball, Yankee Stadium was awarded the All-Star Game, a fitting farewell to the place that hosted more history than any other. On the night of Tuesday, July 15, just before first pitch, the 55,632 folks crammed into the old yard saw a golf cart emerge from the stadium's bowels and begin a full lap around the warning track. When they realized who was inside they began to stir, then cheer, then roar. George Steinbrenner was sitting in the second row with his daughter Jennifer at his left and his son Hal in the back. The roar picked up steam as Jennifer beamed and held her father's arm; Steinbrenner waved a few times but was mostly overcome, weeping the whole ride. At the end of the cart's journey, it stopped at the pitcher's mound, where Steinbrenner hand-delivered four baseballs to the four men who would throw out the ceremonial first pitch, all of them Yankees Hall of Famers—Yogi Berra, Whitey Ford, Reggie Jackson, Goose Gossage.

Every one of them gave Steinbrenner a hug.

Then he was gone, to one last wave of acclaim, one final roll of thunderous applause at a place where they'd once chanted his name in derision.

CHAPTER 28

I just don't fly off the handle as much. But I'm capable.
—HANK STEINBRENNER

Howard Rubenstein was speaking in his own voice now in October 2007, not on behalf of the boldest of his bold-faced-type clients, George Steinbrenner.

"George has said it for a few years, he wants to let the young elephants into the tent. He's doing that now."

The elephants in question were fifty-year-old Henry George Steinbrenner III and thirty-seven-year-old Harold Zieg Steinbrenner, and they were the scions of the Steinbrenner baseball family. The previous month Hal was named chairman of the board, though for now that was simply a matter of protocol; all four Steinbrenner children were equal partners. It was assumed Hal, when the time was right, would be moved to the top and become the face of the team—quietly, as was his preference, and without much rancor.

In the meantime, it would be his older brother who would provide the voice.

Hank would take Rubenstein's comments as literally as possible, happily morphing into the biggest elephant in any room he walked in, trouncing those rooms with various opinions and observations before heading outside for a satisfying smoke.

"I'll pay more attention to the baseball part," Hank said soon after his brother's appointment as chairman. "The stadium, the business end, that's more Hal. Basically, everything will be decided jointly."

That was fine with Hal.

"I don't ever want to be somebody who walks down the street and somebody recognizes," said the son of one of the most recognizable figures in American sports. "I'm a pretty private person."

Hank was not. Hank had a lot of thoughts on a lot of things. And what quickly became apparent was that Hank was every bit the back-page gold mine his father had been—maybe more so. He was happy to hand out his cell phone number to reporters, happier to take their calls, downright gleeful at returning calls he'd missed, and happiest still to fill empty notebooks with gold.

A few of his greatest hits:

When Torre flew to Tampa to face his reckoning after the '07 season, the Yankees brain trust—including the brothers, Brian Cashman and team president Randy Levine—decided not to fire him, but rather offered to let him keep his job, at a pay cut, with the option of earning most of it back with incentive bonuses. Torre turned them down, wasn't at all happy about how this had been handled, wasn't at all shy about sharing that—though he took care to show immediate deference and gratitude to George, sitting quietly at his end of the table. Soon he took a job managing the Los Angeles Dodgers. None of the Yankees brass was happy with how that turned out.

It was Hank who said the quiet parts out loud.

"Where was Joe's career in '95 when my dad hired him?" Hank raged. "My dad was crucified for hiring him!" He called Torre an "ingrate."

A few weeks later Hank was asked about Alex Rodriguez's pending decision opting out of the rest of the ten-year, $252 million deal the Yankees inherited when they'd brought him in from Texas.

"Alex has to decide," Hank said, "does he want to go into the Hall of Fame as a Yankee or a Toledo Mud Hen?"

That one was funny enough that the Mud Hens—Triple-A affiliate of the Detroit Tigers—offered Rodriguez a mock contract. Hank wasn't laughing a few days later when Rodriguez and his agent, Scott Boras, took advantage of the final game of the World Series to upstage the Red Sox's sweep of the Colorado Rockies to announce that he would, in fact, be opting out:

"It's clear he doesn't want to be a Yankee. He doesn't understand the privilege of being a Yankee on a team where owners are willing to pay $200 million to put a winning product on the field. I don't want anybody on my team that doesn't want to be a Yankee."

He took a long drag on a cigarette.

"We're not going to back down," he promised. "It's goodbye."

Asked the next day if there was a chance he'd change his mind? "Not a chance."

That didn't seem to matter to Hank a few weeks later when the Yankees actually offered Rodriguez ten years and $275 million (a deal they would later regret deeply). He kept chattering. He ripped Brian Cashman for keeping prized flamethrower Joba Chamberlain in the bullpen, rather than starting him. When right-handed starter Mike Mussina had a poor start to 2008 Hank offered his star pitcher should throw more like soft-tossing southpaw Jamie Moyer of Philadelphia, to which Mussina had said, "I guess I could throw underhand left-handed if I had to."

When asked about "Red Sox Nation"—Sox fans were more ubiquitous than ever after winning a second title in four years in 2007—Hank made another slew of headlines.

"Red Sox Nation?" he said. "What a bunch of shit that is. That was a creation of the Red Sox and ESPN, which is filled with Red Sox fans. Go anywhere in America and you won't see Red Sox hats and jackets, you'll see Yankees hats and jackets. This is a Yankees country. We're going to put the Yankees back on top and restore the universe to order."

> **INTERLUDE:** Hank really was a columnist's best friend. Once, searching for an idea on a random Tuesday, my boss, Greg Gallo, said, "Call Hank. See what he has to say."

"About what?" I asked.

"About anything," Gallo said.

I called Hank, he picked up right away, and for twenty-five minutes he provided me that day's column, which became the next morning's back page: HANK UNPLUGGED! After we were done, as I was hammering my laptop to beat deadline, my phone rang. It was Hank. "And a few other things..." And by the time he was done I had about fifteen minutes left to finish the column. It ran a little long that day.

In his office a few doors down at Legends Field from his big brother, Hal seemed to get a kick out of Hank, who'd endured a few personal hiccups in his youth and now seemed to be having the time of his life. In his first twenty years working under his father Hal gave exactly three interviews. Now, he was a little more accessible but knew that his dry observations weren't exactly circled with yellow highlighters the next day.

"That's what Hank's for," he said early in 2008. "He's perfect. He's everything you guys want. How many more papers can you sell? Where would you be without him?"

We were about to find out. Alas.

AFTER A WHILE, Hal began spending more and more time at Yankee Stadium in the final weeks and months before its long-appointed date with a wrecking ball. He still didn't say much—Hank was always just a text message away if his thoughts were required—but Hal knew the time was now to begin the final stages of immersion so he could assume solo leadership of the Yankees. Because that day was coming fast.

His father remained in Tampa more and more, his health worsening. The club's Tampa headquarters, Legends Field, had been rebranded George M. Steinbrenner Field. The old Boss attended the Yankees' home opener on April 1 and visited the new park across the street, but after his tour around the warning track at the All-Star Game in July he never returned. There would be no playoff games to tempt him—under Joe Torre's successor, Joe Girardi, the Yankees missed the postseason for the first time since 1993. And he chose to stay away from the star-studded stadium finale September 21, too.

Tellingly, so did Hank. Hal and Jennifer represented the Steinbrenner family that night. On November 20, Hal officially became the Yankees "control person"—first among equals among the other general partners, after Major League Baseball said there could be only one managing general partner. The siblings put the matter up to a vote.

Hank voted for his brother. That was that.

"I realize it's a great responsibility," Hal said when he officially became the New Boss. "My dad, needless to say, is a tough act to follow. But I'm going to do my best."

Of his father, Hal also said: "He's been slowing down the last couple of years."

Hank, too, would soon be slowed, and quieted, if not completely silenced. Respecting his brother meant keeping his own commentaries to a minimum. Hal might not have the loudest voice in the room but his was the only one that mattered now. Hank would still have a say in Yankees business, as would his sisters, but Hal would have *final* say.

The first time Hal truly cleared his throat was to rectify the disappointing final chapter his ball club scripted in its last season at the old stadium. By Christmas, he would expand the team's budget, sign off on Brian Cashman spending $423.5 million on CC Sabathia, a workhorse lefty who was the plum of that year's free agent class; Mark Teixeira, a perennial All-Star first baseman and a genuine slugger; and A. J. Burnett, a hard-throwing righty who would neatly complement Sabathia. Hal stated on multiple occasions that long-term he was going to demand more fiscal restraint than his old man showed but that was for later on. For now he put distance between his 2009 team and the eighty-nine-win, third-place team that preceded it. He also had a sparkling new stadium to fill, one with the highest price points anywhere in the sport. This was no time to squeeze nickels and dimes.

"I guess I can sit up here and say if we don't make the World Series we've let our fans down," Hal said. "I *will* stand up here and say that. That's certainly the mentality of everyone in this organization. And everyone in this family."

A few months later, he borrowed another page out of the family playbook when asked about how he'd grade Girardi midway through his second season: "Joe knows what's expected of him. We expect to win every year. Joe knows who he's working for."

The team was good enough to back up the boasting of the bantam Boss. They lost the first game played in their new house on April 16, 2009—a 10–2 thrashing by Cleveland, observed, from the new owner's box, Box 44, by an old Indians fan named George Steinbrenner. After a slow start the Yankees stormed to 103 wins, then defeated the Twins and Angels in the American League playoffs. When they eliminated Anaheim in Game 6 of the ALCS, Hal briefly appeared in the triumphant home clubhouse at Yankee Stadium to let a few of his players spray him with champagne.

Then he said, "What a terrific year. Let's get the last one!"

Hank?

Hank was last heard from in February, responding thusly to Boston owner John Henry's suggestion that maybe baseball could use a salary cap: "Along with a few other teams, we're basically baseball's stimulus package."

That was it. He changed his phone numbers, and this time kept the digits to himself. Howard Rubenstein would dutifully pass along messages, always with the caveat: Don't hold your breath.

"He's just decided he's really going to defer to his brother," Rubenstein explained, and Hank stayed in Tampa all during the Yankees' playoff push.

His father, however, wanted one more taste of a Yankee Stadium October. At 7:09 on the evening of October 28, Game 1 against the Phillies, a black Town & Country minivan specially equipped to hold a wheelchair in the back rolled through the basement at Yankee Stadium and pulled up to the VIP elevators. Dr. Andrew Boyer was with him along with daughter Jessica and her third husband, Felix Lopez. The group went straight up to Box 44. On the field, the ground crew wore T-shirts that said WIN ONE FOR THE BOSS. After the top of the first inning the stadium's huge scoreboard beamed a message: WIN IT FOR THE BOSS. But Steinbrenner's image wasn't shown, and by the team's request the Fox TV cameras never showed him, either.

When the series returned to New York for Game 6, the Boss stayed home. But Hank went. When the Yankees clinched their twenty-seventh World Series with a 7–3 win over Philadelphia—the seventh under the auspices of George M. Steinbrenner III—Hank renewed acquaintances with his old friends from the press. When asked literally fifteen minutes after the final out if he thought the Yankees would repeat as champions in 2010, he answered exactly as you'd expect he would.

"Of course we will!"

Then he turned quiet and talked about his father.

"This means a lot to my dad," said Hank. "This is maybe the *most* special one for him because we dropped there for a while, we had to come back and we had to rebuild. He was looking forward to this, this one as much as any of them."

Added Jennifer: "This means the world to him."

The message at the stadium dominating the scoreboard as the Steinbrenner siblings accepted another Commissioner's Trophy said it all: BOSS, THIS IS FOR YOU! Hal, fresh off the phone with his father, said, "Dad is very, very happy."

HIS FINAL CAPTAIN would afford George Steinbrenner the last of his endless, priceless moments—and mementos—as Boss, even if he now went by Boss Emeritus. George Steinbrenner had, after all, made the unilateral decision to install Thurman Munson as captain thirty-five years after Lou Gehrig's death. Steinbrenner the erstwhile Big Ten coach never could shake his football instincts and viewed captains differently, and more fondly, all of them: Graig Nettles and Willie Randolph, Ron Guidry and Don Mattingly.

Now Derek Jeter.

One last time, Steinbrenner made the flight to New York. Once, as a young businessman crammed into a middle seat in coach, he'd sworn as his plane from Cleveland descended into LaGuardia Airport that he'd one day fly first class. Now, he'd made this trip thousands of times in his own jet. Once, the deciding factor for Gabe Paul to migrate from Cleveland to New York to help the young Boss build the foundation for this billion-dollar bonanza was how taken Paul—a fairly unimpressionable man his whole professional career—was with the forty-two-year-old version of this anonymous Ohio shipbuilder.

"There was a long period of time of 'I will' . . . 'I won't' . . . 'I will' . . . 'I won't' because the club's books were so discouraging," Paul said in April 1973. "Then I thought about George, who had nothing, whose father's shipping business was nearly broke. He bought a secondhand car and drove to New York. He stayed at the YMCA because it was all he could afford. Finally, he found a small banker who loaned him a half million dollars to buy his father's business, and he saved it. A man who could do *that* was worth going along with."

Now he was three months shy of eighty and required a wheelchair. But he wasn't going to miss the home opener of the 2010 season, April 13. By now, the Boss Watch had been abandoned, so he arrived in Box 44 comfortably.

Soon he was joined by two special guests.

Jeter and Joe Girardi walked the forty or so steps from the Yankees' clubhouse to the VIP elevator, stepped in the Boss's suite and surprised him. They wanted to personally present his World Series ring. Jeter noticed the Boss was wearing two rings: one for the 2000 Yankees and one an Ohio State ring. Jeter looked into Steinbrenner's eyes and laughed when he said, "Boss, take off that Ohio State ring."

Steinbrenner's eyes brightened. He pointed at Jeter.

"Michigan," he said to Jeter, a son of Kalamazoo and nearly a Michigan Wolverine before the Yankees signed him out of the 1992 draft. Jeter took the 2000 ring off instead, replaced it with the 2009 one, and everyone applauded. Later, in the bottom of the third, before Jeter stepped to the plate the scoreboard camera captured Steinbrenner wearing sunglasses in his box as "My Way" played over the public-address system. Jeter waited a respectful amount of time for the 49,293 to roar for the Boss.

Then swung at the first pitch and dunked one over the wall in right-center.

Years later, after another similarly theatrical moment in his last at bat at Yankee Stadium, Joe Girardi would say of Jeter: "His life is a movie." Now he'd save one of his favorite plot points for Steinbrenner's final moment in the Bronx.

"None of us would be here, the stadium wouldn't be here, if it wasn't for him," Jeter said. "He'll always be the Boss."

Ninety-one days later, sitting behind a podium at the All-Star Game, Jeter had this to say about that boss: "I was eighteen. Suddenly here he is, walking toward me, addressing me by name, and said, 'We expect big things from you.' I'll always remember that."

Jeter was stone-faced. The news he'd received he'd been dreading for a long while, same as everyone around the Yankees. It might not have been stunning that George Steinbrenner died earlier that day, July 13, 2010, of a heart attack at his home in Tampa; it was still hard to immediately calibrate. He'd turned eighty just nine days earlier.

After a few respectful days, it also became clear that the Boss left a remarkable legacy for his family, which you might call priceless except it absolutely had one. The federal estate tax expired the previous January, and that would've cost the family around a half billion dollars had the Boss passed in 2009. Had he died in 2011, the renewed law was to be upped to 55 percent, so it would've siphoned $600 million. Without an inheritance tax the Yankees remained comfortably in the hands of his children.

It was a perfect bookend for an initial investment of $168,000.

"One of a kind," Reggie Jackson said.

"A life almost impossible to imagine," said his friend Donald Trump.

"I still hate his guts," said Howie Spira, who planned on holding his grudge long into the next life and beyond.

CHAPTER 29

*There are people that get up in the morning
and have their good day or bad day depending
on how the Yankees did the night before.*
—GEORGE STEINBRENNER

This was about a month after his father died, late August 2010. Hank Steinbrenner was back in New York, making a rare appearance at Yankee Stadium. The cause was a good one: the first-annual "Boss's Cup," a game that on this day featured twenty-two underprivileged New York City teenagers who'd taken part in "Hank's Yanks," a foundation Hank developed the year before to bring baseball to youngsters who otherwise might've never been touched by the game. It would be the great joy of his adult life. Several of the kids drawn to baseball by Hank's Yanks—the uniform looked just like regular Yankees pinstripes, only instead of the famous interlocking "NY" logo the "N" was flattened to an "H"—wound up drafted by big-league clubs. Most notable was Brooklyn's Williams Jerez, who starred at Grand Street Campus High School, was taken in the second round by the Red Sox in 2011 and appeared in twenty-nine major-league games with the Angels, Giants and Pirates in 2018–19. He earned a win in his only big-league decision, July 18, 2019, against the Mets.

"I remember when I was in college my father told me 'America is supposed to be the land of milk and honey, but for a lot of people it just isn't.

That's got to change,'" Hank said, sitting in the first base dugout while Hank's Yanks warmed up for a game against Mariano Rivera's Dominican Foundation team. "I hope Hank's Yanks made him proud. I think it did. I think it's what he was trying to teach me years ago."

Hank was reluctant to speak too freely about the Yankees out of respect for his brother and the organizational chain of command. Still, sitting in the stadium, it was impossible for him to ignore the big pennant flapping in the breeze in center field, emblematic of the team's World Series win the previous October.

"Our plan—myself, my brother, my sisters, the entire staff of the Yankees—it's always going to be the same. We play to win and do what we have to, to win. We don't make a lot of money because of revenue sharing and we don't shy away from paying salaries. We're building up the farm system, too. The objective is the same. Win. Every year."

Hank figured this was the least they could do to pay tribute to the Boss, whose absence he took especially hard, even forty-five days later.

"I was the first and we did everything together when I was a kid, long before he bought the Yankees," he said wistfully. "When he was in his hospital bed I wasn't thinking about the Yankees or all that stuff that's on TV. That's my *dad*. As I walked around the room after he passed, it was like he kept following me. That was the hardest part."

Hank caught himself before his voice could crack.

"He's just not there anymore."

IT WASN'T LONG after when that sentiment—a beautiful and uncomplicated tribute from a son to a father—was co-opted by a vast faction of Yankees fans who studied Hal closely, who wanted reassurance that when he and his brother spoke of maintaining Yankees excellence that they weren't simply following a script authored by their father. It may have been Hal who approved the near-half-billion-dollar spending spree that helped yield the 2009 title, but the old man was still alive then. Whether it was true or not, the belief was Hal still had to answer to his father; that was *exactly* the kind of aggressive approach the Boss would've made.

It was important to Hal, from the start, that Yankees fans understood what they were getting in him. By the time he became the primary face of the Yankees he'd settled into a mostly quiet life with his second wife, Christina DiTullio, and much of his time away from the Yankees was spent with many of the same philanthropic causes his father had been involved in.

One thing Hal has an affinity for that his father most certainly did not—especially after what happened to Thurman Munson—is flying. Flying is Hal's chief hobby—he owns a GTO single-engine and a Cessna high-wing plane—and at thirteen thousand feet a lot of Yankees business can be pondered in the comfort of a cockpit.

"I loved my father," he says, "but I also knew I could never pretend to be him. That's neither my nature nor my inclination. That doesn't make either style better. That doesn't mean I agreed with all of what he did, or disagreed with it. If I tried to be my dad it would come across as phony because it would *be* phony. People would spot that from a mile away. And I wouldn't be able to do my job."

While it was George who established the family's base in Tampa, he also had a taste for New York and had a habit of winding up in the city's gossip columns simply by being an aficionado of the kinds of places where paparazzi tended to prowl as part of their regular rounds. The Boss was never shy about complaining about things that annoyed him, but he never—not once—bitched about seeing his picture in the paper after a night on the town. Hal, in his way, best embodies Derek Jeter's old philosophy: You won't ever see him on Page Six, let alone page one.

"I don't shy away from who I am," Hal said, "and I have never shied away from my last name. Maybe it's because being a Steinbrenner is all I've ever known? I certainly take the responsibility of the family name seriously."

Hal was shrewd: He didn't agree to underwrite the richest team ever assembled in order to satisfy his father, but because it was smart business. They had a new ballpark to fill, and they filled it: 3,719,358 customers in 2009. In the reduced capacity of the new park the Yankees played to 98.6 percent capacity, easily the highest in their history (exceeded in 2010 when they played to 99.4 percent). Winning was the Yankees' business. Joe Girardi took uniform number twenty-seven when he was hired as manager because he intended to lead the Yankees to their twenty-seventh championship; as soon as he did, he changed to twenty-eight. Team president Randy Levine, echoing the Steinbrenner family, said midway through the 2010 season, "We view any season that doesn't end in a championship as coming up short," which fell slightly south of the way that was generally misquoted—"any season without a championship is a failure"—but the point was unambiguous.

Yankees fans heard that loud and clear.

They also saw this: After the Yankees failed to make it to the World Series in either 2010 or 2011, the team played a little bit of hardball with Derek Jeter when his contract expired in 2010, realizing Jeter didn't want to play anywhere else. Jeter settled for four years and $51 million guaranteed, with the opportunity to kick that up as high as $65 million. Hank Steinbrenner said cryptically the following spring, "Sometimes you celebrate too much, players concentrating on building mansions and not concentrating on winning." Jeter had by that point constructed a huge estate near the Yankees Florida complex—the tabs coined it "St. Jetersburg"—so there was little mystery who Steinbrenner was talking about. Jeter took that with a laugh, but that was the last Hank was ever heard from on matters pertaining to the Yankees.

Hal didn't mean for the Jeter negotiation to serve as a harbinger. In both 2010 and 2011 the Yankees were the lone team with a payroll north of $200 million, to which luxury-tax penalties added close to another $50 million to the tab. The Yankees never allowed money to stand in the way of their annual goals, and George Steinbrenner had proven time and again that he would brook no objections to writing a check when he wanted to. Like Hal, he had to answer to a partnership that comprised about 40 percent of the whole Yankee pie; unlike Hal, when the Boss annually told his partners to forget about dividends he was mostly tweaking his wealthy benefactors, not depriving them. The 1977 Yankees, dubbed "the Best Team Money Could Buy," had a total player payroll of about $3.5 million. Even adjusting for inflation, that translated to

$13,260,379.54—or, roughly, what the Yankees were scheduled to pay Alex Rodriguez for the first two and a half months of the 2012 season.

The Yankees payroll for 2012: $201 million. Plus luxury tax.

Privately Hal said: "Having a $200 million payroll every year simply isn't sustainable, especially when that's more like two fifty with taxes." He told confidants it was his goal to reduce Yankees payroll to where it fell under the $189 million tax threshold in time for the 2014 season, at which point the Yankees' tax bill would be reset and they could count on more flexibility going forward.

By the following spring, he went public with that.

"I'm looking at it as a goal, but my goals are normally a requirement," he said. "Is it a requirement with baseball that we be at $189 million? No. It's not a requirement. But that is going to be the threshold and that's where I want to be. That's a real number and we're going to be shooting for it."

A few weeks later, he was even more pointed.

"How many World Series–winning teams the last ten years had a payroll over 189?" Steinbrenner asked, before answering his own question: "One. Us. In 2009. You don't need to have a $200 million payroll to do that. I'm a big believer in that."

He was always quick to add something else, though:

"We will always—always—field a championship-caliber team."

Hal understood Yankees fans would likely misinterpret these words, so used were they to decades of bottom-line-be-damned spending. But he also knew something else. In 2010 the San Francisco Giants won their first World Series in fifty-six years with a payroll of just under *$100 million*. The 2011 champion St. Louis Cardinals weighed in at $105 million. To the Steinbrenner family, it wasn't outrageous to think the Yankees could figure out a way to win with a payroll $50 million clear of those two teams, and not twice as large.

In a vacuum, it was perfectly sensible.

Still, after thirty-seven years of George Steinbrenner, a lot of Yankees fans didn't live in a vacuum, they lived in a bubble. For the first time, you began to hear a refrain that would accompany almost every Yankees season for the next decade and a half.

"*If only George were still alive . . .*"

IT IS SOMETHING Hal Steinbrenner has had to deal with ever since. His father would sooner have shown up to Yankee Stadium bedecked head to toe in a Red Sox uniform than utter the word "budget," so there was that. Fact is, Hal is by nature a far more patient soul than his old man ever was, by a multiple of infinity. It was Hal who personally invited Joe Torre to the dedication of George Steinbrenner's massive plaque in Monument Park in September 2009, officially ending a two-year-old cold war between the team and the man who, five years later, would enter the Hall of Fame largely on the strength of the dynasty he'd helped build in the Bronx.

Hal allowed Joe Girardi to manage the 2017 season after he'd missed the playoffs in three of the previous four years, with one brief wild card appearance. Ironically, it would be after Girardi guided the Yankees to Game 7 of the 2017 ALCS that he approved Brian Cashman's decision to fire Girardi after ten seasons. In the moment that felt like an old-school Steinbrenner stroke, but in truth insiders around the team believed Girardi's message had stopped getting across to his clubhouse a few years earlier. If anything, the axing came a few years too late in their view.

And when Girardi's replacement, Aaron Boone, began a habit, early in his tenure, of refusing to rip—or even criticize—his players even after the most egregious losses, he fell out of favor in a lot of precincts, too, his approval ratings plummeting even as he averaged ninety-five wins a year his first six full seasons on the job.

Loosely translated: *Where have you gone, Billy Martin?*

"If only George were still alive," some fans grumbled, "he wouldn't stand for this."

INTERLUDE: Perhaps no figure in baseball history has seen his reputation more completely sanitized over time than Billy Martin—with the notable exception of George Steinbrenner himself, who by the end of his life was mostly absolved of whatever transgressions had moved Yankees fans to, at various times, fill Yankee Stadium with chants of "STEINBRENNER SUCKS!" and "NO MORE BOSS!" Hal Steinbrenner found this all quite amusing.

"There were many years fans weren't happy with my dad. The door swings both ways," he told me in 2019. "I absolutely have desire to win. Everyone in my family does, I'm just a little quieter about it." He smiled. "But that doesn't mean I won't throw my shoe at the TV every now and again. Believe me."

Brian Cashman?

Bring up Cashman's name around a gaggle of frustrated Yankees fans and you'd think Cashman was a piker who'd been bilking the Steinbrenner family for years (twenty-eight of them, as of 2026, an astonishing career when you consider the first twelve came at the pleasure of the Boss), rather than a general manager who, across those twenty-eight seasons, had produced twenty-three playoff appearances.

"Anyone can win with the Yankees' resources," went the refrain, even when it's pointed out that among the Mets, Cubs, White Sox, Dodgers and Angels—the five teams, like the Yankees, who inhabit the richest baseball markets—in the twenty-eight years in question, they'd qualified for October only seventeen times. This included thirteen straight from 2013 through 2025. Still, every three years, every four years, Cashman's contract comes up for review, and every time, Hal Steinbrenner signs up for more.

Even though, as of 2025, it was sixteen years since the last championship.

"If only George were still alive," those same fans howl, "he wouldn't put up with that!"

If you point out that, from 1982 through 1994, the Yankees missed the playoffs thirteen straight years while employing eight different general managers . . .

"Sure. But he cared about winning! Hal doesn't care! None of the Steinbrenners do!"

Well, that's when Hal Steinbrenner actually gets a little red in the face, and where he'll raise his voice ever so slightly.

George Steinbrenner's trips to New York were often carefully planned and almost always well publicized. Reggie Jackson used to call him "the man with the boats," and when the man with the boats was on his way to New York it was usually to raise a little hell, to put a manager on notice, to hold one of his Rockne talks in the clubhouse. And then he would be gone. He'd spend most of his time during those trips to New York on the back page, and so it was obvious how much he "cared."

Hal's trips north are rarely big deals because he makes them frequently.

"I'm in New York at least once a home stand," he says. "I like talking to the players. I like talking to Cash. And I want to have a feel for what's going on in the day-to-day. I think it's possible to be visible without interfering."

When the Red Sox won their fourth championship in fifteen seasons in 2018, Hal said, "that pisses me off," and added, "I never want a division rival to outdo us, especially *that* division rival."

It was Cashman who, in the winter of 2023, took umbrage to the notion that the Yankees care any less about winning championships than they ever did under the Boss.

"I'm proud of our people and proud of our process," he said. "It doesn't mean we're firing on all cylinders, it doesn't mean that we're best in class. But I think we're pretty fucking good."

To which Hal said: "I don't condone the cussing, but I do like the passion. There are too many false narratives out there about our organization, pushed by uninformed and uninvolved people. It is, needless to say, frustrating."

Yankees fans were unmoved. Twice during the 2022 season, Hal was booed before full houses at the stadium, once on the day they retired Paul O'Neill's number, once when they honored Derek Jeter for making the Hall of Fame. What irked Hal was the perception he didn't *care* as much as his father did. Hal probably doesn't help his case by refusing to say publicly anything that doesn't reflect the family's philosophy about running a baseball team in 2025, which differs wildly from 1996, or 1977.

"There's a lot of multibillionaire corporations and owners coming into the game now," Steinbrenner said in the winter of 2025 after one of those new-age corporations, the one fronting the Dodgers, engaged in an endless spending spree that made even some of the Boss's vintage binges seem like discount-bin scouring by comparison. "This is not a secondary hobby business for my family. *This* is our business. Everything we have is tied up in this. At some point it gets hard for the vast majority of owners to compete with certain things.

"And that includes my family as well."

He will immediately follow with: *Show me the year we* didn't *try. Show me the year we punted. Show me the year where we had a losing record* (and unless you go back to 1992, you can't). That $189 million goal he'd spoken of so adamantly and for so long? After the Yankees finished out of the playoffs in 2013 he smashed that tote board with a hammer and approved deals for Carlos Beltrán, Brian McCann and Masahiro Tanaka that sent the 2014 payroll soaring to $204 million, no questions asked. A few years later, tired of the distraction that Alex Rodriguez became—both as an aging player and drawing a full-year suspension for steroid use—Hal agreed to pay A-Rod to *not* play baseball for a year for the Yankees, simply to make him go away. When the Yankees desperately needed an ace following the 2019 season, he approved a nine-year, $324 million deal for Gerrit Cole, the richest contract ever awarded a starting pitcher.

And, tellingly, when it became apparent in December 2022 that Aaron Judge—fresh off a staggering sixty-two home run season—required one extra year and $36 million more than had already been approved to keep him from jumping to the San Francisco Giants, Hal personally called from Italy to close that deal.

Of course I care!

A year later, there came a two-day period where both sides of this innate juxtaposition were visible.

On a Tuesday he said, "I do believe that a team shouldn't need a $300 million payroll to win a championship."

And on Wednesday he green-lit a Cashman trade that brought Juan

Soto, a twenty-five-year-old outfielder who was among the top five or six everyday players in the sport, and just one year from free agency, to the Yankees from San Diego, nudging the payroll to—naturally—$309 million.

"It's not often you can say that one player can significantly impact a ball club and increase their chances of winning a championship," Hal said. "You can say that in this case, however."

The wolves stopped baying for a second.

But they were only catching their breath.

CHAPTER 30

*I've got ears. I know what's expected
of me. We listen to our fans.*
—HAL STEINBRENNER

It is the oddest job in professional sports, in so many ways. It has its perks, of course. When you are the owner of a franchise, you oversee a public trust. The team itself may be—and now, in almost every case, is—worth billions of dollars. When times are good, there is probably no grander job on earth than being the person who signs the checks of a freshly crowned champion.

When things aren't so good?

That's the tricky part. If an athlete fails, repeatedly, he faces ultimate consequence: traded, released, demoted. When a manager, a general manager, a coach loses over a period of time, or simply fails to meet expectations? He gets fired. His contact isn't renewed. The pressure becomes so great they simply resign. There is turnover everywhere in sports. There is constant churn.

Except in one place: inside an owner's box.

"I kid with people and sometimes they take this the wrong way," James Dolan, who owns both the NBA's New York Knicks and the NHL's New York Rangers, told me one day in 2013. "Only one person can fire me, and you're looking at him. And I don't expect to fire myself anytime soon. So we might as well get used to each other."

Theoretically, fans understand this. Logically, they get it.

But there is very little logic attached to being a sports fan. There is very little reason applied to the visceral reactions that watching, and caring about, and fervently following teams can yield. And so, quite often, the frustration bubbles to the point that groundswells are formed to convince owners to sell the team. There is little point to this, mind you. James Dolan was the one who said it. But all owners feel the exact same way.

"I think enough people have seen how I react to games we win and games we lose to know one thing," says John Mara, who has been a 50 percent owner of the New York Giants of the NFL since 2005, when his father, Wellington, passed away at age eighty-nine. "They have to see that I live and die with these games. I take every one of them *personally*. I go nights at a time without sleep during the football season because I can't get the tough losses out of my mind. I *suffer*. Say anything else you want about me, but I care every bit as much as the most rabid fan."

This didn't shield Mara from battalions of angry Giants fans who, during an increasingly barren era of Giants history in the 2020s, began to turn on him. It was, in fact, the passion to which he refers that caused him, with HBO's *Hard Knocks* cameras rolling, to tell his GM, Joe Schoen, in the spring of 2024, that if the Giants lost star running back Saquon Barkley to the rival Eagles he was going to have many sleepless nights; that was played and replayed on an endless reel of mockery when Barkley not only signed with the Eagles but immediately led them to the Super Bowl championship. Yet even this owner who freely shows his devotions in public, who has, quite literally, been a Giants fan from the cradle, stood accused of simply not caring enough when another lost Giants season was shoved into a wood chipper.

Such will be the likely fate of Hal Steinbrenner for as long as he is the man on top of the Yankees' organizational flowchart. Such will likely be the fate of any Yankees owner, within the Steinbrenner family or without, for as long as there are still fans old enough to remember George Steinbrenner's reign—even if most of those recollections, as the years pass, become a bit more detached from reality.

"We look at this as a blessing," Hal said of the caretaking role he and his family have with the Yankees, which he calls a profound civic trust. "It was something given to us, not necessarily something we earned. And that's the way I approach every day with my job. We hold a great deal of responsibility to ourselves and to our own actions, and we take none of it for granted. We understand the history and the tradition of the team, but it's also a history and tradition of fifty years of my family and now we've got the third generation involved, numerous of George's grandkids. It's going to carry on the way he would want."

Hank Steinbrenner, who inherited the more colorful strands of his father's DNA, died after a long illness on April 14, 2020. He was remembered fondly, a kind soul who'd done well in the other arms of the Steinbrenner family business, whose brief, blusterous time as the Yankees' chief unofficial spokesman provided a welcome comic relief to what can sometimes be the wildly overserious world of Yankees baseball.

But Hank always agreed: Hal was clearly the right choice to lead the Yankees once the Boss was ready to pass the baton. The value of the team has quadrupled on his watch. With the exception of an 82–80 blip in 2023, the Yankees have fielded contending teams every season since 2017. And while Steinbrenner continues to believe that annual payrolls north of $300 million are unsustainable, the Yankees cracked that barrier in 2024, and in 2025, and did so without apology, and will likely do so from now on.

That 2024 season culminated on October 19, Game 5 of the American League Championship Series in Cleveland. The Yankees spotted the Guardians an early 2–0 lead, rallied to tie at 2–2 and in the top of the tenth inning put two runners on with two outs. Juan Soto battled Hunter Gaddis through six pitches and faced a 1-and-2 count, and on the seventh pitch launched a ball that tried to climb over the sky before settling into the stands at Progressive Field. The Yankees won, 5–2, clinching their first World Series berth in fifteen years.

Afterward, Hal Steinbrenner was jubilant—although his was a different manifestation of jubilance than his father would've displayed when he was fifty-four years old. Meredith Marakovits, the sideline reporter for the YES Network, interviewed Hal on the field immediately after the clinching, and while his players were celebrating madly just steps away, Hal remained fairly stoic. He is who he is, and has never tried to be otherwise.

"Listen, that was surreal on a different level than what I've experienced in fifteen years since the last pennant we won," he said a few months later. "I'm in New York, I'm there every home stand; I'm down in the clubhouse a lot and I observe what's going on. I have a good idea of how much work they put in throughout the course of a year. And I was just excited for them. It's the culmination of a long season. You saw that. You saw it in the eyes of everybody else involved, including my sisters and Cashman, and it was."

He laughed.

"It was a very good night."

Across the next two weeks, though, the Yankees fell in five to the Dodgers in the World Series. They were five hard-fought games, but the Yankees could win only one of them—and they permitted decisive Game 5 to turn during an ugly fifth inning in which they allowed five unearned runs—so much of the good feeling evaporated quickly after that.

It didn't help that it was the Dodgers who'd humbled the Yankees, who'd brought them to their knees on the vast October stage. From the moment they first tangled in a World Series in 1941, the Dodgers and the Yankees have been the sport's two most successful franchises, on the baseball field and in the bank coffers. Walter O'Malley was roundly vilified for moving the team from Brooklyn to Los Angeles in 1958, but he'd struck gold in California. By 2024 the team was owned by the Guggenheim Baseball Management consortium, and they and the Yankees were at their usual perch atop the list of MLB's mightiest moneymakers. The Yankees generated $679 million in revenue in '24, the Dodgers $549 million; the Dodgers' operating income was $26 million, the Yankees $2.1 million. Both teams spent a lot—a *lot*—but still landed in the black.

But it was the Dodgers who'd begun to land most of the big-name free agents, notably the Japanese triumvirate of Shohei Ohtani (who won the MVP in 2024), Yoshinobu Yamamoto and Roki Sasaki.

Then Juan Soto officially filed for free agency.

And another challenger to the Yankees' decades-long status as the team with the most financial might in professional sports was officially heard from.

IN THE OLD days, there would have been a predictable rhythm to how the next few weeks played out, culminating with the Mets—*the Mets!*—prying Soto away from the Yankees with a fifteen-year, $765 million deal that was finalized on December 11, 2024. The Yankees made a competitive offer—one more year, $5 million less—but Soto opted for the richer deal that could exceed $800 million by the time it's done.

For the Mets were now owned by Steve Cohen, whose hedge fund company, Point72, had yielded him a personal fortune of more than $14 billion by the time he bought the Mets from the Wilpon family for $2.4 billion in the fall of 2020. Four years later he'd already tasted massive failure (his 2023 team had the richest payroll ever but lost eighty-seven games and he sold off many of his richest assets at the trade deadline) and sublime success (in 2024 the Mets reached the NL Championship Series and actually took one more game off the Dodgers than the Yankees would a round later). Not insignificantly his personal wealth had grown by 50 percent, to $21 billion. He was determined to take Soto away from the Yankees, regardless of cost. And did.

In the old days, George Steinbrenner would have unleashed holy hell on the city's back pages—ripping Soto; ripping his agent, Scott Boras; ripping the Mets. And dependent on which era of his reign we're talking about, he'd have sought immediate retribution either with a series of visceral overpays in free agency or some splashy trades.

But in the old days, Steinbrenner *was* Cohen, a lone wolf, unapologetic that he sat on a pile of riches no other team in the sport could fathom. Nobody was going to hold a telethon for the Yankees as 2024 clicked to 2025, but the facts were they were now competing against the sport's single richest man in their own market *and* a conglomerate with bottomless pockets on the other coast in the nation's number two market (with Blue Jays CEO Edward Rogers III and his $11.5 billion in assets lurking in Toronto and also promising to start spending more).

It went differently this time, mostly because it had to. Spending for the sake of spending would be folly. Across the next few weeks the Yankees quietly but methodically redistributed the funds that had been earmarked for Soto elsewhere: to Milwaukee's fine closer, Devin Williams; to the ex-Braves ace Max Fried; to a pair of former MVPs in Cody Bellinger (to play center, allowing Aaron Judge to replace Soto in right) and Paul Goldschmidt (to play first). By the time Cashman was done acquiring, and Steinbrenner was done approving, they managed to quell much of the anger that had boiled in the wake of the Soto defection. Rather than do as his father had done in past generations—offer ready-fire-aim contracts to the likes of Jack Clark, Jacoby Ellsbury, Kevin Brown and Dave Collins that wound up being yearslong millstones—Hal tried to be reasonable while also keeping his checkbook open for players who made sense in overall roster construction.

And if you didn't already know Hal Steinbrenner was the Yankees' managing general partner, you might not have known that Steinbrenner was the Yankees' managing general partner. He happily ceded the back pages to his players. If he heard any strand of the usual mantra—*If only George were still in charge*—he still refused to acknowledge them.

"First of all, I've been doing this for a long time now, so I guess I'm immune to a lot of that," Hal said. "But the reality is we are two very different people. I've tried to make that clear from day one. I'm less of a shoot-from-the-hip kind of person. These types of decisions are big decisions, and a lot of factors need to be considered. So I don't make any of them sporadically or quickly. And you know what? Maybe that's not a good thing sometimes, but that is who I am and it's going to be hard to change that."

Truth be told, father and son had two very different jobs, too.

In George's time, it became something of an inside joke when he'd have to make a cash call of his partners because, say, a few more dollars had to be shaken loose in order to close a deal with Reggie Jackson. Dividends? Even as late as 2003, Steinbrenner made light of the occasional complaint from the odd partner about the dearth of dividends he'd seen over the years.

"What I tell them," the old man said with a laugh, "is that's the cost of getting really good seats to Yankees games."

Still, when George assembled the 1977 Yankees—instantly dubbed "the Best Team Money Could Buy"—the total operating budget, players included, was around $4 million. Even factoring in inflation, that's around $20.7 million, or approximately what the Yankees will pay Aaron Judge through the end of July 2026. When you're talking about offering one player $765 million—a losing bid at that—these are entirely different conversations Hal is having with *his* partners.

It is a different world, a different time, a different *sport*. *Forbes* magazine's most recent valuation of the Yankees was $7.1 billion, meaning the Steinbrenners' share, at around 70 percent, is a cool $4.97 billion. And growing. But even under George, while it would be wrong to call the Yankees a mom-and-pop shop, it was certainly a simpler corporate structure. Across most of the Boss's tenure, the Yankees were just that: a baseball team. The most successful baseball team, the richest baseball team, but a baseball team all the same. Now, the bundle under the umbrella of the Yankees' hat-and-a-bat logo includes 25 percent of YES Network, 20 percent of NYCFC of Major League Soccer, a minority stake in Legends Hospitality (which the Yankees cofounded in 2008 alongside that other great monolith of American sport, the NFL's Dallas Cowboys) and a 10 percent share of the Italian soccer club AC Milan.

Hal operates baseball's version of Apple, while his father ran an apple cart.

Relatively speaking, of course.

"Look, we have great partners, some of whom have been with us since the seventies, and I've had few problems with any of them," Hal said. "They do understand coming in because it's explained to them that we put money into the payroll to try to field a championship caliber team every year. We don't do distributions. That's not the kind of partnership we are and if we continue to do what we've been doing for years and continue to succeed, the value, the value of what you put in will increase every year. It's not about getting a check every quarter because that's not going to happen."

Of course, these are the Yankees, and so they encounter some unique issues. In the spring of 2025, for instance, Hal Steinbrenner sent shock waves through much of his fan base. Not because of a trade. Not because of a firing. Not because he'd engaged with, say, Aaron Judge in a back-page war of words.

Because of hair.

Beards, specifically.

You'll recall that one of George Steinbrenner's first controversies as owner in 1973 involved identifying and, in essence, publicly shaming some of his players—including two, Bobby Murcer and Gene Michael, with whom he would become close friends—for their long hair. Grooming was a big deal to the Boss. Hair couldn't drift past the ears. Mustaches were allowed but that was it: no goatees; no beards. He ignored the rule once—quietly allowing a petulant Thurman Munson an eleven-day growth in 1977 before Munson finally grew tired of the look. He waived the rule once—permitting Jack McDowell to retain his goatee—and when McDowell's brief stay with the Yankees in 1995 went sideways (highlighted by him flipping the finger to a booing Yankee Stadium) that was it.

But on February 21, 2025, Hal altered that policy, after years of quiet grumbling among players forced to shave their beards after being acquired by the Yankees, and after consulting some present and former Yankees, some of whom believed the policy might hinder recruitment of future players.

"Ultimately the final decision rests with me, and after great consideration, we will be amending our expectations to allow our players and uniformed personnel to have well-groomed beards moving forward," Hal announced.

A few weeks earlier, Hal had told me: "We know that everything we do is a little extra enhanced because we're the Yankees. We demand a lot of our players, and our fans demand a lot out of us. There are a lot of traditions people care a lot about. We respect that. But we also know we live in the modern world. It's a challenging balancing act."

And it will stay that way for a while. More and more Steinbrenner grandchildren have joined the Yankees in recent years. None has been anointed as Hal's successor yet—he is, after all, just fifty-five years old; at fifty-five George was barely a third of the way into his reign, although Steve Swindal Jr., son of Jennifer and Steve Sr.—himself once an heir apparent to the Boss' office—has been cited as a likely candidate. And when Swindal talked to Joel Sherman of the *Post* in spring training 2024, it was obvious that he'd long listened to his uncle and taken notes.

"Hopefully, Hal's not going anywhere for a long time because I think he's really good at this. And I don't think he gets the credit he deserves because he's not as outspoken as my grandfather was," Swindal said. "What I know is that we've got a bunch of us in my generation. We want to tackle this thing [in supporting roles] right now and provide value to get wins now."

"Not a bad legacy at all, I'd say," Hal Steinbrenner said.

Steve Swindal Jr. and the others of his generation of Steinbrenner will find that out soon enough, and will reap the benefits of a baseball dynasty built and crafted by their grandfather, sustained and maintained by their uncle. They will also learn the ongoing truth that breathes forever inside the corridors of the House of Steinbrenner: ninety-four wins and a playoff series victory over the detested Red Sox—which the Yankees accomplished in 2025—may be good enough for most of the twenty-nine other clubs in Major League Baseball.

In New York—specifically the Bronx—it makes a lot of people wistful for a time when the Boss still ruled, and the Boss still roared.

POSTSCRIPT

The Hall of Fame? No, son, I don't belong in the Hall of Fame. The Hall of Fame is for the players. It's the players that make this such a great game. If it were up to me I'd disallow anyone for the Hall of Fame who wore a tie to work at the ballpark instead of a full uniform. And you can start that rule with me. It'd be foolish to put me in there.
—GEORGE STEINBRENNER, 2003

There was a long while when I agreed with the Boss on that one. That quote was the last part of the telephone conversation I detailed at the start of this book, the one that woke me with a start in my hotel room in San Diego. There was enough time between his not-quite-permanent ban from baseball in 1990, and the Yankees had by then added four championships, and so the idea of Steinbrenner earning admission to the Baseball Hall of Fame in Cooperstown, New York, started to gain a little traction.

When I asked about it, he actually laughed.

While I didn't tell him this, the whole idea once seemed pretty laughable to me, too. For years the notion of George Steinbrenner earning a spot in the Hall of Fame's Plaque Gallery—the sport's most sacred space—sounded like some kind of elaborate practical joke. What was it that Groucho Marx said? "I don't care to belong to any club that will have me."

And Steinbrenner—at least on the record—seemed to agree with Groucho.

Still, for years I've believed, and written, that Pete Rose deserves to at least be put up for consideration for the Hall and, if elected, the sins he committed against the game should be included on his plaque, along with noting he'd been barred for years because of those transgressions, notably betting on Cincinnati Reds games when he was the Reds' manager from 1985 to 1989. That feels like an equitable carriage of justice to me. I actually got to ask Rose one time if that would be an acceptable condition to his getting in the Hall, and Rose didn't even pause before saying "Fuck, yeah!" (Commissioner Rob Manfred removed Rose from baseball's permanently ineligible list in May 2025, paving the way for him to be considered for the Hall.)

And here's the thing: If I'm going to grant Pete Rose an olive branch like that, I must do the same for George Steinbrenner.

Even if it's on his permanent record that he was twice suspended from the game—once for a conviction on illegal campaign contributions, once for hiring a small-time hustler to try to blackmail his best player. Even if he was too often bombastic, and bellicose, and a bully, to his own ballplayers and his office employees and fellow owners and league presidents and commissioners. Even if there were too many years when he engaged in self-sabotage, "George-ing" many teams good enough to win pennants.

I'd never been quite sure how the Hall can simply ignore this. Look, for most fans, the lasting memory of Steinbrenner is a cuddly old curmudgeon who'd break Joe Torre's balls a little and cry a lot when his team won big games. The folks entrusted with casting these votes are supposed to remember the whole George—the fulsome George, the flighty George, the George who could be so publicly cruel to his employees. And while it would be wrong to minimize his impact on turning the Yankees back into the Yankees—*twice*—it is also important to note that those eras of prosperity were mostly done while he was absent. Twice. The spirit of the

"Steinbrenner" character invented by Larry David is that the Yankees were often good in spite of the Boss. There's an element of truth to that, too.

And, yes, he got thrown out of baseball twice.

But in the same way those transgressions shouldn't be ignored, neither should it be forgotten that Steinbrenner, in his day, a day that lasted for thirty-seven years and seven months, was the quintessential sports owner in New York, in Major League Baseball—and, probably, the world.

The Yankees he bought (with so very little of his own money) in 1973 were a mess: They'd totally ceded the town to the Mets; they played in a crumbling ballpark. There was talk of them moving to New Orleans and, worse, there was little public outrage about the possibility. There's a reason CBS took a loss on them. They were toxic.

Inside of three years they were pennant winners.

In four they were champions.

In five they were back-to-back champs.

By the end of his life his tidy little $168,000 investment turned him into a billionaire.

Yes, you can talk about all the empty years connecting 1982 and 1996, and that's all on the record, all on the Boss, all a part of his dossier. But remember: He isn't assessed for his Hall of Fame credentials for his baseball acumen, any more than Bud Selig or Happy Chandler or Kenesaw Mountain Landis were. He isn't being judged by his primacy on a baseball field any more than Tom Yawkey or Bill Veeck or Jacob Ruppert—Steinbrenner's historical antecedent and, in many ways, his generational clone. Ruppert earned admission in 2013, seventy-four years after his death. It was about fifty years tardy. The other owners in the Hall are a mixed bag:

◊ **BUD SELIG** brought baseball back to Milwaukee but earned his (somewhat dubious) enshrinement for his tenure as commissioner.

◊ **WALTER O'MALLEY** broke Brooklyn's heart when he bolted for LA, but under his watch the Dodgers aggressively widened integration, and he did expand baseball's borders thirteen hundred miles west.

◊ **BARNEY DREYFUSS** owned the Pirates for thirty-three years and is credited with inventing the idea that became the World Series.

◊ **J. L. WILKINSON, CUMBERLAND POSEY, RUBE FOSTER, ALEX POMPEZ AND EFFA MANLEY** were prominent figures in the Negro Leagues.

◊ **BILL VEECK** was a baseball impresario who had four separate tenures owning three different teams.

◊ **TOM YAWKEY** was a paternal owner of the Red Sox for forty-four years and is also among the most controversial enshrines because he was an unrepentant racist who held out for twelve years before integrating the team in 1959.

◊ **LARRY MACPHAIL** was briefly co-owner of the Yankees and was the man who introduced night baseball while an executive in Cincinnati.

◊ **BRANCH RICKEY** broke baseball's color barrier by signing Jackie Robinson.

◊ **CLARK GRIFFITH** owned the Washington Senators for thirty-five years but before that was a borderline Hall of Fame pitcher who won 237 games.

◊ **CHARLES COMISKEY** owned the Chicago White Sox for thirty-one years but his parsimonious ways have long been blamed for the Sox engaging with gamblers looking to fix the 1919 World Series.

Ask yourself: Would George Steinbrenner's career really not match up with any or all of them? For what it's worth, Steinbrenner's teams won seven World Series in his thirty-seven years as owner. The others on this list, combined, won eleven.

And then ask yourself:

Who has ever been more natural in the job of boss than the Boss? Even now, a decade and a half after his passing, you want to call an especially active member of your fantasy football league a nickname, do you use "Jerry," as in Jones? "Cuban," as in Mark?

No. Odds are good you call them "Steinbrenner." Still.

An old St. John's University president who hired multiple basketball coaches on his watch was nicknamed "Father Steinbrenner." The helicopter father who has a few too many opinions about his daughter's travel soccer team and loves to share?

"Oh god," you whisper to the other fathers. "Here comes Steinbrenner."

On it goes.

Yes. George Steinbrenner belongs in the Hall of Fame, although the Hall has been slow to agree. Three times since his death in 2010 Steinbrenner appeared on Veterans Committee ballots, which is where executives are judged. All three times he's fallen short of the twelve out of sixteen votes required. He belongs with a plaque that details all the good he brought to the Yankees and to the game of baseball; but also detailing why he was such a controversial figure. Let those two facets battle it out forever in the corridors of Cooperstown.

"You can't write the history of baseball without mentioning 'George Steinbrenner,'" says Hal Steinbrenner, admittedly not an objective voice but what he says is 100 percent true. "To me, that tells you whether he should be a Hall of Famer, doesn't it?"

George Steinbrenner won't be eligible for another vote until 2027, when the Veterans Committee will gather names for "Contemporary Baseball Managers/Executives/Umpires."

The vote should be yes.

Even if the Boss would call all those ayes fools.

ACKNOWLEDGMENTS

I tell this story a lot, only because it was the most important day of my life. This was the summer of 1974, and my father surprised me: He'd told me we were visiting my grandmother in Corona, Queens, and that already meant it was going to be a good day. But he hadn't revealed the punch line. We were having breakfast with Nanny, but we were really only parking the car at her house. Soon the two of us would be hoofing it to Shea Stadium to watch a Mets–Cardinals game on Old-Timers' Day. I was seven years old, and I remember every moment as if it all happened fifteen minutes ago: so many sights, so many smells, all of it overwhelming. At one point, my father started pointing out the various ballpark features: *There's the bullpen. There's the tarp. There's the dugout. There's the press box. There's the . . .*

"Press box?" I asked. "What's a press box?"

"You know the stories you read in *Newsday* and the *Long Island Press* every day about the Mets and Yankees?" he asked. "They're written by sportswriters. And they write their stories in the press box."

And, as they say, I was *gone* . . .

So in many ways, this book is very much a product of that day—June 29, 1974, Mets 4, Cardinals 0—and the immediate and intense understanding that *that* was precisely what I was going to do with my life. Since 1989, I've had the great good fortune to earn a living writing about all sports, but baseball has always been the foundation. The great Dave Anderson of *The New York Times* once told me, "If you can write baseball well, everything else is just warm-up."

I am a hopeless junkie of both history and of baseball, so this project was a delight in almost every way, mostly because of the unique way the reporting and research was done. I've written three books in the past, and many of those were heavily dependent on long hours spent in musty microfilm rooms. Some of that was the case for this book, of course, since I didn't start to cover baseball until the 1990s. So it is important to give thanks here for the extraordinary work so many New York baseball writers did in the 1970s and 1980s, at a time when newspapers were the undisputed kings of news gathering, in an era when daily back-page battles often drew blood, not all of it figuratively. For that I am grateful to generations of writers at the following newspapers: the *New York Post*; New York *Daily News*; *The New York Times*; *Newsday*; the Newark *Star-Ledger*; the Bergen County, New Jersey, *Record*; and the Westchester, New York, *Journal-News*. For much of the text of the book for the years before 1995, when I started covering New York baseball myself, I relied on the work of those who came before and worked for those newspapers. A lot of the quotes they gathered in real time are in this book; in many other instances they were the root for a surplus of questions I'd ask sources in the fleshing out of the narrative. Almost all of what is contained here after 1996 is a product of my own reporting.

What made this book unique for me was the fact that for much of the last thirty years I've had a front-row seat to just about every act of the daily drama/thriller/comedy known as the Steinbrenner Yankees. I've gotten to know professionally so many of the people featured and quoted in this story, and it was their frank (and often on-background) recollections that helped provide much of the tone of the story. I'm indebted to all of them for serving as the lifeblood of so many of my newspaper columns over the last three decades, and for allowing me to write this book the way I wanted to write it. I'm also grateful to both Jason Zillo of the Yankees as well as Hal Steinbrenner, who was especially generous with his time. Henry Hecht, who lived through so many of the tabloid wars of the 1970s and 1980s, was an invaluable sounding board as were, through the years, my late colleagues Vic Ziegel, Maury Allen and Dave Anderson.

This is not a biography; if you want the best and most complete version of the life of George Steinbrenner I recommend *Steinbrenner: The Last Lion of Baseball* (Harper, 2010), written by Bill Madden, a member of the writer's wing of the Baseball Hall of Fame. Other books that helped serve as guideposts for this one include *Billy Martin: Baseball's Flawed Genius*

(HarperCollins, 2016) by Bill Pennington; *All Roads Lead to October: Boss Steinbrenner's 25-Year Reign Over the New York Yankees* (St. Martin's Press, 1998) by Maury Allen; *Now Pitching for the Yankees: Spinning the News for Mickey, Billy and George* (Total Sports, 2001) by Marty Appel; and *Pinstripe Empire: The New York Yankees from Before the Babe to After the Boss* (Bloomsbury, 2014), also by Appel. In addition, a terrific book by longtime Cleveland *Plain-Dealer* sports columnist Bill Livingston, *George Steinbrenner's Pipe Dreams: The ABL Champion Cleveland Pipers* (Kent State University Press, 2015), is a wonderful look at the Boss's short-lived but unforgettable ownership of the Cleveland Pipers of the American Basketball League, where he developed so many of the tics and the traits he'd display a decade later once he moved to New York.

I'm indebted to my literary agent, Joe Perry, a fellow acolyte (um, make that alum) of St. Bonaventure University who reached out one day, wondering if I'd like to resume writing books after a thirteen-year sabbatical. He was a good sport as I weeded through some less-than-inspired ideas and then was an all-in advocate once we determined what the best possible project was. I'll forever be grateful for that jump-start.

It is Sean Desmond at Harper, however, whose fingerprints are all over these pages. I've been blessed in my career to work with a number of gifted and talented editors but Sean exists by himself, in his own category. Not only was he the originator of the idea of writing about the Steinbrenner family and their legacy, he was the one who suggested I write these thirty chapters "like thirty of your newspaper columns." No coach has ever given a more meaningful pregame speech. And as we advanced deeper and deeper into the manuscript it was clear that we were reading the pages through similar eyes—his were just a bit sharper sometimes, more focused, and so much of his input is apparent throughout. It is a rare gift to work with an editor you trust implicitly, and I look forward to this being the start of a long and prosperous partnership. I would also like to express my appreciation for Harper assistant Jackie Quaranto, whose gentle guiding hand is all over this book, and for Erica Ferguson, who was charged with the unenviable (but essential) task of fact-checking and copyediting the text, and performed that task as expertly as Don Mattingly, circa 1985. Thanks also to Beth Silfin, Harper's vice president, deputy general counsel (and a fervent Yankees fan), who lent the manuscript one final, thorough and critical set of eyes.

As fortunate a life as it is to write books, it almost seems like an excess of riches that I also have a day job that I treasure. Chris Shaw has my back every day that I write a column for the *New York Post*, and that occasionally means having to wade into difficult and uncomfortable waters together. I have worked for two sports editors in twenty-three years at the *Post*, and while it was Greg Gallo who hired me and opened the door to the only career I've ever dreamed of—a debt I'll never be able to come close to repaying—Shaw has helped make those dreams a daily reality. Together with Mark Hale, Dave Blezow and Josh Egerman they run the best sports section in America, and our bosses at the paper—publisher Sean Giancola, editor in chief Keith Poole and editor in chief/print Steve Lynch—encourage us to remind everyone in New York City that even now, a feisty sports section can still kick a little ass every day.

Every day I appear in that newspaper is a joy, and honors the memory of my father, Mickey, who took me to that game in 1974, encouraged my dreams from the start and helped foster them by bringing the *Post* home with him every day. It is my humble honor to work alongside a top-flight team of baseball writers at the *Post*: Joel Sherman, Jon Heyman, Mike Puma, Greg Joyce, Dan Martin, Mark W. Sanchez and Peter Botte. The daily encouragements of Larry Rocca, Don Burke, Drew Loftis, Ted Holmlund, Harrison Goodman and Justin Terranova all bring me to a better place with my words and my work.

I've been so fortunate to surround myself with dear friends in the newspaper/media business who every day help me to look a little bit smarter than I really am. Chief among them are Les Carpenter, Brian Costello, Jack Curry, Bob Klapisch, Dave Lennon, Tom Missel, Ian O'Connor, Steve Politi, Joe Posnanski, Bob Ryan and Adrian Wojnarowski. I would also like to mention a hero who became a mentor who became a friend, the late John Feinstein, who crafted the blueprint for all of us who write books anchored in the world of sports. Ours is a proud fraternity/sorority, even if it seems to shrink in numbers by the day, but for now and forever I wish to salute the folks who are not only my friends but continue to make this such an honorable vocation, notably: Laura Albanese, Dominic Amore, Marty Appel, Harvey Araton, Stef Bondy, Tim Bontemps, Zach Braziller, Larry Brooks, Pete Caldera, Mark Cannizzaro, Rich Chere, Ken Davidoff, Ryan Duleavy, Mike Fannin, Pat Forde, Kevin Gleason, Dan Graziano, Vahe Gregorian, Jerry Izenberg, Tyler Kepner, George King, Kevin Manahan, Dinn Mann, Andrew Marchand, Jeff Passan, Chuck Pollock, Steve Popper, Ed Price, T. J. Quinn, Lenn Robbins, Michael Rosenberg, Paul Schwartz, Jaret Schwartz, Steve Serby, Michael S. Schmidt, Dan Shaughnessy, Ben Shpigel, Mike Sielski, Tara Sullivan, Barry Svrgula, Wright Thompson, Dave Waldstein, Mollie Walker, Charlie Wenzelberg, Dan Wetzel and Steve Wright—and, always, the late Anthony Causi. My thanks also to Alex Mead of the *New York Post*, who helped furnish the archival photographs in this book.

And it isn't just newspaper folks who help a guy out with a project like this, so I am eager to also recognize Charlie and Loraine Albanese; Peter Barrecchia; Marc and Linda Berman; D. J., Kevin and Brian Bisaccio; Brian Burns; Eddie Burns; Amy Carr Wojnarowski; Chris and Gioia Cassidy; Aaron and Bethanne Chimbel; Pauline Coppola; John and Christie Coyle; Pamela Curry; Nick and Caren Cusano; Brendan, Greg, Mike and Rich Daniels; Ariste and John Egan, Esquire; the late Dr. George Evans; John Finnin; Bill and Donna Going; John and Natalie Hammersley; Patty Hogan; Audrey Hursey; Gavin Hursey; Kris Hursey; Paul and Lori Hursey; Chris and Kari Johnston; Dick and Mo Kearns; Matt Kramer; Brother Robert Lahey; Sean Lapham; Chris LaPlaca; John and Susanne Lovisolo; Scott and Laura Lowy; Mike and Maura MacDonald; Scott and Michelle Mackenzie; the late Dr. Jim Martine; Doug and Meghan Mauch; Tom and Amy McKenna; Gloria McMahon; Neil and Allicia McMahon; Tim and Daura McMahon; Geri Mulea; Todd and Dena Nordt; Mary Beth O'Donnell; Tom Pecora; Linda Penn; Rob and Michaela Ricco;

Father Dan Riley (RIP); Melanie Rolli and Hayo Hummerjohann; Jeanine and Josh Rotolo; Paul and Katie Sabini; Kevin and Marie St. Pierre; Mike St. Pierre; Brian Sanger; Gary Schreier; Charlie and Jane Silecchia; Dr. Richard Simpson; Teresa and Michael Specht; Don and Donna Thompson; Jane Thompson; Stephen and Diana Vaccaro; Dave and Anne Viganola; Glen, Joe, Neil, Peter and Tim Villari; and Cynthia and Tom White.

I would be remiss without offering a profound appreciation for an unparalleled team of physicians and therapists who, through their collective talents and patience, allowed me to continue to pursue this professional life I've cherished for so long: Gianna Bracco; Jacqueline Corcoran; Dr. Carol D'Aquino; Dr. Richard Goldstein; Dr. Anthony Lee; Cynthia Macaluso; Shane Matta; Dr. Mitul Patel; Joe Reda; Marybeth Ryan; and Dr. Marcus Williams.

This is the first book I've written since the passing of my mother, Ann (1934–2019), who was a constant source of strength, faith and optimism, a glass-half-full soul in a glass-half-empty world. The pride in her eyes when I presented my three previous books to her—"I'm going to *buy* them," she insisted, and I always let her—is the lone source of sadness associated with this project, since I won't have that moment this time. But she'll know. I know she'll know.

Then there is Leigh Hursey Vaccaro, who found herself exploring the "for better or worse" and also the "in sickness and in health" portions of our vows a little more literally than she probably intended to these past few years. To say she was both the inspiration and conscience behind this book may be accurate, but also represents only about 1 percent of what she's meant to me these last few decades. I hope the good folks at Harper will understand that as proud as I am of this book, it will only be the second-greatest part of 2025 for me. In August we'll be married thirty years. I'm glad I took the over.

Mike Vaccaro
Hillsdale, New Jersey
May 2025

INDEX

Aaron, Henry, 63, 107
Abbott, Jim, 263
ABC, 126
Adidas, 288
Affleck, Ben, 41
AL Championship Series (ALCS), 16, 33, 98–99, 165, 291, 309–312, 315, 329, 338, 345
AL Division Series (ALDS), 170, 269, 272, 275, 321
Alexander, Doyle, 317
Allen, Janet, 40
Allen, Maury, 29, 40, 58, 72
All-Star Games, 120, 133, 322, 327, 332
Alomar, Sandy, 73
Alou, Matty, 39
Altobelli, Joe, 200
American Basketball League, 15
American League (AL), 12, 36, 45, 51, 53, 60, 67, 73, 82, 176, 193, 194, 221
American Ship Building Co., 39, 61
Anderson, Dave, 107, 127
Anderson, Sparky, 186, 267
Andrews, Mike, 51–52
Angelos, Peter, 267
Anheuser-Busch, 22
Anti-Trust Exemption (1922), 90
Appel, Marty, 19, 64, 166
Arizona Diamondbacks, 290, 302
Armstrong, Michael, 235
Atlanta Braves, 6, 92, 258, 275
autograph seekers, 88–89
Autry, Gene, 105, 177–178

Baltimore Orioles, 12, 38, 43, 49, 59, 62, 71, 74, 92, 95, 97, 100, 109, 164, 194, 275, 281, 305
Barber, Red, 17

Barkley, Saquon, 344
Barnett, Larry, 39
Baseball Writers' Dinner, 41
Bass, Kevin, 228
bats, illegal, 196–198
Bauer, Hank, 83
Baylor, Don, 103, 200, 201, 207–208
Beame, Abe, 98
Beane, Billy, 259
Belcher, Tim, 269
Bellinger, Clay, 289
Bellinger, Cody, 348
Beltrán, Carlos, 341
Bench, Johnny, 38, 99
Benzinger, Todd, 250
Bergesch, Bill, 207
Berra, Carmen, 93, 204, 210
Berra, Dale, 209, 291–292
Berra, Yogi
  ceremonial first pitch, 323
  firings, 93, 204, 209–210
  Hall of Fame induction, 229
  Martin and, 83, 112, 117, 206, 207, 211, 229
  as Mets' manager, 44, 78, 84, 93
  Michael and, 190
  Steinbrenner and, 292–293
  as Yankees manager, 204–205, 206–209, 282
  Yankee Stadium boycott, 247–248, 291
Bird, Doug, 124
Blair, Paul, 116
Blessitt, Ike, 79
Blomberg, Ron, 36, 48
Bloomberg, Michael, 314
Boggs, Wade, 259, 262
Bonds, Barry, 258
Bonds, Bobby, 68, 71, 73, 91, 258
Bonilla, Bobby, 268

364 INDEX

Boone, Aaron, 338
Boras, Scott, 253, 326
Boss Watch, 304–305, 315–317, 321, 330
Boston Braves, 10
Boston Red Sox, 13, 36, 43, 44, 51, 72–73, 93, 116, 132, 141, 218, 220, 305–306, 308–312, 315, 326
Boswell, Dave, 79
Bouton, Jim, 290–291
boxing, 11, 56, 238
Boyer, Andrew, 315, 329
Bremigan, Nick, 204
Brett, George, 158–159, 196–198, 201, 203–204
Brinkman, Joe, 159, 197, 203
Broderick, Edwin, 233
Bronfman, Charles, 105
The Bronx Is Burning (TV show), 322
The Bronx Zoo (Lyle), 173–174
Brooklyn Dodgers, 13, 64, 83, 90, 173
Brosius, Scott, 302
Brown, Bob, 137
Brown, Bobby, 291
Brown, Kevin, 348
Budig, Gene, 270
Burke, Michael, 14, 16–18, 20–23, 26, 27, 29–31, 32, 35, 37, 46–47, 67, 76–77, 81, 146
Burnett, A. J., 328
Burroughs, Jeff, 78
Bush, George H. W., 246
Butcher, Rob, 277–278

Cablevision, 265–266, 295, 298
Cagney, Jimmy, 254
California Angels, 91, 105, 121, 183–185
Callison, Johnny, 50
Cannon, Jimmy, 83
Carbo, Bernie, 73
Carew, Rod, 88, 147
Carlton, Steve, 36, 236
Carney, Don, 201
Carpentier, Georges, 56
Carson, Johnny, 41
Cashen, Frank, 174
Cashman, Brian, 279, 281, 286, 288, 295, 311, 325–326, 328, 338–342, 348
CBS, 5, 8, 14, 16–17, 20–23, 31–32, 46, 67, 109, 166, 294
Cepeda, Orlando, 36
Cerone, Rick, 170–172, 196, 224
Chamberlain, Joba, 321, 326
Chambers, Raymond, 297

Chambliss, Chris, 60, 73, 91, 116, 122, 133, 140, 173
Chandler, Happy, 64, 354
Chass, Murray, 58, 129–130, 137, 149
Chernoff, Mark, 292
Cherry, J. Carlton, 70–71
Chicago Cubs, 14
Chicago White Sox, 64
Cincinnati Reds, 29, 99, 250, 353
Clark, Jack, 348
Clemens, Roger, 288, 297, 300–301, 308, 321
Cleveland, Reggie, 123, 135
Cleveland Cavaliers, 11
Cleveland Guardians, 15
Cleveland Indians, 15, 25, 29, 33, 38, 60, 66–67, 132
Cleveland Pipers, 2, 15, 18, 118–119
Coble, Drew, 203
Coffey, Wayne, 307
Cohen, Steve, 347–348
Cohn, Roy, 202
Colangelo, Jerry, 274
Cole, Gerrit, 341
collective bargaining, 90, 214
Collins, Dave, 7, 185, 348
Colorado Rockies, 259
Comeback Player of the Year, 160
Comiskey, Charles, 355
Cone, David, 7, 258, 259, 268, 274, 276–277, 297–298
contracts, 70–71, 108, 171
Contreras, José, 305
Cooper, Joseph W., 154–156
Copacabana, 83
Corbett, Bob, 78
Corbett, Brad, 74, 80
Cosell, Howard, 28, 126
Costello, Robert, 255–256
Cronin, Joe, 53
Crown, Lester, 32
Cunningham, Patrick J., 64–65, 74–75
Cuomo, Mario, 285
Curran, Paul, 244
Curry, Jack, 57–58, 274, 289, 296
"Curse of the Bambino" myth, 26
Cy Young Award, 70, 78, 90, 157, 258, 288

Daily News, 23, 28, 33, 49, 55–56, 58, 65, 72, 90, 95, 115, 141, 157, 235, 239, 241, 257, 271, 278, 289, 296, 307, 320
Daley, Richard J., 157

INDEX

Dallas Cowboys, 8, 11
Dallas Mavericks, 11
Damon, Matt, 41
David, Larry, 3, 15, 238, 278, 354
Davis, Al, 3–4
Davis, Sammy, Jr., 83
Della Femiina, Jerry, 174, 219–220
DeLorean, John Z., 31
Dempsey, Jack, 56
Dempsey, Rick, 73, 317
Dent, Bucky, 133, 141, 142, 161, 237, 241
Denver Bears, 59
Detroit Tigers, 43, 45, 52, 76–77, 82, 119, 267
Devery, William "Big Bill," 12–13
Dickey, Bill, 229
Dickman, Bernie, 248
Dillard, Harrison, 186
DiMaggio, Joe, 38, 85–86, 291–292
DiTullio, Christina, 335
Dobson, Pat, 49, 60
Dolan, Charles, 265, 294–295, 298
Dolan, James L., 6, 343–344
Doubleday, Nelson, 146, 173, 174
Dowd, John, 242–243, 248, 254, 257
Down, Rick, 273
Dreyfuss, Barney, 355
Durocher, Leo, 64
Dwyer, Jim, 284

Eisenhardt, Roy, 191, 192
Ellis, Dock, 91, 92
Ellis, John, 33, 38
Ellsbury, Jacoby, 348
Epstein, Theo, 305–306, 308
Erolino, Heather, 201
Evans, Dwight "Dewey," 94
Evans, Thomas, 31, 32, 98

fans, 33, 35–36, 44–45, 49, 88–89, 127–128, 146, 165, 183–185, 212–213, 286–287, 296, 335–336, 337–338, 344, 353
Farrell, Frank, 12–13
Fenway Park, 36, 43, 51, 116, 132, 141
Ferraro, Mike, 158–159, 167, 179, 228–229
Fielder, Cecil, 278
Figueroa, Ed, 91, 92
Fingers, Rollie, 103, 171
Finley, Charles Oscar, 51–53, 61, 69, 70–71, 74–75, 89, 91–92, 96, 162
Fishel, Bob, 19, 101

Fisk, Carlton, 44, 94
Forbes (magazine), 8, 349
Forbes Field, 10
Ford, Whitey, 83, 84, 323
Foster, Rube, 355
Franks, Herman, 20–21
Frazee, Harry, 13, 26, 308
Frazier, George, 203
free agency, 7, 25, 69, 90, 102, 175, 176, 200, 347
Fregosi, Jim, 178
Freiman, Ron, 145–146
Frey, Jim, 180
Fried, Max, 348
Frohman, Al, 214, 235
Fugazy, William, 104

Gaddis, Hunter, 345
Gaherin, John, 89
Gallego, Mike, 258
Gallo, Greg, 326–327
gambling, 12, 243
Garciaparra, Nomar, 308, 309
Garfunkel, Art, 16
Garland, Wayne, 103
Gaston, Cito, 267
Gehrig, Lou, 93
George M. Steinbrenner Field, 327
Giamatti, Bart, 239
Giambi, Jason, 311, 320
Gifford, Frank, 28
Giles, Warren, 68
Gillick, Pat, 112, 200
Girardi, Joe, 274–275, 328–329, 331–332, 336, 338
Giuliani, Rudy, 285, 286, 299, 314
Gold, Bob, 242
Goldklang, Marvin, 252, 253
Gonzalez, Luis, 302
Gooden, Dwight, 212, 219, 278, 300
Gossage, Goose, 7, 133, 143–144, 159, 187, 188–190, 196, 201, 225, 323
Graham, Otto, 315
Grant, Cary, 98, 254
Grant, M. Donald, 44, 115, 146, 173, 210
Green, Dallas, 236
Greene, Harvey, 224
Grich, Bobby, 98, 102, 105
Griffey, Ken, 185, 203, 207
Griffith, Clark, 119, 355
Guidry, Ron, 147, 175, 183, 195, 203, 224, 265, 330

Guiver, Jill, 201, 210
Gulf + Western, 266
Gullett, Don, 103

Haas, Moose, 172
Hagar, Ray, 149
Hall, Mel, 241
Hall of Fame, 2, 6, 38, 71, 77, 96, 138, 185, 203, 229, 264, 297, 306, 323, 338, 340
Hamilton, Alexander, 56
Hank's Yanks, 333–334
Hargrove, Mike, 78
Hart, Jim Ray, 49
Hartman, Sid, 48
Hawkins, Burt, 79
Hayes, Charlie, 259
Healy, Fran, 113, 117
Hearst, William Randolph, 56
Heath, Mike, 134, 191–192, 195
Hecht, Henry, 129–130, 136, 137, 149
Hegan, Mike, 49, 50
Henderson, Rickey, 187, 191, 205, 209–210, 211, 221, 224, 236, 262–263
Hendricks, Elrod, 112
Henry, John, 305, 306, 308, 309
"Here Come the Yankees" (song), 16
Hernandez, Keith, 218, 221
Hernandez, Orlando, 281, 288
Heyman, Jon, 296
Hill, David B., 11
Hilltop Park, 12
Hoffberger, Jerold, 74
Holtzman, Ken, 92, 109–110, 317
Home Box Office (HBO), 295
Hooton, Burt, 126
horse racing, 11
Horton, Willie, 82
Hough, Charlie, 126
Houk, Ralph, 45, 48, 49–50, 52–53, 69, 77–78, 167, 200
Houston Astros, 172
Howard, Elston, 116, 118
Howe, Steve, 255–256, 268
Howser, Dick, 86, 116, 120, 123, 134–135, 156, 158, 159, 161, 163–164, 167–169, 179, 197–198, 206, 217, 251
Hrabosky, Al, 134–135
Huggins, Miller, 151
Hunt, Nelson Bunker, 31, 32
Hunter, Jim "Catfish," 8, 69–71, 73, 89, 91, 92, 95–96, 100, 109, 113, 131, 153, 157
Huston, Tillinghast L'Hommedieu, 13, 15

Iglehart, Joseph, 109
International League, 29, 147
Irabu, Hideki, 288–289

Jackson, Reggie
  with Baltimore Orioles, 95
  with California Angels, 183–185
  ceremonial first pitch, 323
  injuries, 147, 176
  with Kansas City Athletics, 52, 91–92
  Martin and, 116–117, 119, 129–131, 134–136, 141–142, 143, 148–149, 150–151, 153–154
  "Mister October," 125–126
  Reggie! candy bars, 131–132
  Steinbrenner and, 100–106, 127–128, 133, 140, 332
  suspensions, 135
  with Yankees, 7, 106–107, 109–110, 122–123, 124–128, 144, 159, 161, 170, 172–173, 174, 175–176, 182
Jackson, Shoeless Joe, 64
Jacobson, Steve, 58, 86
James, Dion, 269
Jaworski, Leon, 59
Jenkins, Fergie, 78
Jerez, Williams, 333
Jeter, Derek, 8, 258–259, 263, 264, 274–275, 286, 297, 302, 306–308, 310, 315, 330–332, 335–336, 340
John, Tommy, 125, 147, 223
Johnson, Alex, 74
Johnson, Ban, 12
Johnson, Cliff, 124–125, 135, 143–144
Johnson, Davey, 219, 221
Johnson, Nick, 311
Jones, Edwin, 83–84
Judge, Aaron, 8, 341, 348–349

Kaat, Jim, 266–267
Kalmbach, Herbert, 58
Kane, Bill, 60–61
Kane, Charles Foster, 11
Kansas City Athletics, 25, 51, 84
Kansas City Royals, 60, 119, 124, 134, 158–159, 169, 195–196, 251, 258
Katz, Lewis, 297
Kauffman, Ewing, 167
Kaufman, Steve, 244
Kay, Michael, 316
Kehoe, Gregory, 254–255

INDEX

Kekich, Mike, 39–42, 49
Kekich, Susanne, 39–41
Kelly, Roberto, 258
Kenney, Jerry, 33
Key, Jimmy, 259, 262, 264
Kidd, Jason, 2
King, Clyde, 190–191, 206, 217
Kingman, Brian, 192
Kingman, Dave, 115
Kleinman, Leonard, 248, 254, 255
Kluttz, Clyde, 70
Knoblauch, Chuck, 281
Koch, Ed, 254
Koufax, Sandy, 173
Kriegel, Mark, 257
Krivacs, Jim, 273
Kroc, Ray, 70–71
Kubek, Tony, 266–267
Kucks, Johnny, 83
Kuhn, Bowie, 53, 59, 61–63, 66, 69–70, 72, 74–75, 87, 89–90, 92, 145, 156, 174, 199, 247, 249

Lamoriello, Lou, 296
Landis, Kenesaw Mountain, 64, 354
Lansford, Carney, 250
Lasorda, Tommy, 186
Lawn, Jack, 256
Layton, Eddie, 166
Le Club, 166
Lee, Bill, 94, 113
Lee, Spike, 33, 285, 297
Legends Field, 2, 5, 320, 321, 327
Legends Hospitality, 349
Lehman Brothers, 20–21, 23
Leiter, Al, 300
Lemon, Bob, 137–138, 142, 144, 148, 150–151, 171, 178–181, 182, 186–187, 206, 282
Lemon, Jerry, 148
Leonard, Dennis, 158
Levine, Randy, 325, 336
Lindsay, John V., 23, 49
Lisker, Jerry, 136
Little, Grady, 310
Lloyd, Graeme, 278–279
Loaiza, Esteban, 310
LoCasale, Al, 3
lockouts, 90, 94
Lopez, Felix, 329
Los Angeles Angels, 96
Los Angeles Dodgers, 141–142, 181–182, 346–347

Lucchino, Larry, 287–288, 303–306, 308, 312
Luciano, Ron, 82
Lupica, Mike, 157–158, 235
Lyle, Sparky, 37, 41, 67–68, 120, 149, 157, 173
Lynn, Fred, 74

MacPhail, Larry, 16, 77, 355
MacPhail, Lee, 31, 33, 35, 37–39, 41, 45–46, 47, 49–50, 53, 67, 73, 77, 79, 101, 109, 193–195, 198–199, 202, 203–204
Madden, Bill, 257, 296
Maddox, Elliott, 60
Maddux, Greg, 258, 259, 275
Madison Square Garden (MSG), 146, 266–267, 295, 296, 298
Major League Baseball (MLB), 11, 24
Manfred, Rob, 353
Manley, Effa, 355
Mantle, Mickey, 38, 68, 78, 83, 84, 111, 131, 228–229, 290–291
Mara, John, 344
Mara, Wellington, 145
Maraesca, Orest V., 202
Marakovits, Meredith, 346
Maris, Roger, 106, 126–127, 131
Marriott, J. Willard, 58
Martin, Billy
  affairs, 78–79, 201
  Berra and, 83, 112, 117, 206, 207, 211, 229
  death, 231–233
  with Detroit Tigers, 76–77
  drinking and fighting, 77, 83–85, 148–150, 154–156, 210–211, 215–216, 228–229
  firings, 6, 77, 80, 82–85, 119, 156, 162, 217
  Jackson and, 116–117, 119, 127, 129–131, 134–136, 141–142, 143, 148, 150–151, 153–154
  with Minnesota Twins, 76
  "Mister October," 83
  Number 1, 162, 163
  as Oakland Athletics manager, 157, 162–163, 187, 191–192
  Paul and, 118
  personality, 81–82
  racism, 79
  reputation sanitization, 338–339
  resignation, 137
  Steinbrenner and, 80–82, 107, 110–114, 117–118, 119–121, 123–125, 131, 136–138, 158, 159, 162–163, 182, 192, 225, 232
  as Texas Rangers manager, 78–80, 82

Martin, Billy (*continued*)
  traded to Kansas City Athletics, 84
  as Yankees manager, 82–87, 93–99, 102–103, 120–128, 129–134, 138–140, 151, 193–201, 210–212, 228–229
Martin, Billy Joe, 233
Martin, Gretchen, 85
Martin, Jill, 231, 233
Martinez, Edgar, 269
Martinez, Pedro, 308, 309–310, 315
Martinez, Tino, 274–275, 302
Martinez, Tippy, 317
Mason, Jim, 74
Matsui, Hideki, 308–309, 320
Mattingly, Don, 195, 200, 203, 204–205, 209, 211–212, 221–222, 226–228, 236–237, 249, 260, 264, 268–269, 274–275, 330
Mauch, Gene, 177–178
May, Rudy, 317
Mayor's Trophy Game, 173–174, 187, 220
Mays, Willie, 21, 258
McCann, Brian, 341
McCarthy, Joe, 151
McClelland, Tim, 196–198, 203
McCovey. Willie, 107
McDowell, Jack, 268, 350
McDowell, Sam, 49
McGee, Willie, 187–188
McGraw, John J., 13
McGregor, Scott, 317
McLendon, John, 18, 118–119
McNally, Dave, 90
McNiff, Phil, 233
McRae, Hal, 203
Meacham, Bobby, 207, 209
Medich, Doc, 60, 91
"Meet the Mets" (song), 16
Merchant, Larry, 23–24
Merrill, Carl Harrison "Stump," 241, 251
Merrill, Robert, 37
Messer, Frank, 36, 196
Messersmith, Andy, 90, 92–93, 105
Michael, Gene, 37, 44, 135, 147, 156, 167–168, 172, 176–180, 186–188, 190, 227, 249, 251–253, 255–256, 258–259, 261–263, 268, 272–273, 299
Michael, Gene "Stick," 69
Michaels, Al, 158
Milbourne, Larry, 161, 170
Millar, Kevin, 310
Miller, Marvin, 25, 63, 89, 178, 223
Miller, Rick, 74

Millus, Albert, 215
Milwaukee Brewers, 120, 141, 170–171
Minnesota Twins, 76, 78, 79, 88, 93
Molloy, Joe, 259, 318
Monahan, Gene, 119, 229
Moore, Marianne, 16
Morabito, Mickey, 98, 140–141
Moran, Sheila, 41
Morgan, Joe, 99
Morris, Jack, 222
Moses, Jerry, 33
Moss, Dick, 222–223
Most Valuable Player (MVP), 28, 78, 103–104, 218, 258
Moyer, Jamie, 326
Mueller, Bill, 310
Munson, Thurman, 37, 38, 44, 72, 91, 93, 103–104, 105, 106–108, 110, 113–114, 116, 121–122, 125, 127, 133–134, 140, 143, 147, 151–152, 171, 197, 264, 330, 335, 350
Murcer, Bobby, 28–29, 37, 38–39, 41, 43, 60, 68, 152–153, 163–164, 350
Murderers' Row, 286
Murray, Dale, 195–196
Murray, Jim, 80
Musselman, Bill, 148
Mussina, Mike, 316, 326
Myers, Randy, 250

National Basketball League (NBA), 15
National Hockey League (NHL), 11
National Industrial Basketball League, 15
National Labor Relations Board, 267
National League (NL), 12, 33, 36, 176, 194
NBA Finals, 2
NBC, 116, 117
Nederlander, James M., 7, 31, 32
Nederlander, Robert, 249, 259
Nettles, Graig, 25, 33, 38, 48, 60, 72, 73, 91, 101, 106, 108–109, 133, 160, 161, 173, 196–197, 224, 330
network partnerships, 265–267, 288, 296
New Jersey Devils, 2, 296–297
New Jersey Nets, 2–3, 296–298
newspaper strike, 141
"New York, New York" (song), 166–167, 312
New York Giants, 12–13, 20, 56, 145, 173, 344
New York Highlanders, 12, 13
New York Knicks, 2, 6, 34

INDEX

New York Mets, 11, 16, 17, 33, 36, 43–44, 46–47, 49, 52, 78, 94, 115–116, 136, 146–147, 173–176, 187, 204, 218–221, 268, 291, 299–301, 314, 347–348
New York Mirror, 56
New York Newsday, 28, 33, 56, 58, 86, 253, 289, 296, 320
New York Police Department (NYPD), 12
New York Post, 2, 23–24, 28, 29, 33, 40, 41, 44, 56, 57, 58, 65, 72, 83, 115–116, 129, 136, 141, 220, 257, 259, 289, 296, 311, 320, 350
New York Rangers, 6
The New York Times, 33, 57, 58, 83, 107, 127, 129, 141, 157, 255, 274, 296, 304, 306
New York Yankees
  ALCS games, 16, 33, 98–99, 165, 291, 309–312, 315, 329, 338, 345
  ALDS games, 170, 269, 272, 275, 321
  Banner Day, 238
  Berra's tenure as manager, 204–205, 206–209
  as a big-market team, 7
  brawls, 194–195
  CBS ownership, 5, 8, 14, 16–18, 20–23
  celebrity first pitches, 16, 323
  championship wins, 3, 14, 98–99, 191, 275, 287, 289–290
  fans, 33, 35–36, 44–45, 49, 88–89, 127–128, 165, 183–185, 212–213, 286–287, 296, 335–336, 337–338, 353
  fight song, 16
  franchise worth, 8–9
  George's ownership, 5–6, 7–8, 15, 17–18, 21–26, 46, 50, 52–54, 61–62, 71–75, 89–99, 102–106, 110–114, 117–121, 156, 194, 199–201, 208–209, 212, 221–225, 317, 341, 348–349, 352–356
  George's ownership partners, 27–34, 37, 46–53, 283
  Green's tenure as manager, 236–237
  Hal's ownership, 8–9, 328–329, 334–342, 344–351
  Martin's tenures as manager, 82–87, 93–99, 102–103, 120–128, 129–134, 138–140, 151, 193–201, 210–212, 228–229
  Mayor's Trophy Game, 173–174, 187, 220
  media coverage, 48–49, 186, 188–189, 211, 297
  Murderers' Row, 286
  name change from Highlanders, 13
  network partnerships, 265–267, 288, 296
  "New York, New York" song, 166–167, 312
  Old-Timers' Day, 84, 85–86, 138, 162–163, 229, 290–291

  personal appearance code, 37–38, 47–48, 95–96, 121–122, 350–351
  Piniella's tenure as manager, 217, 219, 222–225, 227
  player scandals, 40–42
  rivalries, 44, 89, 93, 94, 147, 218, 308–312
  Ruppert's ownership, 11, 13–16
  strikes, 265, 267–268
  Subway Series, 291, 299–301
  victories, 43–44, 60, 68, 286–287
  World Series, 3, 6, 14, 16, 56, 125–128, 141–142, 181–182, 214, 264, 275, 287, 290, 296–297, 300–301, 334, 345–347, 356
Nicolau, George, 255–256
Niekro, Phil, 213
Nigro, Ken, 195
Nixon, Richard M., 31, 58, 233, 254
NL Championship Series (NLCS), 44, 299, 347
No, No, Nanette, 25–26

Oakland Athletics, 39, 44, 51–52, 69–70, 91, 162, 187, 191–192, 194–195, 246, 250
Oakland Raiders, 3, 5
O'Brien, Pete, 207
O'Connor, Ian, 272, 274, 321–322
O'Connor, John, 233
O'Dowd, Mary, 213
Ohtani, Shohei, 347
O'Malley, Walter, 354–355
O'Neill, Paul, 258, 260, 262, 264, 281, 297, 340
O'Neill, Steve, 132
Ortiz, David, 308, 310–312
Osmond, Herb, 92
Otis, Amos, 124

Pacific Coast League, 84
Pagliarulo, Mike, 209
Paley, William, 16, 17, 18, 22–23, 30, 32, 48, 283
Palmer, Jim, 97, 143, 158
Patterson, Joseph Medill, 55
Paul, Gabe, 26, 29–33, 38, 46–53, 60–61, 65, 66–70, 75, 79–80, 81–82, 84–86, 91, 98, 99, 102, 112, 118, 120, 126, 132, 152, 172, 200, 247, 249, 330
Payson, Joan Whitney, 34, 36, 46–47, 58, 146
Pepe, Phil, 23, 49, 58, 72, 149
Perez, Pascual, 241

Pérez, Tony, 99
Perry, Gaylord, 82
Peterson, Fritz, 39–42, 49
Peterson, Marilyn, 39–41
Pettitte, Andy, 263, 297, 302
Phillips, Dave, 203–204
Piazza, Mike, 291, 300–301
Pienciak, Richard T., 241
Pine Tar Game, 196–198, 201
Piniella, Lou, 94, 108, 122, 140, 152, 163–164, 182, 211, 216, 217, 219, 222–225, 227, 229–230, 243, 250–251, 269, 319
Pittsburgh Pirates, 44, 59, 91
Platt, Oliver, 322
Players Association, 176, 264
players' union, 25, 89, 309
Polo Grounds, 12–13, 33
Pompez, Alex, 355
Porter, Darrell, 135, 159
Posada, Jorge, 263, 291, 297
Posey, Cumberland, 355
Pulido, Alfonso, 226, 317

Quantrill, Paul, 310
Quisenberry, Dan, 204

racism, 78, 83, 118–119, 153
Raines, Tim, 278
Ramirez, Manny, 308, 309
Randolph, Willie, 91, 116, 124, 133, 140, 158–159, 211, 224, 274, 330
Rasmussen, Dennis, 209
Ratner, Bruce, 298
Reagan, Ronald, 231
Reedy, Bill, 231–232
Reinsdorf, Jerry, 257–258
Reno Evening Gazette, 149
reserve clause, 25, 68, 89–90
Rice, Jim, 116
Rice University, 17
Richman, Arthur, 273
Richman, Milton, 40–41
Rickey, Branch, 355
Rieber, Anthony, 271
Righetti, Dave, 176, 195, 225–226, 317
Rivera, Mariano, 263, 297, 302, 310, 334
Rivers, Mickey, 91, 140
Rizzuti, Philip C., 242
Rizzuto, Phil, 19, 36, 137, 186
Roach, Jay, 41

Roberts, Dave, 310
Robertson, Andre, 186, 209
Robinson, Frank, 66
Robinson, Jackie, 83
Rochester Tribe, 29
Rockefeller, Nelson, 58
Rodón, Carlos, 8
Rodriguez, Alex, 309, 325–326, 337, 341
Rogers, Edward, III, 348
Rookie of the Year, 78, 195, 218, 225, 288
Rose, Pete, 99, 147, 236
Rosen, Al, 132–133, 136–137, 140, 142, 149–150, 172, 353
Ross, Steve, 237
Royko, Mike, 157
Rozelle, Pete, 28
Rubensein, Howard, 296, 303–304, 315, 316, 324, 329
Rudi, Joe, 102–103, 105
Rules of Procedure, 256–257
Ruppert, Jacob, Jr., 10–11, 13–16, 354
Ruppert Brewing Company, 11
Ruth, Babe (George Herman), 10, 13–14, 26, 63, 218, 233, 308, 313
Ryan, Nolan, 115

Saban, Lou, 172
Sabathia, CC, 7, 328
Saigh, Fred, 22, 62
salary caps, 7
Salas, Mark, 224
Sanders, Deion, 237
San Diego Padres, 70–71, 175, 287
San Francisco Giants, 21, 68, 70, 246, 258, 337
Sapir, Eddie, 83, 85, 150, 156
Sasaki, Roki, 347
Saturday Night Live (TV show), 6, 249–250, 278
Sax, Steve, 232
Schaap, Dick, 28, 129
Scheffing, Bob, 44
Schiff, Dorothy, 56
Schilling, Curt, 308
Schmidt, Mike, 236, 304–305
Schoen, Joe, 344
Scott, Dale, 269–270
seagulls, 201–202
Seattle Mariners, 165, 187, 269, 272, 302
Seattle Pilots, 22
Seaver, Tom, 36, 71, 115–116, 218
Seinfeld (TV show), 3, 238, 278

Seitz, Peter, 69, 89–90, 115
Selig, Bud, 257, 287, 322, 354
September 11, 2001 terrorist attacks, 301–302
Shales, Tom, 250
Shea Stadium, 33, 36, 49, 52, 60, 72–73, 94, 146, 173, 285, 286, 299, 300
Shecter, Leonard, 290
Sheffield, Gary, 308
Sheppard, Bob, 138, 190, 212–213
Sherman, Joel, 57, 259, 296, 311, 350
Shirley, Bob, 223
Short, Bob, 78, 84
Showalter, Buck, 188, 241, 251–252, 256, 259, 261–262, 265, 267, 272–273, 276
Silvestri, Joey, 83–84
Simon, Paul, 16
Sinatra, Frank, 166–167
Slaton, Jim, 172
Smalley, Roy, 203
Smoltz, John, 264
Snyder, Ruth, 55
Soderholm, Eric, 160–161
Soriano, Alfonso, 316
Sosa, Elias, 126
Soto, Juan, 341–342, 345, 347
Sotomayor, Sonia, 267
Spikes, Charlie, 33, 38
Spinks, Michael, 238
Spira, Howard, 233–236, 239–240, 242–243, 248, 254–255, 332
Splittorff, Paul, 124
Sport (magazine), 110, 113
SportsChannel, 266–267
Sports Illustrated, 82, 226, 259, 260, 267
Springsteen, Bruce, 297
Standard Brands Confectionery, 131
Stanley, Fred "Chicken," 73–74, 140
Stanley, Mike, 258, 274
Stanton, Frank, 16
Star-Ledger, 289, 297
Steinbrenner, George M., III
  author and, 1–9, 352–353
  background, 14–15, 17
  Berra's firing, 93, 204, 209–210
  The Boss, 157–158, 208–209, 296, 303–306
  Burke and, 17–18, 21–23, 47, 81, 146
  Davis and, 4–5
  death, 6–7, 81, 332, 333
  as deserving of Hall of Fame, 352–356
  elevator attack, 181–182
  expulsion, 244–245, 246–249
  fines, 199
  game attendance, 35–39, 71–74, 88, 93, 131, 254, 285, 304, 329–332
  health issues, 315–317, 327
  Howser's firing, 168–169, 179
  impressions of, 3, 15, 238, 278, 354
  indictments, 59, 61
  lawsuits against, 214, 231, 234
  Lemon's firing, 187
  Martin's death, 232–233
  Martin's firings, 6, 82–85, 156, 162, 217
  media coverage, 23–24, 28–29, 33, 47–49, 56–58, 65, 86, 95, 115–116, 157–158, 253, 262, 270, 278, 289, 295–296, 304–306, 320–321, 335
  Michael's firings, 178–181, 190
  New York Post guest column, 220
  No, No, Nanette mentions, 25–26
  offers to buy Yankees, 237
  Paul and, 67–69
  personality, 15, 42, 64, 66, 68, 80–81, 118–119, 153, 159–161, 170–172, 244
  political contributions, 58–59, 61
  presidential pardon, 231
  reinstatements, 87, 260–261
  Saturday Night Live appearance, 249–250, 278
  successor search, 317–320
  suspensions, 8, 62, 63–65, 66, 69, 71–72, 74–75, 85, 88, 195, 290
  Yankees ownership, 5–6, 7–8, 15, 17–18, 21–26, 46, 50, 52–54, 61–62, 71–75, 89–99, 102–106, 110–114, 117–121, 156, 194, 199–201, 208–209, 212, 221–225, 294–297, 317, 341, 348–349, 352–356
  Yankees ownership partners, 27–34, 37, 46–53, 283
Steinbrenner, Harold Zeig (Hal), 317, 322
  as board chairman, 319–320, 324–325, 327
  father's legacy and, 7, 8, 295, 339–341, 344–345, 356
  Martin's death, 232
  personality, 7–8
  Yankees ownership, 8–9, 328–329, 334–342, 344–351
Steinbrenner, Henry, 15, 80
Steinbrenner, Henry George (Hank), 226, 231, 247–248, 317–318, 329, 333–334, 336, 345
  as board chairman, 324–327
Steinbrenner, Jennifer, 316, 317, 318–319, 322–323, 328, 330, 350
Steinbrenner, Jessica, 316, 317, 318

Steinbrenner, Joan, 247, 316
Steinbrennerfication, 145–147
Stengel, Casey, 84, 99, 151
Sterling, John, 314
Stewart, Sammy, 164
St. Louis Cardinals, 22, 51, 62, 337
Stottlemyre, Mel, 36, 60, 100
Stouffer, Vernon, 29
Strawberry, Darryl, 218, 268, 278
strikes, 170, 265, 267–268
Subway Series, 291, 299–301
Sugar, Bert Randolph, 45
Sullivan, Joseph, 203
Summer of Sam (film), 297
Super Bowls
   XXXVIII, 3–5
The Superteams (TV show), 110
suspensions
   Howe's, 255–256
   Jackson's, 129–131, 135–136
   Steinbrenner's, 8, 62, 63–65, 66, 69, 71–72, 74–75, 85, 88, 195, 290
Sutton, Don, 126, 172
Swindal, Haley, 316
Swindal, Steve, 318–319, 350
Swindal, Steve, Jr., 350
Swoboda, Cecilia, 39–40
Swoboda, Ron, 39–40
Sykes, Bob, 188

tabloids, 7, 21, 28, 55–58, 65, 220, 271–272
Tammany Hall, 11, 12
Tampa Bay Buccaneers, 3, 4–5
Tanaka, Masahiro, 341
Tartabull, Danny, 268
Taylor, Brien, 252–253
Teixeira, Mark, 7, 328
Tellem, Arn, 320
Texas Rangers, 74, 78, 79–80, 168
Thorne, Gary, 269
Tiant, Luis, 36, 98, 143, 147, 160, 163, 306
Tidrow, Dick, 60
Topping, Dan, 16, 77, 210
Torborg, Jeff, 202
Toronto Blue Jays, 112, 201–202, 212–213, 262, 267
Torre, Frank, 276
Torre, Joe, 5, 271–272, 273, 274–282, 286, 295, 321–322, 325, 338, 353
Torre, Rocco, 276
Torres, Rusty, 33, 38

Torrez, Mike, 125
The Trade (film), 41
Trump, Donald J., 237, 254, 262, 303, 332
Turner, Ted, 92
21 Club, 27–28, 103–104, 166
Tyson, Mike, 238

Ueberroth, Peter, 223, 239
umpires, 82, 194–195, 196–197, 203–204, 269–270
US Olympic team (2004), 3

Valentine, Bobby, 301
Veeck, Bill, 354, 355
Velez, Otto, 94
Vincent, Fay, 238–241, 242–245, 246–248, 251, 254–257, 317
Virdon, Bill, 53–54, 59–62, 67–68, 71–72, 73–74, 81, 85–86

Waldman, Suzyn, 260, 292
Walters, Barbara, 254
Ward, Gary, 224
Ward, Robert, 110, 113
Washington, Claudell, 224
Washington, U. L., 158, 195–196, 203–204
Watergate investigation, 58–59, 61, 244
Watson, Bob, 158, 273, 277–279
Weaver, Earl, 92, 155, 164–165, 177, 186, 194, 251
Webb, Del, 16, 77, 210
Weiss, George, 84
Welch, Bob, 141–142
Wells, David, 280–281, 286, 288
Werner, Tom, 308
Wetteland, John, 268
White, Bill, 36, 99
White, Roy, 38, 82, 106–107, 140
Whitson, Eddie Lee, 214–216
wife swapping, 40–41
Wilkerson, Curt, 206–207
Wilkinson, J. L., 355
Williams, Bernie, 8, 241, 249, 259, 263, 274–275, 297
Williams, Devin, 348
Williams, Dick, 50–53, 59, 61, 96, 155, 186, 264
Williams, Edward Bennett, 59, 63–64, 305
Williams, Stan, 179

Wills, Maury, 165
Wilpon, Fred, 173, 174
Wilson, Willie, 158
Winfield, Dave, 175, 176, 195, 202, 204–205, 213–215, 219, 221–222, 224, 229, 231, 233–236, 239, 241–242, 291
Witt, Mike, 242
Wolf, Warner, 316
Wong, Howard, 154, 156
Woodward, Woody, 223–224
World Series, 3, 52
  1904, 265
  1919, 64
  1938, 14
  1953, 83
  1956, 299
  1964, 93
  1974, 68
  1977, 125–128
  1978, 141–142
  1981, 181–182, 214
  1983, 200
  1986, 218, 220–221
  1989, 246
  1990, 250
  1998, 287, 296
  1999, 6, 296
  2000, 296
  2001, 290
  2024, 346–347
  Yankees in, 3, 6, 14, 16, 125–128, 141–142, 181–182, 214, 264, 275, 287, 290, 296–297, 300–301, 334, 345–347, 356
Wynegar, Butch, 217
Wynn, Jimmy, 117

Yamamoto, Yoshinobu, 347
Yankee Entertainment and Sports Network (YES), 298, 349
YankeeNets, 2, 296–297
Yankees ownership
  George's ownership, 294–297
Yankee Stadium (new), 313–315, 316, 335
Yankee Stadium (old), 2, 16–17, 19–20, 45, 93–94, 100, 102, 194, 282, 283–285
Yawkey, Tom, 308, 354, 355
Young, Dick, 24, 90, 115–116

Ziegel, Vic, 23
Zimmer, Don, 167, 274, 309–310

ABOUT THE AUTHOR

MIKE VACCARO has been the lead sports columnist for the *New York Post* since November 2002. He's authored three previous books: *Emperors and Idiots: The Hundred-Year Rivalry Between the Yankees and Red Sox, From the Very Beginning to the End of the Curse* (2005); *1941—The Greatest Year in Sports: Two Baseball Legends, Two Boxing Champs, and the Unstoppable Thoroughbred Who Made History in the Shadow of War* (2007); and *The First Fall Classic: The Red Sox, the Giants, and the Cast of Players, Pugs, and Politicos Who Reinvented the World Series in 1912* (2009). He lives in New Jersey.